Rational Piety and Social Reform in Glasgow

Rational Piety and Social Reform in Glasgow

The Life, Philosophy, and Political Economy
of James Mylne (1757–1839)

BY
Stephen Cowley

FOREWORD BY
David Fergusson

WIPF & STOCK · Eugene, Oregon

RATIONAL PIETY AND SOCIAL REFORM IN GLASGOW
The Life, Philosophy, and Political Economy of James Mylne (1757–1839)

Copyright © 2015 Stephen Cowley. All rights reserved. Except for brief quotations in critical publications or reviews, no part of this book may be reproduced in any manner without prior written permission from the publisher. Write: Permissions. Wipf and Stock Publishers, 199 W. 8th Ave., Suite 3, Eugene, OR 97401.

Wipf & Stock
An Imprint of Wipf and Stock Publishers
199 W. 8th Ave., Suite 3
Eugene, OR 97401

www.wipfandstock.com

ISBN 13: 978-1-62564-997-3

Manufactured in the U.S.A.   07/06/2015

Some Quotes from James Mylne's Lectures

"I have no objection to common sense, as long as it does not hinder investigation."
—Lectures on Intellectual Philosophy

"Hope never deserts the children of sorrow."
—Lectures on the Existence and Attributes of God

"The great mine from which all wealth is drawn is the intellect of man."
—Lectures on Political Economy

Portrait of James Mylne by John Linnell (1835) copied from Sotheby's catalogue (1985), accessed through Scottish National Portrait Gallery, © courtesy of Sotheby's, London. The original was last known in the possession of a private collector, Virginia, U.S. in 2011.

Contents

Foreword by David Fergusson | ix
Acknowledgements | xi
Abbreviations | xii
Introduction | 1

PART 1 The Life, Philosophy, and Influence
of James Mylne (1757–1839) | 13
  1 Early Life and Education | 15
  2 Deputy Chaplaincy | 30
  3 Ministry in Paisley | 41
  4 Professor in Glasgow | 63
  5 Whig Politics and Activity | 79
  6 Family, Church, and Succession | 97

PART 2 Philosophy, Politics, and Political Economy | 121
  7 The Lectures on Intellectual Philosophy | 125
  8 Encounters with Condillac and Thomas Reid | 142
  9 The Active Powers and Moral Philosophy | 162
  10 Faith, Belief, and Freedom | 177
  11 Political Influences and Doctrines | 194
  12 Political Economy | 217

Conclusion | 247

Appendix: Collation of James Mylne's Introductory
Lecture on Moral Philosophy | 259

Bibliography | 267

Index | 291

Foreword

After serving as minister of Paisley Abbey, James Mylne (1757–1839) held the Chair of Moral Philosophy in the University of Glasgow for over forty years. He was the most significant figure between Thomas Reid and Edward Caird in a distinguished tradition of 18th–19th century philosophy in Glasgow. Yet Mylne's career is marked by a paradox of eminence and obscurity. As a Church of Scotland minister, political activist, university teacher, and popular lecturer, he was an influential public intellectual in the early 19th century. His interests were not confined to metaphysical speculation; they extended to the most pressing social, political and religious interests of the day. To this extent, he was an impressive exponent of what George Davie has called 'the democratic intellect'. Viewed with suspicion by some, he was held in high esteem by many. Testimonies reveal him to be of an independent, questioning spirit and reluctant to be closely identified with any single party. Many of his students found their way into positions of professional leadership. Others held important posts in philosophy throughout the English-speaking world. Yet since the mid-19th century, Mylne has become a shadowy and virtually unknown figure of the Scottish philosophical tradition. The main reason for this is certainly that Mylne never left a body of published work for later generations to read and inwardly digest. This absence has consigned him to obscurity. Our principal mode of access to his philosophy is through several sets of student handwritten lecture notes, deposited in different libraries.

In this meticulous study, Dr Stephen Cowley has succeeded in bringing Mylne out from the shadows. After years of painstaking research on lecture notes, press reports, minutes of meetings, and testimonials, he has produced an integrated account of Mylne as philosopher, political economist, churchman and social reformer. What emerges is a thinker who attributed more to the organising powers of the rational mind than did his predecessor, Thomas Reid through his so-called common sense philosophy. This places Mylne between the traditions of Scottish realism and the later emergence of idealism in Glasgow via the study of Kant and Hegel. More broadly, it also locates Mylne, who was much influenced by his reading of French philosophy, in a longstanding Scottish intellectual tradition that developed through close contact with continental Europe.

As a social reformer, Mylne identified with the Whig Party and participated prominently in 'Fox dinners' in the west of Scotland. His commitment to press freedom, constitutional reform, and Catholic emancipation placed him on the left of Scottish politics, not always a comfortable position for a professor or minister of the Kirk at that time. Within the Church of Scotland, he appears to have sympathised with revisionist tendencies on doctrines such as the work of Christ, the Trinity and hell as everlasting punishment. This led to accusations of doctrinal heterodoxy, the advancement of a sterile rational religion, and the undermining of the faith of ordinands who attended his lectures. Doubtless, the fear of censure in the courts of the church contributed to his decision not to promote his views in print—a similar strategy had been employed by the controversial theologian John Simson, a century earlier in Glasgow. And yet Mylne did not seek to confine his views to the solitude of his study. He was active in public life, participating in reforming movements and lecturing regularly in the evenings to the merchant classes of Glasgow.

We are greatly indebted to Stephen Cowley for this rounded and sympathetic portrait. As the standard point of reference for our understanding of his life and work, Cowley's monograph is unrivalled as the most significant study of Mylne. Not only has he drawn attention to a leading philosophical figure in the history of modern Scotland, he has given us a richer understanding of the intellectual, religious and political life of this period. Mylne's independence of spirit, political awareness and academic rigour, together with the intellectual vitality of the period, provide us with much to ponder and admire in this study.

—David Fergusson

Acknowledgements

I WISH TO THANK my supervisor, Professor David Fergusson, and examiners Dr. James Harris and Professor Stewart J. Brown for guidance on the content and final form of this work. The staffs of the libraries and archives overleaf were of great assistance to me.

Abbreviations

BL	British Library, London
EUL	Edinburgh University Library
FES	Fasti Ecclesiae Scoticanae
GChr	Glasgow Chronicle
GC	Glasgow Courier
GJ	Glasgow Journal
GM	Glasgow Mercury
GUA	Glasgow University Archives
GUL	Glasgow University Library
JSP	Journal of Scottish Philosophy
ML	Mitchell Library, Glasgow
NAS	National Archives of Scotland, Edinburgh
NCL	New College Library, Edinburgh
NLS	National Library of Scotland, Edinburgh
PCL	Paisley Central Library
PRO	Public Records Office, Kew Gardens, London
StUL	St. Andrews University Library, St. Andrews

INTRODUCTION

The Need to Recover James Mylne's Philosophy

Introduction

THE PHILOSOPHER JAMES MYLNE (1757–1839) vindicated the rational powers of humanity against the skeptical and "common sense" philosophies of his Scottish predecessors and earned the trust of his Whig contemporaries for his interventions in political debate. Many considered him a significant and original figure. Mylne and the largely neglected philosophy and political economy classes he taught in Glasgow hence clearly merited closer study. This book contains a biography of James Mylne and interpretative essays on his lectures on moral philosophy and political economy and on his political views and activities.

James Mylne attended St. Andrews University where he acquired a liberal education in the Scottish tradition and a particular knowledge of theology. He became a Deputy-Chaplain with the 83rd Regiment of Foot during the American War of Independence and his experience sheds light on his later advocacy of a militia. Thereafter he served for fourteen years as a minister in Paisley where he was exposed to the literary culture of Glasgow and the radical-tinged politics of the French revolutionary era. From 1797 until his death he was Professor of Moral Philosophy at Glasgow University, where he delivered effective lectures on moral philosophy and political economy. The impact of his teaching was enhanced by student exercises in essay writing, following the method of George Jardine. He was also active and influential in the Whig politics of the day. Mylne broke with the political caution of Adam Smith, Thomas Reid (1710–96), and James

Beattie (1735-1802).¹ Smith's warning of a "daring, but often dangerous spirit of innovation" in politics² contrasts with the "speedy and substantial reform" advocated by Mylne, who extended the Whig thought of John Millar (1735-1801).³

The lectures contain material common to Scottish traditions of mental philosophy. However, Mylne's philosophy is anchored in a tradition of "rational piety" that places individual judgments at the core of mental life and in a philosophy of history that sees intellectual progress at the heart of social, economic and political developments. In place of the skepticism of David Hume (1711-76) and the common sense of Thomas Reid and Dugald Stewart (1753-1828), he proposed a constructive account of experience, developing directly from John Locke (1632-1704) and his French follower Condillac (1714-80). In two particular respects, Mylne's thought diverges from the "moral sense" and "common sense" traditions associated with Francis Hutcheson and Thomas Reid in Glasgow. These are his doctrine of the external world and his account of free will and providence. Mylne draws on Condillac to argue that there is no need to draw on common sense to explain belief in an external world as this is explicable by an analysis of touch. He considers that the mind is determined to act by rational motives and the concept of freedom without motive is incoherent.

As a result of these views, Mylne reinstates reason as the guiding principle of conscience and argues for utility as the predominant criterion of morality. His views of political reform and the concept of value in his political economy lectures on the emerging market economy are related loosely to these features of his philosophy.

The influence of Mylne's teaching was extensive both in Scotland and the English-speaking world. This can be documented by acknowledgements and reminiscences by his students, many of whom who went on to teach themselves and by comparison of their published works with the content of

---

1. Thomas Reid, *Dangers of Political Innovation* in Arthur, *Discourses on Theological and Literary Subjects*; Beattie, *Elements of Moral Science* vol. 2.

2. Smith, *Theory of Moral Sentiments*, 232. Smith's sympathies with Burke, with whom he corresponded and whom he succeeded as Rector at Glasgow, and hostility to Richard Price, are evaluated in the context of the 6th edition of *TMS* by Daniel Brühlmeier's essay "Price, Burke, Smith, Millar: Réactions Britanniques face à la Révolution Française" in *La Révolution Française dans la Pensée Européenne*.

3. George Jardine (1742-1827), professor of Logic to Rev. Robin Hunter, letter of 16 July, 1801 wrote on Millar's death: "though I am sensible we have suffered of late in public opinion by his Politics and those he brought over to his side—yet with all his faults—our society has sustained an irreparable loss: as a Professor we shall never see the like of him" (GUL:MSGen507/Letter 124). [I have kept European-style dates in the footnotes for help with references.]

Mylne's teaching. More distantly, I argue that Mylne had an indirect influence on the ethos of the early Idealist movement in Glasgow. Mylne's philosophy evinces a sense of the unity of experience, drawn initially from the universal elements of sensation and judgment, but with religious overtones. His commitments to inquiry and social reform and critique of the common sense school prepared the ground for the Glasgow idealists.

The Case for Recovering the Philosophy of "Old Sensation"[4]

THE NEGLECT OF MYLNE creates a vacuum in Scottish intellectual history that spills over into contemporary popular culture. For example, the bicentenary commemorations of the French revolution in Scotland generally represented the Scots as camp followers of Burke or Paine.[5] This underestimation of Scottish thought continues in the tourist displays of New Lanark, which are silent, for example, on Mylne's connection with David Dale and influence on his grandniece, Frances Wright.[6]

Knowledge of Mylne's philosophy has survived through a slender chapter in James McCosh in *The Scottish Philosophy* (1875) and other incidental reports in the literature on "Scottish philosophy."[7] A key limiting factor for his reputation in the long run though, has been his failure to ensure publication of his work. During his life, this was normal, for lectures in Scotland were a personal asset and publication was thus often posthumous.[8]

I will outline the history of his reputation. Many contemporary witnesses generally held a high view of Mylne as a teacher, even where they opposed his political or religious positions. His student James McCosh (1811–94) identifies the religious and political character of this influence alongside mental and moral philosophy, "Opposed to the national creed of Scotland, and an admirer of liberal principles, he was regarded as a dangerous man by the government of the day. [. . .] for upwards of forty years he delivered to large classes in Glasgow a course of lectures which set many

---

4. Anon., "Sir Daniel Keyte Sandford," 403.

5. Crawford, *Boswell, Burns and the French Revolution*, for example shows little development from Henry Meikle's *Scotland and the French Revolution*.

6. Personal visit, 2009.

7. For example, Fraser, *Biographia Philosophica*, and on education: Davie, *The Democratic Intellect*, chapter 1.

8. The cases of Thomas Brown and William Hamilton in Edinburgh bear this out. However, there were partial exceptions, such as Thomas Reid and Dugald Stewart. The legal grounds of this practice were established in a court case led by Edward Caird.

minds a working."⁹ That Mylne "set many minds a working" is abundantly verifiable. The historian of philosophy, John Daniel Morell (1816–91), who studied at Glasgow within two years of Mylne's death, confirms Mylne's reputation as a "metaphysician of great ability." He corroborates Mylne's influence in Glasgow: "From what I have learned of those who attended his lectures, and what I have seen of the impulse they gave in prosecuting the work of intellectual analysis, I think there can be little doubt but that his mind told forcibly upon the philosophy of Scotland during the many years of his professorship."[10] Indeed, Mylne was compared favorably with his leading philosophical contemporaries in Scotland. The *Kilmarnock Mirror* recorded:

> The qualities of Mr. Mylne's mind are great depth and clearness. [. . .] Mr Stewart seldom seems to get to the bottom of a subject. Mr Mylne always does. At times one cannot help doubting, whether Mr Stewart clearly comprehends what he is about; of Mr Mylne, there is never such a doubt. Of the two, Mr Mylne is the more original thinker, in so far as the phrase signifies thinking for oneself, rather than adopting the thoughts of another. Mr Stewart enters upon a discussion with all the prejudices of his school; Mr Mylne is the disciple of no school, follows no system but his own.[11]

The author not only prefers Mylne over Dugald Stewart (1753–1828) who represented the common sense school, but extends the favorable comparison to Thomas Brown (1778–1820):

> It is one of Mr Mylne's greatest excellencies that he keeps always to the subject in hand. This is more than can be said for Mr Stewart or his successor in office. These gentlemen, particularly the latter, never omit an opportunity of flying off from their immediate business for the sake of fine writing. Dr Brown's lectures are certainly the finest specimens of composition we have ever heard, but they are no more to be compared with Mr Mylne's,

---

9. McCosh, *The Scottish Philosophy*, 363–65. The opening phrase suggests a religious consensus that existed neither amongst philosophers nor in the country at large, where in Paisley and Glasgow alone there were not only many Seceding congregations, but also Catholic, Unitarian, and Quaker chapels. Indeed Mylne's most vociferous opponent, Ralph Wardlaw, was a Congregationalist.

10. Morrell, *Historical and Critical View*, 390.

11. From article "On the University of Glasgow: Moral Philosophy Class" in *The Kilmarnock Mirror and Literary Gleaner* (Kilmarnock 1819) 176–80.

for the closeness of their logic, than a piece of mere declamation, to the essay on the Human Understanding.[12]

Stewart and Brown's reputations, despite the edition of Stewart's works by William Hamilton and the posthumous publication of Brown's lectures, have declined for the reasons the author predicts.[13] The Episcopalian Reverend Michael Russel (1781–1848), who graduated from Glasgow in 1806,[14] compared the teaching at Edinburgh at this time, where "there is neither a question asked nor an essay written throughout the whole session" very unfavorably with that of Glasgow, and the other Scottish universities.[15] In the following generation, Mylne's students went on to occupy teaching chairs in philosophy at Glasgow, Edinburgh, Belfast, London, and elsewhere. A history based only on published writings may thus misrepresent the moral philosophy effectively taught in Scotland.

The Decline of Mylne's Reputation after His Death

One common observation was Mylne's rejection of Reid's common sense. This situation was reversed under Mylne's successor in Glasgow William Fleming, under whom "common sense" was reinstated, as in another context by William Hamilton in Edinburgh. John Daniel Morrell (1816–91) took the moral philosophy class of Fleming within two years of Mylne's death,[16] having already absorbed John Locke and Thomas Brown. He later reminisced:

> Induced by the lively admiration I had conceived for the Scottish metaphysics, I proceeded to the University of Glasgow, and studied philosophy in the classrooms which had been honored by the presence and enlightened by the genius of Reid and Smith. Here the veneration for Brown began to subside; I felt that there was a depth in the philosophy of Reid which I had not fully appreciated, and that the sensational tendency of the

---

12. Ibid., 178. The reference is to Locke's *Essay Concerning Human Understanding*.

13. The *Kilmarnock Mirror* author accurately predicts the trajectory of Stewart's reputation: "We have certainly no wish to underrate the talents of Mr Stewart, but we submit, that if he had paid less attention to the graces of writing, if he had rendered his lectures as instructive as they were certainly amusing, he would have done much for philosophy and the permanency of his own fame that he has left undone" (ibid, 179).

14. Addison, *Matriculation Albums*, entry 6184.

15. Russel, *View of the System*, 119.

16. Morrell, *Historical and Critical View*, iv.

former, though it added popularity to his thoughts, was an ill exchange for the incipient spiritualism of the latter.[17]

This mentions the "popularity" of sensationalist philosophy. Some of Morell's criticisms of Brown—on his deduction of the external world and the irrationalism of his ethics—are such as would derive from Mylne's thought, of which he says in the chapter on "The Scottish School of the Nineteenth Century": "The tendency of his influence was decidedly sensational [. . .] of this character, also, was his firm support of utilitarianism in morals; yet, we believe, he explained his views in such a manner as not materially to injure those great principles of belief for which Reid had so earnestly contended."[18]

This brief account is accurate as far as it goes and Morrell notes Mylne's influence on John Young and similarity to Rev. John Bannatyne. The general standpoint of *Historical and Critical View of the Speculative Philosophy of Europe in the Nineteenth Century* (1846), including its treatment of "Scottish philosophy," is plainly based in substance and terminology on the philosophy of Victor Cousin. Morrell adopts Cousin's classification of philosophies into sensationalism, idealism, skepticism and mysticism and reflects Cousin's own purported synthesis of eclecticism. For example, he classifies Reid as an opponent of skepticism and characterizes his philosophy as an "incipient spiritualism."

Three thinkers contributed to the eclipse of Mylne's reputation. First, William Fleming (1791–1866), Mylne's immediate successor at Glasgow, acknowledged Mylne generously as a teacher in an inaugural article published in the Tory students' journal *The Peel Club Papers* (1840). As a Tory, Fleming obviously did not identify with Mylne's political engagements. J. D. Morell records the return of Reid's influence with Fleming in the 1840s: "Glasgow and Edinburgh have both come back, with little exception, to the philosophy of Reid; and seem to be recanting the sensational heresy they began to imbibe under the impressive genius of Brown and Mylne."[19] Fleming did not publish Mylne's lectures, which as deputy lecturer he must have had access to in some form. Indeed, Mylne's literary effects seem to have been mislaid. Fleming did publish two philosophical works though, a *Manual of Moral Philosophy* (1854) and *The Vocabulary of Philosophy: Mental, Moral and Metaphysical* (1857). The first of these reproduces the content of the latter sections of Mylne's course, leaving out the metaphysics from the start. What is lacking in this work is the urgent sense of addressing the beliefs

17. Ibid.
18. Ibid., 390.
19. Ibid., 707.

guiding the actions of the society around him. What remains is a series of "timeless" meditations on duty, immortality, free will, etc.

Second, James McCosh, in his influential work *The Scottish Philosophy* (1875), draws a barbed picture of Mylne. His history of Scottish philosophy follows Cousin in relating the subject particularly to the Presbyterian tradition. Within this limitation, McCosh represents Mylne's religion in a particularly unfavorable light. For many years, Mylne was college chaplain. McCosh writes, "The students felt his preaching and that of his substitutes to be cold, and regarded him as secretly a rationalist or a Socinian."[20] This passage suggests that McCosh is tying Scotland in a theological straitjacket rather than aiming for a "broad church." Some scattered aphorisms though, suggest that Mylne downplayed revelation. Thus from 1799 he says. "We have no reason to say that nations are civilised only as having a communion with the internal parts of Asia where there was revelation. Thus China."

Yet his thought on the whole evinces great piety, and like that of Condillac, is suffused with religious concerns. Elsewhere, McCosh describes Mylne as "the first professor of mental science who impressed me favourably, which he did by his cool intellectual power."[21] However, *The Scottish Philosophy* was the most accessible account he left and does Mylne less than justice.

Third, George Gilfillan (1813–78), an evangelical minister and prolific editor of poetry, wrote on Mylne in several essays. The first was a biographical essay published in 1849 on the Reverend David Young of Perth, with whom he had studied under Mylne. He wrote, "What a clear, solid system he built before his students, year after year, from the first faint sensation of the infant up to the poet's dream of immortality and the philosopher's theory of God."[22] Gilfillan's *History of a Man* (1856) copies much of the wording of this. While appreciative of Mylne as a thinker, it is vicious on his religious beliefs. I here cite this directly autobiographical version:

---

20. McCosh, *The Scottish Philosophy*, 365. The term "Socinian" is a traditional term for denial of the divinity of Christ. It was applied to the Unitarians by Ralph Wardlaw in *Discourses on the Socinian Controversy* (1814). It is found also in Hume (see Jones, *Hume's Sentiments*, 16) and Voltaire, *Lettres Anglaises*, chapter 7; both writers whom Mylne mentions in his lectures. Mylne's colleague Boog considered them believers though in *Discourses*, 266.

21. McCosh, *Philosophical Papers*, 436.

22. Gilfillan, "Reverend David Young," 194. Gilfillan was United Presbyterian minister in Dundee (DNB). It seems more reasonable to suppose that he wrote about his colleague than that he plagiarized someone else's work. David Young is Matriculation No 11428 in Addison, *Matriculation Albums*, for 1824, a year before Gilfillan.

> Arrived at Glasgow, I lost no time in joining Milne's [sic] Moral Philosophy Class, and soon became interested, if not very much in the study, much in the idiosyncrasy of my Professor. He was a fine-minded old man; clear, original, acute, but cold rather— at all events, careless. At the morning hour, to which he came sometimes scarcely dressed, he seldom seemed fully awake; yet the snorings of his slumber were often noble. [. . .] He was, if common report did not belie him, although a clergyman, a sceptic; and indeed, he set himself, in a quiet but effectual way, to shake the belief of his students.

The qualification "if common report did not belie him" does not appear in the biography of Young and thus represents a retreat, despite the continuing negative tone. The first and last sentences of the following passage offer new justifications:

> He openly denied and argued against eternal punishment, and sneered at some of the cardinal doctrines of Christianity besides. Few came away from his class without sharing, more or less, in the infection, if not of his actual doubts, at least of his cold, sceptical, materialistic spirit. The Moral Philosophy Class was a kind of ice-bath, in which we shivering novices were plunged; some of the weaker perishing, and even the stronger more chilled than strengthened by the operation. I have heard eminent Doctors of Divinity confessing that, years after they had entered the ministry, the recollection of some of Milne's half-hinted doubts, sly suggestions, words when more was meant than met the ear, came back at times upon them, and threatened to darken their faith and paralyse their exertions.[23]

I will argue that Gilfillan's varied metaphors of "coldness," typical of mid-Victorian evangelical rhetoric, spring from a misapprehension of the Glasite Christianity embodied in Mylne's lectures. Mylne's teaching was not materialist, for he defended immortality, nor skeptical, save in a narrow sense of denying some literal interpretations of the Bible, particularly in Genesis. What Mylne said about eternal punishment was: "He, who suffers it to take possession of his mind that the almighty has doomed a number of his fellow creatures to misery cannot be very ardent in duty. But he who believes on the other hand that God wills all to be happy[,] that it is the folly and absurdity of man which introduces misery, then he exerts himself

---

23. Gilfillan, *History of a Man*, 89–90.

to banish that folly and its consequences, co-operating with the grand and benignant design of the great Eternal."²⁴

Despite these criticisms, Gilfillan returns abruptly to a positive assessment of Mylne in his concluding peroration, "As a preacher, he sometimes approached the verge of very high eloquence. His sermons were too philosophical, but they were carefully composed, elegant in language, and occasionally very effective: one on the text, 'Ponder the path of thy feet,' was, we understand, a masterpiece of sound wisdom, chaste fervour, and happy illustration. [. . .] Farewell 'Old Sensation,' as thy students called thee! Well I knew thee, and owe thee a debt of considerable gratitude."²⁵ In a later biography of John Morell Mackenzie published in 1867, he comes to a still more positive assessment of Mylne as a philosopher, writing that from him one could, "learn a great deal as to metaphysical facts, and as to the *limits* of human knowledge, from one who was at once one of the boldest and most sensible of thinkers."²⁶

Gilfillan rescinded his criticism further in an essay from 1873, where he said that Mylne "although accused of seeking to shake the faith of his students, only fixed it the deeper in the stronger of them, as the blast confirms the roots of the mountain pine,"²⁷ but only the harsher *History of a Man* is cited by Murray in his authoritative *Memories of the Old College of Glasgow*.

Sources within the Scottish churches endorsed the high opinion of Mylne. More than twenty years after Mylne retired, the *United Presbyterian Magazine* (1857) published an essay on *Scotch Metaphysics and their Influence on Scottish Theology* that judged Mylne a desirable complement to the common sense school of Reid and Stewart, "Professor Mylne of Glasgow [. . .] had the reputation of an acute and profound metaphysician. His system occupied a middle position between the excessive simplifications of some of the French philosophers and the more extended classifications of Reid and Stewart. There was no mystification about him; everything was elegantly simple and perspicuous; and he was admirable on the passions."²⁸ The same publications later compared Mylne with Hamilton of whom it held a high but not uncritical opinion.²⁹

---

24. Pollok's notes, lecture of 8/3/1821: GUL:Spec.Coll/MSGen1355/103, 8.
25. Gilfillan, *History of a Man*, 91.
26. Gilfillan *Remoter Stars in the Church Sky*, 123.
27. Gilfillan, *Life of the Rev. William Anderson*, 25.
28. *United Presbyterian Magazine* (Edinburgh, Oliphant, 1857), 109, article signed "RESH."
29. Ibid., 258

As late as the twentieth century, the long-lived Alexander Campbell Fraser (1819–1914) wrote in his reminiscences, "In 1833 Mylne was probably the most independent thinker in the Scottish philosophical professoriate, although he makes no appearance in histories of philosophy, or even in the philosophical library."[30] Independence of spirit suggests philosophical originality. The early Glasgow Idealist, James Hutchison Stirling, not someone given to undeserved praise, corroborates the substance of this, writing: "Independent he may have been, but 'old Mylne' was certainly spoken of in the college courts as something more than usual in his place."[31]

In terms of philosophy in Glasgow, scholars by the twentieth century commonly overlooked the period from Millar's death in 1801 to the arrival of John Veitch in 1864 and the return of Edward Caird two years later. The few who do not are scathing, giving the impression of a collapse in original philosophy. C. A. Campbell for example, writes of the period, "Certainly the contribution to the advancement of philosophic thought made by this particular series of incumbents can hardly be underestimated."[32] I will argue that that is precisely what Campbell does! Since the 1980s, essays by James Somerville, Charles Stewart-Robertson and James Harris, based on readings of the Glasgow manuscripts, have identified Mylne as an original opponent of Reid, though without doing justice to his political economy or Whig politics.

Conclusion and Plan of the Book

In his heyday, Mylne was an effective and influential teacher. The lack of publication sealed Mylne's literary fate when those who knew him personally had gone.[33] The recovery of Mylne's views may thus reverse this situation and I include contributions towards this recovery as an appendix to the present book. Extensive further transcriptions and collations are bound with my thesis and can be consulted at Edinburgh University Library.

On the question of influence, Mylne's students were prominent in the churches, politics, and academia—as merchants and lawyers. In the West of

30. Fraser, *Biographia Philosophica*, 42.

31. Stirling, "Review of Alexander Campbell Fraser's *Biographia Philosophia*," 87. Stirling also mentions Alexander Scott ("A J Scott of Woolwich"), another pupil of Mylne, as a religious influence "He awed us to the deepest religious trust and absorption" (ibid., 87). Scott was associated with the theologian John MacLeod Campbell, also Mylne's pupil (see Tulloch, *Movements of Religious Thought*).

32. Campbell, *Fortuna Domus*, 116.

33. Millar had spoken from notes and it is possible Mylne did the same, hence the lack of manuscript material. This is speculation however.

Scotland, they were a large part of the opinion-forming and tradition-bearing part of the middle class, but they were present also in Edinburgh, England, Ireland, America, Canada, and Australia.[34] This reputation justifies a more thorough investigation of the origin and nature of his doctrines. I initially take a biographical route to investigation of their origin and dissemination. Thereafter, I discuss what is original in their content in separate essays.

---

34. Addison, *Matriculation Album*; MacLehose, *Memoirs and Portraits*.

PART 1

The Life, Philosophy, and Influence of James Mylne (1757–1839)

Rational Piety and Social Reform

Introduction

IN THIS FIRST PART, we shall trace James Mylne's life chronologically in relation to his thought. This leads us through chapters on his early life in Kinnaird in Perthshire and education at St. Andrew's University in Fife; his chaplaincy with the 83rd Regiment of Foot, during the American War of Independence; his ministry with the Church of Scotland in Paisley, from 1783 to 1797; and his occupancy of the Chair of Moral Philosophy at Glasgow University thereafter up to his death. The overall picture that emerges from this biographical approach is of a scholar whose ideas on the malleability of the mind are partly explicable in terms of the revolutionary era in which he lived, as well as by his reading. I devote separate chapters to his later personal affairs and public involvement in the Whig politics of Glasgow. The chapters on his professorship and political commitments should be read in conjunction with the interpretative essays on his mental philosophy, political creed, and political economy.

CHAPTER 1

James Mylne

Early Life and Education

JAMES MYLNE WAS BORN in the parish of Kinnaird, in September 1757.[1] The parish is in the rich farmlands of the Carse of Gowrie in East Perthshire between Dundee and Perth, bounded to the north by hills and to the south by the river Tay. Mylne was a son of the manse and the namesake of his father, the Reverend James Mylne, who had been called to Kinnaird in 1736 by the Presbytery of Dundee, subject to the Synod of Angus and Mearns and a branch of the established Church of Scotland.

James Mylne's father (hereafter "Mylne senior") had been ordained by the Presbytery of Haddington in East Lothian. George Hill, the leading Scottish theologian of his son's era at St. Andrews was also ordained by Haddington, which may suggest a connection with St. Andrews University.[2] The previous minister of Kinnaird, James Adams, had taken a degree at St. Andrews at the end of the seventeenth century and had been presented to the parish by the Laird of Fingask and Kinnaird around 1707. Adams produced a sequence of pamphlets, starting with *The Snake in the Grass* (1719) that addressed the emergence of the Independent Glasite or Sandemanian movement from the Marrow controversy.

---

1. Scott, *Fasti Ecclesia Scoticanae* gives 3 September, 1757. However, the two editions of *Fasti* contain contradictory information on Mylne's date of birth. I follow the later and more specific edition. For material in earlier edition: Vol 3, Synod of Glasgow and Ayr, 169. I draw the information on his family from *Fasti* and the memoirs of Frances Wright.

2. Cook, *Life of the Late George Hill*, 70.

Adams died in 1734. Prior to this, a probationer, George Blaikie,[3] had preached several times at Kinnaird with his approval, meeting with general, though not universal, acceptance. However, Blaikie then took the unpopular step of having himself presented to the Parish by royal permission.[4] The Parish Session and heads of local families objected to Dundee Presbytery, the next level up in the Presbyterian court system, declaring that they would "always oppose the Man who accepted of a presentation."[5] They seem to have been led by a Colonel Ogilvie, who exercised a kind of charismatic authority. The Presbytery authorized hearing of other probationers for a new minister, following which Blaikie employed a lawyer claiming that this constituted "a Covenant enter'd into against King and the Law."[6] The Presbytery referred the matter to the Synod of Angus and Mearns, who remitted it again on to the General Assembly.

The Kinnaird parishioners, in presence of the Presbytery, chose James Mylne senior as prospective minister in February 1735,[7] the first choice candidate, George Aitken, having been in the meantime transferred to Montrose.[8] At Forfar in April 1735, the Presbytery received his testimonials and agreed to put him through trials. These involved an "exercise and addition" (exegesis and thesis) on Hebrews 7:2–3[9] and delivering a popular sermon on 2 Timothy 1:10.[10] The scrutiny given to the work submitted seems to have been robust and would have contributed to the sense of authority and identity typical of Scottish professional life.

In May 1736, the General Assembly rejected Blaikie's case and Mylne senior's position was secured. The Presbytery met in November 1736 to confirm Mylne's candidature. Mylne senior was thus appointed minister of Kinnaird at the wishes of both parishioners and Presbytery, to whom responsibility for establishing procedures for the appointment of ministers reverted ("*jure devoluto*") in the absence of agreed parochial arrangements. Some time later, Blaikie was accepted by a nearby parish.[11]

---

3. Also written "Blackie."

4. Church of Scotland records, Kinnaird Settlement Case. This contains 54 pages of records ff178–237. NAS CH1/2/72 f188.

5. NAS CH1/2/72 f178.

6. NAS CH1/2/72, f178.

7. NAS CH1/2/72, f210.

8. NAS CH1/2/72, f190/196.

9. NAS CH1/2/72 f186 & Presbytery of Dundee records CH2/103/11/213.

10. NAS CH2/103/11/217.

11. Scott, *Fasti* (1920), 3:346.

The Kirk session and heads of families who had called Mylne senior put on a celebratory procession to the Presbytery meeting to represent "their firm and cordial adherence to the said call and earnest desire to have the said Mr Mylne speedily settled amongst them."[12] This reflected popular feeling at the time,[13] and is in contrast to the common sense philosopher Thomas Reid, who was reputedly ducked in a horse-pond at New Machar in similar circumstances to Blaikie.[14] In view of Mylne's later advocacy of extending the franchise, it may be worth noting that his father's experience of Presbyterian democracy was both beneficial to him and relatively benign in its dealing with the transferred minister.

Family Life

Five years later, in 1741, Mylne's father married minister's daughter Janet Faichney. Janet bore ten children in her marriage, nine of them within the eighteen years following 1742. There were seven sisters and three boys, of which children James Mylne junior was the third youngest. When he was born, he had five elder sisters. They were: Elizabeth, then aged fifteen and five months; followed by Isobel, just turned fourteen; Mary, almost twelve, who later married a minister; Janet, ten, who at the age of seventeen married the Dundee merchant Alexander Wright and whose famous granddaughter was Frances Wright; and Anne, almost eight. James also had an elder brother John, five years his senior, soon a younger brother George, almost three years James' junior and later by a little sister Margaret, who like Mary went on to marry a minister.[15]

Infant mortality was common in Scotland then. Another sister, also named Margaret, had died two years previously to James' arrival, just short of two years of age. His elder brother John died in September 1764 aged thirteen, nine days after James' seventh birthday. When he was eleven, in October 1769, his sister Janet died at the age of twenty-two leaving a small family to be taken care of by relatives. Two years later, his elder sisters

---

12. NAS CH2/103/283.

13. A Sandemanian noted "Any zeal about the Christian religion that appeared in Scotland at that time was for the National Establishment and Covenants, for the Presbyterian form of church government, for the call of the People in opposition to Patronage, etc" (John Handaside to William Sandeman 3/8/1784 in *Letters of Correspondence: Robert Sandeman and John Glas* (1851, Copy in NLS)). Mylne colleague John Snodgrass reckoned two thirds of Ministers supported patronage (Snodgrass, *An Effectual Method for Recovering our Religious Liberties*, 6).

14. Fraser, *Thomas Reid*, 30–31.

15. Scott, *Fasti* (1920).

Elizabeth and Anne died, in June and August 1771 respectively, just after James had successfully completed his first year of study at St. Andrews University before he turned fourteen. It would not be surprising if grief over the loss of his sisters contributed to his decision six months later, in February 1772, to renounce his bursary at St. Andrews and abandon his studies for a year. The college records offer no other explanation.

The minister's stipend in the 1790s was £37 and seems not to have materially changed for many years. Mylne and his brother George did not settle their father's estate until ten years after his death and the records they handed in indicate no material inheritance.[16] This would be typical of a minister with a large family who did not own the manse in which he lived: Adam Smith praises the parsimony of the Scottish Church in this respect. James Mylne thus began life poor but well educated and it speaks for his religious values that he entered the ministry knowing the relatively poor financial prospects.

Political Economy

When we cast our eye beyond the family home to the surroundings in which Mylne grew up, we find that Kinnaird Parish, along with the rest of the Carse of Gowrie, was predominantly agricultural, though there was a small weaving industry.[17] Literacy was widespread, though far from universal: five of six elders could sign Mylne senior's draft call from Kinnaird in 1735, but only 29 heads of families, with another 41 heads of families declaring they could not write.[18]

Trade was increasing: in 1734, several Kinnaird parishioners were at Perth for the Midsummer market day,[19] whilst for the local farmers, family farms were slowly being displaced by commercial production of grain and livestock for the growing market of Dundee. By 1804,[20] the Carse of Gowrie

16. Testament Dative in Commissary Court of St. Andrews records (NAS: CC20/4/27/256-7). The phrase "Summa inventar[ii] patet" indicates only one sum of money was involved (£5 owed to Mylne senior by a merchant Walter Ogilvie in Dundee) and that the matter was effectively closed.

17. I draw this account from the chapter on Kinnaird in the Spence, "South and East Perthshire, Kinross-shire," 11:280–88, who succeeded Mylne senior as minister of the Parish; and Spence, "Perth," 10:228–32.

18. NAS CH1/2/72/212.

19. NAS CH1/2/72/235 Letter to Blaikie.

20. I draw the following information from James Maitland (Lord Lauderdale) *An Inquiry into the Nature and Origin of Public Wealth*, 478 et seq. Lauderdale was an ally of Mylne's political association in Glasgow.

was estimated to have approximately 30,000 acres under cultivation, plus around 1,000 acres of orchard, and a human population of not more than 8,000. The principal crops were wheat, peas or beans, barley with red clover and ryegrass, grass for horse and cattle fodder, and oats, with one acre in six left fallow. The money value of the crop was reckoned to be worth around £133,000. These crops, particularly grain, were sent in bulk to Glasgow, Leith, and London. Except in respect of population, this undoubtedly marks a significant increase from Mylne's time there as steady improvements in transport and drainage were made.

Writing in the 1790s, the local minister David Spence describes the locals admiringly as "in general sober, honest and industrious;" and as "judicious and discerning, especially in farming," adding that "a new practice, that is generally adopted in the Carse, may be depended upon as a solid improvement."[21] Early in his lectures, Mylne expresses the view that a farmer may acquire knowledge by an extended process of observation, without formal experimentation. This view may go back to conversations with the local farmers or even his own experience, as his father's stipend as minister included a glebe of eight or nine acres. Mylne in later life experimented with the use of kelp as a fertilizer, glossed by a commentator as an "interest in gardening" but apparently conceived more grandiosely by Mylne himself as of potential significance for the Highland economy.

The gradual increase of rents by landowners, accompanied by the amalgamation of farms, led to the work of family members being increasingly supplemented or replaced by wage labor. Political conflict contributed to this. A local Jacobite family, the Threiplands, owned an estate which produced rent of £538 per annum, mostly in "kain" (i.e., kind, or farm produce) and out of which ministers' stipends and other expenses were paid.[22] As a result of their participation in the 1715 rising, this estate was confiscated by the government and sold on to the York Building Company for £9,606. However, the family leased the estate back from the Company for £480.

Religion

Several sources point to the religious belief of the local people as typically steady and informed, untroubled and undemonstrative. James Mylne senior's predecessor, James Adams, for example, wrote that: "tho' the Generality of them, in the view of the world, are very little concerned about the *One Thing Needful*; yet converse them upon a sick-bed, all is well with

---

21. Sinclair, *Statistical Account*, 11:288.
22. Chambers *The Threiplands of Fingask*, 32–34.

them, they believe in Christ."[23] This he intended as a criticism that their faith was shallow and may indicate a tension with some parishioners. Two generations later, Rev. David Spence observes that the "natural genius" of his Kinnaird parishioners was "favourable to tranquillity and contentment of mind." Specifically of their religious sensibilities, he noted: "Their religion may be often tinctured with superstition, but is seldom heated with enthusiasm. If, where it is in truth, it is accompanied with little fervour, it however operates as a calm rational, steady principle of wise and virtuous conduct."[24] These impressions then are probably applicable to some of Mylne's early acquaintances. It may thus be that Mylne's observations in his lectures against superstition refer back in part to this early period of his life. It may also be that the "coldness" that some evangelical students found in his preaching arose in part from the temper of such a congregation.

However, one religious movement based in the nearby towns of Perth and later Dundee, drew many followers, whilst also embodying a "calm, rational, steady principle." The nearby town of Perth was the centre of a proselytizing religious movement known as the Glasite church after its founder Reverend John Glas (1695–1773). Glas had studied at Perth Grammar School and graduated from St. Andrews in 1713, studying theology at Edinburgh thereafter. He opposed the idea of a national church in his first book *Testimony of the King of Martyrs* (1729). This led him to an Independent position, according to which the civil magistrate has no role in the church, a position contrary to chapter 23 of the *Westminster Confession of Faith*, the doctrinal standard of the Established Church. Glas was deposed from the ministry of the Established church in 1730. He drew a congregation in Dundee and for a time in Perth, where he met his most noted follower, Robert Sandeman. The General Assembly removed the sentence of deposition in 1739, though the Glasite church remained voluntarily independent thereafter.

James Adams had contributed to several religious and political controversies in five pamphlets.[25] The first two of these addressed the "Marrow" controversy in the Church of Scotland, a dispute about the meaning of the promises given in Christian revelation that sheds light on Mylne's concept of belief.[26] Adams considered the Glasites an offshoot of the Marrow-men. Edward Fisher's *Marrow of Modern Divinity*, republished in Scotland, was

23. Philip, *The Evangel in Gowrie*, 175–76, quoting Adams' *Snake in the Grass*.

24. Sinclair, *Statistical Account*, 11:288.

25. Scott, *Fasti Ecclesiae Scoticanae*, 5:345.

26. Adams, *The Snake in the Grass, or remarks upon a Book entitled "The Marrow of Divinity"* and *The Cromwellian Ghost conjured [. . .] and put from creeping into Houses.* In reply appeared: *The Viper shaken off* etc.

condemned by the Established Church in 1720 and 1722 and the debate shifted into a debate on Independency, or the authority of the Established Presbyterian Church. Adams' pamphlets reflect this, demonstrating familiarity with debate at the fringes of the Established Church. In his third pamphlet, *Marrow-Chicaning Display'd* (1726), he transfers the antinomian accusation of offering forgiveness without repentance from the Marrow-men to the early Glasites, still at this time within the folds of the Established Church. Whilst some of the Marrow-men joined the Secession Church of 1733 (the "anti-burghers"), this was not true of all and certainly not in Perthshire.[27] This pamphlet makes it clear that, in Adams view, the Glasite church grew directly from the "Marrow fraternity."

Two years later, in *The independent Ghost Conjur'd* (1728), Adams addresses the incipient Glasite movement directly. Two points emerge clearly from this pamphlet: the energy with which the Marrow doctrine was canvassed in Perthshire and the direct relationship between the Marrow men and the Glasite church. Adams writes: "Some years ago we were stuff'd and cramm'd, even to nauseating, with the *Marrow of Modern Divinity*, smoothing the *Antinomian* Doctrine to us; And now by a *Rump* of the same Men, we have got some of the worst parts of the *Independent Scheme* brought upon the Stage."[28] The pamphlet indicates that Adams had met Glas in person. Before leaving Adams, we might speculate that his pamphlets circulated in Kinnaird and that his thought that "there is nothing in our Constitution to hinder a Man from being a Philosopher, and at the same time a true-pac'd Presbyterian"[29] might have made an impression on Mylne's mind. The significant point in relation to Mylne is Glas' intellectualist view of religion, of which Adams complained: "your notion of faith will never make any true believers in a Gospel sense."[30] We will develop these ideas on their own account when we discuss Mylne's theory of belief.

Turning briefly to the founder of the Glasite church, Glas was noted as a kindly man and his followers were present in Perth and Dundee. There were two editions of his *Works*.[31] The movement was noted for its female followers. James Adams implied as much when he described the Glasites as those who "creep into houses, and lead captive silly women,"[32] later toning

---

27. Professor Donald Macleod of Free Church College, lecture at New College on Reformed Theology in Scotland, 26 November, 2009.
28. Adams, *Independent Ghost Conjur'd*, iv.
29. Ibid., 67.
30. Adams, *Marrow-chicaning*, 39.
31. First edition Edinburgh, 1761 (4 vols.); second edition Perth, 1782 (5 vols.).
32. Adams, *Snake in the Grass*, title page, from *Tim* 3.6.

down his description of those who testified for the Marrow to "a few well meaning women and tradesmen."³³ The Glasites counted women equally with men in the votes of elders. They shared broth in extended communion meals, whence their local name of the "kail kirk." In Adams' view, these meals—to which anyone was invited—undermined the discipline of the established Kirk, which refused communion to unrepentant sinners and were "a common receptacle for Clean and Unclean." This he connected with the Marrow doctrine of unconditional forgiveness of believers, giving as an instance a wife beater who had mocked the rebuke of his parish authorities and instead joined the Glasites.³⁴

The Glasite church soon acquired its most accomplished exponent, Robert Sandeman (1718–71). His views too are worth reviewing, not only as Mylne was probably aware of them early in life through his church environment and the theology teaching at St. Andrews, but as they influenced another philosopher, William Godwin,³⁵ whose work Mylne absorbed in the 1790s shortly before preparing his lecture course.

Politics

Turning to matters of state as seen from Kinnaird, the Jacobite movement was present in strength locally and "the feeling in Perthshire was pretty strong in favour of James."³⁶ We have mentioned one local family of landowners, the Threiplands of Fingask, who received the Pretender in 1715, but there was no consensus on Jacobite politics. Unlike the Laird, who had participated in the 1715 Rising, James Adams opposed the Jacobite activity that divided Perthshire, as apparently did Mylne senior himself in his role as clergyman in the '45.³⁷ Supporters perhaps included some in Kinnaird Parish, to the dismay of Adams, who denounced them from the pulpit.³⁸ Adams also criticized the "Marrow men" in this respect, insinuating in 1720 that "I find you highly commended by *Jacobites*, who expect to see our Church quickly destroyed by her pretended friends."³⁹

33 Adams, *Cromwellian Ghost Conjur'd*, 85.

34 See Ross: *A History of Congregational Independency*; idem, "Glasites" in *Encyclopaedia Britannica* (1911).

35 See Godwin's "Autobiography," in *Collected Novels and Memoirs*, vol 1.

36 Philip, *The Evangel in Gowrie*, 171.

37 Presbytery of Dundee minutes NAS:CH2/103/12/187.

38 We know this as Rev. Adams is recorded as having been active against it "being a Covenanter of a somewhat fiery type"(Scott, *Fasti* (1925), 5:345.)

39 Adams, *Marrow-Chicaning Display'd*, 13, 26.

Mylne himself was close to at least one former Jacobite family, into which his sister Janet had married and from whom his grandniece Frances Wright derived. Given the vulnerability to confiscation of landed property after the 1745 rebellion, it would be natural for such families to prefer towns and trade over agriculture and this appears to have been the case with the Wrights.[40] The Wright family was politically radicalized in the wake of the French revolution.[41] This contrasts with the interpretations by Mylne's contemporaries Walter Scott and James Hogg of the Jacobite movement as unequivocally Tory.[42] At college, Mylne's reading included the *Works* and *Letters* of the former Jacobite sympathizer Lord Bolingbroke.[43] These contain an account of the differences in foreign policy between the Hanoverians and Jacobite camps and also an advocacy of the emerging system of political parties. Mylne was decidedly internationalist as a professor. He may also have derived from Bolingbroke the ideas of foreign policy opposed to the imperial project and more conciliatory to France and Austria, the more progressive Catholic powers of the Continent, as well as of a political party and in particular of a "loyal opposition" that characterized his own Whig politics.

Education at St. Andrews

In 1770, at age 13, Mylne matriculated at the University of St. Andrews where he learned from several notable teachers over the next nine years. Mylne was one of four students offered a Foundation bursary at United College this year after a trial.[44] The benefit was financial and included the right to a "plate and spoon at the bursar's table" for 16s 8d. He was classed as a

---

40. See Frances Wright's autobiographical recollections in *Life, Letters and Lectures* for Mylne's sister's (Wright's grandmother) marriage with the Wilson family. Wright comments: "all the various and conflicting political convulsions of Europe have invariably tended to throw into the New World the most daring spirits and noblest energies of the Old" (n. 9).

41. James Mill (1773–1836) was another such case from the same shire: "It is said that Isobel Fenton's [Mill's mother] father had fallen from much better circumstances, in consequence of joining the Stuart rising of 1745" (Bain, *James Mill*, 4).

42. James Hogg for example, described his *The Jacobite Relics of Scotland* as "the unmasked sentiments of a bold and primitive race, who hated and despised the overturning innovations in church and state" (quoted in GC 5/12/1818). A similar line was taken by Walter Scott in *Waverley*.

43. St. Andrews Library borrowers' records for James Mylne (LY 207).

44. Minutes of United College 1765–1773 (St. Andrews UL: UC400) Meeting of 6/11/1770: "This being the day appointed for the bursar trial, the four following persons were preferred as most deserving [. . .] James Miln [. . .]" (592). The meeting was attended by Young, Morton, Watson, Forrest, and Cook.

"ternar," the ordinary students then distinguished from the sons of peers (primars), and landed and upper professional fathers (secondars). St. Andrews is a seaside town and its landmarks include the impressive remains of the medieval cathedral after which it is named. In several respects the education he received there stayed with him in later life.

Mylne spent the first two academic years from 1770 to 1772 in United College. This offered an arts curriculum and, in the Scottish tradition, Mylne's education there was generalist.[45] He studied Greek under Alexander Morton in 1770/71 and the record of his library borrowings shows a familiarity with Latin. The university had a high reputation for mathematics: its teachers had included the famous David Gregory (1712-65) on whose death the poet Robert Fergusson wrote an *Ode*.[46] James Mylne returned to St. Andrews in the early 1790s to meet the mathematician James Brown and the natural philosopher and mathematician John Leslie—later involved in a famous controversy over a remark on Hume's theory of causation.[47] Throughout his life, Mylne continued to acquire books on mathematics, and his early lectures show an interest in mathematics.

In March 1772, Mylne is recorded as leaving United College, his bursary passing to another student.[48] Unusually, when he returns in 1773, he enrolls in St. Mary's College, which offered theological education for intending ministers, funded by a bursary from that college.[49] It seems likely however, that Mylne completed the Arts curriculum. St. Mary's College was at that time conducted under Professor Murison (d. 1779).[50] At any rate, Mylne took the logic class of Robert Watson (1730-81).[51] Watson is better known

45. Davie, *The Democratic Intellect*, passim.

46. Robert Fergusson, *Ode on the Death of David Gregory*. Mylne was also a student during the visit of Samuel Johnson in 1773, which Fergusson satirized.

47. Brown *Thomas Chalmers*, 6; Hanna *Memoirs of Chalmers*, 1:465-7 and Morrell "The Leslie Affair," 70-71). See also Letters chiefly addressed to James Brown in EUL, Dc.2.57 and Chalmers papers at New College Edinburgh (TCP, CHA 2 Hanna Letters J Miller to W Hanna 21/1/1848).

48. Minutes of United College 1765-1773 (UC400): Meeting of 17 February, 1772: "Allowed a seat at the bursar table, vacant by James Miln's leaving the College, to Duncan McFarlan" (631).

49. Minutes of St. Mary's College 1774-1785 (SM400/1). Meeting of 8 November, 1773: "This being the day appointed for filling up the vacant bursaries—the meeting [...] nominate Mr Miln and Mr Fleming to be foundation bursars" (321).

50. I am grateful to Rachel Hart, archivist at St. Andrews UL and to Robert Reid, for conversations on the College records over several years. Robert Smart's typescript *Biographical Register of St. Andrews 1747-1897*, on the subject has been invaluable in accessing the records.

51. Mylne is recorded as "ex classe" Robert Watson in the matriculation records for 1774/75. For Watson, see Anderson, *Matriculation Roll*.

as a historian than a philosopher, being the author of *History of Phillip 2nd of Spain*,[52] the subject of which is best known for sending the Spanish Armada against Elizabethan England. Watson's book covers the "last Mediterranean age,"[53] the period after William Robertson's *History of Charles the Fifth*, of which Mylne later had a copy. Watson's was a popular work in its day from which Mylne drew an example of the corrupting influence of education on conscience in his lectures on moral philosophy[54] and apparently relies on in several places in his political economy course. Watson's course had four parts: "1. To explain the powers of the understanding; 2. Species of evidence on which our assent is founded in the several branches of truth and knowledge; 3. Causes and species of error; 4. Practical observations concerning reading and the other means of improvement."[55] He also introduced his class to the ideas of Bacon, Hume and Reid, albeit at an elementary level. For example, Watson finds a happy illustration of his Reidian critique of Hume's view of belief as a "lively conception." He comments: "But this is mistaken—a novel may be livelier than history without evoking belief."[56] These subjects were treated in much greater depth in Mylne's own teaching.

Having studied under Watson, Mylne is likely, given the normal curriculum, also to have taken the moral philosophy class of John Cook (d. 1815), professor of Ethics and Pneumatics from 1773 to 1815 and who previously taught humanities.[57] Cook's lectures were remembered as effective and animated.[58] The content was based on the Mental and Ethical Philosophy sections of Francis Hutcheson's Latin *Synopsis Metaphysiciae, Ontologium et Pneumatologiam Complectens* (Glasgow: Foulis, 1762).[59] They show Cook finding an answer to Hume's skepticism in Hutcheson's terms, but at the expense of the vitality of the rational powers as a whole. The course would have illustrated for Mylne the process of detailed, critical scrutiny of

---

52. Watson, *History of Phillip 2nd of Spain*, 1777, and later editions.

53. Braudel, *The Mediterranean*.

54. See *Dict. Of Nat. Biography*, 2:940. The work went through seven editions prior to 1812 and was translated into French, German, and Dutch. Mylne's reference is found in 1799/1800 lectures, 264–65: "When Philip the Second came to his kingdom, he testified his joy by an [265] *Auto da fe* and looked back on this with a feeling of approbation."

55. Watson, *A Compend of Logic and Universal Grammar* (StUL:MS BC.6.W1).

56. Watson, *A Compend of Logic and Universal Grammar* (StUL:MS BC.6.W1), 51.

57. Anderson, *The Matriculation Roll*, LXXVIII.

58. "We remember well the high classical acquirements, the unambitious and neglected, yet acute and even animated lectures of Cook the Moralist" ("Notes on the current State of St. Andrews," *Edinburgh Magazine*, January 1826, 92).

59. This can be determined by the page numbers and translations cited by Cook. There is a copy of the 5th edition in St. Andrews UL.

a densely written philosophical text, whilst raising the problems of "moral sense" theory. Cook's discussions of God, freedom and immortality and his division of duties into those to God, mankind and ourselves are taken up in Mylne's lectures at Glasgow.

Mylne is recorded at St. Andrews for the two academic years between 1773 and summer 1775. The library records indicate that he withdrew around four books a month. It seems he turned first to Roman literature. The first author in whom he showed deep interest was Virgil.[60] He perhaps compared the Epicurean shepherds of the *Eclogues*, and their pagan sacrifices with the Christian farming community into which he was born. He also borrowed Plutarch's *Lives of the Philosophers*, which contains an account of Epicurus. Mylne borrowed Cicero's *Opera* and he was referred to in John Cook's moral philosophy class in respect of *De Fato*. Mylne later set prize essay questions on passages from Cicero for his moral philosophy class in Glasgow. Cicero describes the Stoic philosophy sympathetically and strongly prefers it to the Epicurean system. Mylne's students were regularly asked to expound one or other system or to reconcile them.

Turning to modern literature, Mylne borrowed Samuel Butler's comic poem *Hudibras* in 1772. Many Scottish philosophers known to Mylne mention *Hudibras*[61] and David Hume gives it a key role at the end of his *History of England*, calling it "one of the most learned compositions, that is to be found in any language."[62] Mylne too quotes from the poem[63] and we know that its manner was recognizable to his contemporaries.[64] The poem tells of

---

60. He borrowed three separate editions of Virgil (those of Andrew, Martin, and Pill) from St. Andrews University Library in his first two years (LY207/1).

61. Smith, *Theory of Moral Sentiments*, 198. Thomas Reid mentions it (*Active Powers*, 14 "sir Hudibras's dagger"; as does Dugald Stewart (*Philosophy of the Human Mind*, chapter 5 "Association of Ideas," 1.4.2 "Of rhyme") and it is singled out for praise by Beattie (*Elements of Moral Science*, 164, 166). Mylne's pupil William Hamilton quotes from Hudibras in "Philosophy of Perception" in *Discussions on Philosophy and Literature*, 64; and also "Oxford as it might be" (ibid., 784).

62. This is located prominently in the prominent concluding peroration of David Hume's *History of the Stuarts* that concludes his *History of England*, 6:544.

63. The citation that he gives was a standard instance of ludicrous juxtaposition:
"Like a lobster boiled the morn,
From black to red began to turn."   Samuel Butler, *Hudibras*, 146; [Part 2, Canto 2].

Despite the humor of the comparison, the image of a "red sky in the morning" also evokes the bloodshed and thus the violence in the contemporary religious culture of England.

64. Mylne's friend the Congregationalist minister Ralph Wardlaw also wrote an unpublished poem, described as "in the Hudibrastic manner" on a pamphlet *The New Light Examined*, by Rev. William Porteous (see Alexander, *Memoirs of the Life*, 37).

the English Civil War, "When civil dudgeon first grew high/ And men fell out, they knew not why," and satirizes Christians:

> Such as do build their faith upon
> The holy text of pike and gun
> Decide all controversies by
> Infallible artillery

By which he means the English Presbyterians and Independents ("Puritans") and their Scottish supporters. The poem thus deplores the resort to force in religious debate. However, Butler also uses the weakness of reason to justify the Anglican settlement:

> For when we swore to carry on
> The present reformation
> According to the purest mode
> Of churches best reformed abroad
> What did we else but make a vow
> To do we knew not what nor how?
> For no three of us will agree
> Where or what churches these should be.[65]

The popularity of this poem amongst Scottish Churchmen and secular intellectuals indicates a will to rise above Protestant denominational antipathies. Yet the weakness of reason was not conceded in the dissenting tradition from which Mylne later drew.

Mylne borrowed weighty volumes of theology such as the undogmatic Genevan Benedict Pictet's *Theology*, a standard work of Calvinist theology in Scotland;[66] John Calvin's *Institutes of the Christian Religion*; the works of Edward Stillingfleet (1635–99), an Anglican critic of John Locke; the sermons of Samuel Clarke and some similar volumes.[67] There was also an active student theological society.[68]

James Mylne is not recorded as present for the three following academic years to 1778. It may be that he studied elsewhere for these three years or worked as a tutor, as often happened. It may also be that he was still at St. Andrews, as there is no record of his bursary being transferred or resigned. He borrowed Voltaire's *Lettres anglaises* (1734) and his personal library indicates that he owned several books published on the Continent at this time. He may thus have visited Europe, though the evidence is only

---

65. Samuel Butler, *Hudibras*, 76 [Part 1 Canto 2].
66. Whytock, *An Educated Clergy*, 107, 127–28.
67. St. Andrews library records, LY 207.
68. Cant, *The University of St. Andrews*, 97.

circumstantial. He was present again for 1778/79. Mylne ended his student career by winning the highest prize for an essay on the question "Under what limitations may Popery be tolerated in a Protestant country?"[69] He was the only student to submit an answer.[70] Perhaps it reflected time spent on the Continent in the preceding years. In the last two decades of his life Mylne was a public supporter of Catholic emancipation in Great Britain and Ireland, at the expense of some personal opprobrium.[71] However, he thought the Catholic Church inimical to economic prosperity in his political economy lectures. The subject however, suggests a willingness to take a measured line on subjects where Scottish opinion was apt to be driven by hidebound passions.

There is strong evidence of an interweaving of academic and political influence throughout Mylne's career. For example, politically, John Cook was later a Dundas supporter, though Henry Dundas did not establish his influence before the 1780s.[72] Mylne may also have known George Hill (1750–1819), at that time professor of Greek, but later Principal of St. Mary's, Moderator of the General Assembly of the Church of Scotland and considered "the outstanding Scottish theologian of his day."[73] As with Cook, Hill had a "close association" with the "Dundas despotism," both being considered "managers."[74]

---

69. Minutes of St. Mary's College 1774–1785 (SM400/2) Meeting of 14/12/1778: "This being the day appointed for prescribing the premium discourses for the two highest classes, the meeting prescribed to the 4th or highest class, a question, "Under what limitations may Popery be tolerated in a Protestant country?" (115).

70. Ibid. SM400/2: Meeting of 15 February, 1779: "This day the prizes were determined for the two highest classes when (only one being given in for each class and no competitor) they were judged worthy of a premium. The transcribers being called declared that for the 4th or highest class belonged to Mr Miln."

71. See *GC* 25/1/1821. The toasts at the "Anniversary of Mr Fox" at which Mylne spoke included: "A liberal and conciliatory Government to Ireland," followed by "Catholic emancipation." He was criticized for attending the O'Connell dinner in Glasgow in 1835.

72. On Cook's electoral support for a Dundas electoral candidate, see Melville papers at St. Andrews, letter 4446.

73. Cant, *The University of St. Andrews*, 99. In 1803, Hill published *Theological Institutes*, a brief summary of his course. His *Lectures on Divinity* (1821) were published posthumously by his son Alexander Hill and went through many editions. In 1826, an observer of St. Andrews wrote: "Hill, and Cook, and Lee are certainly proud names in the Theological literature of the same University" ("Notes on the Present State of the University of St. Andrews," in *Edinburgh Magazine*, January 1826, 91).

74. Cant, *The University of St. Andrews*, 99. For correspondence between Hill and Robert Dundas, see Melville Papers, Letters 4832, 4854.

Mylne thus emerged into adult life in 1779 as a young man with a sound general education and an informed view of Christian theology and church history. The American War of Independence had broken out in 1776 and was still going on. Elements from a recently formed regiment, the "Royal Glasgow Volunteers" were present in Dundee and Mylne must have come across them.

CHAPTER 2

Deputy Chaplaincy

IN DECEMBER 1779, JAMES Mylne became deputy chaplain of a Scottish regiment, the 83rd Regiment of Foot, raised for the American War of independence but stationed in the Channel Islands. He spent three years, aged 22 to 25, with this regiment. Here he was exposed to first-hand experience of several regiments of the British Army, the Jersey Militia, and the Royal Navy. This sheds some light on his advocacy of militias and naval defense and perhaps on his publicly expressed hopes for an end to war.

The Raising of the 83rd Regiment of Foot

James Mylne was ordained as a minister of the Church of Scotland by the Presbytery of Dundee in May 1779, aged 21. In December that year he became deputy-chaplain of the 83rd Regiment of Foot, also known as the "Royal Glasgow Volunteers,"[1] which had been headquartered in Dundee earlier that year.[2] The troops had joined up when the Corporation of Glasgow offered a bounty to prospective recruits.[3] Originally under the command of

---

1. Scott, *Fasti* (1920), 3:169.

2. *Glasgow Mercury* (*GM*), 18/3–15/4/1779: Recruiting parties were ordered back to Dundee headquarters on 18 March, 1779, when "the corps expressed their willingness to go wherever the service of their country called them, by three cheers" (92).

3. *GM*, Thurs 8/1/1778 on raising of money under auspices of Town Council "to enable his Majesty to quell the present unnatural rebellion in America," 5; £50 contribution from weavers received same date, 6; £9,600 raised, 21; first reference to 'Glasgow Volunteers' 29/1/1778, 30; to "Royal Glasgow Volunteers" recruiting at Saracen's Head Inn, 19/2/1778, 55.

a Lieutenant Alexander Leslie,[4] they were one of 12 new British regiments raised in 1778[5] at the behest of the government.[6] By July 1778, they were about 900 men strong and deemed "efficient in manoeuvres."[7]

The 83rd Regiment was divided into ten companies of around 100 men of which two, the grenadiers and light infantry, selected by height and marksmanship respectively, were considered the elite. We can gather from lists of deserters[8] that the recruits were typically aged 17 to 35 with an average age just short of 25 on recruitment. The older men generally had manual trades,[9] the younger often none. They were drawn from all over lowland Scotland, including Argyle, Ayr, and Lanark, but with a majority from Counties Armagh and Antrim in Ireland. They were armed with muskets and wore coats of red broadcloth over white or buff clothing. The uniform promoted *esprit de corps*, but also made deserters identifiable. Standard pay for a private was 8d a day of which, after 2d deductions, 6d was left for subsistence.[10]

In October 1778, four companies at Ayr and Irvine marched for Edinburgh to quell a mutiny of a Highland regiment.[11] Thereafter they witnessed a further attempted mutiny of a Highland regiment in the Firth of Forth. A description records: "About 50 of Fraser's Highlanders came down to be shipped in the transports, and incorporated with the Glasgow regiment. They absolutely refused to go." This was an example of "drafting," unpopular with soldiers, who lost control of their situation.[12] The mutineers demanded payment of arrears of pay. After being both reasoned with and intimidated, shots were discharged and around twenty Highlanders killed, along with "several Fencibles and a Captain."[13] The Highlanders never

---

4. Leslie's command *GM* 5/2/1778; he declines post of Colonel *GM* 18/6/1778,

5. Curtis, *Organisation of the British Army in the American Revolution*, 67, citing National Archives, Kew, London: PRO WO.24.494.

6. Curtis, *Organisation*, citing Fortescue, *History of the British Army*, 3:245; 36 *Commons Journal*, 613–15.

7. *GM*, issue 26, 2/7/1778, 206.

8. Thirty-three deserters named in *GM* 25/6/1778, a further one in *GM* 8/10/1778.

9. These included: weaver, flax dresser, shoe maker, wheelwright, labourer (*GM* 25/6/1778).

10. Reid, *British Redcoat 1740–1793*, 7. 12d =1shilling; 20 shillings=1pound.

11. *GM*, 15/10/1778, 327. The Seaforth Highlanders were involved.

12. Curtis, *Organisation*, 79. Fortescue's *History* cites a letter of General Oughton to the Secretary of State of 20/4/1779.

13. *GM*, 22/4/1779: These events do not seem to be mentioned in Prebble's work on Highland mutinies.

fired.[14] The remaining Highlanders were court-martialled under Lt.-Col. Ralph Dundas. Three were sentenced to death, but the King later granted a free pardon,[15] a practice condemned by William Godwin, whom Mylne later read. Strengthened by the Highlanders, the 83rd Regiment sailed to the Channel Islands in April 1779 with no further desertions.[16] They had settled there when Mylne was appointed deputy chaplain in December 1779.[17] Soon, five companies of the regiment were based in each of the two principal islands of Jersey and Guernsey. At this time French or a dialect thereof was the predominant language on the Channel Islands and Mylne's knowledge of French may owe something to this.

Chaplaincy, Officers, and Men

The chaplain of the 83rd Regiment from July 1778 was Robert Small (1732–1808), who had been educated at Dundee Grammar school and St. Andrews University and married in 1764.[18] He was a classical scholar who published on mathematics and astronomy, interests he shared with his assistant Mylne. Robert Small served as Moderator of the General Assembly of the Church of Scotland in 1791, which was addressed by Thomas Muir on the M'Gill controversy. In Dundee, he later co-founded a local medical dispensary and his publications include also a sermon *The Importance of the Poor* (Dundee, 1794) and a contribution to Sinclair's *Statistical Account*. He addressed the General Assembly again in 1800 in defense of his conduct in admitting elders of known reformist views into the church.[19]

---

14. *GM*, 22/4/1779, 132.

15. *GM*, 3/6/1779, 179.

16. *GM*, 18/3–15/4/1779, 92 on move from Dundee and Montrose; 116 "To the honour of this corps, not a man has deserted from it since they received orders for embarkation"; 123 convoy expected in a few days. 22 April 1779: "The first division of the Glasgow regiment marched from Dundee, on Monday, and last division on Tuesday, for Burntisland, in order to embark upon the transports lying there ready to receive them." (132). By 29 April they are reported as embarked (*GM*, 29/4/1779, 140) and sailed Friday 18 June under convoy. (*GM* 24/6/1779, 204) See also *GM* 15/10/1778, 327 for danger from American privateers.

17. *GM*, 2/12/1779 publishes a letter from a Gentleman of the Glasgow regiment in Guernsey dated Nov 18 1779: "Our barrack-rooms are tolerable, and we live very happily" (388). Mylne was appointed Deputy Chaplain at the start of December.

18. Scott, *Fasti*, vol. 5, *Synods of Fife, Angus and the Mearns* (1925), 316–17.

19. Small, *Defence delivered by Dr Small at the Bar of the General Assembly 1800*.

Small wrote a book, *Kepler's Astronomical Discoveries* (London, 1804) of which Mylne owned a copy,[20] dedicated to the Earl of Lauderdale. In this, Small adopts a historical approach to science by interpreting Kepler's work as a series of revisions of the views of his predecessors tested by means of new calculations and observations. Small writes that, in addition to its historical interest, Kepler's work: "Claims attention for another reason, that it exhibited, even prior to publication of Bacon's *Novum Organum*, a more perfect example, than perhaps ever was given, of the legitimate connection between theory and experiment; of experiments suggested by theory, and of theory submitted without prejudice to the test and decision of experiments."[21] Small describes Kepler's examination of the assumptions and hypotheses of Ptolemy, Copernicus and Tycho Brahé on the geocentric or heliocentric orbits of the planets. After discovery of the heliocentric orbits of Mercury and Venus, controversy focused on interpreting Mars, in the light of which new observations were made and old ones reinterpreted. The book has considerable factual and mathematical content. In his lectures, Mylne appeals to astronomy as an example of a science where experiment strictly so-called, as opposed to observation, is not possible and he shared Small's interest in mathematics. Mylne also owned Adam Smith's *Philosophical Essays* (1795) which contains Smith's "History of Astronomy," but Small's book is considerably more detailed and may also be a source of his views.

The other deputy chaplain was James Playfair (1752–1812), with whom Mylne had common interests in Virgil, Shakespeare, French literature, and natural history. Playfair moved from Guernsey to Jersey by July 1781, preferring the latter where he lodged outside the garrison and where apples, pork, beans, and parsnips were grown and bread and milk were plentiful.[22] His colleague Mylne probably made the reverse journey and shared a similar diet. Playfair later became a minister at Bendochy, about five miles from Mylne's birthplace,[23] where he married and created the literary persona of a studious rustic minister in an unpublished manuscript *Of the Care and Knowledge of Bees*, which still survives.[24] Along with a study of beekeeping, it contains detailed and original discussions of the anatomy and senses of bees. Playfair tells us that "there is a kind of Divine pleasure in contemplat-

20. Skirving Catalogue of Books of the late Professor Mylne 1840 (GUL:Sp.Coll/BD17-h.11).

21. Small, *An Account of the Astronomical Discoveries of Kepler*, 2. Mawman also published Leslie's *Experimental Inquiry into the Nature and Propagation of Heat* at this time that caused a famous controversy at Edinburgh on Hume's account of causality.

22. Letter to his parents in Balleine, *History of Jersey*, 197–98.

23. Scott, *Fasti*, near Cupar Angus in Meigle Presbytery.

24. NLS: Manuscript MRB.214.

ing the ways of God, even in the smallest of his works."[25] In a sermon on the centenary of the 1688 Revolution, he evoked God's benevolence in terms drawn from the philosophy of mind: "how amazing his goodness in the endowment of our souls! their memory! their faculty of reasoning! their power of imitation and invention! their powers of investigation, even into the stupendous objects that are in heaven!"[26] He observes, "Our civil government is the admiration and envy of all nations," a view many would have endorsed at the time. James Playfair was distantly related to John Playfair (1748–1819)[27] the professor of natural philosophy at Edinburgh University. Mylne thus shared elements of a common ecclesiastical culture with both his chaplaincy colleagues and, we shall see, some political views with Small.

The commissioned officers of the 83rd Regiment were appointed by the Crown.[28] The commanding officer from July 1778 was Colonel George Scott who had been transferred with promotion from the 61st Regiment of Foot stationed at Gibraltar, with Alexander Fotheringham Ogilvie as Lieutenant-Colonel.[29] The other senior officers above lieutenant were also transferred from other units. In August 1781, Scott was appointed Lieutenant-Governor of Windsor Castle.[30] In June 1781, Henry Fanshawe replaced Ogilvie.[31] Fanshawe went on to serve with distinction under Russian command as Colonel of the Elotzkoy Regiment at the time of the Russo-Turkish war.[32] In short, the senior officers of the Regiment were well-connected career soldiers.

According to a press report in January 1781, the garrison on the Channel Islands comprised: 900 effective men of Lord Seaforth's 78th Regiment; 780 men of the 83rd Regiment under Colonel Scott; 600 men of the 95th Regiment under Colonel John Reid (c. 1722–1807), a veteran soldier and composer who succeeded Moses Corbet as Lieutenant-Governor; and 570 men of the 96th under Colonel Whyte. In addition, 240 "invalids" and a

25. NLS: Manuscript MRB.214, introductory sections.

26. Playfair, *Sermon on the Centennial Say*, 8.

27. James' grandfather was John's father's brother: see Rogers *The Scottish Branch*, 24–25 and *Four Perthshire Families*, 83.

28. Curtis, *Organisation of the British Army in the American Revolution*, citing *Correspondence of Geo. III with Lord North*, Letter of 24/1//1778.

29. *London Gazette* (London, England), 21–25/7/1778; Issue 11894; Gale Doc Ref: Z2000735964. This lists all officers of the 83rd at that date.

30. *London Chronicle* (London, England), 21–23/8/1781; Issue 3857.

31. *Morning Chronicle and London Advertiser* (London, England), 11/6/1781; Issue 3765. Gale Doc Ref: Z2000858748.

32. *The World* 29/7/1789, citing *London Gazette* 28/7/1789 Gale Doc. Ref. Z2001516215.

7,000 strong local militia is noted.[33] The Jersey Militia cooperated with, but did not consider itself under the command of, the regular forces.[34] The 78th regiment, partly or wholly Gaelic-speaking highlanders from Ross-shire, was also divided equally across the two islands and encounters with them may have contributed to Mylne's later interest in the Highland economy.

The Battle of Jersey

In January 1781, elements of the 83rd stationed at Grouville in Jersey saw action during an abortive French attack on Jersey, during which seven members of the regiment and around twenty French soldiers were killed.[35] The French were led by a Baron Rullancourt, described as "an adventurer," who was killed in the abortive attack. The deep Guernsey harbor, through which smuggling between Britain and France was conducted and which was visited by privateers, would have been the main military prize.[36] The French apparently had allies on the Islands who had communicated British troop strengths to them.[37] Rullancourt used this information to persuade the Lieutenant-Governor, Moses Corbet, to surrender, but not before Corbet had dispatched Captain Hemery to inform the 83rd and other troops, though without transmitting orders. However, subsequent to Corbet's surrender, he issued a capitulation and an unsigned order to surrender that "threw the officers of the 83rd into the utmost perplexity what to do." A witness testified that: "They argued that, if they should obey it, they were liable to be broke; on the other hand, if they surrendered to the enemy without at least an acknowledged superiority, [it] would be cowardice."[38] In the absence of Colonel Scott, they concluded that "it was a palpable absurdity that a man, deprived of his liberty, should give any order," and the Regiment marched in support of Major Pierson. The grenadiers of the 83rd, with

33. *London Chronicle* (London, England), 20- 23/1/1781, Gale Doc Ref: Z2000573787.
34. "Lettres Inédites Relatives à la Bataille de Jersey," in *Société Jersiaise Bulletin Annuels* 5:27–30, Lemprière letter of 13/2/1781, 278.
35. *GM*, Issues 159-61, 11-25/1/1781. "The French on the 6th Inst attacked the island of Jersey." Many were reported drowned on landing in the dark (19–20). The governor "had just time to dispatch him [Col. Hemery] with the intelligence to Grenville Bay, to the 83rd Regiment and another messenger to La Hague, to the 95th Regiment."
36. *Lloyd's Evening Post* (London, England), 22–24/1/1781; Issue 3681.
37. *Actes des États de l'Ile de Jersey* 1780–1785: "il semble que l'ennemi avait des alliès à Jersey," 5–6, 59; letter of 13/2/1781 of William-Charles Lemprière in "Lettres Inédites Relatives à la Bataille de Jersey" in *Société Jersiaise Bulletin Annuels* 5:27–30, 282.
38. Evidence of Francis La Coutour, in Williamson, *Trial of Moses Corbet*, 14.

support: "attacked a party of the enemy at La Roque, being part of a second debarquation, many of whom were killed, others fled into the country, and the rest surrendered prisoners. [. . .] About fifty of the regulars were killed, and about twenty of the militia, and several wounded."[39] A later report states that the attack was a bayonet charge, with about twenty French killed and thirty taken prisoner in the attack by the Glasgow Regiment, out of the 300 or so French troops who landed.[40] Seven grenadiers of the 83rd Regiment were killed and a memorial stone was later erected to them at Grouville Parish church. Corbet was later put on trial and superseded as Governor, while victory was celebrated in song and on the London stage. Mylne was thus witness to a bloody military confrontation. The battle was the subject of John Copley's painting, *The Death of Major Peirson*.[41]

Peace Returns

At this point, the fog of war descends on the history of the 83rd Regiment, though it appears to have remained in the Channel Islands. There were rumors of a second invasion attempt in April 1781.[42] In July 1781 James Playfair wrote to his parents, "You need not be alarmed at any reports of our Regiment going abroad; the newspaper accounts are often false, as they mistake one Regiment for another. [. . .] I have no desire to go to an unhealthy climate and upon my present pay, it is impossible for me to go."[43] Two much later sources state without providing sources that the Regiment sailed for New York, but contemporary documents tell against this.[44] Hostilities in America had come to a virtual end with the surrender of Cornwallis at Yorktown on October 19, 1781. In July 1781 and April 1782, the *Parliamentary Register* records expenditure paid to Scott for forage for the 83rd regiment whilst it was in Guernsey and Jersey.[45] Army Returns of Stations and the

39. *GM*, 11/1/1781, 20.

40. *GM*, 25/1/1781, 29.

41. John Copley's (1738–1815) painting, *Death of Major Peirson* (Tate Gallery, London).

42. *Lloyd's Evening Post* (London, England), 18–20/4/1781; Gale Doc Ref: Z2000529376 col. 2.

43. Cited in Balleine, *History of Jersey*, 197–98.

44. Mayne, *The Battle of Jersey*, 43 and Chichester's *The Records and Badges of every Regiment and Corps in the British Army*, 780, do not cite sources or take account of PRO records. Fortescue's *A History of the British Army 1763–1793* and Thomas Jones's *History of New York during the Revolutionary War* do not mention the 83rd Regiment in America.

45. *Parliamentary Register* (London, 1781), Vol 2, 172; 1782, 677.

Amherst papers locate the 83rd Regiment in Guernsey and Jersey throughout 1782, with no order to sail given.[46]

The Amherst papers and Jersey records indicate a breakdown of relations between soldiers and the islanders and their authorities over the cost of provisions in 1782, with Major John Whyte of the 83rd playing a negotiating role.[47] In December 1782, Robert Small was replaced as chaplain of the regiment by Playfair,[48] around which time Mylne must have left. After the surrender of Cornwallis to General George Washington and protracted peace negotiations thereafter, the Royal Glasgow Volunteers were ordered to sail for India. The *Glasgow Mercury* reported in December 1782, "The 83rd Regiment of Foot, or Royal Glasgow Volunteers, commanded by General Scott, are under orders to embark immediately for the East Indies."[49] There are records of this order, though Scott was a Colonel.[50] The *Glasgow Mercury* reported that ships for Madras were proceeding to Portsmouth.[51] However, contemporary newspaper records are again confused, with reports of a "secret expedition" under General John Dalling (1731-98), a former Governor of Jamaica.[52] In February 1783, the 83rd were "part at Fareham & Titchfield, part on board at Spithead,"[53] but they were returning home. The mutiny of an English regiment was reported as having broken out on January 27, 1783, though this was not admitted in the *Glasgow Mercury* until a year later: "The 77th regiment of foot at Portsmouth mutinied, and refused to go on board for the East Indies, and by the mediation of Lord Maitland, they were discharged."[54] In March 1783 an Irish Regiment, given the same order in the south of England, also mutinied.[55] The Lord Maitland involved was James Maitland (1759-1839), better known as the politician

46. Amherst papers PRO/WO34/108/29,48,58,60 for Guernsey returns Jan-Mar 1782; Return of Stations: PRO/WO379/3/74,80,85,88,91,94,97,99 for Dec 1779 & June-Dec 1782, all locate 83rd Regiment in Channel Islands.

47. Correspondence in Amherst papers PRO/WO34/108/18,35,44,65,69,74.

48. *The British Magazine and Review* Vol 1 (London, 1782-1783), 479.

49. *GM*, Issue 261, 26/12/1782. The General John Scott, who acquired wealth in India, played whist with David Hume and whose daughter married the future Tory Prime Minister George Canning (1770-1827) seems to be a different person.

50. PRO/WO379/3/102: the 83rd is "under orders for [Hilica Barr]."

51. *GM*, Issue 225, 23/1/1783.

52. *Morning Herald and Daily Advertiser* (London, England), 16/1/1783; Issue 692.

53. Army Return of Stations: PRO/WO379/3/106

54. *GM*, issue 314, 8/1/1784, in its review of the year for 1783.

55. The Irish 104th Regiment also mutinied at Guernsey according to the *Glasgow Mercury* Issue 274 27/3/1783 (109). The men wished to be discharged, fired at their officers, but eventually surrendered, being subdued by the 18th regiment

and political economist Earl (thereafter Lord) Lauderdale, who had visited Paris and studied at Edinburgh, Oxford and Glasgow University under John Millar,[56] qualifying as an Advocate in 1780. Maitland was at that time a Whig MP and supporter of Fox's East India Bill. We may conjecture that this may have been when Mylne first heard of Lauderdale. Mylne later drew on Lauderdale's work in his political economy lectures,[57] discussing his *Inquiry into the Nature and Origin of Public Wealth*, which appeared in Glasgow bookshops in 1804.[58]

In January 1783 there were considerable changes in the officers of the 83rd Regiment of Foot.[59] No regimental history exists and unusually its muster rolls and other records appear to have been lost.[60] The Glasgow politicians who had been instrumental in raising the Regiment do not appear to have been informed of its fate.[61] This would be consistent with an official cover-up following some unrecorded challenge to the order to embark for India, which was clearly beyond the reasons for which the Regiment had been raised.[62] In March 1783, the 83rd Regiment was ordered disbanded on the usual terms whereby a register of men and officers was made, arrears of

56. Craig, "Account of the Life," xcii.

57. Lauderdale is mentioned in both surviving student notes of Mylne's course in 1804 and 1815/16.

58. *GC*, 3/3/1804.

59. Following the December 1782 order to sail to embark for the East Indies, the *Glasgow Mercury* reports three replacements of the officer corps (James Stanley to replace Herbert Whitfield as Captain; John Gilfillan to replace David Carnie as Lieutenant & new Ensign: Issue 264, 16 /1/1783; interpreting "vice" as "replacing"); a further three (with identical ranks) on 6 February (issue 267, 6/2/1783); another three a month later (Issue 271, 6/3/1783); two changes (Adjutant and deputy) a month later (issue 276, 10/4/1783); and two new appointments (Major Gordon appointed Lieutenant Colonel and new Major) two weeks after that (issue 278, 24/4/1783).

60. It is not in the exhaustive catalogue of Kitzmiller, 1988. Farmer (1901) mentions the 83rd's existence (200), but White's *Bibliography of Regimental Histories of the British Army* records no regimental history. Usual records include the muster book, pay list, pension related records, and records of deserters.

61. The Glasgow City Council Minutes, held at Mitchell Library, refer to the raising of the Volunteers on 29 December 1777 (Mitchell Library: C/1/36, 28–30), but there are apparently no military references in 1783 to shed light on its fate, with the Volunteers not in the A-Z index either. According to Chichester's *Records and Badges*, "its colours are, or were not very many years ago, still in possession of the corporation of Glasgow" (780).

62. Henry Dundas was "a leading member of the board" of the East India Company following the passing of the India Bill in August 1784 (B Lenman, *Scotland 1746–1832*, 80). It is possible, though unlikely, that reported government views of Mylne owe something to the events of this time.

pay made up and arms returned;[63] thereafter they marched for Carlisle due to arrive on April 25 and disappear from the public record.[64]

As a former deputy-chaplain, Mylne spoke from experience when he addressed military affairs in his lectures on Moral Philosophy and Political Economy. In the former, he questioned the justification of both war and empire. In a discussion dated 1799 of the question 'Will general philanthropy ever prevail?' he says:

> Commerce too tho' it has been the cause of wars yet finally will not continue so. Smith showed the real interests of nations and in 25 years since this was published the notions of [awhile] are altered and men are convinced of the folly of monopolies of colonies, of the advantages of free trade, etc. If these were fully understood many causes of war would vanish, nations would see their common interests in peace. War may be favourable to a few merchants as a fire is to a timber merchant or a mildew to a few farmers.[65]

The condemnation of colonial policies is taken from Smith's *Wealth of Nations* (1776), a work Mylne greatly admired,[66] while the remark about some merchants benefitting from war adds imagery to the anti-belligerent view of John Millar in a posthumous work jointly edited by Mylne.[67]

After his discharge from the army, Mylne returned to Scotland. Relating to this period, Mylne's library indicates that he owned a copy of the *Mutiny Act and Articles of War* (Edinburgh, 1744).[68] The only two books he owned that were published in Dublin date from 1783 and 1784, which suggests a route by which he may have made his way to Paisley. This time, from July 1782 to July 1783, was the height of the volunteer militia movement in Ireland. As result, Britain relinquished its claims over the Irish government, so that, according to John Millar: "By these alterations, Ireland became an independent kingdom, connected by a federal union with Britain, but possessing within itself a supreme legislative assembly, and supreme courts

---

63. PRO/WO26/31/362–66 (Royal Orders).

64. PRO/WO379/3/112. Joe Fisher, *Glasgow Encyclopaedia*, 215. The *Glasgow Mercury* lists active British regiments in issue 309, 27/11/1783, with the 83rd not amongst them.

65. GUL, 1799 notes: MS 207, 434–35.

66. See James Mylne, *Outline of Lectures on Political Economy*, preface. For Smith on colonies, see Adam Smith, *Wealth of Nations*, book 4, chapter 7.

67. Millar, *Historical View of the English Government*, 706.

68. See Skirving Catalogue of Books of the late Professor Mylne 1840 (GUL:Sp. Coll/BD17-h.11).

for the distribution of justice."⁶⁹ In his political economy lectures, Mylne covers military policy in some detail in the context of public expenditure. He takes issue with Adam Smith's preference for a standing army over a militia and neglect of the navy (for Mylne the "Wooden walls of England"). His enthusiasm for a militia is surprising in the light of his general opposition to war, but it may have been influenced by the American, Irish or Jersey militias that he knew of or had met. The British regiments themselves showed something of a militia spirit marching on St. Helier without orders and perhaps by refusing to sail for India. In his discussion, Mylne weighs the dangers to freedom of separating civil and military professions, concluding that a militia: "would effectively prevent all the just privileges and rights of the people from being lessened or com[muted] by the oppression and tyranny of in[solent] rulers."⁷⁰ He quotes Andrew Fletcher's view that a free man must be allowed to bear arms and cites Machiavelli, who's *Works* he had borrowed from the college library, but the strength of his views suggests they derive from personal experience.

---

69. Millar, *Historical Views*, 698.
70. Lectures on Political Economy (NCL:MS/BOGU3), Lecture 47.

CHAPTER 3

Ministry in Paisley

FOLLOWING HIS RETURN TO Scotland from military service, James Mylne was presented as Minister of the second charge of Paisley Abbey Church on March 27, 1783,[1] a few days before the formation of the Fox-North coalition in London in April, a post he held for fourteen years.[2] Mylne's close involvement with the life of the town impacted on his intellectual development and widened his circle of contacts. This was the era of the French Revolution when, according to Henry Cockburn: "Everything rung, and was connected with the Revolution in France; which, for above 20 years, was, or was made, the all in all. Everything, not this or that thing, but literally everything, was soaked in this one event."[3] However, the vitality of the indigenous Whig tradition should not be underestimated. Indeed, the educational project to which Mylne contributed falls naturally into the sequence of a British reformist tradition. The sparse evidence relating to Mylne personally from this period thus forms a coherent narrative in connection with later developments on which we have greater visibility. In this chapter, I shall sketch his personal life and ministry, before looking more broadly at the economic and literary life of Paisley and Glasgow.

---

1. Scott, *Fasti* (1920), 3:169.
2. Scott, *Fasti* (1920), 2:1, 201.
3. Cockburn, *Memorials of his Time*, 80.

Domestic Life

Turning first to personal matters, after six years of bachelorhood Mylne married in August 1789,[4] but the marriage was cut short by tragedy. The couple married shortly after her thirtieth birthday and before Mylne turned thirty-two, when the newspapers were full of the outbreak of revolution in France. His bride was a widow of some years standing, Mrs. Grizel Hamilton (*née* Davidson), a daughter of the manse from Old Kirkpatrick. We may perhaps glimpse the impression Grizel made on Mylne from a description written by her father for Sinclair's *Statistical Account*:

> All the young people of the parish dress well. The men wear hats and coats of English cloth. The young women put on silk and calico gowns, and black caps and cloaks. They meet together occasionally and make merry. Their chief amusement is dancing, and upon these occasions there is a pleasing cheerfulness and innocence among them.[5]

Grizel was the daughter of the Reverend John Davidson, the minister of Old Kilpatrick since 1745 and Margaret Hamilton, who had married in September 1754.[6] Her three brothers, Robert, James and Christopher, were four to seven years younger than Mylne.[7] James became a solicitor and Christopher a captain with the 26th Regiment of Foot.[8] John Davidson's views in the *Statistical Account* show that he was convinced from personal observation of the economic benefits of the increase in commerce activity and agricultural improvements he had witnessed.[9] He had helped to introduce the practice of inoculation into the parish, starting with his own family.[10] Grizel's mother was Margaret Hamilton, a daughter of Hamilton of Barns, a family also involved in trade who owned property locally.

---

4. NAS/SPC: Old Parish Registers: Proclamation of Banns & Marriages 559/0040, confirmed by marriage notice, *GM* 25/8/1789. The name is variously spelt, "Grizall" being the main variant.

5. Davidson, "Dunbartonshire," 71.

6. NAS Births: 501/0020/0062 [hard to read] notes her baptism and names of her parents on 30 June 1759. Scott, *Fasti* (1920), 3:354, notes her first marriage to Hamilton. There are no other Grizall Davidsons recorded from this parish from this time.

7. NAS Parish births, 501/0020/0081 and 501/0020/0085.

8. Scott, *Fasti* (1920), vol. 3. No such information is recorded of Robert, though a Robert Davidson was promoted to captain of a company of the 83rd Regiment of Foot in February 1783 (*Public Advertiser* 5/2/1783), which would be one explanation of how Mylne heard of the vacancy at Paisley Abbey.

9. Davidson, "Dunbartonshire," passim.

10. Ibid., 71.

Old Kilpatrick was associated historically with Paisley Abbey and local tradition, as retailed by Davidson, alleged it was the birthplace of Saint Patrick of Ireland.[11] His wife Margaret died in June 1788 and he in May 1793. These in-laws gave Mylne two connections with literary and academic life, as John Davidson was the brother of Principal Archibald Davidson[12] and the parish records show that Ilay Campbell, Advocate, had been admitted elder of the local Kirk Session in September 1759.[13] Archibald Davidson had graduated MA from Glasgow in 1752, going on to be a minister at Paisley from 1758 and Inchinnan from 1761. From 1785 to his death in 1803 he was Principal of Glasgow University and his son, Robert, was Mylne's colleague and professor of Law from 1801 to 1842. Ilay Campbell was involved in University affairs as Rector and correspondence on Mylne's appointment as Professor of Moral Philosophy survives amongst his papers.

Grizel's first husband had been James Hamilton, whom she had married in December 1781 in Old Kilpatrick. Hamilton was a merchant in Glasgow[14] and by November 1786 had left her a widow.[15] The inheritance could have been a tricky subject given the recent date of the marriage. In June 1783 he made a verbal bequest (a "testament testamentary" in Scots law) in the presence of Ilay Campbell, the Reverends John and Archibald Davidson and several local merchants including William French, a former Lord Provost, authorizing them to act as his trustees.[16] The document makes no reference to any children from his marriage or to property.

There were no children in Mylne's first marriage and Grizel died the following year.[17] There is no record of the cause of death. Complications surrounding pregnancy would be one explanation though mortality from other causes was not negligible even amongst healthy young adults at this

---

11. Ibid., 61–62.

12. Bruce, *History of the Parish of West*, 125.

13. Ibid., 108.

14. NAS 501/0020/0593, which describes both parties and Hew Scott, *Fasti* (1920), 3:169.

15. NAS CC9/7/73/257-260. Eleven other James Hamiltons are recorded dying between June 1783 and November 1986 in Glasgow or Dunbarton (NAS records).

16. NAS CC9/7/73.

17. Scott, *Fasti* (1920), 3:169 gives the name Grizel Davidson and year of death 1790, adding that there were no children.

time.[18] In November of the same year, his mother died.[19] His faith was again tempered by misfortune.

The Church in Society

The social role of the Church of Scotland for which Mylne worked was broader then than nowadays. Drummond and Bulloch state: "Those elements of local government which touched the mind and the pocket of the ordinary man most closely, education and poor relief, fell to the Church."[20] This included both schools and universities[21] and gave rise to a literature on educational theory.[22] The Poor Laws were roughly equivalent to the modern social security system and involved an element of social work. Leading Scottish politician Henry Dundas wrote: "if I was to name what circumstance was of the most essential importance to the peace of the country, I would name the influence of the clergy over the people properly exercised."[23] It is not surprising in the light of this that the wealthy sought to influence the Church and this gave rise to social tensions, with patronage supported by the Moderate faction.[24] Another consequence was that the careers of many public figures cross the boundary between religion and politics, as with the Scottish lawyer Thomas Muir, whose actions impacted on Mylne's circle.[25]

18. Mylne had a Latin dissertation from this time, dedicated to John Millar, *De morbi venerei natura* (1789) by Richard Millar, a local doctor who later wrote on typhus and the history of medicine (see Skirving catalogue). Local newspapers record significant mortality for all age ranges.

19. Scott, *Fasti* (1920), 3:346.

20. Drummond and Bulloch, *The Scottish Church 1688–1843*, 82. This remained the case until the Poor Law (Amendment) Act 1845, which followed closely on the 1843 Disruption (ibid., 176).

21. On schools, the Synod of Glasgow and Ayr publicly thanked Reverend Dr. McCulloch in 1800 for vindicating the rights of the Church in relation to schoolmasters by a decision of the House of Peers (GC10/4/1800). Many clergymen, including Mylne, were university teachers.

22. For example, Chapman *Treatise on Education* (advertised in *GM* 11/11/1794); Reverend Michael Russel *View of the System of Education at present pursued in the Schools and Universities of Scotland*. Mylne's colleague Stevenson MacGill wrote on "Elementary Education" and "The Qualifications of the Teachers of Youth" (in *Discourses and Essays on Subjects of Public Interest*).

23. Fry, *The Dundas Despotism*, 179.

24. Ministerial appointments in the Church of Scotland had been subject to Patronage since the Patronage Act of 1712. This had been implemented by the Moderate faction within the Church, led at first by William Robertson and later by George Hill of St. Andrews, known to Mylne since his student days.

25. The two leading statesmen mentioned by Mylne, Edmund Burke, and Charles

Robert Boog and the Abbey Parish

Paisley was the context for Mylne's work as a minister. Mylne's fellow minister and senior[26] there was Robert Boog (1746–1823), who was engaged in a series of innovative charitable works. The two men kept up a friendship throughout their lives. Boog (pronounced "Bogue") was from Edinburgh and, after general and theological studies at the University there, had taken a "jaunt to London"[27] in 1772, the year in which he was licensed by the Presbytery of Edinburgh. He was ordained Minister of the Second Charge at Paisley in 1774 and married Mary Fulton, daughter of a silk manufacturer, in 1781. The couple had eight children, from one of whom, William, a merchant in Rio de Janeiro, fragments of a correspondence with Mylne survive.[28] The year before Mylne's arrival Boog had transferred to the first charge, with Mylne soon appointed as his replacement. Mary died in 1827, the same year as Mylne's second wife. Mylne later praised Boog's achievements:

> The judicious and equitable plan which, many years ago, he formed and perfected for the support of the numerous poor of his parish, for whom the law made no adequate provision, and from whom, at that time, it seemed almost to withhold a provision; the expedients which, on different occasions, he suggested and superintended for the relief of the operative classes, when suffering under a general or local depression of their industry; the formation of the Paisley Medical Dispensary; the erection and management of the Paisley House of Recovery—will be long remembered as instances of his benevolent exertions.[29]

Robert Boog spoke out also on the challenges of urbanization and industrialization to the town. Of cotton spinning he says:

> Ignorance, disease and mortality, are but too likely to be the effects of this manufacture, if carried on by unfeeling and selfish men. The characters of the gentlemen engaged in it in this neighbourhood give reason to hope, that every method will be

---

James Fox, likewise addressed church government in their parliamentary speeches and writings. Fox's posthumous *Historical Work* dealt with the 1688 revolution in church and state.

26. Mylne was minister "of the second charge," Boog "of the first charge" (Scott, *Fasti* (1920), 2:1, 199, 201).

27. Introduction to Boog's *History of the Abbacy of Paisley*.

28. Scott, *Fasti* (1920), V3:166.

29. James Mylne, preface to Boog's *Sermons*, introduction, x.

employed which humanity and good sense can suggest to prevent these evils.[30]

This is the individual humanity identified in Mylne's lectures as a form of benevolence.[31] We also know from Frances Wright that Mylne's family knew the family of the most famous local philanthropist of the era, David Dale (1739–1806). Boog's contribution to this voluntary effort was exhortation of factory owners, and the institution of Sunday schools for the children of weavers. Boog also describes a system of voluntary poor relief.[32] He wrote: "to the honour of the more affluent inhabitants of the town and Abbey parish, let it be said that every plan to supply the wants, or mitigate the distresses of the indigent or the destitute, has always met with their hearty concurrence, and most liberal support."[33] The minister of nearby Eastwood, Stevenson MacGill (1765–1840) later Mylne's colleague as Professor of Divinity at Glasgow, also wrote on social subjects,[34] including poor relief. When Mylne lectured on the poor law, drawing on and criticizing the work of Lord Kames, he did so on the basis of practical experience.

Robert Boog also played a major role in the Sunday school movement in the town. On one occasion, he preached to nearly 2,000 local children.[35] Mylne's former colleague Robert Small supported this movement in Dundee and published a sermon, *The Importance of the Poor* (1794)[36] to encourage funding, noting that the increased use of child labor increased the importance of education and Sabbath observance. Sunday schools had been instituted in Glasgow in 1787[37] and their history in Paisley seems to have dated back to Mylne's time there.[38]

---

30. Boog, in Sinclair, *Statistical Account*, 7:850–51.

31. Dale's activities are reported in the *GM* and noted by Strang, *Glasgow and its Clubs*: "Perhaps among the many philanthropists for whom Glasgow has been so celebrated, none held a higher place than David Dale" (364–66).

32. He records the intention of the system: "It is a matter of vast importance, that, while they receive an adequate subsistence, industry is not discouraged" Boog, in Sinclair, *Statistical Account*, 7:830.

33. Ibid., 7:860. The parish records substantiate this, giving quarterly lists of the donors to and recipients of parish funds. (Register House, Edinburgh NAS/CH2/490 has a very incomplete series of the account book and session records.)

34. MacGill, *Discourses on Subjects of General Interest*.

35. *GC*, 22/7/1813; Sabbath and Weekday Evening School Society.

36. Small, *The importance of the poor illustrated*.

37. *GC* 1/1/1799.

38. *GC* 22/7/1813; text from Ps 119:9. The society had existed "for upwards of 15 years" in Paisley.

Boog's literary and intellectual interests included local history, poetry, and astronomy. He wrote an unpublished history of the town and was later on the Committee of the Wallace Tower along with former Lord Provost Kirkman Finlay.[39] Paisley Abbey church, from which he and Mylne operated and the fabric of which he helped preserve, long pre-dated the Reformation.[40] Boog wrote that it "held a distinguished place among the religious houses in Scotland" and wrote a history of it. Mylne noted that Boog did not relish the confrontational politics of the Church of Scotland. However, Boog attended the local Synod and General Assemblies in 1795, 1809, and 1818, on the latter occasion with Mylne's colleagues Principal Taylor and Professor Jardine.[41] He was awarded the degree of D.D. by Glasgow University in 1812. Mylne and Boog's friendship continued after Mylne moved to Glasgow. The week following Mylne's appearance on the front page of the local newspapers in 1815, for his supposedly "Napoleonic" sermon, he turned to Robert Boog. On Wednesday May 17 Mylne borrowed Montesquieu's *L'Esprit des Lois* and a travel book from the college library for him.[42] This was before publication of Mylne's *Statement of the Facts*.[43] They met on two further Wednesdays that year, since in July Mylne borrowed Boswell's *Life of Johnson* (1791) and in October a radical Whig History of Britain from the library for him.[44] After Boog's death in 1823, Mylne edited some of his sermons for publication, under the title *Discourses, Selected from the Manuscripts of the Late Robert Boog D.D.*, prefaced by a short biography.

The parishioners in Abbey Parish seem to have consisted mostly of families of manufacturers, their employees, and subcontractors. One contemporary observer wrote that "only two noblemen are proprietors in the Abbey church to a considerable amount; yet their residence here is but seldom and of short duration," adding that "though they possess a humane disposition, yet I never heard of any 'Paisley weavers' that supplicated their

---

39. GC 16/3/1819.

40. Some degree of patriotic feeling is suggested by the memory in local histories of the town's association with William Wallace and of the burning of the Abbey by English forces in 1307. There is little specific contemporary Scottish patriotic material associated with Mylne's circle, though the Literary and Commercial Society heard a talk "On the Results of the Union between England and Scotland" in November 1826.

41. GC 27/3/1795, 30/3/1809, 12/5/1818.

42. GUL: Professors' Receipt Books. William Paterson: *Narrative of Four Journeys to the Country of the Hottentots and Caffraria*.

43. Advertised in GC 23/5/1815.

44. William Belsham's *Memoirs of the Kings of Great Britain*. Mylne returns the other books at the same time and records who they are for.

favour."[45] Another, writing in 1789 that Paisley was "destined to be torn in pieces and inflamed by parties and factions" included the "sessions and church measures" in his satire, observing that "the demon of pride, selfish views and party-spirit has prevailed" in them, which suggests that the effects of the French revolution manifested themselves even within the walls of Mylne's church.[46] Another account of the intrusion of secular politics into the Kirk survives from Dundee, where Robert Small, Mylne's former colleague as Chaplain of the 83rd Regiment, was accused of enlisting elders from amongst the political reformers. A debate at the General Assembly in May 1799 resulted in Small's condemnation in his absence. He delivered and published his defense in 1800. Mylne was a commissioner to the General Assembly[47] in that year. Small was accused of seeking elders: "out of the inferior order of the community, and particularly from that class of people who were but too open to receive seditious, turbulent, and disloyal impressions, in preference to the more opulent and respectable;"[48] Small described the accusations against him further:

> We had been industrious, and well known to be industrious, in preparing and [finding] for this purpose, those that were notorious for seditious principles and disaffection to our happy Constitution, and some of them even under suspicion of being active in pulling down the Royal Oak, and planting the tree of liberty.[49]

Small replies that he did not "sound" people for their political views. The Assembly ruled that he was wrong to ordain Elders on the basis of general questions, without requiring subscription to the *Confession of Faith*. Even a former Moderator of the General Assembly then, was not safe from reproof. The episode shows that the Church of Scotland clergy known to Mylne were not uniformly conservative.

Paisley Presbytery

The Abbey Parish was part of Paisley Presbytery, the next level up in the Presbyterian system. Other ministers in the Presbytery included John Snodgrass (1744–97), who attended the General Assembly with Boog in

---

45. William Taylor, *An Answer to Mr Carlile's*, 34.

46. PCL: Paisley Pamphlets Vol 2:13 "On the Spirit and Manners of the Town of Paisley."

47. GUL: GU Senate Minutes SEN 1/1/2, 299.

48. Small, *Defence delivered by Dr Small*, 14.

49. Ibid., 14.

1795; John Monteath (1752-1843); and Stevenson MacGill. Snodgrass was author of *An Effectual Method for Recovering our Religious Liberties* (1770) a polemical work against patronage dedicated to "the Elders of the Presbyteries of Dumbarton and Paisley who have signalised themselves on the Cause of Religious Liberty." He published a similar pamphlet[50] and an essay distinguishing Christianity from natural religion[51] in Dundee, where he knew Robert Small.[52] John Monteath had been presented, after election by the parishioners, by Archibald Speirs of Elderslie, the son of a banker and "Tobacco Lord" and later Mylne's Whig ally as an MP in Glasgow.

Stevenson MacGill was Mylne's colleague as Professor of Divinity from 1814 and his career typifies the establishment sympathies and charitable initiatives of many clergymen of Mylne's era.[53] MacGill had won a prize at Glasgow College in 1785 for an essay on the genealogy in the Gospel of Matthew.[54] He was ordained minister of Eastwood in 1791 by the Presbytery of Paisley[55] and preached at the General Assembly the following year.[56] He published *The Spirit of the Times* (1792), calling for political moderation. His *The Connexion of Situation with Character, considered with a View to the Ministers of Religion* (1796) shares its subject matter with Mylne's talk "On the Formation of Character" to the Glasgow Literary and Commercial Society, though it is related to a dispute about the conduct of the Secession Church in relation to the right to hold public meetings. MacGill knew Professors Jardine, Richardson and Arthur through educational work.[57] He wrote *Remarks on Prisons* (1810), with the Scripture citation "I was in prison and ye came unto me."[58] In 1814, he succeeded Robert Findlay as Professor of Theology at Glasgow University.

50. Snodgrass, *The Means of Preserving the Life and Power*.

51. GC 26/3/17n95&11/4/1795; Snodgrass, *The Leading Doctrines of the Gospel* (1794). Only his posthumous *Commentary on Part of the Book of Revelation* (1798) is recorded in Scott, *Fasti* (1920), 3:179.

52. Small, *Defence delivered by Dr Small*, 22.

53. He was Secretary of the Magdalene Asylum, which assisted both women and destitute boys (GC 4/11/1813) and President of the Old Man's Friend Society (GC 17/12/1816).

54. GM 28/4/1785.

55. GM 3/4/1791.

56. GM 15/5/1792 (also 3/5/1792).

57. GM 3/6/1794 for MacGill's subscribing a report on an Eastwood school from the three college professors.

58. Stevenson MacGill, *Remarks on Prisons*: advertised in GC 1/2/1810.

The Synod of Glasgow and Ayr

In April 1785, James Mylne accompanied Robert Boog to the Synod of Glasgow and Ayr.[59] This regional body covered seven Presbyteries and was intermediate in authority between Presbytery and the General Assembly. It met twice yearly in April and October and had both ministers and lay members. On this occasion attendance was 75, of whom 49 were clergy and the rest elders and a clerk.[60] It addressed routine business and occasionally spoke out on issues of the day.

At this meeting, Mylne would have encountered several ministers with literary or intellectual ambitions. The Reverend Dr. James Meek of Cambuslang, later Dean of Faculties at the University was present for Hamilton.[61] The most impressive literary contingent though, was from the Presbytery of Glasgow. This included Robert Findlay (1721–1814), Glasgow's Professor of Divinity from 1782 and successor of William Leechman (1706–85), the friend and biographer of Francis Hutcheson. Findlay had studied at Glasgow and Leyden in the Netherlands, becoming a minister in 1744 in Paisley and thereafter Glasgow.[62] He wrote a book against Voltaire and several other tracts.[63] The Glasgow contingent also contained William Thom, the minister of Govan and the author of essays and satires sending up the pretensions of the College professors, collected in 1799.[64] He and Findlay had both subscribed to the posthumous edition of Francis Hutcheson's *System of Moral Philosophy* (1755) which Mylne owned, and which also contains Leechman's biography.

The future reformer Reverend William Dunn was present, later to play a role in the trial of Thomas Muir, and his future opponents Drs William Porteous and William Taylor, the latter Mylne's rival for the professorship of moral philosophy and Principal of the College. William Porteous was the chief mover of the insertion in Synod minutes and publication of an unqualified denunciation of "French principles."[65] He wrote *The New Light Examined* (1800) and was described as having "a warm attachment to our

---

59. Synod of Glasgow and Ayr records 1761–1803: NAS:CH2/464/4, 197–203. Lay and clerical members attended from Irvine, Paisley, Hamilton, Dumbarton, Lanark, Glasgow, and Ayr presbyteries.

60. Synod of Glasgow and Ayr records 1761–1803: NAS:CH2/464/4/197 Sederunt.

61. For his appointment as dean, see *GM*, 4/4/88.

62. Scott, *Fasti* (1920), vol. 3 Synod of Glasgow and Ayr (1920), 174, 439.

63. Obituary in *GC*, 21/6/1814.

64. Thom, *The Works of the Rev. William Thom*. The satire included the founding of Glasgow College chapel, of which Mylne was chaplain from 1809 to 1819.

65. Synod minutes 8/4/1794, 301–5.

constitution and laws, an inviolable love of order and a dread of rash and presumptuous innovations."[66] The sermon at the Synod meeting was delivered by Alexander Ranken, who spoke on the parable of the tares.[67] In March 1788, Ranken took part in the Glasgow Presbytery decision to petition Parliament on the African Slave trade. The Presbytery stated that they:

> view with the most sincere regret the unhappy situation of their fellow men who, without any fault of their own, are deprived of the natural rights of mankind and reduced to a state adverse to [the] intellectual and moral improvement of rational beings.[68]

The slave trade from Britain was regulated by law from August 1788.[69] Ranken was Moderator of the General Assembly in 1811.[70] His main literary work was an eight volume *History of France* (1801–20) from 486–1715, from the conversion of Clovis to the death of Louis XIV,[71] which Mylne later borrowed from the College library.[72]

The Early Cases of Thomas Muir in Church and College

At the meeting, Mylne heard of the first of three causes pursued within the courts of the Church by the young advocate Thomas Muir of Huntershill (1765–99) prior to his better-known political role after the outbreak of the French Revolution that ended with his transportation to Australia. This first case involved College administration. Muir also helped keep alive the issue of patronage in a long running case involving Cadder Parish. Robert Boog took a leading role in the third, the case of William McGill. These are worth covering for the light they shed on later divisions within the local political reform movement in which both Muir and Mylne played parts.

---

66. Obituary in *GC* 19/1/1812.

67. Matt 13:27.

68. Glasgow Presbytery minutes held at Mitchell Library CH2/171/14, 399. Meeting of 19 March 1788, with McCaul and Ranken present

69. 28 Geo III c. 54, subsequently renewed.

70. The first two advertised in the *GC* 25/11/1788 and 29/1/1799. For moderatorship, see *GC* 18/5/1811.

71. The first volume appeared in 1801, volume 2 the following year, volume 3 in 1804; volumes 4 to 6 by Blackwood in 1819 and volumes 7 to 8 by Blackwood and Cadell in 1820. Blackwood was a conservative publisher, most closely associated with the magazine of that name.

72. Mylne borrowed the first three volumes from the College Library in 1822 (GUL:Professors' Receipt Books).

The principal subject of discussion at the April 1785 Synod arose from a crisis at Glasgow University. Having resigned as Professor of Divinity, William Leechman was College Principal. He had been accused by Professor Anderson. former professor of Oriental Languages and then professor of Natural Philosophy and author of an *Institutes of Physics*,[73] of irregular financial dealings with the College. This led to a meeting of graduates at which a demand was made for a Royal Visitation.[74] There was soon a suggestion that the local merchants, traders and manufacturers would support a petition to the same effect.[75] Thomas Muir used the case to raise objections against the college administration. Leechman's defenders however, increased their activity on his behalf and Anderson was left isolated.[76]

A divinity student, David McIndoe, and Thomas Muir were expelled, Muir going on to complete his legal studies in Edinburgh. Glasgow Presbytery however, wished to take McIndoe on for public trials, which met with opposition from Ayrshire.[77] At the April 1785 meeting, the Synod rejected Glasgow's position, leading to a protest, supported by William Thom and others, who wished to take the matter to the General Assembly. The Synod appointed William Porteous, William Dunn and the well-liked Robert Balfour[78] to speak for their position in public. At a second meeting later in April, Boog and Mylne asked for their names to be added to the dissent.[79] The General Assembly decided against McIndoe, who was later ordained a minister in Newcastle.[80]

Professor Anderson left a legacy on his death in 1796 to found Anderson's Institution, whose first teaching was a mathematical course and a "ladies' course of physical lectures."[81] The first professor of natural philosophy

73. This went through five editions by Anderson's death (*GC* 16/4/1796).

74. *GM*, 20/1/1785 or student meeting and 3/2/for participation of professors. Minutes of the meeting were to be sold.

75. *GM* 17/2/1785.

76. *GM* 24/2/1785 for Leechman's defense. See 3/3/1785 for denial of embezzlement claim and statement that only one professor disagrees with the others.

77. NAS:CH2/464/4. Ayr had written alerting the other Presbyteries to their proposal, objecting to McIndoe on grounds of character, citing his expulsion from the College.

78. Balfour was the subject of an affectionate eulogy by Alexander Ranken (*GC* 24/10/1818) and of Ralph Wardlaw's *Sermon on Reverend Balfour* (advertised in *GC* 7/11/1818).

79. NAS:CH2/464/4/197 et seq.

80. *GM* 5/10/1790.

81. *GC* 29/3/1796.

was Thomas Garnett (1766-1802).⁸² In 1830, Mylne attended and spoke at a meeting and lecture by Andrew Ure at the Institution.⁸³ Ure's mechanics class at Anderson's Institution included introductory lectures on "Christianity and Learning"⁸⁴ and he wrote on "the general diffusion of Philosophical Knowledge and the importance to a Commercial Community of a Popular Institution."⁸⁵ The institution continued to offer a rival educational agenda to Glasgow University throughout Mylne's life.

Thomas Muir's first involvement with the patronage issue came with a dispute at Cadder Parish in Glasgow, with the patrons pitted against the heritors and elders over the choice of minister.⁸⁶ Glasgow Presbytery eventually referred the matter to the General Assembly.⁸⁷ Although the Cadder issue rumbled on,⁸⁸ it was soon overtaken by the M'Gill case. In 1782, Paisley was ahead of its neighbors in raising the question of lay patronage.⁸⁹ James Craig, Preses of the Several Societies or Incorporations of Trades of Paisley, said that "the great bulk of the inhabitants of this populous and increasing town have expressed their earnest desire of the abolition of this law." He went on to state that law on patronage was "intolerable to every man that has any sense of religious liberty remaining within him."⁹⁰ In 1783 the Synod of Glasgow and Ayr also stated that Patronage had led many thousands to abandon the Established Church and emigrate to America.⁹¹

Thomas Muir and the M'Gill Case

The Reverend William M'Gill of Ayr had been awarded the degree of doctor of divinity at Glasgow University in 1785.⁹² The following year, he pub-

82. For Garnett, see Smith "Retaking the Register," 318.
83. *Edinburgh Literary Journal* 27/3/1830, 194-95.
84. GC 3/11/1808.
85. Ure, *Outlines of Physical Science*, advertised in GC 30/10/1806.
86. Muir is named as an elder in GM 14/12/1790&24/5/1791.
87. GM 24/5/1791.
88. There were disturbances there in 1797 over establishment of a Scottish Militia with reference to "unlawful oaths" in terms of the 1796 Act on Mutinous or Seditious Oaths (GC 24/8/1797).
89. In 1782, the general session of the town of Paisley resolved to oppose the Law of Patronage, observing that the situation made people "an easy prey to fanatics, who can give no sufficient security, either of their loyalty to government, or of their attention to good morals" (GM 16/5/1782, 168).
90. GM 26/8/1784.
91. GM 3/4/1783.
92. GM 31/3/1785.

lished *A Practical Essay on the Death of Jesus Christ* (1786). This gave rise to a major controversy that was dragged through the Courts of the Church over many years, partly by the industry of Thomas Muir. Its theological content is the central theme of McNair's *Scots Theology in the 18th Century*. M'Gill visited the High Church at Paisley in or prior to 1792,[93] and Robert Boog took a leading role in trying to defuse the controversy his book caused, which only fizzled out with Muir's transportation to Australia on charges of sedition at the commencement of the French revolutionary wars. Muir denounced Boog at the General Assembly over the case.

M'Gill's *Practical Essay*—never since reprinted—addressed the central Christian mystery of the Atonement of Christ and is plainly a serious contribution to theology. It cites Joseph Butler's *Analogy of Religion* and John Locke's *The Reasonableness of Christianity*[94] and his rational treatment places it naturally in the Moderate camp of Scottish theology. Scottish theologians often reflect on the Passion narrative.[95] However, in his treatment M'Gill seemed to deny the divinity of Christ, a view known as "Socinian." This term of reproach was later used against Mylne.

The book was "spread with much industry"[96] in Scotland and led to considerable anxiety. Meetings were held to discuss possible action against M'Gill. Along with opposition to the African slave trade, it was the leading ecclesiastical issue of its day. Opponents posed the question in stark terms:

> Whether we are to believe the Scripture, where it is asserted, that our Saviour, Jesus Christ, is the great God, co-equal, co-essential and co-eternal with the Father; or to believe Dr M'Gill and his Socinian brethren, that Jesus is only a person of our own order and a man like ourselves.[97]

The Reverend James Moir published *The Scripture Doctrine of Redemption* (1787), a book length restatement of orthodox Calvinism. In 1788, the dissenting Associate Synod issued *A Warning against Socinianism*, which soon went through two editions.[98] At the University, the College prize

---

93. "Liberty without Licentiousness" (1792) in PCL:Paisley Pamphlets vol. 3.

94. M'Gill, *Practical Essay on the Death of Jesus Christ*, on Butler, 366, on Locke, 370.

95. This point is made in Principal Tulloch's *Religious Thought in Britain*, lecture 4.

96. Anon., *A Memorial and Remonstrance Concerning the Proceedings of the Synod of Glasgow and Ayr, and of the General Assembly ... in the Case of Dr. William McGill*, 4.

97. Ibid., 2.

98. *GM* 5/8/1788; second edition 16/12/1788.

offered the following year was for the best essay on the "Arian" controversy, an older name for Socinianism.[99]

The matter was pursued at the instigation of Muir through the courts of the Church until, in April 1790, it ended up at the Synod of Glasgow and Ayr at a meeting in Ayr. At this point, Robert Boog took the initiative in forming a committee to agree with M'Gill a form of wording to defuse the issue.[100] An agreement was reached and the Synod duly published M'Gill's Apology, along with sections eight and nine of the *Westminster Confession of Faith* on the dignity of Christ and Atonement.[101]

The matter was not allowed to rest, as Muir and his supporters hounded M'Gill relentlessly. This was the subject of Robert Burns' lively but obscure satires *The Twa Herds* and *The Kirk's Alarm* and the name M'Gill is preserved in James Hogg's *Memoirs and Confessions of a Justified Sinner* (1824). In January 1791, Thomas Muir took the part of the complainants and a new writ was presented to the Synod of Glasgow and Ayr. The ministers gave the lay complainants the frostiest of receptions. "Mob" and "rabble" were reputedly the most civil of the terms used by the Reverend James Lapslie.[102] The complaint was dismissed, but taken to the 1791 General Assembly,[103] whose Moderator was Robert Small. An eloquent speech survives by Thomas Muir to the General Assembly asserting the right of congregations over ministers. He argued that "religious establishments had no divine sanction" and were unjust.[104] Turning to the Synod compromise, he argued that Boog had orchestrated a fudge that left the offending book at large. Whilst Muir spoke eloquently, it was hard not to feel that the real theme was the question of Patronage. The General Assembly dismissed the case. Soon, Muir's political activities led to his arrest, trial and transportation, with James Lapslie re-

---

99. GM 30/4/1788. Matching doctrine with pastoral concerns, another prize was offered for a sermon on Titus 2:6, "Young men likewise exhort to be sober minded."

100. For Boog's initiative, see Anon., *A Narrative of the Whole Process respecting some late publications of the Rev. Dr. William McGill*, which records Boog as moving "that as Dr M'Gill had shown a disposition to make some suitable acknowledgements for the sake of peace, a Committee be appointed to converse with him.," 46. Boog's role is confirmed in Anon., *The Procedure of our Church Courts in the Case of Dr William M'Gill of Ayr*, 38. The Synod minutes indicate that Boog was a member of the committee, along with Gilbert Lang, James Wodrow, John Snodgrass, Robert Balfour, and William Dunn.

101. GM 14/4/1790.

102. Anon, *The Procedure of our Church Courts in the Case of Dr William M'Gill*, 117.

103. GM 12/4/1791 and 3/5/1791.

104. Anon., *The Procedure of our Church Courts in the Case of Dr William M'Gill*, 134.

jected as a witness. Without Muir's stimulus, the issue seems to have fizzled out. The Socinian controversy was later reawakened on religious grounds by one of Mylne's students, the English dissenter James Yates and his friend and later rival, the theologian Ralph Wardlaw in the form of the Unitarian controversy. Some evangelicals accused Mylne of sympathy with the views of Yates and they thus form part of the context in which he taught.

The General Assembly and Travels in Scotland

James Mylne attended the General Assembly in Edinburgh in May 1793 with Robert Davidson, Advocate,[105] perhaps the son of Principal Davidson who succeeded John Millar as Professor Law at Glasgow from 1801 to 1842. Also present from Glasgow was Archibald Arthur, the Professor of moral philosophy at Glasgow.[106] Mylne's father had died almost ten years earlier in December 1783 when he was on the point of leaving the chaplaincy.[107] Some months following the 1793 General Assembly, Mylne and his brother George finally settled his father's affairs through St. Andrews Commissary Court, appointing John Law, a merchant and Provost of Perth to act on their behalf as cautioner (i.e., guarantor).[108] Mylne is also recorded as present in St. Andrews in the mid 1790s where a student remembers him discussing politics with the Reverend James Brown, then an assistant to the Professor of Mathematics, and the mathematician Sir John Leslie in the presence of Thomas Chalmers. Brown was a Foxite Whig and later moved to Glasgow.[109] We may conjecture that Mylne may have been interested in academic appointments as this would explain not only his presence at St. Andrews, but also his wide reading, particularly in mathematics, and his capacity to prepare at short notice a comprehensive course of moral philosophy for delivery in Glasgow in 1797. Mylne attended the General Assembly again in 1797. This year, Professor Adamson of St. Andrews was Moderator, but the local press records no political discussions.

---

105. GC 23/3/1793.

106. GC 9/4/1793.

107. Scott, *Fasti*, 3:346.

108. Scott, *Fasti*, has December 1783 for his father's death, which is confirmed by the first part of the Testament Dative. This document however, dates from October 1793 (NAS/Scotland's People Centre: CC20/4/27). The reason for the almost ten year delay is not clear.

109. In Chitnis, *The Scottish Enlightenment*.

Sandemanianism and Dissent in Renfrewshire

The religious life of Paisley was both varied and vibrant, with many denominations represented.[110] The radical Reverend William Dunn observed that, "The existence of Seceders, and of seceding meeting houses, has perhaps no bad effect upon the manners and sentiments of the people," and felt that they were "in some degree spies and checks upon the members of the established church."[111] Their presence may have loosened any sense of doctrinal rigidity held by the local Kirk ministers.[112]

Sandemanian ideas were present in Glasgow through Robert Ferrier (1741–95), a former minister in Fife who had separated from the Established Presbyterian Kirk in 1768. Ferrier moved to Glasgow where he became the minister and "colleague" of David Dale, the manufacturer, philanthropist and later friend of Mylne and his family.[113] Ferrier explained his reason for adhering to the Glasite church in a preface to a posthumous edition of Glas's *Testament of the King of Martyrs* (1777). He describes how he heard the deathbed confession of an old clergyman who regretted that he had not joined the Glasite church and his heartfelt urging to read *Testament of the King of Martyrs*. He duly acquired a copy and soon resigned his ministerial charge in the established Kirk. Ferrier joined the Glasite church.[114] The matter of relevance for Mylne is Ferrier's objection to the *Westminster Confession* description of the "principal acts of saving faith" as "accepting, receiving and resting upon Christ alone." In contrast, Ferrier argued that faith is not a complex but a simple act consisting of the acceptance of a truth of fact upon sufficient testimony.[115] He argues that "in the believing this gospel, possession thereof is obtained."[116]

In the 1790s, another group of Independents emerged in Paisley—known as the "Pen' folk" from their meeting in a place known as the

---

110. McCarthy, *A Social Geography of Paisley*, records a Roman Catholic chapel from 1808 and Unitarian meetings (33 et seq.).

111. Dunn, "Kirkintilloch," 80.

112. For example, Boog says that the Christian temper does not consist in "having decided opinions on obscure and difficult matters" (*Discourses*, 344). See Strang, *Glasgow and its Clubs*, 347 et seq. for the ecumenical spirit of the times in Glasgow.

113. Ross, *History of Congregational Independency*, 35. A church in Paisley associated with the Pen folk and founded by "seven members of the Abbey Close Independents" was known as "Dale's kirk" (Gilmour, *Reminiscences of the Pen' Folk*, 42.)

114. See Smith, *The Case of James Smith*, chapter 4.

115. Ross, *History of Congregational Independency*, 34.

116. Smith, *The Case of James Smith [. . .] and of Robert Ferrier*, 11.

Pend—amongst whom William M'Lerie was a leading figure.[117] Though they were "not Baptists originally," their participation in a dispute on "believer baptism" prior to Mylne's departure suggests Sandemanian ideas.[118] Eight of the group travelled to Edinburgh in 1793 to sign the National Convention and some attended the trials of Muir and Gerald. M'Lerie reportedly "had to abscond for a time for having been a member of the National Convention."[119] The Pen folk later adopted as a motto "Let brotherly love continue," a phrase on which Mylne had given a sermon, though it was also associated with the contemporary masons.[120]

Literary Culture and Mylne as Reader in Paisley

At a day-to-day level, Mylne described the life of a minister as "simple and uniform"[121] and he sought out intellectual stimulation at the Literary Society of Glasgow from 1787 at the latest. This was the major literary society of its day in Glasgow and indeed the West of Scotland and it brought him again into contact with academia. Many philosophers, including Thomas Reid, George Jardine and Archibald Arthur were present, along with churchmen, merchants and lawyers.[122] John Strang wrote:

> to those acquainted with the state of Glasgow for the last forty or fifty years, it is well known that the labours of this society have been eminently successful in training for public usefulness a large portion of the men who have taken an active share in political and municipal affairs.[123]

Mylne's involvement with the Society and its successor body was sustained through much of the remainder of his life.

---

117. M'Lerie has "trained under Dr Ferrier" and his Independent group was also reformist in politics. However, according to Baptist historian Brian Talbot (*The Search for a Common Identity*, n. 50), this was a Dr. William Ferrier, local minister from 1787–1835, though he does not cite his sources in full. Talbot notes that William Ferrier was an "anti-Burgher," i.e., part of the original Secession church of 1733 some of whose founders were former "Marrow-men."

118. Gilmour, *Reminiscences*, 41.

119. Ibid., 29.

120. The contemporary masons were at pains to stress their adherence to Christianity and (when pressure was applied by the government) political loyalty.

121. Preface to Boog's *Discourses*, vii.

122. Duncan, *Notices and Documents*, 134. The appendix of original papers, no. 5, indicates that Mylne joined between 1783 and 1787.

123. Strang, *Glasgow and Its Clubs* (1864), 315 n.

The literary culture of Glasgow has also left considerable local evidence of itself through the records of its circulating libraries, reading rooms and periodical literature. The circulating libraries developed as commercial businesses from which the reading rooms were an offshoot. The reading rooms featured the London periodical literature of the day. Prior to 1800, when new technology became available, these monthly magazines had British circulations of 3,250 to 5,000.[124] The adverts of bookseller John Smith and of the Trongate Literary Museum, run by John Murdoch, indicate that even after the restrictions on publishing put in place in the early 1790s, the periodicals available in the reading rooms were a source of reformist and radical ideas. Mylne owned copies of these only after 1797, when his income greatly increased, but it seems unlikely that his interest began so late.

The *Analytical Review* (1778–1799), to which Mylne subscribed in its final years and John Millar contributed,[125] was considered "the most important radical review adopting the encyclopaedic format." Other names known to Mylne and associated with the *Analytical Review* were Richard Price and William Godwin. Its editor, Joseph Johnson (1738–1809) also published Joseph Priestley's writings and promoted those of Thomas Paine, both writers whose works Mylne owned.[126] Mylne also subscribed to the *Monthly Magazine* (1796–1843).[127] Its editor, Richard Phillips, had endured imprisonment for selling Paine's *Common Sense* and considered it "an enterprise on behalf of intellectual liberty against the forces of panic conservatism." Amongst writers cited by Mylne, his contributors included Joseph Priestley and the historian of philosophy William Enfield (1741–97).

Lord Stanhope's patenting of an iron printing press and the invention of a paper-making machine, both in 1798, reduced publication costs, leading to a fresh outbreak of periodical publishing in the early nineteenth century.[128] Mylne's student Robert Buchanan wrote at this time:

> Blessed be the man whose genius divine
> Invented first the monthly magazine
> And planned the guillotine of stern reviews
> For erring sages and the pilfering muse.[129]

124. Sullivan, *British Literary Magazines*, xvi.

125. Millar, *Origin*, 86–87. Mylne owned copies for 1797–99, according to the Skirving catalogue I-56.

126. "Joseph Johnson" in *DNB*.

127. "In politics, the Magazine was antiministerial; in religion, Dissenting and Unitarian." (Sullivan, *British Monthly Magazines*, 2:315. For Mylne's copies, see Skirving catalogue.

128. Ibid., 1:xv.

129. Robert Buchanan, *Satirical verses* (GUL:MSGen656), 4.

Before the *Edinburgh Review* (1802—) took off, Robert Sibbald published the *Edinburgh Magazine* (1785–1803), which reflected liberal views, for example against slavery, public executions and to restrict the death penalty. After 1803, it merged in the *Scots Magazine*. Mylne subscribed to the *Edinburgh Review* all his life.

For his time in Paisley we have only the Skirving catalogue to indicate what Mylne was reading, and this gives no certainty on date of purchase.[130] We also have the records of his early lectures to indicate what made most impact on his mind. The Skirving catalogue indicates that his reading ranged over Roman history, English and French literature, natural philosophy, mathematics, mental philosophy, and politics. His interest in the ancient world is evidenced by Ferguson's *Roman Republic* (1783) and Horace's *Opera* (1792). Of English literature, we find Johnson's *Lives of the Poets* (1783) and the *Works* (1789) of Alexander Pope. Simson's *Euclid* (1781), Cronstedt's *Mineralogy* (1790), and the *Algebra*'s of Maclaurin (1738), Saunderson (1792) and Frend (1796) indicate his interest in science.

Of religious works, his sense of church history probably owes something to Mosheim's *Ecclesiastical History* (1774). He owned *Le Vray Système de l'Église* (Dordrecht, 1686) by the French Protestant Pierre Jurieu (1637–1713), a reply to Nicole.[131] This had appeared just after the Revocation of the Edict of Nantes in 1685 by Louis XIV (1638–1715), which may help explain Mylne's lively detestation of this monarch in his political economy lectures. He owned John Toland's Deistic *Christianity not Mysterious* (London, 1702) and Anthony Collins' *Discourse on Free Thinking* ((London, 1715), but also the orthodox Joseph Butler's *Analogy of Religion* (1740) and an eleven-volume edition of Samuel Clark's *Sermons* (1749). He owned the *Sermons* of Hugh Blair (1781) and James Bell (1790). The former is a classic of Scottish Moderatism. The latter was "sermons preached before the University of Glasgow."[132] Bell argues that sermons and "the writings of moralists" should be based on observation and illustration. He wrote:

> Characters, good and bad, must be accurately drawn from life. Manners must be pourtrayed as they exist in nature. The

---

130. The Skirving catalogue (1840) may include books he inherited from his father on his death in 1783, the same year he arrived in Paisley. The catalogue gives the date of publication of books owned by Mylne at his death, which may have been bought at any time after publication. Archibald Arthur's library, from which he may have drawn was auctioned and a catalogue printed (GC 18/11/1797). However, most books are bought within two years of printing, owing to short print runs and initial advertising, so the evidence is at least indicative in bulk, though indecisive for any given book.

131. Nicole, *Les Pretendus*.

132. GM 12/4/1791.

principles of human actions must be defined [...] together with their appearances, simple and combined with one another. The ruling passion, the key which unlocks so many secrets of the heart, must be explained.[133]

The student of "spiritual maladies and their cure" should follow the physician, who takes into account the circumstances and history of his patient in inquiring into the cause and proposing treatment of an ailment. Mylne applied this in his lectures and perhaps also in his preaching.

In mental philosophy, he owned old editions of Fénélon, Buffier, and Spinoza, perhaps from his father's library. Of great significance for his lectures on moral philosophy is William Godwin's *Enquiry concerning Political Justice* (1796). Works published in the Paisley years in the catalogue include Thomas Reid's *Intellectual Powers* (1785) and *Active Powers* (1788); Dugald Stewart's *Outlines of Moral Philosophy* (1792) and Adam Smith's *Essays* (1795); and the English dissenter William Enfield's *History of Philosophy* (1791). France contributes Helvetius' *Oeuvres* (1784); Rousseau's *Émile* (1783), both mentioned in the lectures, and *Nouvelle Heloise* (1793); 100 volumes (!) of Voltaire's *Oeuvres* (1791) and Condorcet's *On the Human Mind* (1795). He also owned Condillac's *Oeuvres* (1777) and perhaps bought his posthumous historical and mathematical works (1798) as they were issued.

Of political works, we find John Millar's *English Government* (1790), Thomas Paine's *Common Sense* and *Rights of Man* (1792), Joseph Priestley's *Lectures on History and General Policy* (1793), and the much advertised *Anecdotes of the Founders of the French Revolution* (1797). His interest in political economy seems to have been dormant, perhaps overshadowed by purely political projects.

Conclusion

When we survey the events of James Mylne's fourteen years in Paisley we can more easily make sense of his later achievements as a professor and convictions as a Whig intellectual. He had considerable opportunity for intellectual stimulation through the Church and the debates in the Glasgow Literary Society and his extensive reading in British and French mental philosophy and political theory would enable him to compose an original course of moral philosophy in 1797.

---

133. Bell, *Sermons*, v.

More speculatively, a familiarity with Sandemanian ideas would explain Mylne's sympathy to their presence in the writings of William Godwin. Thomas Muir's hounding of William M'Gill and the Terror in France would push Mylne in the direction of the moderate Whig advocacy of Parliamentary reform. Mylne's moral philosophy, that placed investigation above reliance on "common sense" and his promotion of the study of social problems through his lectures on political economy are rational and measured responses to the impasse of opposed revolutionary and conservative ideologies and to rapid changes in society and the economy.

CHAPTER 4

Professor at Glasgow

Introduction

IN THIS CHAPTER WE cover the circumstances of Mylne's appointment as Professor of Moral Philosophy at Glasgow University and his conduct of the class. In studying the personalities involved in the appointment we will indirectly illuminate the expectations colleagues and others placed on a Professor of Moral Philosophy. In describing the conduct of the class, we lay the basis for explaining his influence on former students, which is summarized in the final section of the book. This leaves his domestic life; relations with the Churches; retirement and succession; and involvement in Whig politics for the remaining biographical chapters.

The Competition for the Glasgow Chair of Moral Philosophy

In 1797 Mylne resigned from his Paisley ministry and became Professor of Moral Philosophy at Glasgow University where he taught a generation of students from 1797–1837. Education at the University was distinguished into "Literature and Philosophy" and professional classes in the Church, law, and medicine.[1] Moral Philosophy was part of the culmination of the general or liberal education. Mylne taught a rationalist version of moral philosophy, combined with political economy in supplementary lectures.[2] His

---

1. This is the structure of the adverts of college classes in the local press (e.g., *GC*). A contemporary description is in Hay, *Inaugural Addresses*, introduction.

2. The earliest surviving student lecture notes date from 1799/1800.

moral philosophy retained a wide scope, drawing on French achievements to engage critically with the common sense of Thomas Reid, whilst in political economy he modified the commercial theories of Adam Smith.

The appointment was contested by seven candidates. They were: William McTurk (d. 1841), from a local merchant family, who had won the Ethics class prize in 1784,[3] trained for the ministry and served as Glasgow College Chaplain and Professor of Civil and Ecclesiastical History; George Jardine's son, whom Jardine vetoed; George Hamilton, minister of Gladsmuir; William Taylor,[4] minister at Glasgow; Lockhart Muirhead (1766–1829), College librarian; a Mr. Allan from Edinburgh, to whom Professor Millar was initially sympathetic; and James Mylne.[5] Thus at least four had trained for the ministry. The educational, political, and professional interests won over by Mylne persisted well into his professorship.

The Masters of the College

The Masters of the College decided the appointment.[6] Humanities Professor William Richardson (1743–1814) was originally from Perthshire. He had travelled in, and written on, Russia. At Glasgow, he taught both Latin and modern literature. Richardson applied Lord Kames' distinction, in *Elements of Criticism* (1762), between the description of a passion and its imitation in his *Philosophical Analysis and Illustration of some of Shakespeare's remarkable Characters* (1774), dedicated to the Whig lawyer Robert Graham. His play, *The Indians*, was performed at the local Dunlop Street Theatre. William Taylor said around this time that "Mr Richardson looks to the Principality."[7] Richardson's moral and religious principles "yielded him consolation in the season of affliction, and in the view of death."[8]

The Professor of Greek was John Young (1750–1820) also ventured into modern literature. He wrote *A Criticism on the Elegy written in a*

---

3. *GM* 29/4/1784.

4. There were two Reverend William Taylors in Glasgow at this time. Obviously this can cause problems of identification.

5. Letter of George Jardine to Hunter: GUL:MSGen507: letter 105, dated 24/8/1797, mentioning "our poor unfortunate friend Arthur's death." Jardine writes: "We have had a great deal of bustle about his successor [after so] many candidates appeared." And he goes on to list them.

6. "The Rector, the Dean, the Principal and the Professors of the College" says John Hay, describing the situation in the 1830s in Hay, *Inaugural Addresses*, xxxviii.

7. ML:Succoth papers/TD/219/294.1 (may be 296.1) Taylor to Campbell 28/3/1800.

8. *GC*, 5/11/1814.

Country Churchyard (1783, 1810)[9] a wide-ranging essay in the Johnsonian tradition of literary criticism. Young describes the function of the literary critic as "not to discover what has been said, but what may be said justly."[10] This is done by individual judgement, "Of fine writing, the perfection is not so well promoted by abstract canons, as by individual illustrations; by the inculcating what should be written; as by the examination of what has been written."[11] Mylne owned Johnson's *Lives of the English Poets* and probably Johnson's edition of Shakespeare (1766) and describes Shakespeare in his lectures as a "great metaphysician as well as poet."[12] Mylne and Young shared further cultural reference points in Milton, Italian literature,[13] Hume,[14] and Rousseau, though not the "Whiggish prejudices" Young found in Gray, commenting "Of liberty, the idea is so vague and the dimensions so little settled, that the poet may make of it what he will."[15] Young rebuked Shaftesbury for raising morality to batter revelation and Gray for suggesting that morality teaches us "how to die": this is the proper office of religion alone. Late in his life observers saw "the old man's eyes streaming with tears under the oratory of Chalmers, when that illustrious man first appeared in Glasgow and 'struck it like a planet.'"[16]

At Glasgow College, students took the class of George Jardine (1742–1827), the Professor of Logic, in their third year, before moral philosophy. Jardine was an innovative and widely admired teacher.[17] He had met Hume and Helvetius in person. His course strongly developed the analytical and essay writing skills of students.[18] It also explains the note-taking skills of some of Mylne's students, this being one of Jardine's first class exercises.[19] The Whig lawyer Francis Jeffrey, a former student, praised Jardine very highly;[20] whilst the Tory *Blackwood's Magazine* noted that his teaching

---

9. The two editions are: John Young, *Criticism on the Elegy written in a Country Churchyard* (London: Wilkie, 1783; Edinburgh: Ballantyne, 1810).

10. Young, *Criticism* (1810), 16.

11. Ibid., 145.

12. Wicksteed MS, lecture 30, 27.

13. In particular Petrarch in Young's case, comedy in Mylne's.

14. Hume's *Essays and Treatises on Several Subjects* is mentioned by Young, though the name of its author is not.

15. Young, *Criticism* (1810), 70.

16. *Hogg's Weekly Instructor*, 1845, 1:403.

17. Davie, *Democratic Intellect*, 9–25.

18. Some student MSS survive. Davie discusses his methods in *Democratic Intellect*, chapter 1.

19. See Jardine, *Outlines*, part 2, first order of "themes."

20. Jeffrey's inaugural address as rector in Hay, *Inaugural Addresses*.

methods turned his class from "a dull, yawning, fidgetting congregation of listless and fretful idlers" into one "'instinct with spirit', full of animation, gladness and delight, resounding with clear and unfaltering voices."[21] Jardine outlined the intellectual faculties of the mind, an account which Mylne developed in his class. These teaching methods became widely influential and are described in Jardine's *Outline of a Philosophical Education* (1818, 1825). Mylne thus shared considerable common intellectual ground with these three influential College Masters, many of whom he would have met at the Glasgow Literary Society, which met at the College.

Professional and Political Interests

Members of two Scottish professions, the law and the Church, had a voice in the election. The legal profession was relatively weak in Glasgow, as the main courts of the country were in Edinburgh and justice was administered from there through the circuit system. However, John Millar, the professor of law was a major cultural figure and the foremost advocate of political reform in Glasgow College. He had debated philosophy with Reid, but was "a zealous admirer of Mr Hume's philosophical opinions."[22] Indeed, he had also known Hume personally.[23] The philosophy which Millar took over from Hume involves the rejection of intuitive, *a priori* propositions. The justification of belief belongs instead to experience and this led both Hume and Millar to history as a repository of experience.[24] Mylne took Millar's side in this against Reid, describing Millar later as the "brightest ornament" of the university, rivaled only by Adam Smith. Francis Jeffrey also compared Millar favorably with Reid.[25] Mylne wrote of Millar that:

> A spirit of Philosophical Inquiry, ingenious and profound, guided all his researches, and enabled him to discover those simple, general principles in the feelings or the circumstances

21. *Blackwood's Magazine* no. 16, July 1818, as quoted in GC, 25/7/1818.

22. Millar, *Origin of the Distinction of Ranks*, 61; Dugald Stewart's "Life of Reid," in *Biographical Memoirs*, 426.

23. "He [Hume the philosopher] paid for David [the nephew]'s education at Glasgow University under Professor John Millar and proudly watched his progress in law" (Mossner, *Life of David Hume*, 575–76).

24. Millar's view was cast into a conservative mold in the law lectures of Hume's nephew, Baron David Hume (1757–1838), in which form, they passed into popular literature in the *Waverley Novels* of Walter Scott. For Scott and Hume see Lockhart's *Memoirs of the Life of Scott* (1837), 1:45: "Such an architect has Mr Hume been to the law of Scotland" etc.

25. Hay, *Inaugural Addresses*, 6.

of mankind, which serve to unfold the origin and the nature of the legal and political institutions which it was his province to investigate.²⁶

Millar agrees with Smith in supporting liberal education as a counterweight to the effects of specialization. He relates moral philosophy to law in his essay on "The Progress of Science relative to Law and Government" in *Historical View* and concludes by advocating historical inquiries, such as those of Montesquieu, Kames, and Adam Smith. It would seem that he would support a moral philosophy in which inquiry supplemented or replaced reflection. Elsewhere, he describes lawyers as typically "bred up in the habits of a gainful profession"²⁷ and notes the "direction of financial transactions," along with settlement of disputes and conveyancing ("transmission of property"),²⁸ as their major concerns. This would give weight to his view that political economy should be taught in Glasgow College. Mylne's lectures responded to Millar's concerns on inquiry and political economy.

Another leading Scottish lawyer and political figure, Ilay Campbell (1734–1823), was also aware of and interested in the appointment process. Campbell had studied at Glasgow University and was Rector from 1797 to 1801. He had been dismissed from office in 1783 by the Whig coalition of Lord North and Charles James Fox and was thereafter politically aligned with Henry Dundas. He served as MP for Glasgow Burghs from 1784, as President of the Court of Session from 1789 and also as Lord Advocate. Henry Cockburn said of Campbell "Of all the old judges he was the only one whose mind was thoroughly opened to the comprehension of modern mercantile jurisprudence."²⁹ Thus, despite his conservative allegiances, he would likely have sympathized with Millar and Mylne's view that political economy be taught at the College. As we have seen, Campbell had also come across Mylne through family and business connections with Reverend John Davidson of Old Kilpatrick.

In terms of commercial interests, there was a separate Mercantile Academy. Its director James Morrison's book, *Elements of Bookkeeping*,³⁰

---

26. "Account of the Late Professor Millar" in *GC*, 13/6/1801. It is signed "M, Glasgow College," but Mylne's authorship is established by the attributed quotation from the article in Craig's *Account of the Life and Writings of John Millar* in Millar's *Origins* (1806), cxxix.

27. Millar, *Historical View of the English Government*, 279–80.

28. Ibid., chapter 4.4.

29. Cockburn, *Memorials of his Time* (1856), 125–30.

30. Author of *Elements of Bookkeeping*, advertised in *GC* 21/12/1811. Morrison was not a member of the Literary Society, where political economy was discussed. The Scottish College of Commerce merged with Strathclyde University only in 1964.

shares some common ground with Mylne's lectures on the development of commerce. Science and engineering had trade organizations which seem to have had looked more to Anderson's Institution (as Strathclyde University was then called), which was already specializing in science and technology. There is little evidence of the medical profession taking an interest in moral philosophy.[31]

Turning to the Church, several Glasgow academics were also ministers. One leading figure was Principal Archibald Davidson, previously minister of Inchinnan. He also had personal knowledge of Mylne through his niece and Mylne's spouse Grizall Davidson and perhaps also his son Robert Davidson. Davidson and Dr Findlay, the Professor of Theology, were reckoned government supporters by William Taylor.

However, beyond the Scottish Presbyterians, Glasgow was an important destination for numerous students from English dissenting denominations, who were supported by the Williams scholarship, established by Dr. Daniel Williams.[32] Presbyterian scholars in England were vociferous against perceived irrationalist tendencies in Glasgow philosophy, dating back to the opposition to Hutcheson's sentimentalism in Richard Price's *Review of the Principal Questions of Morals* (1757) and John Taylor of Warrington's *Examination of Dr Hutcheson's Scheme of Morality* (1759). The argument was that on Hutcheson's scheme, morality would be based only on the will and not the intellect of God and thus would be arbitrary. This rationalist tradition was renewed against Thomas Reid in Joseph Priestley's *Examination of Dr Reid's Inquiry* (1774). Mylne's vindication of reason accompanied by a mature appreciation of Reid responded to these criticisms and concerns.

Turning to purely political interests, Tory and Whig agendas were undoubtedly at work in Scottish academic appointments at this era. Indeed, perhaps any political agenda implies an educational project. Henry Dundas (1742–1811), 1st Viscount Melville was the leading figure in Scottish politics in the 1790s. Identifying with the Tory patriotism and traditionalism of William Pitt and Edmund Burke, Dundas played a role of world significance in steering the defeated British Empire towards India and against revolutionary France. Despite a sympathetic recent biography,[33] he remains to this day an opaque, even menacing figure in Scottish historiography. In light of this, the revival of Charles Macklin's (1710–97) comedy *The Man of the*

---

31. One of Mylne's students, the physician George Redford, did write a book *Body and Soul* (1847) on the medical knowledge of the relations of mind and body. An article in *The Lancet* (London, 1841), 567–75, applied Mylne's ideas to the classification and treatment of insanity.

32. Coutts: *History of the University of Glasgow*, 208–9.

33. Fry, *The Dundas Despotism*.

World (1764)[34] in Glasgow in 1793,[35] a satire on the ruthless political fixers of the Scottish-led Bute Ministry, may be seen as directed at Dundas.

The Dundas papers indicate that Dundas was interested in academic appointments in Edinburgh, St. Andrews[36] and, through his local representative James Graham, the Duke of Montrose (1755–1836), in Glasgow. However, Montrose reported to Dundas in January 1797, "it has been my system and my practice, not to interfere with the Elections at the College of Glasgow, except when I thought an attempt was making to introduce men of wild principles."[37] Montrose had been educated at Eton and Cambridge and succeeded his father as Chancellor of the University from 1781 to 1836, being succeeded in turn by his son. Letters passed between Montrose, the future Principal William Taylor (1744–1823) and Ilay Campbell on the moral philosophy appointment.[38] William Taylor had been Minister at the High Church at Paisley from 1772 to 1780 when he transferred to Glasgow. He was a Visitor charged with examining the College accounts and for this reason had been passed over as Principal in 1785 in favor of Archibald Davidson, whom he succeeded as Principal from 1803 to 1822. In 1798 he was Moderator of the General Assembly. However, Taylor's manoeuvrings in this case came to nothing.

On the side of reform, the Whigs were not powerless. Mylne's political sympathies would have put him in the good graces of the Whig faction headed by Millar. It would seem that he may in addition have held such political cards as he was then carrying close to his chest: Jardine shortly afterwards states only that he was "suspected" of reformist sympathies. Following his appointment however, William Taylor identified Mylne as an

---

34. Macklin, *The Man of the World* (1793).

35. *GC* 11/6/1793: "The paper notes that the play "produced more laughter and applause than any other that has been performed for a considerable time." Theater reviews were uncommon at this time in the Glasgow press.

36. Dundas claimed in 1801 to have influenced the appointment of "every professor in the universities of St. Andrews and Edinburgh" for "more than 20 years" (quoted in Emerson, *Academic Patronage in the Scottish Enlightenment: Glasgow, Edinburgh and St. Andrews Universities*, which covers the period from 1690 to 1806.). Emerson's helpful account of Mylne's appointment is let down by his gratuitous assumption that Mylne must have chosen between Reid's common sense and the sentimentalism of Hutcheson and Adam Smith in his lectures. No such exclusive choice faced him.

37. Montrose to Henry Dundas 29/1/1797: Melville Castle Muniments, NAS/GD51/6/1205. For Glasgow, see also Emerson, "Politics and the Glasgow Professors 1690–1800" in Hook and Sher, *The Glasgow Enlightenment*.

38. Succoth papers, Mitchell Library.

opponent of the government in a list of the political sympathies of the College professors sent to Ilay Campbell in 1800.[39]

In terms of public speaking and teaching capacity, Mylne's duties as a minister would have equipped him well, whilst some of the appointing panel knew of Mylne's abilities beforehand through the Literary Society. One of his students, George Gilfillan, describes another such early essay:

> [H]e once read us an early essay written by him on Beauty, developing the theory of Alison, which had been formed by him previously and on independent grounds, and which was written so tenderly, elegantly, in a style so chastely yet richly adorned, that the class were taken by surprise, and, contrasting it with his ordinary prelections, could solve the problem in no other way than by supposing, that when he wrote it he had been in love.[40]

It was presumably on some such favorable assessment of his philosophical and teaching abilities, the latter no doubt developed by his preaching in Paisley, that Mylne was appointed.[41] In any event, Mylne was elected by a margin of one vote.

The Moral Philosophy Class

Mylne thus succeeded Archibald Arthur (1744–97) who had taught moral philosophy after Reid's retirement in 1780. Glasgow had an established reputation in scholarship to rival its growing reputation in industry and commerce. In 1802, a Swiss visitor recorded that: "Glasgow est devenue à la fois le Birmingham, le Manchester, le Sheffield, et même *l'Oxford* de l'Ecosse."[42] Describing the students, the American Benjamin Silliman wrote in 1806 "the young men wore gowns of scarlet cloth, most of which were so old and rusty, as to give them a slovenly and ridiculous appearance."[43] This suggests that many students were not wealthy. However, they were full of literary ambition. Mylne's student Robert Buchanan (1785–1873), later Professor of Logic, but then training to be a teacher, expressed this in verse:

---

39. Mitchell Library, Succoth Papers/TD/219/6/294/2, cited in Emerson *Academic Patronage in the Scottish Enlightenment*.

40. Gilfillan, *History of a Man*, 80.

41. On Mylne's appointment, the Senate minutes record only the bare fact, with a unanimous vote (GUA/GU Senate minutes, vol. 80:195–96; 333; 391). There is a computerized index of the minutes in GUA.

42. Pictet *Voyage de Trois Mois en Angleterre*, 89.

43. Silliman, *Journal of Travels*, 2:276.

> From the long gloom of literary night
> Rise Glasgow! Crowned with intellectual light
> See the grim shades of ignorance decay
> And science bursting in a flood of day
> From garret high, thy rival Drury Lane
> The studious High Street pours its letter'd train
> And upstart authors swarm in patten'd state
> [i.e., wearing clogs]
> From Enoch's Temple to the Gallowgate.[44]

The teaching methods of James Mylne and George Jardine nourished this ambition, though directing it on the whole more to prose than to poetry or drama. Another observer noted that Hutcheson, Smith and Reid had given "a decided bias, at Glasgow, to moral and metaphysical research."[45] James MacIntosh as Rector told students in 1823 that "the study of metaphysics has nowhere been more rationally or successfully cultivated than amongst you."[46] The published version of this speech was placed in the Ethics class library.[47] Mylne had much to live up to when he set to work and described the duties of such a Chair as "arduous."[48]

The Old College (near the current High Street Station) where Mylne taught is described in J. G. Lockhart's *Peter's Letters to his Kinsfolk* (1819). The basic form of two connected quadrangles with gardens attached was copied over into the present building on Gilmorehill.[49] Silliman noted in his journal that "Their appearance is venerable and impressive."[50]

Following his appointment,[51] Mylne subscribed the *Confession of Faith* appointed for professors at Glasgow Presbytery[52] and the University Senate required a Latin dissertation from him on "The Use of Moral Sci-

---

44. GUL:MSGen656, 1.

45. Craig, "Account of the Life," lvii-lviii.

46. Hay, *Inaugural Addresses*, 31.

47. Ibid., list of subscribers.

48. James Mylne, Letter of 24/8/1815 in John Young, *Testimonials in favour of John Young*, 21.

49. Lockhart, a Tory, also gives an imaginary dialogue with a "philosophical weaver" (perhaps Mylne himself), and describes the teaching of Mylne's colleagues Young and Jardine, and the preaching of Thomas Chalmers.

50. Silliman, *Journal of Travels*, 2:276.

51. For the appointment on 18 August 1797, see GUA:GU Senate Minutes Vol 80, 196.

52. Presbytery of Glasgow Records, held at Mitchell Library. On 3 January, 1798: "Appeared Mr James Miln, [sic] professor of Moral Philosophy in the University of Glasgow and subscribed the Confession of Faith and Formula appointed to be subscribed by professors." NAS:T-PRES CH2/171/15, 155.

ence" as a trial.⁵³ Mylne began his first year of moral philosophy lectures in October 1797. The lectures were at 7:30 am in the winter, which may help explain Gilfillan's description of them as an "ice bath"! By 1799, the course ran to over 100 lectures, delivered between October and April or May each year. The lectures were successful, though Mylne's innovations drew comment. Soon after his appointment, his colleague George Jardine wrote, "Our new Professor or M[oral] Philosophy pleases much and would please much more generally were there not some suspicions of his favouring the new opinions both in Politic[s] and Philosophy."⁵⁴ Jardine himself was reckoned fairly neutral in his politics at this time. As we shall see, there are many freely offered positive accounts of Mylne's teaching abilities. According to the recollection of an early student:

> I believe that it was in his class that my mind was first taught to think; and that, under God, I owe mainly to him whatever strength of character I possess, and whatever name and reputation I may have in the world. I know that many who hear me could echo the sentiments I have just expressed.⁵⁵

Several other reminiscences and letters home from students remark on or give sketches of the class. In 1818, an English student, Theodore Rathbone wrote to his family that he rose at 6:00 am. After studying mathematics for an hour, lectures started at 7:30 am. There was:

> An hour's lecture on Moral Philosophy, and an hour's lecture on Natural Philosophy. Then breakfast; a lecture or rather class three times a week on the higher branches of mathematics, and lecture twice a week upon geography, elements of astronomy, etc from 10 to 11, and from 11 to 12 a second lecture or rather examination into, and discussion of the subject of the morning's lecture on Moral Philosophy. From 12 to 2, two hours for private classical reading, and from two to three a most interesting and useful lecture upon the Greek language and its philological bearings.⁵⁶

---

53. GUA:GU Senate Minutes Vol 81: 52; 117.

54. George Jardine, Letter of 28 April 1800 to Rev. Robin Hunter (GUL, Special Collections: MSGen507, Letter 114.)

55. *The Christian Pioneer* (Glasgow, 1829) Vol 3, 451 (reported speech of Mr Cooke). Probably Henry Cooke (1788–1868), GU Matric. 6316.

56. TW Rathbone Letter from Glasgow December 1818. Rathbone papers RP VIII 1.1A. Sydney Jones Library, University of Liverpool. Rathbone refers also to more casual studies of anatomy and French.

Rathbone goes on to say that he spends two hours in the evening on preparatory reading connected with Mylne's class. Rathbone was an unusually diligent student[57] and as he lodged with Mylne no doubt felt obliged to study hard. His account of the student itinerary is confirmed by other sources. One seceding English student, John Collingwood Bruce, confirms this in outline writing home in 1824/25 that he "found the work of the Moral Philosophy class very hard."[58] Bruce also mentions studying mathematics and Greek in the same year. As concerns Moral Philosophy, these accounts are confirmed by contemporary timetables[59] and by the University Commissioners' Report of 1831, which notes five lectures a week, supplemented by six hours of teaching including one hour on Saturday.

As well as lecturing for an hour from Monday to Friday, Mylne followed Jardine's methods and examined students at a separate discussion hour, marking and commenting on student essays.[60] Of these, two hours a week were devoted to recapitulation of the lecture material in more conversational style, though he found that the students "in general have an indisposition to undergo examination." The Reverend Michael Russel describes the result of examination hours in Glasgow: "By going over the subject in different language, by varying the illustrations and by introducing familiar analogies, he [the professor] can hardly fail to render the drift of his reasoning familiar to every capacity."[61] Like Jardine though, Mylne thought "the second hour devoted to exercises of various kinds to be not less, but rather more important, for the instruction of his students than mere lectures."[62] There was also a "morning hour on Saturdays."[63]

The class also read texts in the classical languages.[64] Three remaining hours were spent reading the first book of Bacon's *Novum Organum* and Cicero's *De Officiis*.[65] According to Russel, this served the "double purpose of making the student cultivate or retain his acquaintance with the Latin language, and of giving the professor an opportunity of setting forth the

57. He won class prizes in both Logic (1818) and Ethics (1819).
58. Bruce, *Life and Letters of John Collingwood Bruce*, 24.
59. The published college timetable confirms the times of Mylne's class, Meikleham's natural philosophy class, Millar's second mathematical class and Young's private Greek class. I have checked the 1807 timetable, but there is little change over the years.
60. He gave evidence on this to the 1826 Scottish Universities Commission, covered by Davie, *Democratic Intellect*.
61. Russel, *View of the System of Education*, 124.
62. *Commission of Inquiry into the State of the Universities of Scotland*, 247.
63. Hay, *Inaugural Addresses*, xxxix.
64. Ibid., xl, drawing his account from the Parliamentary Commission.
65. Russel, *View of the system of education*, 119–121.

doctrines of the old philosophy, as well as the principles of the new."[66] According to Murray, Mylne also "insisted on his students reading in class parts of Plato and Aristotle in the original."[67] J. G. Lockhart, whom Mylne helped win a Snell exhibition at Oxford following his performance at the Blackstone examination, comments that the standard of classical languages at Glasgow was high.[68] Another source claimed that Mylne could "tauk Greek as forthily" as Professor Young.[69] Mylne would have learned New Testament Greek for the ministry and the College Library records suggest someone keeping up a reading knowledge of the language, borrowing an early edition of Plato's *Works* (1570) in 1819 and Aristotle's *Ethics* and *Rhetoric* in 1821–22, along with Greek and Roman historians and dramatists.

In 1803, Mylne had an edition of Francis Bacon's *Novum Organum* published for the use of his students,[70] whilst his colleague George Jardine brought out an edition of the Latin rhetorician Quintilian.[71] Mylne set class essays on specific passages of the *Novum Organum*. One was on Bacon's rejection of a blank slate for a reconstruction of knowledge.[72] In 1818, there was a prize essay on *The Best Account of Bacon's Idols*. An essay in the following year was on aphorism 49 of *Novum Organum*: that, "The human intellect is not of the character of a dry light, but receives a tincture from the will and affections [. . .] in short, the affections enter and corrupt the intellect in innumerable ways, and these sometimes imperceptible."[73] There is reference in 1813 to a compilation by Mylne "from the philosophical works of Cicero and Lucretius, among the ancients, and from those of Bacon and Hutchison [*sic*] among the moderns,"[74] though I have not traced a copy of this. There is though an edition of Cicero's *De Officiis*, which appeared in 1824 for the use of students.[75] The lecture course began with a lecture on "the Stoics and the Epicureans," drawing on Diogenes Laertius for the latter.[76]

---

66. Ibid., 119.
67. Murray, *Memories of the Old College of Glasgow*, 81.
68. *Peter's Letters*; "Life of Lockhart," in *Quarterly Review* 116 (1864), 446
69. "Professor Young" in *Notes and Queries* 2nd series, 96 (London: Bell, October 1857), 354.
70. *Fransisci de Verulamio Novum Organum* (Glasguae: Scrymgeour, 1803).
71. Murray, *Memories of the Old College of Glasgow*, 81 n.
72. For Mylne's class essays, see reports in *GC* each May 1805–10.
73. *GC* 4/5/1819. Ethics class prize.
74. Russel, *View of the system of education*, liii.
75. *De Officiis* bound with *Novum Organum* (Glasguae: Duncan, 1824).
76. GUL: Mackenzie MS & MS Murray 207.

The six surviving sets of manuscript notes made by students indicate that the course evolved over time, around a constant basic structure.[77] In content, Mylne's moved the intellectual philosophy sharply away from Reid towards a modified version of Condillac. An evangelical student, Thomas Durant, wrote in 1820:

> Mr Mylne [. . .] is altogether one of the most fascinating men I have ever met with. [. . .] His lectures are original, and ingenious in the highest degree. [. . .] He has nothing to do with "*Common Sense*," and I am very glad of it; as I confess this appendage has always seemed to me a most awkward excrescence on the science of the human mind.[78]

There may be a pattern of English students from dissenting backgrounds being accustomed to reject the appeal to common sense in philosophy. In his lectures, Mylne indicates in passing something of the intellectual focus of his method of teaching when he says, "It is wrong for a teacher of morality to appeal to the moral feelings, and to ask if the rules laid down are not consistent with their feelings, because this supposes man's moral feelings to be something like instinct."[79] Another dissenting English student, John Kendrick qualifies this when he notes in particular the "prominence which he gave to the opinions of his predecessor, Dr Reid" which was useful to English students who were liable to know of Reid only through Priestley's denunciations of him.[80]

This was combined with appreciation of Mylne's originality. For example, another English student, Lant Carpenter, noted with pleasure in 1800 that: "Few are so liberal in departing from the common standard of philosophical orthodoxy as Mr Mylne."[81] Carpenter returned the following year and attended further private classes under Mylne.[82] Several other students

---

77. In his earliest lectures for example, Mylne speaks of abstraction as a fourth fundamental faculty of understanding. However, in the later courses, abstraction is subordinated to memory and judgement. McCosh reports his later view that: "Abstraction is nothing more than the attention directed in a particular way" (McCosh, *The Scottish Philosophy*, 366).

78. From Durant, *Memoirs and Select Remains of an Only Son*, 208–10. I quote from the American edition, section "Extract of letters written during the session 1820." Durant, who died in tragic circumstances, resided with Mylne's theological sparring partner Ralph Wardlaw.

79. GUL:MSGen466 (Mackenzie notes of Mylne's lectures), 9.

80. Kendrick, "Memoir of the Late Rev. William Turner Jun., MA" in *The Christian Reformer*, March 1854, 131.

81. Carpenter, *Memoirs of the Life of Lant Carpenter*, 43.

82. Ibid., 48.

endorse the liberating effect of Mylne's teaching. A Unitarian student from Ireland who took Mylne's class in 1811, Joseph Hutton (1790–1860) recalled that the teaching there "contributed in an eminent degree to open his mind and give him the command of his faculties."[83] In 1820, the future author of the poem *The Course of Time* (1827), Robert Pollok (1798–1827), took Mylne's class to which he had "looked forward with great pleasure and high expectations," having "often heard of the clear head, and clear thinking and writing of Professor Mylne."[84] The young poet was not disappointed. Belonging to a Secession church, Pollok is another example of Mylne's appeal to the dissenting community. Pollok, who "was not given to the indiscriminate praise of any-thing,"[85] praised the independent spirit and his brother later recalled him saying:

> Till I heard Mylne lecture I never thought of calling in question the opinion of an author. If it differed from mine I thought it must be right and my own wrong. But in Mr Mylne's class I was set free, for ever, from the trammels of book authority; I lost all deference to authors, and opinions, and names; and learned, not only to think and decide for myself, but to test severely my own opinions.[86]

Pollok was allowed to submit essays in verse and reckoned his powers of communicating ideas clearly had increased greatly, a result more usually attributed to Jardine's class. Pollok went on to win a prize in the class along with Thomas Durant[87] and his lecture notes are amongst the surviving sets. Gilfillan records another instance of a verse submission, when Mylne one year offered a class prize to a poem by George Gray on burial at sea, "which he read to his class, and by which they, as well as the old, arid, although profound and ingenious philosopher, were perfectly electrified."[88] John Kendrick wrote that, "Mylne laid down no system to be demonstrated, but in clear, simple and impartial summaries, brought the chief systems of metaphysical and ethical writers before his class."[89] It seems then, that he

---

83. *The Christian Reformer, or Unitarian Magazine* (London, 1860), 298. Hutton's scattered writings reflect an even-handed and rational approach to religious questions.

84. Pollok, *Life of Robert Pollok*, 56.

85. "Reminiscences of Robert Pollock" in *Belfast News-Letter* 2/1/1835.

86. David Pollok, *Life of Robert Pollok*, 57.

87. Scott, *Life, Letters and Remains of Rev. Robert Pollok*, 97.

88. "The Life and Poetry of William Falconer" in Gilfillan, *Poetical Works of Beattie, Blair and Falconer*, 173–74.

89. Kendrick, "Memoir of the Late Rev. William Turner Jun., MA" in *The Christian Reformer*, March 1854, 131.

sought to approximate the "cool" style of Hume's *Inquiries*. Despite his impartiality though, the lectures do put across a coherent body of doctrine.

Mylne mentions in a testimonial the attributes he valued in a successful teacher of young students, including the ability "to awaken their love of the knowledge which it is his endeavour to communicate and diminish [. . .] their apprehension of the difficulty of acquiring it."[90] In the lectures he mentions as a particular duty of a teacher the removal of his own ignorance and it is apparent from the lectures that he kept up his knowledge across a range of disciplines. John Wilson mentions Mylne's "notes," but no direct description of Mylne's method of delivery survives. One student, William Turner who particularly admired Mylne as a lecturer and was "probably influenced by his recollections" of him in his own lectures was said to, "lecture extemporaneously, in a conversational and familiar manner, but from carefully arranged notes, often introducing extracts from the writers with whom he wished to make his class acquainted."[91]

John Craig notes a similar lecturing style by John Millar, who spoke from notes, finding that this made it easier to add new material to his lectures, thus keeping them up to date.[92] Millar described Adam Smith's lectures as delivered ex tempore, saying that: "each discourse consisted commonly of several distinct propositions, which he successively endeavoured to prove and illustrate" and would perhaps have passed this on to Mylne as advice.[93] To conjecture some similarity with Mylne's style is consistent with the variety of expression of the lecture notes, dictation being suggested only by the presence of occasional quotations, and the tenor of all contemporary descriptions. However, it is possible that at times he simply read from notes, as Thomas Reid had done.[94]

Students had easy access to books, though for a fee. An American visitor in 1806 who was shown around Glasgow College noted: "There is a fine library of about seventy thousand volumes, which are arranged very advantageously in a large room."[95] In addition, there was a separate Ethics class library, part of a system which Mylne "strongly supported"[96] and that still continues. Mylne had a catalogue of the books in the Ethics class

---

90. NLS:Traill Papers MS19344 f49.

91. Kendrick, "Memoir of the Late Rev. William Turner Jun., MA" in *The Christian Reformer*, March 1854, 133.

92. Craig, "Account of the Life," xiv-xvii.

93. Stewart, "Account of the Life and Writings of Adam Smith," 15.

94. Stewart, *Biographical Memoirs*, 428.

95. Silliman, *A Journal of Travels in England, Holland and Scotland*, 2:276.

96. Murray, *Memories of the Old College of Glasgow*, 166.

library printed in 1815[97] which helps us to identify many references in the lectures.[98]

The academic year concluded in April with the class voting on prizes. A description of this for 1799/1800 survives from Lant Carpenter, with Mylne increasing the number of prizes and reading out some of the best essays.[99] The distribution of College prizes was a major public event attracting crowds of up to 1,200, including many women.[100]

In the evenings, Mylne lectured on political economy.[101] These latter lectures form an unbroken thread from Mylne through to Edward Caird, who also lectured on the same subjects.[102] We shall discuss these in a separate chapter.

Conclusions

Mylne attempted with some success to modify the perceived defects of the sentimental and common sense philosophies associated with his predecessors. He also followed George Jardine's innovations in teaching methods. There is strong evidence that students benefitted from this. As a result, Glasgow students went on to occupy the chairs of philosophy in Edinburgh, Belfast and well beyond in the generation after Mylne. Thus the distinctive content of Mylne's teaching influenced debate for two generations. We shall demonstrate the extent of this influence on philosophy when we consider Mylne's legacy.

---

97. Mylne supported the class library system. Murray writes: "Professor Mylne considered that they greatly saved the wear and tear of the books in the general library, and that the provision of several copies of the books most sought after was very beneficial to the students" (Murray, *Memories of the Old College of Glasgow*, 166.)

98. *Catalogue of Books belonging to the Ethics Class Library* (Glasgow, 1815), copy in GUL.

99. Carpenter: *Memoirs of the Life*, 40 et seq.

100. Description in "Glasgow College Prize Exhibition: Job and no Job" in *Caledonian Mercury* 6/5/1833.

101. Murray, *Memories of the Old College of Glasgow*, 43. One copy of these lectures by James Yates (in shorthand) is in the National Library of Scotland (Manuscripts, ADV.) and another with the Bogue papers at NCL.

102. *Report of the Royal Commissioners Appointed to Inquire into the Universities of Scotland* (Edinburgh: HMSO, 1878.) Vol 3. Caird's evidence. He gives a 30–40 lecture course on political economy in alternate years, but cannot keep up with the literature (209). Shorthand versions of two such lectures survive as MSGen 178–80. Notes of William Fleming's course, which followed Smith closely, also survive at GUL (MS Gen 93), Fleming being the intervening occupant of the chair of moral philosophy at Glasgow.

CHAPTER 5

Whig Politics and Activity

Introduction

WE TURN NOW TO another aspect of James Mylne's life: his contributions to the Glasgow Whig agenda, under which "talent" and "virtue" would supplant, without altogether replacing, "wealth" and (aristocratic) "rank" in society. Mylne's contribution was not only to articulate these ideals, but to contribute to their realization. To this end, I will describe the political program of Mylne and the Glasgow Whigs and then narrate Mylne's role in the political vehicles they adopted, including the informal group of Whigs known variously as the "Fox Club," "Friends of Mr Fox," or "Friends of Civil and Religious Liberty," later constituted as the Glasgow Reform Association. Their activity led to the 1832 Reform Acts and realization of the Whig agenda. This biographical chapter should be read in conjunction with the chapter on Mylne's political influences and doctrines.

The evidence for liberal and reformist opinion associated with Mylne is (a) newspaper reports of his political speeches and activities; (b) David Bogue's minutes of Mylne's 1815/16 course on political economy at Glasgow College and Mylne's 1815 *Statement of the Facts*; (c) his reading, according to the Skirving catalogue and Professors' Receipt Books; (d) the prize essay subjects for political economy; (e) press reports of speeches and toasts at the Fox dinners; and (f) the reminiscences of Peter Mackenzie, John Strang, and John McAdam on the Glasgow reform movement.

The "Napoleonic" Sermon

Mylne followed practical politics as a minister from at least the early 1790s, though public political activity is recorded only after 1815. This chronology is suggested by the newspapers and the reminiscences of Peter Mackenzie (1799–1875), the chronicler of the Glasgow Reform movement who knew of Mylne through both the *Literary and Commercial Society* and probably the Glasgow reformist groups. On Sunday March 26, 1815, Mylne led the service at the College Chapel as usual. However, this propelled him onto the front pages of the local newspapers as he was accused of expressing the hope that Napoleon's landing in France in 1815 would succeed. Mylne spoke on Acts of the Apostles 11:19 and in a sermon "deprecated the needless spilling of human blood."[1] Use of the lines of the 107th Psalm culminating in "that they might to a city go, wherein they might abide" and the words of the 26th paraphrase:

> Behold he comes, your leader comes,
> With might and honour crowned,

apparently gave such offense to one listener, a professor's wife according to some,[2] that a complaint was made to the authorities. This resulted in a precognition, with Mylne and other witnesses questioned, that could have resulted in a charge of sedition or treason. When word was out, leading figures in the town, including Robert Grahame, the lawyer who had defended Thomas Muir in 1793, spoke out in his favor. Mylne defended himself in print, at first through letters to the press collected with other material in his *Statement of the Facts connected with a Precognition taken in the College* (1815). In this pamphlet, he mentions fear of a charge of "sedition, if not high treason," which echoes the language of the 1790s. His students and the student theology society rallied in his support. As his colleagues also backed his version of events, matters soon blew over. Peter Mackenzie reminisced in later life on the effect of the precognition and the support that the students gave Mylne, that:

> it very much encouraged, as we often heard him declare, his *political* faith; and for many years afterwards, down to the period of the passing of the Reform Bill, Professor Mylne was one of

---

1. *Caledonian Mercury* 8/4/1815, citing *Glasgow Chronicle* 6/4/1815. Gale Doc Ref: BB3205367489.

2. Wilson, *Noctes Ambosianae*, 1:382 refers to "Barbara."

the small but choice band which led every popular movement in Glasgow.³

This confirms my impression of a relatively private "political faith" prior to 1815, with Mylne rising to the fore of political agitation in Glasgow only after that date. My survey of local newspaper records of the period indicates that Mylne's profile in the local press prior to 1815 was purely academic or charitable, but that by 1820 at the latest he was playing a public part in Glasgow Whig politics. Prior to that however, he taught political economy to classes composed of a mixture of his students and the general public, sometimes touching on politics in a non-partisan spirit.

Mylne on Whig Political Theory and Practice

In 1815, in his political economy lectures, Mylne sketched a political program based on popular education of the citizenry: "It is not necessary only for legislators or politicians to be acquainted with such principles, but for all citizens of a country." His reasoning is that the political class responds to the opinions of the rest of the community: "How many foolish legislative enactments have been made because the people wished them [. . .] In every country of Europe, indeed, the public opinion is felt by the government, however despotic the government may be in its nature."⁴ He goes on to enumerate the channels through which the influence of opinion operates in Britain: "In our happy country of justice to obtain redress of grievances we have always a legislature ready to receive our petitions; and generally a fair press."⁵

Mylne describes normal political action as involving the press, public meetings and petitions to Parliament as a prelude to legislation. However, these were subject to controversial legal restrictions by Parliament. Despite this, Mylne speaks with a genuine pride of the British Parliament: "Other [nations] have their King and their nobles, but England alone the House of Commons. In England alone do [manufacturers] and merchants arise to such distinguished honour as to [be] the representatives of the people and the Legislators of the land."⁶ These proud remarks place Mylne firmly in the Whig tradition of John Millar in which sovereignty rests with the

---

3. Mackenzie, *Reminiscences of Glasgow and the West of Scotland*, 1:468.
4. Mylne, Lectures on Political Economy, (NCL:MS/BOGU3), Lecture 1.
5. Ibid.
6. Ibid., Lecture 25.

representatives of the people gathered in Parliament with the Court and royalist interests granted only a subsidiary position.

To do justice to Mylne's political thought then, we must first survey the component parts of the system of redress whose inadequacies led to his support for the reform of the representation of the people later embodied in the 1832 Reform Act. These are: public meetings, petitions, and the press.

Political campaigns generally involved press coverage of an issue which resulted in public meetings and in petitions to Parliament which were themselves reported in the press. The petition was publicized, signatures collected and the document delivered to a sympathetic local politician for presentation to the House of Commons.[7]

Public Meetings and Petitions

Following the radical agitation of the early 1790s, curbs were placed on public meetings. In 1795, a controversy broke out over William Pitt's "Bill for the More Effectually preventing Seditious Meetings and Assemblies." Leading Whigs Charles James Fox and Lauderdale argued against this that the right to petition for the redress of grievances was fundamental.[8] This was the context of Edmund Burke's letter against the Duke of Bedford and Lauderdale. Legal restrictions were imposed for a period of three years. The three-year limit was itself a concession to widespread public opposition to the measure. There was a further act in 1799.[9]

By the early 1800s, the evidence of the local newspapers suggests that this legislation had effectively stymied the public life of Glasgow. The situation in the early 1800s was recalled by Lord Archibald Hamilton at a landmark meeting in Glasgow also addressed by Henry Brougham and James Mylne. Reflecting in 1823 on the last twenty years, Hamilton said that, "at one period of his recollection it was hardly possible to assemble twenty persons in favour of honest and liberal principles, without being slandered as a radical, an enemy to social order, hostile to the constitution, and disloyal to the crown."[10] Some major issues did still generate petitioning activity. In February 1805, 7,000 petitioners from Paisley opposed the Corn Laws.[11] However, petitions did not include political reform. Despite Hamilton's use of the past tense in 1823, official inertia and obstacles to the

---

7. Examples include the agitation on Burgh reform in the early 1790s.
8. *GC* 26/11/1795.
9. The "Act for Suppressing Seditious Societies" (*GC* 13/8/1799).
10. *Liverpool Mercury* 19/9/1823, citing the *Scotsman* and *Free Press*.
11. *GC* 28/2/1805.

promotion of political aims still existed. The reformer John McAdam reminisced of the period prior to 1832 that, "The Assembly Rooms, Trades Hall, and churches, were mainly in the disposal of parties unfriendly. Even the right of meeting in the Green was disputed."[12] As we shall see, from 1811, the Fox Club was one of the means of recovering the situation for the cause of reform and re-establishing the tradition of public meetings.

The Newspapers and Freedom of the Press

Mylne acknowledged the political role of the newspaper. In 1815, he said that Britain had "generally a fair press,"[13] though he also spoke with contempt of the "hireling authors of our own day."[14] Mylne mentions also "many complaints indeed of the fetters put on the freedom of our press."[15] The "Friends of Mr Fox" annually toasted "the Liberty of the press" at the Fox dinners from 1815. In 1819 they toasted "May an affected zeal for religion never be made the cloak for political persecution of the Press" and the following year "may its benefits be kept open to the rich and poor of all nations." In 1821, the advocate Alexander Dunlop gave a speech in defense of press freedom.

The newspapers were a more immediate means of communicating political intelligence than books and periodicals. In the Tontine Coffee Rooms in Glasgow, a public meeting place designed by the architect William Hamilton RA, who also designed David Dale's house in Charlotte Street, an unseemly struggle broke out in 1793 when the papers announcing the execution of Louis XVI and the outbreak of war with France arrived.

Initially, the Glasgow newspapers were mostly of the establishment. For example, the editor of the *Glasgow Mercury* stated that he had an abhorrence of inflammatory statements.[16] As with public meetings, restrictions dated from the 1790s. Thereafter, the tone of the newspapers, for example in the coverage of the trial of Viscount Melville in 1808, increasingly fell into sycophancy. Stamp duty was imposed on newspapers in 1796. This raised the price of publications, but was partially circumvented by the establishment of reading rooms, though these too had to be registered. The reading rooms had become established in the 1790s as places of discussion. Thomas Chalmers in 1820 lamented that "the reading rooms of sedition and infi-

12. McAdam, *Autobiography*, 4.
13. Mylne, Lectures on Political Economy, (NCL:MS/BOGU3), Lecture 1.
14. MS Gen1355/103/26; MS Murray207/454.
15. Mylne, Lectures on Political Economy, (NCL:MS/BOGU3), Lecture 26.
16. *Glasgow Mercury* 20/9/1796.

delity are now open every Sabbath."[17] The requirement to register printing presses and to affix the name and address of the publisher and the date of publication to each document dates from this period. Mylne's colleague Meikleham was a partner in the *Glasgow Courier*, which advertised college courses. Mylne used the paper to advertise his evening lectures. It supported him in 1815 in the alarm over his "seditious" sermon in the college chapel. John McAdam commented that, prior to 1832, "unless a very mild article from the *Chronicle* occasionally, nothing emanated from the Press unless permitted as an article at the maximum rate."[18] The Radicals in 1819 alleged that "the whole newspapers in the West of Scotland were venal and corrupt"[19] and proposed setting up their own independent rival.[20] In the case of the *Courier*, coverage of the reformers became more sympathetic in early 1820, as outright opposition to reform became untenable.

The Friends of Mr. Fox

The main vehicle of Whig opinion in Glasgow from 1811 was the "Friends of Mr Fox," or "Fox Club," named after Charles James Fox, the leading Whig statesman of the era, which existed ostensibly for the purpose of commemorating Fox's birthday around the 25th of January each year.[21] Such dinners were key events publicizing and cementing local reformist sentiment in the political calendar.[22] The date coincided with Burns' Suppers which—to judge by the publicity—they rivaled in popularity. The Glasgow Fox Club was less aristocratic in membership than its Edinburgh equivalent, with more commercial and Scottish toasts, though less radical than in Tayside.[23]

The chronicler of the time, Peter Mackenzie, notes that Mylne stood out amongst the churchmen of the city. He writes:

> It was difficult to get any of the city clergymen to grace the Fox Club—they rather preferred the Pitt one—but in order to

---

17. Drummond and Bulloch, *The Scottish Church 1688–1843*, 165, citing Chalmers' "Importance of Civil Government."

18. McAdam, *Autobiography*, 4.

19. GC, 24/8/1819.

20. They recommended instead Wooler's *Gazette*, the *Manchester Observer*, *The Statesman* and the *Belfast Irishman* to their audience (see GC, 28/8/1819).

21. See GC 28/1/1819 for meeting on 25 January and similar adverts for other years.

22. See Hughes, "James Hogg," for further examples.

23. Trent Orme, talk on "Toasting Fox" at EU, 27/10/2011, based on doctoral thesis at Edinburgh University on Scottish Whigs, forthcoming.

prevent the Tories from saying, as they sometimes tauntingly did, that the Whigs, or the Foxites, were nothing but "a graceless and a godless set," Professor Mylne pretty regularly officiated at the Fox anniversary, by asking the blessing "for the good things of this life," and he in consequence got the name of the "Whig chaplain."[24]

Mylne's Christianity may have contributed a moderating effect. With respect to the "hireling authors" mentioned above, he said for example: "Truth must be supported with dignity, gentleness, philanthropy and perseverance. Let us not hope to overthrow error in one instant."[25] Mackenzie identifies Mylne as one of four Whig professors at the college in 1815, out of twenty.[26] He wrote:

> These four gentlemen were of the liberal, or Whig school. They rather admired the principles of the Right Honourable Charles James Fox: and they attended the anniversary of his birth given regularly by a public dinner, at one guinea per head, in the Black Bull ballroom, then a very celebrated place in Glasgow. In fact the occasion of the celebration of Mr Fox's birth-day in Glasgow was almost the only occasion at that remote period of ventilating anything in the shape of *Politics*, or political sentiments of any kind whatever.[27]

This confirms the decline of public meetings since the 1790s. Mackenzie generally has an eye for a story and would probably be relying on second-hand information for these years, but the relationship of Mylne and the Fox Club is confirmed by contemporary newspapers and other witnesses. John Strang, another sympathetic observer close to Mylne, refers to the leaders of liberal opinion post-1832 as being "from the class of old, steady Whigs, who had countenanced Fox dinners and Reform meetings during the worst of times" and names Mylne as a prominent member,[28] as does John McAdam. This group included several prominent business people.

Mylne's public involvement dates from at the latest 1820, though he knew Robert Grahame, one of the prime movers, ten years earlier.[29] The Fox Club agenda corresponds closely to Mylne's personal views from the

24. Mackenzie, *Reminiscences of Glasgow*, 1:459.
25. MS Gen1355/103/27.
26. The others being George Jardine, James Millar, and Richard Miller.
27. Mackenzie, *Reminiscences of Glasgow*, 1:458. Mackenzie gets Mylne's name wrong here.
28. Strang, *Clubs of Glasgow* (1856), 548–49.
29. *GC*, 17/1/1809, Glasgow Public Library committee.

outset. In 1814 a toast is given to "Sir Thomas Graham and the University of Glasgow, and may public spirit always predominate in the universities of Scotland" and the Mylnean thought "May neither precedent nor antiquity be a sanction to errors pernicious to mankind" is the subject of a speech.[30] Graham (1748–1843) was a Whig MP with a military background and Rector of Glasgow University at the time.

After 1811, public life begins to recover vitality. In the same year, the Tory hold on the press was challenged by the founding of the *Glasgow Chronicle* and political campaigning revived with the debate on renewal of the East India Company monopoly. In 1812, the *Glasgow Chronicle* noted "upwards of one hundred gentlemen" in attendance at the Fox Dinner.[31] Robert Bell, published his *Commentary on the Election Laws as they relate to the Representation of Scotland* that year.[32] Petitions were raised against the renewal of the East India Company's Exclusive Charter in 1812, including one from the Merchants and Manufacturers of Glasgow.[33] A further petition against alterations to the Corn Laws from the Incorporation of Weavers was presented and in March the following year there were thirty local meetings on the subject.[34] These were subjects covered in Mylne's political economy lectures. In respect of these issues, he was reflecting, or perhaps in some degree leading, politics in Glasgow. Mylne's political economy lectures were themselves a source of reform ideas.

It was only after the impact of these local campaigns on the East India Company and Corn Laws that the question of parliamentary reform was raised again in 1817, accompanied by arrests. A divinity student, Mr. McTear, was arrested but freed without charge.[35] Others arrested included the "itinerant political preacher" Neil Douglas, who had been a member from Dundee at the Scots Convention in Edinburgh in 1796. This time though, prosecutions by government for sedition failed in the Scottish courts.[36] Around this time, the Fox dinners toasted "The British Constitution in its original purity, and may it never be suspended by means of spies and informers." The Friends of Mr. Fox resorted to the Whig theory that monarchy was a manifestation of constitutional principle. Thus a typical toast from

30. *Glasgow Chronicle* 27/1/1814.
31. *Glasgow Chronicle* 25/1/1812.
32. GC 30/1/1812.
33. GC 31/3/12; 12/1/1813.
34. GC 31/5/14; 4–11/3/1815.
35. GC 11/3/1817.
36. GC 18/3 and 29/5/1817. See also published records of trials of Neil Douglas, William [Edgar].

1817 runs "The House of Hanover, and may they never forget the principles which seated them on the Throne." This they soon follow with "The Sovereignty of the People—the only *legitimate* foundation of free Government," and then: "May the people of Scotland soon cease to be inferior to Englishmen in Political Rights."[37]

Mylne publicly officiated at the Fox anniversary commemoration on January 24, 1820 as Steward, the first of a series of reported events from which we can glean his political opinions.[38] The meeting was chaired by Robert Wallace of Kelly, with John Maxwell MP as Vice Preses. Maxwell (1791–1865) was a wealthy aristocrat from the family that eventually bequeathed Pollok House in Eastwood in the presbytery of Paisley to the public.[39] He was MP for Renfrewshire from 1818 until 1830 and was returned from Lanarkshire from 1832–37. Maxwell was also present with Mylne at the Glasgow Fox dinner the following year, having defeated the Tory Boyd Alexander as MP for Renfrewshire in March 1820.[40] Whilst he enjoyed some popularity for his support for reform,[41] he had to defend his character as a reformer following publication of his *Letter to the Honest Reformers of Scotland* (1819) against understandable calls of "desertion of principle" by the reformist paper *The Spirit of the Union*, on account of his disavowal of "riotous, violent, irreligious plundering way" of obtaining reform.[42]

As usual, the toasts at the meeting in January 1820 were published in the press, setting out the reformist agenda of the Friends of Mr. Fox.[43] These first involve conditional recognition of the Crown: "The King. The House of Hanover, may they be mindful of the Principles that seated them on the throne." Thereafter comes the political agenda: "the speedy Reform of the Scottish Boroughs, the Liberty of the Press" and "the speedy removal of all unnecessary restrictions on the liberty of the subject." The legal reform agenda, associated with Sir James MacIntosh in the case of the criminal law and "the Independence of the Scottish Bar" follows.

In the following months, the "Radical Wars" shook the establishment. Thereafter, John McAdam noted that "public opinion had grown steadily for Parliamentary Reform since the ill advised attempt of 1820."[44] Mylne

37. *Glasgow Chronicle* 25/1/1817.
38. *GC* 18/1/1820. His academic title "Mr Professor Mylne" is advertised.
39. More specifically to the National Trust for Scotland.
40. *GC* 18/1/1820; 4/1/21; 23/3/1820.
41. "John Maxwell" by Irene Mavor in *DNB*.
42. Letter in *GC* 11/1/1820.
43. *GC* 25/1/1820.
44. McAdam, *Autobiography*, 4.

also spoke of a shift in public opinion around this time. In December 1820, Mylne was alone among the College professors in appending his signature publicly to an advert asking the Lord Provost to call a meeting at which, in a common formulation, local "Merchants, Bankers, Manufacturers and Inhabitants" could vote a Loyal Address to the King "praying his Majesty to dismiss his ministers and reassemble Parliament without delay."[45] James Oswald (1779–1853), the future MP, was elected to chair the resultant meeting and expressed the Whig creed that they were loyal subjects of a free state. He went on to describe the meeting as an "experiment" in peaceable politics and accused the government ministers of ruling by dividing the country and increasing its military force in order to quell the consequent discontent. Peter Mackenzie too records Mylne's involvement in the meeting on December 13, 1820 objecting to a petition in support of the King being sent in the name of the town.[46] Again, he is found in the company of James Dennistoun, Robert Grahame and his neighbor Charles Tennant, prominent businessmen of the time.

At this time, Mylne's political involvements appear to have put him at odds with his academic colleagues. A few days later, the University of Glasgow published a Loyal Address, lamenting the actions of "a factious and turbulent portion of our fellow subjects to propagate disaffection, to exasperate discontent and to overawe the legislature." They recall the termination of the late war and state that his Majesty's servants have since "conducted the affairs of state, firmly, constitutionally and successfully. This is signed by the Vice Chancellor William Taylor.[47]

Early in 1821, Mylne's fellow reformers, Archibald Spiers and John Maxwell, amongst others, were active in a series of meetings of the County of Renfrew and County of Lanark, attempting with varying success to append criticisms of the government to loyal addresses to the King.[48] Spiers had chaired the Fox dinner in 1814[49] and had been MP for Renfrewshire up to 1818 when he was replaced by fellow Whig John Maxwell.[50] He and Maxwell also shared concerns for banking with Mylne, who lectured on the subject.[51]

---

45. GC 19/1/1820. The advert carries around 350 signatures.
46. Mackenzie: *Reminiscences of Glasgow*, 1:305.
47. GC 28/12/1820. This time, Mylne's name does not appear.
48. GC 6, 9, 18 and 23/1/1821.
49. *Glasgow Chronicle*, reported in *Liverpool Mercury* 4/2/1814.
50. William Frazer, "Memoirs of the Maxwell's of Pollok" in *Glasgow Herald* 1/4/1865. (Gale Doc Ref: BC3203549901). See "John Maxwell" by Irene Mavor in *DNB*.
51. *Glasgow Herald* 3/3/1826.

At the January 1821 "Anniversary of Mr Fox," Mylne was again at the forefront of the speakers at the animated gathering at the Black Bull Inn, chaired by future Lord Provost Robert Grahame, this time under the name *The Friends of Civil and Religious Liberty*. The *Glasgow Courier* reported that the attendance was double the average of previous years.[52] Mylne pushed the reform agenda ahead in a speech advocating "a speedy and substantial Reform in the Representation of the People." This openly raised again the issue of Parliamentary reform. In the following years his phraseology was echoed and appealed to by other reform orators. Mylne rose again to speak on "Mr Brougham and the Education of the People." He had taken on the mantle of Millar as the reasoned academic voice of social and political reform in Glasgow. The meeting offered in return toasts to "The University of Glasgow" and to "the Memory of Professor Millar, and may Constitutional Principles ever distinguish our Scottish Universities."[53]

Mylne gave further speeches to the meeting on "Earl Grey and the Whigs of England" and "The Duke of Leinster and the Whigs of Ireland" and "Robert Wallace," an organizer, as reported in the Whig *Morning Chronicle*.[54] Charles Grey (1764–1845) was a leader of the Whig opposition. The political interests of Augustus Fitzgerald, the third Duke of Leinster (1791–1874) included education and agriculture in Ireland. Clearly, the agenda looked beyond Scotland. Here, Mylne again met publicly with Maxwell, Spiers and other reformers.[55]

At the Fox dinner in 1823, Mylne spoke directly after Spiers' introductory remarks. Newspaper reports state that:

> Professor Mylne very ably introduced the toast in favour of reform. He noted the change that had taken place in the opinions of the higher classes on this vital subject. Such were the distresses of the country that reform was likely to be speedy, and he trusted it would be substantial.[56]

---

52. *GC* 25/1/1821.

53. This account is drawn from the report in the *GC* 25/1/1821.

54. *Morning Chronicle* (London) 30/1/1821, citing *Edinburgh Star*. Wallace was the croupier who assisted chairman Robert Grahame at the meeting.

55. See adverts in *GC* 11&13/1/1821. Mylne and Millar were the only college professors to publicly support the Reformers. The *Courier* records that: "The toasts were given partly from the chair and partly by other Gentlemen, and being generally prefaced by appropriate observations, the meeting assumed the aspect and animation of an English one."

56. *Caledonian Mercury* 27/1/1823; see also *Times* 29/1/1823, reproduced from *Glasgow Chronicle*.

This makes a connection between the economy and political representation. It was well received. Another speaker, Grahame of Gartmore, preferred the formulation a "full, free and radical reform."[57] Grahame went on to be Lord Provost of Glasgow following reform of the franchise.

Alliance with Henry Brougham

Around this time, the common program of popular education and political reform seems to have led the Glasgow reformers, including Mylne, into association with Henry Brougham (1778–1868), the Whig lawyer and Edinburgh reviewer. From 1821, the Glasgow Fox dinners toasted versions of "A cordial union and co-operation of all the friends of Freedom in the cause of Parliamentary Reform." Already the same year, Mylne had spoken on "Mr Brougham and the Education of the People."[58] At this time, Brougham's activities included an investigation of charity schools in London.

Mylne shared a political platform with Brougham in Glasgow in September 1823, at which credit was offered to: "the powerful accession of feeling in Scotland within the last twenty years, in favour of the great cause of reform, of which that able politician was the powerful champion."[59] Brougham then gave a wide-ranging speech. He first recalled "the last of the public meetings, in 1794" held in opposition to the "gagging bills of the day" and the treatment of Mr. Erskine the Advocate who would otherwise have stood at the head of the legal profession. Henry Erskine (1746–1817) was a Whig lawyer, aristocrat and rival to Henry Dundas. Brougham then proposed a "priesthood in middle circumstances," as defenders of freedom, and the need to "diffuse knowledge, and sound principles, by every fair means." According to what appears to be a verbatim report, Mylne then rose to speak for:

> a reform that would place the right of voting in the hands of those who should possess it—a reform which would not deprive wealth, and rank, and talent, and virtue, of the influence they ought to possess, but which would prevent wealth and rank from monopolising privileges, the abuse of which made them objects of jealousy and aversion to the people, instead of being objects of respect and confidence.

57. *Times* 29/1/1823.

58. *Morning Chronicle* (London) 30/1/1821, citing *Edinburgh Star*.

59. *Liverpool Mercury*, 19/9/1823 "Dinner to Mr Brougham at Glasgow," citing the *Scotsman* & *Free Press*.

This is in line with the Glasgow Whig creed that stopped short of levelling, but sought outlets for "talent" and "virtue" in the common interest. The report continues:

> He considered it needless to refine much as to the terms by which such a reform might be qualified; he thought it might very properly be characterised as a substantial reform, and it was equally desirable that it should be speedy. He proposed "A reform of the representation of the people in parliament."[60]

This was followed by other speeches, including one by Mr. Lawless of *The Irishman* in favor of Brougham's policies in Ireland that was the occasion of attack by Mylne's counterpart Professor John Wilson of Edinburgh, whilst Professor Pillans praised Brougham's endeavors to introduce a Bill for National Education in England.

Mylne spoke again at a public dinner following Brougham's election as Rector of Glasgow University in 1825, when Brougham was elected over Walter Scott on the casting vote of the preceding Rector Sir James MacIntosh, though his words are not recorded. Party feeling was clearly predominant at this event, the "Great Unknown" (Scott, who published his novels anonymously) being said to have "cared nothing about the liberty of the human race." Another speaker asked "What had the friends of civil and religious liberty to do with this Great Unknown?" Thomas Campbell, author of *The Pleasures of Hope* was praised to much laughter at the expense of, "artificial and sycophantic verse-mongers and doggrel story-tellers, who instinctively sing the praises of tyranny, and fatten on the solid comforts of subserviency."[61] The results of universal suffrage at the University were extolled at the expense of the presumed results of Professorial suffrage. Despite being accessory to this outburst of party feeling, Mylne did own a few works by Scott, including the novel *Quentin Durward* set in Burgundy, and borrowed others from the College Library.

The Reform Association and the Victory of Reform

Mylne was one of a committee of twelve appointed in 1830 to draw up the constitution of the Glasgow Reform Association.[62] The Reform Association was the most moderate of three reformist bodies in Glasgow at this time,

---

60. *Liverpool Mercury*, 19/9/1823.

61. *The Examiner* (London) 10/4/1825; *Liverpool Mercury* 15/4/1825.

62. Fyfe, in notes to *Autobiography of John McAdam*, 222-23. Fyfe does not mention her sources.

along with the Trades Committee and the Glasgow Political Union, which preceded it and were more vocal and broader-based in membership. John McAdam describes the Association as containing:

> nearly all the Whig gentlemen in Glasgow, many of them eminent in commerce, manufactures and literature, some of them very advanced in political opinion [. . .] differing in some particulars, but all agreed on the [1832] Reform Bill,"[63] adding that most "remained true to their professions" in coming years.[64]

Mylne is named along with his colleague Daniel Sandford and the reform parliament MPs James Oswald and candidate George Crawfurd, whom Mylne voted for in 1832.[65]

After the 1832 Reform Act, the reform parliament introduced bills on a range of subjects. These resulted in the Abolition of Slavery Act (1833);[66] the end of the East India Company monopoly over trade with China; a grant to build schools and the Factory Act (1833),[67] which restricted child labor; and burgh reform (1833). By the end of his life then, Mylne's agenda in politics and political economy was well on the way to realization.

Late Political Encounters

After the 1832 Reform Act, Mylne was an established member of "the Clique" of liberal opinion formers without whose support mercantile or political projects were likely to be stymied.[68] Several later political encounters, from after the 1832 election, confirm Mylne's continuing reformist leanings. In 1832, William Cobbett (1763–1835), the radical journalist and newly elected MP for Oldham, toured Scotland. Mylne owned copies of Cobbett's *Political Register* and Wooller's *Black Dwarf* (1817).[69] A historian says of

---

63. McAdam, *Autobiography*, 6–7.

64. Ibid., 7.

65. Mackenzie, *Glasgow Electors*.

66. "An Act for the Abolition of Slavery throughout the British Colonies," 3&4 Will IV c. 73.

67. 3 & 4 William IV, c. 103.

68. As a prominent liberal, John Strang was well placed to place Mylne in this circle, which he does in *Glasgow and its Clubs* (1856) 549 n. Mylne is well up the list and the only professor of the fifty-seven persons named, which include Robert Grahame, James Oswald, and A Spiers [sic].

69. For Mylne's personal library, see the auction lists of Booker & Skirving 1839–40 in GUL.

the early nineteenth century: that "the writings of William Cobbett and T J Wooler became widely disseminated in the west of Scotland."[70]

In his *Tour in Scotland, and in the Four Northern Counties of England* (1833), Cobbett reproduces an account of his meeting with Mylne on October 20, taken from the local reformist paper *Glasgow Chronicle*.[71] A few days later he reflected on Scottish philosophy:

> I, even I, had strong feelings excited in my mind against Scotland generally (always making great exceptions) by the scoundrelly "*feelosophers*" who preached up a doctrine tending to cause the people of England to be treated like cattle; even I could not make out how it was, that Scotland should spew forth so many of these monsters. I now see to the bottom of the whole thing. [...] The renegade villainous "*feelosophers*" who have come to London, have been, and are, the corrupt tools of the Scotch oligarchy for selling their own country, and of the English oligarchy for pillaging and enslaving the people of England.[72]

He completes the intended sense by referring to "the "land-clearing" and poor-rate-abolishing "feelosophers.""[73] George Davie replies to Cobbett in terms that do not question the identification of "Scottish philosophy" with the common sense school, but here as elsewhere Mylne was probably at one with Cobbett.

Later that year, Mylne appears to have been drawn into an impromptu response to a "hole and corner meeting" on fulfillment of a treaty with Belgium and Holland, held by Mr. Motherwell the editor of the *Glasgow Courier* and reputed "supporters of West India slavery," reported by the *Glasgow Chronicle*.[74] Mylne and others in the Liberal deputation were prevented from entering the meeting. Another meeting in opposition was held and scuffles broke out when entry was again sought to the Black Bull Inn. Little was accomplished, though the representative character of the original meeting was called in question.

The moderate Whig agenda on electoral law did not stop with the 1832 Reform Act. This was the context of a further dinner in October 1834 in

---

70. Alexander Wilson, *The Chartist Movement in Scotland*, 24.

71. Professor Mylne received Mr. Cobbett, and showed him the Museum, the College, the Faculty-hall, etc., all of which Mr. Cobbett seemed much pleased with, and laughed heartily at the prospect of his being elected Lord Rector (Cobbett, *Tour in Scotland*, 148).

72. Cobbett, *Tour in Scotland*, 156.

73. Ibid., 157.

74. *Morning Chronicle* 3/12/1832.

Glasgow, attended by around 1,450 in the Grammar school yard, in honor of John Lambton (1792–1840), the Earl of Durham, who had been earlier greeted by a crowd estimated at 100,000 or more and presented with the freedom of the city. Durham's father had been Preses of the Friends of the People in the 1790s and a supporter of Fox. Durham had expressed himself "a friend to household suffrage, triennial Parliaments and vote by ballot"[75] and was at that time a rival of Henry Brougham. At the dinner, Mylne contributed a "long and reverend" grace and returned thanks. Following a brief meal and the admission of women, toasts agreed in advance by the Stewards were given.[76] Durham discussed the terms of a second reform bill and discussed the predominantly Tory nature of the unelected state in Church, law, and the military. He later spoke again on friendly relations with France. *Rule Britannia* vied with a version of *Scots Wha Hae* as musical accompaniment.[77] JF Ferrier refers to this day in his edition of Wilson's *Noctes Ambrosianae* (1856), describing the crowd as "Glasgow Radicals."[78]

Another public act brought Mylne full circle to his first, prize-winning theological essay on the limits of toleration. Alexander Campbell Fraser recalls it in his brief account of Mylne in the 1830s: "In politics Mylne was a philosophical Radical, and he offended many by going to a Glasgow public dinner in honour of Daniel O'Connell, when the Irish liberator visited Scotland."[79] Fraser's description "philosophical radical" is correct philosophically, though the term "radical" on its own, found in the *Times* article on the event, could be misleading. Mylne had already chaired a crowded meeting in Glasgow Trades Hall on the "Irish Coercion Bill" of Grey's Whig ministry two years prior to this. The meeting agreed unanimously to petition against the Bill, which contained a range of repressive measures.[80] The dinner in 1835 was attended by around 200 people. Mylne's contribution consisted of saying grace at the outset, for which his successor at Paisley Abbey, the Reverend Patrick Brewster returned thanks.[81] Brewster (1788–1859)

---

75. *Caledonian Mercury* 30/10/34; *Morning Chronicle* (London) 1/11/34, citing the *Times*; *Examiner* (London), 2/11/34; *Liverpool Mercury* 7/11/34.

76. Lambton, *Speeches of the Earl of Durham*, 46.

77. *Scotsman* 1/11/1834.

78. Wilson, *Works of Professor Wilson*, 4:208 n.

79. Fraser, *Biographia Philosophica*, 42. This event can be dated to 21 September 1835. See Hamilton, *Life of Daniel O'Connell*, 129.

80. *Johnstone's Political Register*, 8.2 30/3/1833, 46.

81. *Times* 26/9/1835 "Daniel's second Exhibition at Glasgow."

was known then and later by his publications.⁸² Brewster had to defend his presence in print.⁸³

The *Times* took offense at the toast "The Sovereignty of the People" preceding that to the King. O'Connell (1775–1847) was the leading Irish politician of the era and a highly controversial figure. Such was the animosity of the day, that *The Times* of London, normally guarded in its tone, published a poem:

> Scum condensed of Irish bog!
> Ruffian—coward—demagogue!
> Boundless liar—base detractor!
> Nurse of murders, treason's factor!⁸⁴

O'Connell's speech mocked the Aristocracy as "the real swinish multitude"⁸⁵ reflecting the common offense taken in Scotland at Burke's phrase from the 1790s. At this time, liberal opinion in Scotland was sympathetic to O'Connell's views, perhaps influenced by the favorable opinion of Henry Brougham, who had negotiated with O'Connell on the terms of Catholic emancipation.⁸⁶ At this period, he was cooperating with the Whigs at Westminster, Ireland being run at the time in the conciliatory manner long advocated by Mylne and the Glasgow liberals by Thomas Drummond, under-secretary at Dublin Castle.⁸⁷

---

82. Brewster was the brother of the scientist David Brewster. He advocated abolition of the slave trade, repeal of the Corn Laws and Roman Catholic emancipation. In Mylne's day, only *The Heroism of the Christian Spirit* (1833) and *The Claims of the Church of Scotland* (1835) had appeared. His best known work was *Seven Chartist and military Discourses* (1843). From 1898–1817 the minister of second charge at Paisley had been James Smith (1771–1817). Smith's *Evidences of a Special Divine Providence attending the late signal Successes obtained over the Enemy* (Paisley, 1814) suggests a preference for Reid's, rather than Mylne's view of a particular providence (Scott, *Fasti* (1920), 2:1, 201–2).

83. Brewster, *Reply to the Attacks*.

84. Dunlop, *Daniel O'Connell*, 306 et seq.

85. *Times* 26/9/1835.

86. "The papers are full of nothing but O'Connell's progress in Scotland, where he is received with unbounded enthusiasm by enormous crowds," says Greville, see Hamilton's *Life*, 129. O'Connell wrote: "There was one man who has behaved to me in a manner which exceeds all praise: that is Mr Brougham" (O'Connell, *Correspondence of Daniel O'Connell*, 4:63).

87. This policy initially bore fruit in terms of the administration of justice, the Irish legal system and administration being largely under the control of Drummond. When the reform policy failed, he founded the Repeal Association to re-establish Irish self-government in 1840. See also Smeal's "Glasgow's Share."

As late as January 1837, Mylne continued to attend similar events. The last such record we have is of a dinner for James Oswald MP for Glasgow at which Mylne "officiated as Chaplain" in January 1837.[88] After royalty, the toast "The People, the true source of political power" was given. Oswald's speech testifies to the growing strength of the Tories after several years of Whig government and the emergence of the terms "conservative" and "liberal" as party labels. Mylne then, reaffirmed his reformist convictions to the end of his public life.

Conclusions

Chronologically, our incomplete knowledge of James Mylne's political activity shows him engaging in radical-tinged political debate as a young clergyman in the 1790s. After his appointment as Professor in Glasgow College, his institution of lectures on political economy made him a public figure in Glasgow as early as 1801. He was emboldened, rather than intimidated, by the precognition in 1815, which shows a degree of personal courage. From 1820 he was prepared to openly court political controversy through public advocacy of a Whig reformist agenda that included extension of the electoral franchise, popular education and Catholic emancipation.

He sought to do this without rancor. As we shall see, his political principles involved flow naturally from the content of the moral philosophy he expounded in his university lectures and the content of particular reforms is underpinned by the analyses in his lectures on political economy.

88. *Scotsman* 7/1/1837. See also *Glasgow Chronicle*, cited in *Morning Chronicle* 9/1/1837.

CHAPTER 6

Family, Church, and Succession

IN THIS CHAPTER WE look beyond the college classroom at Mylne's domestic circle, amongst many of whom the Whig creed was a commonplace; his relations with leading churchmen and reading in theology; role in the Literary and Commercial Society; and the unfortunate controversies in the 1830s over the succession to his post.

Second Marriage and Domestic Life

James Mylne's first moral philosophy course ended around May 1798. He married Agnes Millar, daughter of John Millar (1735–1801) the professor of law, in a service in Millheugh, near Glasgow on June 26, 1798, conducted by his friend and colleague the Reverend Robert Boog.[1] In 1820 he remarked in the context of a discussion of sympathy that: "it is difficult to say whether self-love or sympathy preponderates in the compound feelings of love of the sexes."[2] This suggests a happy marriage. According to John Craig, Agnes Millar was one of nine children of Millar and his wife, Margaret Craig (c. 1736–95), born after 1760, six daughters and three sons.[3]

Agnes' sisters were described by the brother of William Lamb (1779–1848, Viscount Melbourne) who with his brother Frederick attended Mylne and Millar's classes. Melbourne was Britain's Prime Minister from 1835–41 and a Whig. Incidentally, his biographer considered it "possible that

1. Announcement in *GC* 28/6/1798; location in Millheugh noted in *General Evening Post* of London 3/7/1798 and other London papers.

2. GUL:MSGen466/176.

3. Craig: "Account of the Life," cxxvii, n. The *DNB* article on Millar speaks of four sons and six daughters and a further two children who died in infancy.

Professor Mylne's lectures may have helped to nourish those speculative tendencies and that dreamy fondness for casuistic discussion which characterized Lamb in later years." Frederick felt that in Millar's house "there is nothing heard of in this house but study" and wrote to his mother that, "All the ladies here are contaminated with an itch for philosophy and learning, and such a set of fools it never was my lot to see. One of the Miss Millars is pretty, but they are all philosophers, and the eldest is exactly like Mrs Trimmer."[4] Sarah Trimmer (1741–1810) was an Anglican advocate of Sunday schools. John Millar had celebrated the early stages of the Revolution in France.[5] Mylne joined him in the Whig minority amongst the professors[6] and attended him on his deathbed in 1801.

Of Agnes' brothers, John Craig describes the hounding into emigration of John Millar's eldest son and namesake (1760–95), a lawyer who had written on insurance, in the 1790s:

> It was impossible for the son of Mr Millar, carrying his conviction of the necessity of reform in some degree farther than his father, and equally open and steady in maintaining his opinions, to escape the obloquy with which the violent and interested in political parties always attempt to overwhelm their opponents.[7]

Millar's son died in America and his widow, Robina Craig Millar, returned to Britain, where she was a radical influence close to Mylne in the Millheugh circle. She was a sister of the novelist Margaret Cullen, a friend of Eliza Fletcher and addressee of the letters in Mylne's grandniece Frances Wright's *View of Men and Manners in America* (1821).[8] Mylne was later closely associated with James Millar, who was Professor of mathematics at Glasgow College, through their shared Whig politics. The other son, William Millar served as an army officer in the West Indies and in the Peninsular War, dying through suicide in 1838.

---

4. Dunckley, *Lord Melbourne*, vol. 2, section 3, chapter 2.

5. See Strang, *Glasgow and Its Clubs* (1856), 20 n. 4, quoting *GM* 5/7/1791). He knew John Craig, the biographer of John Millar, through the Literary Society, and probably Thomas Reid, who was also a member.

6. See Emerson, "Politics and the Glasgow Professors."

7. Craig continues: "Averse to contention, hopeless of a pacific change in the political institutions of his country, and finding himself in a state of health which rendered laborious application improper, he resolved, in spring 1795, to emigrate to America" (Craig, "Account of the Life," cxxvi).

8. See Eckhardt, *Fanny Wright*, passim; Rendall, "Women that would plague me," 327.

Mylne moved into a College house adjoining the High Street in 1797.[9] His borrowings of piano music from the College library may suggest something of the sounds around the house. He received visitors. Despite a greatly increased income, he obtained a loan from the College in 1804.[10] By 1814, he had acquired an interest in one of three villas in Fairley (also spelled Fairlie), three miles from Largs on the Ayrshire coast, where he could stay in summer.[11] These are described in a travel book as "in a very uncommon style of elegance, which one should think more adapted to an Italian sky, than to the northern latitude of this part of Britain," which the author takes as "proof of the genial temperature of the air of this place."[12] The property was "held in feu or long lease" from the Earl of Glasgow who lived nearby.[13] Mylne was still resident there in 1837.[14]

Mylne's wife kept in contact with her sisters at Millheugh. Another Millar daughter, Margaret, married Professor John Thomson of Edinburgh. Other daughters, Ann and Janet, remained at Millar's family home at Millheugh after his death. Millar's sons were James (1762-1831), William, and Archibald. The Millheugh circle was an important source of reformist opinion. Eliza Fletcher, wife of Archibald Fletcher (1745-1828), sent her daughter Grace there and recalled, "She used to speak of this visit to Millheugh as the acme of her intellectual existence. The extent and variety of knowledge that as pointed out to her on subjects of taste, politics and morals made her feel, she said, how she had before trifled away time."[15] Archibald Fletcher was a former Glasgow student[16] who served as counsel for some of the 1/93 reformers and became the leader of Burgh reform which Mylne also advocated. Elizabeth Fletcher, originally from Yorkshire, was an impressive figure in her own right. George Ticknor, an American visitor recorded: "Mrs Fletcher is the most powerful lady in conversation in Edinburgh and has a

9. Murray, *Memories of the Old College of Glasgow*, 373.

10. GUA:Glasgow University Senate Minutes, 81:340-1.

11. Robert Burns, *Memoir of Stevenson MacGill*, 320 n. There is a letter from Fairlie dated August, 1815 in *Testimonials in favour of John Young*, 21.

12. Robertson, *Topographical Description of Ayrshire*, 61. The author says also that the villa "belonged to" Mylne. Duncan's *Itinerary of Scotland* describes it as "17 on l[eft]" on the road from Largs to Ayr, 36.

13. Robertson, *Topographical Description of Ayrshire*, 61.

14. See *Largs and Fairlie: Ayrshire Directories*. Reproduced on: maybole.org/history/Archives/1837directory/Largs&fairlie.

15. Richardson, *Autobiography of Mrs Fletcher*, 298.

16. Addison, *Matriculation Albums*, entry 1816.

Whig coterie of her own, as Mrs Grant does a Tory one."[17] Frances Wright also stayed at Millheugh when in Scotland.[18]

The Millheugh circle also included the playwright Joanna Baillie (1762–1851), the daughter of Dr. Baillie, Professor of Divinity for two years prior to his death in 1782, who herself wrote on Christianity. Mylne subscribed to the publication of her poems.[19] Baillie described her earlier plays as an attempt to "delineate the Stronger Passions of the Mind" and attributed the interest of drama to "sympathetick curiosity." Mylne shared her interest in drama, using it to illustrate his lectures on imagination and belief, arguing against Dugald Stewart's account of the suspension of disbelief as involving a real, if momentary, belief in the story on stage.

The Mylne family lodged private students, some from English dissenting merchant families. One was Theodore Rathbone, from a Quaker-turned-Unitarian family, who recorded gratefully his stay under Mylne's "hospitable roof." He refers to Mylne "in whose delightful and in every way improving society, some of my later years were passed, whilst in the college and for two years a student and member of the University."[20] Samuel Parr (1747–1825), "the Whig Johnson," sought out Mylne in Glasgow and admired him "alike for his exemption from affectation and pedantry, and for his distinguished proficiency in useful and ornamental literature."[21] John Griscom, an American visitor in March 1819, praised the "cordiality and simplicity" of his manners, with no offense taken at another professor's remark at dinner that attending sermons was a "waste of time."[22]

In 1824, the Mylne family moved from a College house adjoining the High Street to one in the Professors' Court.[23] After the death of her sister Helen in 1827, a distressed letter informed Joanna Baillie early in November that Agnes too was severely ill.[24] Agnes died later that month,[25] leaving James a widower, who soon expressed a wish to retire and occupied his final years with reading and Whig politics. Mylne thus had a full domestic life, with the house gradually emptying leaving him a widower in his old age.

17. Ticknor, *Life and Letters*, 1:279.
18. See Eckhardt, *Fanny Wright*, 14; Craig, "Account of the Life," lxxii et seq.
19. Millar, *Origin*, 69–70; Baillie, *A Collection of Poems*.
20. Notes by T. W. Rathbone in Rathbone papers, University of Liverpool, advised by Maureen Watry, Sydney Jones Library, University of Liverpool 26 September 2007.
21. Field, *Memoirs of the Life*, 2:230.
22. Griscom, *A Year in Europe*, 2:267.
23. Murray, *Memories of the Old College of Glasgow*, 374.
24. J Baillie to Mrs A Elliot 12/11/1827 (in Baillie, *Collected Letters*, 1:466.)
25. Scott, *Fasti* (1920), 3:169; *Blackwood's* 1828 gives 28 Nov 1827, 271.

Children

If we may rely on non-contemporaneous birth records, Agnes Mylne had a daughter, Margaret, in June 1799[26] and a son, James William Mylne, in August 1800. Another daughter, born in June 1803, was also named Margaret, but this may be a confusion. There seems no further public record of these daughters: they are not mentioned in James Mylne's will and so perhaps predeceased him. Thereafter were born John Millar Mylne in July 1804, William Craig Mylne in November 1805, and finally Archibald Mylne in December 1806.[27]

The eldest son was James William Mylne (hereafter "JW Mylne," 1800–55) who attended Glasgow Grammar School and Glasgow University (1814–19). He was the most exemplary scholar of the brothers and won prizes at both school as "Dux" and at university. His college prizes were for: Greek and the Blackstone examination (Latin) in 1815, the latter being a pass to senior study; junior Logic in 1816; Greek in 1817; Latin and natural philosophy in 1818; and Scots Law in 1819.[28] JW Mylne went on to Oxford University as a Snell exhibitioner (1819–29).[29] He qualified as a barrister in 1827 and practiced in London, living in Bloomsbury Place and reporting technical legal decisions, including those of Henry Brougham, that were published with coauthors between 1832 and 1848.[30] He was on the board of the new University College, London along with Brougham.[31] His Episcopalian sympathies appear in his tract *Oxford and the Scottish Universities* (Edinburgh: Lendrum, 1848) originally from the *Scottish Magazine*, which defends the rights of Scottish Episcopalians to attend Oxford University, "the sun and centre of the Reformed Catholic religion in these kingdoms," through the Snell exhibition. We have not dwelt on Mylne's Anglican acquaintances, but we might mention as instances Mylne's assistant William Galloway Brown (see below) and Archibald Campbell Tait (1811–83), Ilay Campbell's grandson and a future Archbishop of Canterbury, who studied in Glasgow from 1827.[32] Lord Brougham appointed JW Mylne one of the two first "Metropolitan Commissioners" in 1832, jointly responsible with

26. NAS/SPC: Birth records 644-01/0190.

27. NAS/SPC: Birth records 6644-01/0300, listing all five children. The witnesses are Professors George Jardine and John Young.

28. Addison, *Prize Lists*, see index.

29. For this paragraph, see online *Biographies of Legal Lunacy Commissioners and Secretaries 1832–1912* (mdsx.ac.uk); Addison, *Matriculation Albums*, entry 9123.

30. Mylne et al., *Reports of Cases determined in Chancery*.

31. JSTOR minutes of UCL.

32. Davidson and Benham: *Life of Archibald Campbell Tait*, 32

medical appointees for control of London's Madhouses under the 1832 Madhouses Act. The other initial appointee was Bryan Waller Procter (1787–1874), a poet and dramatist,[33] who knew the radical politician Leigh Hunt and essayist Charles Lamb (1775–1834).[34] After his father's death, JW Mylne served as a Legal Lunacy commissioner from 1845 until his death at his home in Oxford Square Hyde Park, London.[35] The playwright Joanna Baillie wrote "he is always friendly and seems always to consider himself as allied and connected with you, which goes a good way in really making him so,"[36] though she also found him "not always agreeable."[37]

The second son, John Millar Mylne (1804–1880) matriculated at Glasgow University in 1820, before serving a legal apprenticeship to the solicitor George Douglas WS (1776–1852) from Garnkirk in Lanarkshire. He became a member of the Society of Writers to his Majesty's Signet (i.e., a Scottish solicitor) in December 1828. His parents did not live to see John's marriage in 1843 to his cousin Margaret Thomson (1806–92). Margaret Mylne wrote an essay "Woman, and her place in Society" for the *Westminster Review* in 1841 around which time she corresponded with her cousins in London. This was published in book form in 1872.[38] John died in Ladbroke Square, London in 1880 and Margaret twelve years later.[39]

The third son, William Craig Mylne (1805–55), also matriculated at Glasgow University in 1820, where he won a junior class prize for exemplary diligence and talents in 1821.[40] Thereafter his interests were commercial, for we find him, aged 22, travelling from Liverpool on the *Britannia* on October 3, 1828[41] and arriving in New York on November 5 in company with William Wood of Glasgow, aged 20, both describing themselves as

33. Under the pen name Barry Cornwall, he published *Dramatic Scenes* (1819) *Poetical Works* (1822), *Portraits of British Poets* (1824) and *English Songs* (1832) and the tragedy *Mirandola* (1822). His poem *Marcian Collona* deals with madness. He also edited *Works of Shakespeare* (1843).

34. For example, he attended the theater with Charles Dickens in 1837 and wrote to Thomas Carlyle in 1843. See Armour, *Barry Cornwall*.

35. *Caledonian Mercury* 5/12/1855.

36. Baillie, *Collected Letters*, 85. The letter is undated, but seems to date from the 1840s.

37. Ibid. She perhaps took exception to Mylne's expression that his wife had "given him a son."

38. Margaret Mylne, *Woman, and her place in Society*. See Ewan et al., *The Biographical Dictionary of Scottish Women*.

39. From: *Register of the Society of Writers to Her Majesty's Signet* [copy in NLS]; Addison, *Matriculation Albums*, entry 10451.

40. Addison, *Prize Lists*, 221.

41. *Liverpool Mercury* 10/10/28.

merchants and giving England rather than America as the country of which they intend to become inhabitants.[42] Along with Wood, he was for a time a partner in the firm of Alexander Dennistoun & Co, merchants of Glasgow, Liverpool and New York.[43] Three surviving judgements in American court cases[44] indicate that the firm imported cotton and grain into Britain and acquired a debt from a slave owner in New Orleans in the American South. William Mylne was a merchant in New York at the time of Mylne's death in 1839.[45] He was later a director of Liverpool Borough Bank,[46] which illustrates the intertwining of merchant and banking capital, as does the career of David Dale in Glasgow. William Mylne died in Falkner Street, Liverpool in 1855.[47]

The fourth son, Archibald Mylne (1806—) won College prizes in mathematics and senior logic in 1825 at Glasgow, though he neither matriculated nor graduated.[48] He was an engineer in Glasgow at the time of Mylne's death.[49] James Mylne had corresponded with the engineer James Watt, making a personal link to the circle of Joseph Priestley[50] and father and son shared an interest in mathematics and natural science. This may be the same Archibald Mylne who contributed technical drawings to a book of essays and drawings *The Engineer and Machinist's Assistant* (Glasgow: Blackie, 1847, 1850, 1856) edited by David Scott, to which the marine engineering firm of Caird & Company in Greenock also contributed.[51] If so, it would establish a professional link between Mylne's family and that of the Glasgow idealists John and Edward Caird.

42. Records held by New York Public Library.

43. See court cases: the other partners were Alexander and John Dennistoun (1850); Robert Dick and Murray Thompson (1834),

44. Dennistoun vs. Stewart on bill of exchange on goods from Alabama in 1850 (U.S. Supreme Court); Guerin's Heirs vs. Bagneries on rights over two women held in slavery (Louisiana); Millbank et al. vs. Dennistoun et al. (New York, 1863) on due care in on-sale of American grain in Britain in 1846.

45. Will of James Mylne as copied 4 December 1840. NAS: SC36/51/17/61.

46. *Liverpool Mercury* 10/2/1854.

47. Addison, *Matriculation Albums*, Entry 10490; announcement of death in *Times* of London 24/10/1855.

48. Addison, *Prize Lists*, 258-60.

49. NAS:SC36/51/17/61.

50. Birmingham Central Library: Industrial Revolution Documentary History Series 3: Papers of James Watt: Reel 27: JWP C6/6 1806-08: Letters from various Scottish correspondents. The letters concern the heating of the Hunterian museum.

51. There is copy in the NLS.

The Wright Sisters

In 1815, the Mylne household was augmented by the arrival from England of his grand nieces Frances Wright (1795–1852) and her sister Camilla, originally from Dundee. They were daughters of James Wright, a merchant who had corresponded with Adam Smith, and Camilla Campbell Wright.[52] Frances Wright went on to play a significant role in the early American republic, speaking and writing on education, finance capital, slavery, and the role of women in a series of innovative public lectures and books.[53]

The character of Epicurus in her early book *A Few Days in Athens* (1822) is said to be based on Mylne. Epicurus featured in Mylne's lectures and Wright also mentioned Condillac in her writings. This suggests that she perhaps found a way to listen in to his lectures or gather his views in some depth and that her early "Epicurean" views may in fact reflect those of Mylne, though her journeys in America and encounters with figures of the stature of Jeremy Bentham and Auguste Comte made her an independent figure in later years.[54]

Mylne felt obliged to travel to Liverpool in an attempt to persuade Wright and her sister from boarding a ship to America, suggesting that they went to Italy instead. The passage across the Atlantic took around four weeks.[55] Perhaps the memory of the early loss of his sisters, perhaps from consumption, made him aware of the dangers of a long sea voyage. Wright knew Mylne's friend Robert Owen (1771–1858) of New Lanark and shared his interest in building new societies, though by 1827 Mylne himself held Owen's views to be "extravagant."[56] In America, Wright founded Nashoba, a colony intended to facilitate the elimination of slavery through education and compulsory labor. Her involvement in this project with Robert Dale Owen brought Mylne again into contact with Robert Owen. Mylne remained close to Frances Wright, though they fell out over her conversion to atheism.[57] He visited Paris, probably in 1822, where he met General La

---

52. Bartlett, *Liberty, Equality, Sorority*, 31.

53. E.g., Wright, *Course of Popular Lectures*.

54. For the relations of Mylne and Wright, inaccurate as regards Mylne, see Bartlett, *Liberty, Equality, Sorority*; for citation of Condillac, 31.

55. Silliman, *A Journal of Travels in England, Holland and Scotland*. In vol. 1, the crossing is from 6/4 to 3/5 (13, 51); vol. 2 from 2/5 to 27/5.

56. Mylne's letter to Julia Pertz, 1827 (Houghton library, Harvard). James Smith, another student (1801–57), inspired by Robert Owen (1771–1858), espoused a new doctrine of "mystical universalism," particularly in a socialistic book *The Coming Man*. See Addison, *Matriculation Albums*, entry 8672.

57. Mylne's letter to Julia Pertz, 1827 (Houghton library, Harvard).

Fayette, leader of the French forces in the American War of Independence, whose biography Wright then intended to write.[58] The American poet Walt Whitman said she was "sweeter, nobler, grander—multiplied by twenty—than all who traduced her."[59] The empiricist side of her work owes something to Mylne's outlook and it is notable that the irreligion of her middle period softens in her later works.[60]

The Literary and Commercial Society

According to Strang's *Clubs of Glasgow*, the Glasgow Literary and Commercial Society was founded in 1805.[61] Mylne was a member, joined in the years prior to 1830 by local literary and public figures such as Ralph Wardlaw (1779-1853), his evangelical opponent; and John Strang (1795-1863), the liberal author of *Germany in 1831* (1836) and *Clubs of Glasgow* (1856). Between 1807 and 1816, Mylne gave talks on contemporary issues in political economy, which we discuss in a separate chapter. He also spoke on: "On the Common Theoretical Account of the Early History of Mankind and the Origin of Civil Society," March 1809; "On the State of the Drama in Italy," April 1810; "On Works of Humour amongst the Ancient Writers," February, 1814 (repeated April 1817); and "Some Observations on the manner in which our ideas of external objects may be supposed to be originally formed," December 1819. The first, second, and last are subjects covered in his lectures, whilst his interests in the humor of the ancients and Italian drama, as far as we know, were kept from his students. The list of talks given to the society indicates enviable intellectual stimulation for its members across an impressive range of subjects. Indeed, the impression is created of the harmonious working together on the common problems of their society and of a wide range of opinion amongst the membership.

---

58. Eckhardt, *Fanny Wright*, 68, quoting Wolfson papers in NLS (740, f.48v). Wright knew the liberal Benjamin Constant (1767-1830) and Countess de Tracy (ibid., 68) and we can speculate that Mylne may have sought out Destutt de Tracy (1754-1836), who also knew La Fayette and whose work Mylne greatly admired.

59. Eckhardt, *Fanny Wright*, 3.

60. She also predicted the return of Scottish self-government in her work *England the Civiliser*, 429, which her American biographer described in 1984 as a "millenial fantasy," commenting: "Those who awaited the Second Coming, however, were more likely to be gratified than Fanny" (Eckhardt, *Fanny Wright*, 280).

61. Strang, *Glasgow and Its Clubs* (1856), Coul Club chapter, 378 n.

Mylne and the Church

From 1809 to 1819, Mylne acted as college chaplain, giving talks on Sundays or arranging for others to do so.[62] The Chapel had a moderate reputation. The Unitarian student, Lant Carpenter, who was present in Glasgow from 1797–1801, recorded that: "The sermons which we heard at the College Chapel [. . .] had, indeed, rarely anything in them but what was quite acceptable to us; and the prayers, as far as my impressions are just, were addressed to God, without reference to a trinity of person."[63] This predates Mylne's occupancy, but indicates the expectations he would have inherited. Under Mylne, the services began with singing a Psalm and combined readings from Scripture, paraphrases, and a sermon by Mylne. In 1815, these were a series of talks on Acts of the Apostles. Peter Mackenzie, a partial witness, says of the students that "many of them liked to hear him wonderfully well, for he was a favourite with most of them."[64] We have seen that one of Mylne's services led to a precognition for sedition, but his conduct as a whole indicates that he voluntarily contributed to an agenda of religious education.

Another future Unitarian minister, John Kendrick, described Mylne as "sufficiently liberal to be an object of great suspicion to the bigoted religious party."[65] James McCosh wrote "After the revival of evangelical faith in the city of Glasgow under Chalmers, loud complaints were uttered as to the doctrine taught in the college chapel."[66] Mylne's relations with his immediate colleagues who attended the chapel seem to have been cordial though. William Fleming, Mylne's successor and College librarian, records being struck by the "calm confidence with which he habitually reposed in the wisdom and goodness of the Great First Cause."[67] The Professor of Civil and Ecclesiastical history was William McTurk, whose intellectual engagement with Mylne is suggested by his reading of Condillac after the former's appointment.[68] In 1814, a former colleague from Paisley, Stevenson MacGill became Professor of Divinity, following the death of Robert Findlay at age 94.[69]

---

62. Senate Minutes, Vol 82, 263 for appointment 10 June 1810; Vol [83], 198 for resignation 11 October 1819. Per computerized abstract of the minutes.

63. Carpenter, "Social improvement," 5–6.

64. Mackenzie, *Reminiscences of Glasgow*, 1:460.

65. John Kendrick "Memoir," 131. Kendrick was in Glasgow from 1807 to 1810.

66. McCosh, *The Scottish Philosophy*, 365.

67. Fleming, "Moral Philosophy Chair," 10.

68. GUL:Professors' Receipt Books.

69. See *GC* 26/11/1814. Chalmers is admitted minister in July 1815 (*GC* 22/7/1815). Findlay had published on Voltaire and other anonymous pieces on Christianity. Obituary in *GC*, 1814.

Kendrick's and McCosh's remarks thus probably refer to those Evangelicals who were most swayed by Thomas Chalmers. For example, James Begg (1808–83), an evangelical student who graduated in 1824,[70] complained:

> Mr. Milne [sic] taught us Moral Philosophy in a somewhat heathenish style, making man pass through all stages from savage to civilised, insisting on the progress of human nature, even in its primitive state, from worse to better, instead of from better to worse; in short, it was very much philosophy without the fall of man and apart from the Bible.[71]

Begg was strongly evangelical and studied theology at Edinburgh under Thomas Chalmers, with whom he was closely associated, serving as Moderator of the Free Church in 1865.

There is also evidence of tension between Mylne and the Congregationalist Ralph Wardlaw, who engaged in several skirmishes with Mylne and his students. Wardlaw taught at the congregational Glasgow Theological Academy, for a while alongside Mylne's student John Morell Mackenzie (1806-43). Although Wardlaw was in writing a fierce opponent of Mylne's views, the two men also cooperated for many years in running the Glasgow Literary Society.[72] They also both sat on the management committee of Glasgow Public Library. Wardlaw also wrote on "universal Atonement," a theme implicit in Mylne's lectures. Furthermore, several of Wardlaw's views in his *Christian Ethics* (1834), for example, his identification of conscience with reason applied to moral subjects, coincide with Mylne. Indeed, Wardlaw's book and Mylne's lectures provide commentary on each other's arguments on several subjects, particularly the relations of religion and ethics.[73]

Wardlaw's first skirmish with one of Mylne's students involved an English minister's son, James Yates (1789-1871), a member of the Literary Society: the so-called Unitarian controversy. The growth of Unitarianism in the nineteenth century is reflected in Mylne's library. He owned *Illustrations of the Divine Government* (1816) by Thomas Southwood Smith (1788-1861), a Unitarian Minister and physician, based on talks on determinism and "universal restoration" given in Edinburgh. Mylne also owned Robert Aspland's *Sermons* (1816). The radical-Whig Aspland (1782-1845) succeeded Thomas Belsham (1750-1829) as Unitarian minister at Hackney. A petition he organized against prosecution of unbelievers was presented to

---

70. Addison, *Matriculation Albums*, entry 10407.

71. Smith, *Memoirs of James Begg D.D.*, vol. 1, chapter 2.

72. This was founded in 1805 according to Strang's *Clubs of Glasgow* (1856), 378 n. See Anon., *Literary and Commercial Society records*.

73. Their view of the Divine command theory of obligation contrast, for example.

Parliament by Joseph Hume, whose biography was written by Mylne's student Charles Badham. However, Mylne also borrowed Burton's *Testimonies of the Ante-Nicene Fathers* (1829), written in opposition to the Unitarians. In Glasgow, Mylne was remembered for "paying marked attention to Mr. Yates, when a student in his class—of introducing him to his friends, and showing them his essays." Some saw in this "a desire to propagate Socinianism," though others saw only "the kindness of Professor Milne's [sic] heart, and his admiration of genius."[74] Wardlaw published *Discourses on the Principal Points of the Socinian Controversy* (1814). The prize essay on the moral philosophy class the following year was for "the best account of the tenets of Arius."[75] In 1816, to Yates' *Vindication of Unitarianism*, Wardlaw replied with *Unitarianism incapable of Vindication*.

Secondly, in 1825 Wardlaw took the occasion of Henry Brougham's "Inaugural Address" as Lord Rector to launch an attack on the concept of belief as involuntary and thus not meritorious[76] that Brougham and Mylne shared and which Brougham had used to bolster the case for freedom of speech. Mylne had recently spoken publicly in praise of Brougham. Wardlaw published *Man Responsible for his Belief: Two Sermons* (Glasgow, 1825), arguing for a "reciprocally influential connection between the understanding and the affections"[77] and attacking the competence of reason as arbiter of morality. This brought forward a rejoinder from Brougham.

Wardlaw perhaps harbored hopes of succeeding to Mylne's chair. Mylne lectured on Samuel Clark's proofs of the existence and attributes of God. In 1831, Wardlaw published an edition of Clark's *Collection of the Promises of Scripture*,[78] followed by *Christian Ethics* (1834), which contains a thinly veiled attack on Mylne's approach to moral philosophy, echoing his 1825 *Sermons*, though the most strident denunciations are relegated to an appendix.[79] The book was attacked in the *Edinburgh Review*. In 1845, Wardlaw took aim at Mylne's views openly in *Memoir of the Late Rev. John Reid*.[80] Reid (1806–40), an intending missionary in India, had entered Mylne's class in 1825 whilst lodging with Wardlaw and felt that the general content of the course was "anti-spiritual" and that Mylne's reduction of desire to concep-

---

74. *The Christian Pioneer* (Glasgow, 1829), 3:451.

75. GC 2/5/1815.

76. Published in Hay's *Inaugural Addresses*, 68.

77. Wardlaw, *Man Responsible for his Belief*, 10.

78. Wardlaw, *Collection of the Promises of Scripture*.

79. His most outspoken remarks, quoted by George Davie, are confined to the notes (esp. note B).

80. Wardlaw, *Memoir of the Late Rev. John Reid*, 56.

tion excluded the possibility of sin. Wardlaw makes it plain that he endorses these views. James McCosh, who shared Wardlaw's evangelical views, makes similar criticisms in *The Scottish Philosophy* (1875). Wardlaw continued to lecture on theology in Glasgow and his posthumous lectures contain a less heated version of his critique of Mylne. Here he observes that secular education is useful both in understanding and communicating scripture[81] and undertakes to "take the lights of nature and of Revelation . . . conjointly."[82]

The leading evangelical Churchman of the day was Thomas Chalmers (1780–1847) who spent the years 1815 to 1823 in Glasgow. He already knew Mylne from early conversations in St. Andrews with the mathematicians there.[83] Another attendee later reminisced of himself and Chalmers that: "The seeds of our reforming notions were then sown in our minds, by our conversation with these men."[84] In the meantime though, Chalmers had strengthened his evangelical convictions after reading William Wilberforce's *Practical View of Christianity* (1797) and moved to the right politically. Wilberforce defended the religious passions against the accusation of being unreasonable "strongholds of enthusiasm."[85] Chalmers renewed his acquaintance with Mylne through the Literary and Commercial Society. His earliest work, *An Inquiry into the Extent and Stability of National Resources* (1808),[86] had argued that the absence of trade better fitted Britain for defense and political independence. This sharply contradicts the advocacy of commerce that Mylne put across in his lectures on political economy. Chalmers had also published *The Evidence and Authority of the Christian Revelation* (1814) which, he stressed, was "chiefly confined to the exposition of the historical argument for the truth of Christianity."[87] The following year, he moved to Glasgow as minister of the Tron Kirk. In Glasgow, Chalmers' early books were soon advertised[88] and supplemented by published

81. Wardlaw, *Systematic Theology*, 1:20–21.

82. Ibid., 1:75.

83. Chalmers' Collection in EUL: Letters chiefly addressed to James Brown, Dc.2.57. See also Brown, *Thomas Chalmers*, 6; Hanna, *Memoirs of Chalmers*, 1:465–67, and Morrell, "The Leslie Affair," 70–71.

84. Quoted by Brown, *Thomas Chalmers*, citing Chalmers papers at New College Edinburgh (TCP, CHA 2 Hanna Letters J Miller to W Hanna 21 January 1848).

85. Wilberforce, *Practical View of Christianity*, 86.

86. Chalmers, *An Inquiry into the Extent and Stability of National Resources*, advertised in *GC* 7/4/1808.

87. Advert in *GC* 29/9/1814. The work had earlier appeared in the *Edinburgh Encyclopaedia*.

88. See *GC* 17/10/1815 for advert for *Address to [. . .] Kilmeny*; *Inquiry into [..] National Resources* and *Other Sermons and Addresses*.

sermons, often reported in the newspapers. Chalmers soon observed in a sermon "the utter repugnance there is between the spirit of Christianity and the factious, turbulent, unquenchable and ever-meddling spirit of political disaffection."[89] Memorably expressed passages of like import directed against the Reform movement are scattered through Chalmers' writings from this time on and influence perceptions of Scottish Church history to the present day.[90]

In June 1816, Chalmers spoke on Christianity and modern astronomy.[91] The following year, his engaging strain of vernacular piety found written expression in his *Discourses on the Christian Revelation, viewed in connection with the Modern Astronomy* (1817), which reached a sixth edition in the same year.[92] Soon, the first four-volume edition of his *Works* (1817), appeared, in which the above volumes on astronomy, revelation and political economy were accompanied by a collection of sermons.[93] We may speculate that some later shifts in Chalmers' views from this edition may owe something to encounters with Mylne at the Literary Society, for example on commerce. In 1823, Chalmers returned to St. Andrews as Professor of Moral Philosophy, his place at the Tron Kirk being taken by the Reverend Daniel Dewar, formerly Professor of Moral Philosophy at Aberdeen and author of *Elements of Moral Philosophy, and of Christian Ethics* (1826).

On Mylne's part, there is evidence of suspicion of Evangelical intolerance. In a letter to Henry Brougham in 1827 about John Hoppus, who was applying for a position at University College, London, he wrote that Hoppus was: "a member of a very prevalent class of separatists of high and zealous Calvinist Orthodoxy" which he thinks raises:

> one point of which I am not qualified to judge and which cannot I hope be regarded as of small importance [. . .] I mean how far he is free from a degree of religious zeal or even perhaps bigotry which I would be sorry to see obtaining any place in the proposed institution.[94]

---

89. From *Thoughts on Universal Peace: A Sermon*, cited in GC 15/2/1816.

90. See for example: Smith, *Passive Obedience*.

91. See notice of a sermon on *The Eighth Psalm and Astronomy* in GC 1/6/1816. The relevant text is: "When I consider the heavens, the work of thy fingers, the moon and the stars, which thou hast ordained; what is man that art mindful of him? And the son of man that thou visitest him?" (verses 4–5).

92. Chalmers, *Discourses on the Christian Revelation*. Sixth edition advertised in GC 1/7/1817.

93. Advertised in GC 13/5/1817.

94. Brougham Papers at UCL, Letter of Mylne to Brougham 3/2/1827, 1446.

We may perhaps refer this attitude back to Mylne's experiences of clerical intolerance dating back to the M'Gill case in the 1780s. However, read as a whole, the letter was supportive and Hoppus was appointed.

Another disagreement with the Evangelicals came in 1829 when Mylne contributed to a joint reference for John Ferrie, then Chaplain of Glasgow University, who had applied to succeed John Young in the chair of moral philosophy at the Belfast Academical Institution. Ferrie had published a sermon on *The Distinction of Rich and Poor* (Glasgow, 1820) and had a reputation as a "rational preacher."[95] His relationship with Mylne is suggested by Mylne's borrowing a book for him when he moved to Belfast.[96] A joint testimonial from several Scottish professors praised Ferrie's ability to put across "that interesting branch of Philosophy which treats of the constitution of the human mind, and the exhibition of mental phenomena." Ferrie's rival, James Carlile (1784–1854), was from Paisley and had been an outstanding student in Glasgow, before taking over the London congregation of John Hoppus, another former student of Mylne. Carlile corresponded with Chalmers and like Wardlaw, objected to Mylne's treatment of moral philosophy as independent from revelation, interpreting this as a tradition in Glasgow that had begun with Hutcheson.[97] Aspersions were cast at Mylne who, it was heatedly said, stood to gain financially from Ferrie's appointment. Chalmers reportedly recommended another candidate, as did Ralph Wardlaw,[98] rather than Ferrie. Controversy over the content of Ferrie's lectures broke out again in 1834, with Chalmers again cited as an authority by the "Orthodox" party,[99] and Mylne styled "heterodox."

Charitable and Other Activities

Mylne was involved in various charitable endeavors. At the end of 1819, he is named in the press when the College had publicly supported private charitable efforts for the "relief of the operative weavers out of employment and industrious poor."[100] He played a role in managing the life of the college,[101]

---

95. *The Christian Pioneer* (Glasgow, 1829), 3:451–52.
96. GUL: Professor's Receipt Book 134.
97. *Belfast Newsletter* 7/8/1829; 18/9/1829.
98. *Belfast Newsletter* 7/7/1829.
99. *Belfast Newsletter* 22/8/1834; see also *Minutes of an Inquiry... respecting the Moral Philosophy Class* (Belfast, 1835); *Edinburgh Review*, 1835.
100. *GC*, 28/12/1819. The Glasgow Bank gave £200. The college professors gave from five to ten guineas each, Mylne giving seven.
101. He writes: "We have generally been compelled to make the most we could of

notably objecting to outside work by staff that would detract from their teaching or other duties.[102] Mylne's interest in Astronomy, expressed in the lectures, is confirmed by his support of an unsuccessful plan to buy Garnethill observatory for the college.[103] An interest in natural history, also discernible in his lectures, is further suggested by fragments of correspondence from 1816 with William Boog, son of Robert Boog and a merchant in Rio de Janiero, which also discusses Latin American politics. The Hunterian museum was established in 1807 and Mylne had written asking for exhibits.[104]

In 1809 Mylne was involved in the managing committee of the first Glasgow Public Library, a year in which an interest in Irish political literature first appears. He became the Principal Curator the following year. This library began trading on virtually identical terms to the commercial circulating libraries, though with restricted opening hours. The merchant Walter Stuting had left funds in 1791 to establish a public library for Glasgow.[105] Specific arrangements in terms of opening hours were made to suit women. The Public Library also established the uniqueness of its offer by offering books for children, a natural follow-on from its encouragement of female readership. It appears to have been associated with the Glasgow Foreign Library, which existed at least from 1820.[106]

He was also on the Glasgow committee of the *Society for the Diffusion of Useful Knowledge*, the only Scottish committee of the society, along with Kirkman Finlay and Robert Grahame, both Lord Provosts.[107] This had

---

old and not very convenient buildings, and besides we have had to struggle with the difficulties arising from very limited means" (Letter of Mylne, 10/10/1825; GUL MS Gen 501/35-36).

102. This occurred with Professor Couper of Astronomy in 1803 (Coutts, *History of the University of Glasgow*, 352–53). In 1823 he is involved in objecting to a new Principal, Rev. MacFarlan, still a minister of Glasgow High Church (ibid., 339).

103. Ibid., 353. Astronomy was relevant to the design argument in theology, and enters briefly into Mylne's lectures in his discussion of the roles of observation and experiment in science. John Nichol (1833–94), of the early idealist circle, was son of the Professor of Astronomy (see below).

104. Ibid., 340. There is reference to the classifications of the French naturalist Buffon, mentioned in Mylne's lectures and of whose *Histoire Naturelle* was in the Ethics class library. Boog replies: "The people submit to everything with the greatest good humour and there is very little danger of them attempting to better themselves. The republican government of Buenos Ayres is not at all in a secure state" (Letter of W Boog to Mylne 6/3/1816. GUL MR 50/7). Further reports of Napoleon on St. Helena follow.

105. *GM* 25/1/1791.

106. See *GC* of 2/11/1820 for notice of its Annual General Meeting. Dr Chrystal of its management committee is presumably the same as the William Chrystal who was still Secretary of the Glasgow Public Library (see *GC*, 2/1/1821) the following year.

107. See local committee lists in the *Penny Cyclopaedia* (London, 1833) published

been established by Henry Brougham in 1826. The Society published cheap editions of improving and educational literature. As we have seen, Mylne was allied politically with Brougham.

Academic Appointments

In addition to John Ferrie, we can discern Mylne's role in several other academic appointments. For example, Mylne wrote a testimonial for John Wilson when he applied to be Professor of Moral Philosophy in 1820 following the death of Thomas Brown. In comparison with the praise offered by John Young and George Jardine, Mylne's testimonial is terse. On April 27, 1820, he wrote: "After so long an interval, during which my personal acquaintance with Mr Wilson has been but very little kept up, it will not be expected that I should now be very particular in my account of the qualifications which at that time he seemed to me to possess."[108]

Mylne does "but justice" to Wilson by invoking his "distinct recollection" of his conduct in class and the "general esteem in which on that account he was held by his fellow-students as well as by myself." This was followed in May 24, 1820 by a much more flattering letter in favor of "my friend," John Young, then teaching in Belfast, than whom he can "scarcely imagine any other candidate can appear on the scene, bringing with him such a weight of proof and evidence of tried and approved fitness for the office."[109] It would not be surprising if the Tory Wilson harbored some resentment at this somewhat grudging praise that overlooks Wilson's subsequent reputation either in literature or as an Advocate. In the event, Wilson won out over the Whig candidate William Hamilton.

Mylne wrote another positive testimonial for Thomas Stewart Traill (1781–1862) in 1832 in connection with his application for the Chair of Medical Jurisprudence in Edinburgh "at the request of a person in Liverpool whom I highly regard."[110] He refers generously to Traill's qualities of character, lecturing abilities and experience in medical practice. He wrote

---

by the Society. In 1833, the other members of the Glasgow committee were Kirkman Finlay, Alexander McGrigor, Charles Tennant, James Cowper, and T Atkinson. In another list of the same year, D. Bannatyne and Robert Grahame (Lord Provost) are added (see Thomas, *Gallery or Portraits*).

    108. NLS:Wilson papers MS21240, f29.

    109. *Testimonials in favour of John Young*, in NCL, May 1820, 35.

    110. NLS:Traill papers MS19344 f49. Traill was appointed Professor of medical jurisprudence in 1832. Mylne was under the impression it was a Chair of Materia Medica.

in favor also of John Lyon for a post as teacher in the educational flagship High School of Edinburgh.[111]

In 1836, Mylne wrote in support of "Rev. Mr Muston" for the Logic chair at Edinburgh,[112] probably Christopher Muston, author of *Recognition in the World to Come, or Christian Friendship on Earth* (1830). Muston was an English student who had matriculated alongside John Hoppus at Glasgow in 1820, studied under Mylne and graduated in 1822.[113] His book applies "reason, guided and enlightened by revelation" to immortality and friendship.[114] Other candidates included William Hamilton, Isaac Taylor, and the phrenologist George Combe.[115] Edinburgh Town Council, as Patrons of the Chair under the Chairmanship of the dissenting publisher Adam Black, endorsed Hamilton. In this case though, Hamilton won.

The Linnell Portrait

There is a description of Mylne's physical appearance from his later years: "with his silvery head, careless dress, lazy demeanour, sagacious face, and unequalled system of severe and masculine thought."[116] This corresponds to Gilfillan's description. However, we need not rely on description, for in 1835 Mylne sat for a portrait by John Linnell (1792–1882), the English portraitist and landscape painter. Linnell had worked closely with William Blake and knew Percy Shelley and William Godwin.[117] The informality of the pose suggests empathy between sitter and subject. Mylne sits holding a document, looking out with a penetrating but kindly gaze. It is an attractive image of a Christian philosopher of advanced age.

---

111. Testimonial in NCL. Ref:Cf/42. Compare Addison, *Matriculation Albums*, entry 6736.

112. Combe, *Testimonials*, 158.

113. Addison, *Matriculation Albums*, 313, entry 10434.

114. Muston, *Recognition in the World to Come*, 1.

115. Combe, *Testimonials*, 158; Deuchar, *Brief Review of Ancient and Modern Philosophy*, 269.

116. *Hogg's Weekly Instructor*, vol. 1 March–August 1845, 403.

117. See Story, *The Life of John Linnell*. Linnell kept sketchbooks of his work, partly as a check against forgery and these are now with the British Museum. Linnell's artistic remains are held partly in the British Museum and partly Fitzwilliam Museum, Cambridge.

Retiral and Succession

In 1833, Mylne told the then Rector, Henry Cockburn, that he had already "for some time past" had it in mind to retire from the Chair of Moral Philosophy, commenting that "if I have not already held it too long, I have good reason to apprehend I may, at no distant period, be unfitted by the increasing infirmities of age."[118] The infirmities seem to have included deafness. The salary of the Moral Philosophy chair in 1835 was reportedly the best in Scotland, standing at £722, exclusive of a free house,[119] having been increased £30 the previous year through a bequest.[120]

The succession was already generating controversy. According to Mylne, he had sought an assistant and judged the prospect of succession to the Chair necessary to attract an appropriate candidate. However, on consulting his colleagues, he hastily and wrongly acquired the impression that an arrangement with Professor of Hebrew William Fleming was acceptable to them.[121] Cockburn soon heard reports that "instead of being thrown fairly open to the competition of all able men" the Chair was to be transferred by an "understanding equivalent to a pledge" to an existing professor. On inquiry, Mylne confirmed to Cockburn that this was true and that the professor concerned was William Fleming whom he praised as a clergyman, librarian, College chaplain and Professor of Oriental Languages, claiming that he was "eminently qualified" for the Chair of Moral Philosophy.

Cockburn was aghast and privately issued a pamphlet outlining his procedural objections that found its way into the press. Mylne, he objected, was making his resignation "conditional on the promotion of a specified individual," whilst only an open competition could establish whether Fleming was indeed *eminent* in relation to other potential candidates. The pamphlet inveighed indignantly against Mylne's behavior, against which the Royal Commissioners had spoken:

> If the promotion of one public officer be made a condition of the retirement of another—these two have the appointment in their own hands. [...] the difficulty of being conspicuously wrong, when the public is the spectator of a contest, is so great, that nearly all the bad appointments which have depressed

---

118. Scotsman 25/12/1837, citing published letter of Mylne to Cockburn.
119. *Gentleman's Magazine*, London, 1840, 222.
120. *Sessional Papers of the House of Lords* (London, 1839), vol. 37, 1837 Report of the Glasgow University Commissioners, 19.
121. "Glasgow College Prize Exhibition: Job and no Job," in *Caledonian Mercury* 6/5/1833.

universities, have been effected by avoiding competition, or by allowing premature pledges.

Mylne dropped his agreement with Fleming and backtracked on his request for an assistant. He gave an unforeseen speech on the subject at the distribution of Prizes in May 1833, regretting that Cockburn's letter had been published rather than addressed to him in person, but expressing agreement that his proposal would be a "bad precedent, though in conformity with previous usage" and claiming that he had behaved with openness and frankness. He concluded that in the light of events he "was determined to keep his chair as long as he lived, and would take good care that no jobs were perpetrated in the College during his life."[122]

However, in 1834 Mylne again expressed a desire to retire, this time to his former pupil William Hamilton to whom he wrote on the subject. Mylne knew Hamilton both as a former student and through his outstanding contributions to the *Edinburgh Review*. He offered to take Hamilton on as assistant to the "chair of Ethical and Political science," with his "full warrant and authority" to apply for the Chair at a later date. His guarded letter stressed the range of subjects on which Hamilton might offer lectures. In the end though, the plan did not come to fruition.[123]

Mylne was now increasingly hard of hearing and William Fleming took over the examination hour in 1833 with extended duties, including the lecture hour, the following year. According to Coutts, Mylne last taught for part of the 1836/37 year, assisted by William Brown Galloway (1811–1903). Brown had graduated at Glasgow from 1831 and published *Philosophy and Religion with their Mutual Bearings comprehensively considered and satisfactorily determined on Scientific Principles* (1837), an original book which adopts Mylne's account of perception as a compound result of sensation, memory, and judgement, but objects to his view of utility as the basis of morality.[124] Brown eventually became the Anglican vicar of St. Mark's Church, Primrose Hill, London where he was considered "an Evangelical"[125] and wrote on geology and biblical history.

In May 1837 there were again press reports of Mylne's having intimated to the Senate of Glasgow University "his anxiety to retire [. . .] on

---

122. *Caledonian Mercury* 6/5/1833, citing *Glasgow Free Press*.

123. Veitch, *Memoir of Hamilton*, 176 et seq.

124. Galloway, *Philosophy and Religion*, 66; 348. The preface is dated 20 December 1836.

125. Coutts, *History of the University of Glasgow*, 382–83; Addison, *Matriculation Albums*, Galloway is entry 11750; St. Marks' parish history (stmarksregentpark.org.uk). Brown also wrote on biblical history and geology.

account of advanced age" and the Church of Scotland was made aware of the situation. J. P. Nichol took steps to find other candidates, including John Austin and Samuel Bailey.[126] Several possible successors were mooted. These included: William Fleming; Isaac Taylor, author of the introductory textbook *Elements of Thought* (1823) and the better known *The Natural History of Enthusiasm* (1829); and William Hamilton, then professor of Logic in Edinburgh.[127] Mylne had borrowed Taylor's book on Enthusiasm from the College library for a female friend[128] and would likely have warmed to Taylor's description of enthusiasm as an invasion by the imaginative powers into the legitimate provinces of reason. However, from November 1, 1837, at the request of the Senate, Fleming took over the moral philosophy class in return for £200 per annum paid out of class fees by Mylne, which the Royal Commissioners noted was a practice "very liable to abuse," recommending that the University Court was a more suitable elective body than either the Crown or the Professors.[129]

Within three weeks of Mylne's death, despite Cockburn's earlier strictures,[130] William Fleming was transferred from the Chair of Oriental Languages by the Faculty of the College.[131] The succession was in the hands of the fourteen Faculty members of Glasgow University, which meant those professors not appointed by the Crown. The then Rector, James Graham, made no protest. Professors J. P. Nichol and Lushington were opposed, with Nichol again seeking other candidates.[132] The *Scotsman* claimed that the Faculty had not advertised the post and objected, echoing Cockburn in arguing that "No merit short of the highest, no reputation less than Euro-

126. Mill, *Earlier Letters*. Letter 204 to Sarah Austin, 28/4/1837, 335: "Would Mr Austin like to be the Professor of Moral Philosophy at Glasgow? The chair is vacant, and it is worth £700 a year, but so long as old Mylne lives (he is 83 years of age) it will only be worth £300. It is in the gift of the Professors, and one of them, my friend Nichol, who is an admirer of Mr Austin has written to me to ask if he would like it and to say that he could perhaps carry Mr Austin's election to the chair with such testimonials as it would be easy to get. If Mr Austin declines, he has nobody better than Bailey of Sheffield, and means to try for him."

127. *Scotsman* 17/5/1837, citing the *Glasgow Constitutional*.

128. GUL: Professors' Receipt Books.

129. *Sessional Papers of the House of Lords*, 1839, vol. 37, 1837 Report of the Glasgow University Commissioners, 17-18, 22.

130. Cockburn, *Letter by the Late Rector*. Murray, *Memories of the Old College of Glasgow* refers also to *The Reformers' Gazette* (1835, 286), 103.

131. *Glasgow Herald* 11/10/1839.

132. Mill, *Collected Works*, 12:409. Letter 265 to John Sterling 2/10/1839,: "The Moral Philosophy Chair at Glasgow is vacant, and my friend Nichol has written to me about finding some fit person to fill it—it is in the gift of the Professors and any good man would be sure of all that Nichol and Lushington could do."

pean, could entitle the patrons to appoint him within a period so short as to preclude the possibility of any fair competition for the office."[133] The speed may be partly explained, though not justified, as coinciding with the start of a new academic year and by Fleming's having given the course for some years previously.

Death and Inheritance

James Mylne died on September 21, 1839.[134] His will[135] indicates that he left £1,000 to each of his four sons before his death. The will includes £674 moveable possessions. Scottish wills do not include land and houses, so there is no information on the house in Fairlie, though there is mention of a property in Dryggate [Street], overlooking the Molendinar Burn in Glasgow.[136] There is no reference to manuscripts in the will. However, the Skirving catalogue of his possessions contains a list of books for auction that sheds light on his literary and scientific interests over the course of his life.[137]

The *Glasgow Argus*, a reformist publication, noted in its obituary that the Chair had previously been occupied by Hutcheson, Adam Smith, Reid, and Archibald Arthur, adding that Mylne had "amply sustained its high reputation." This is supported by reports of his teaching, but the *Argus* also addressed his lack of publications:

> The memory of this amiable and eminent philosopher will be cherished by his pupils with gratitude and reverence; and we only echo the sentiments of the thousands who have had the honour and advantage of attending his lectures, when we say, that the publication of those discourses would be the most honourable of all monuments to his public usefulness and philosophic attainments.[138]

This indicates that Mylne's lectures were believed to exist in written form at this time and it is possible they still exist in private hands. Versions of the *Argus* text were repeated with attribution in the other Glasgow papers and William Fleming published a tribute to Mylne in the Tory *Peel Papers* the following year. However, Fleming in Glasgow and Wilson in Edinburgh

---

133. *Scotsman* 25/12/1839.
134. McCosh, *The Scottish Philosophy*, 365.
135. NAS:SC36/51/17/61 (Will & inventory, 1840).
136. There may be further information in NAS, but not online.
137. GUL Special Collections, Skirving catalogue of Mylne's books for auction.
138. Cited from *Glasgow Herald* 30/9/1839.

both taught versions of common sense philosophy in their moral philosophy classes and their work bears marks of their Tory allegiances.

Conclusions

Looking back over his life as a whole, we can see that Mylne was by no means an isolated figure in respect of his opinions. Many amongst his extended family and wider circle of friends in politics and the Church also supported his approach to social reform and intellectual inquiry. Towards the end of his life, Mylne rode the tide of opinion that led to the 1832 Reform Acts. Yet he knew people with many hues of conservative, reformist, and radical opinion, from Joanna Baillie though Elizabeth Fletcher to Frances Wright, so his opinions were not pre-determined by social pressures. In addition to his classroom teaching, he found further scope as a public intellectual in disputes over modes of preaching in the Churches and in talks to the Literary and Commercial society.

Politically, although the clique of Henry Dundas were not all powerful in Scotland, their views are well represented in published philosophical literature from the period after the outbreak of the French Revolution, through influence on academic and other appointments and other social pressures.[139] Given the preponderance of such conservative voices, it is particularly unfortunate that Mylne, a bold advocate of reform who raised his thought to the level of a distinctive philosophy, should remain in the shadows. Mylne's thought also broadens our idea of "Scottish philosophy" beyond the confinement to common sense that Victor Cousin, James McCosh, and William Hamilton sought to put on it. We will now turn from biography to address the merits of some of his principal arguments.

---

139. For example, Beattie's *Elements of Moral Science* (1793), the 6th edition of Adam Smith's *Theory of Moral Sentiments* (1790) and Thomas Reid's *Dangers of Political Innovation* in Arthur, *Discourses on Theological and Literary Subjects* (Glasgow, 1803).

PART 2

Philosophy, Politics, and Political Economy

Introduction

WE HAVE NOW EXAMINED Mylne's life and the public institutions and events that lent his thought significance and sketched the educational uses of his ideas. We now turn to a thematic consideration of Mylne's moral philosophy, politics and political economy. The annual moral philosophy course contained material similar to other Scottish courses and books on moral philosophy alongside original material. The division of duties into those to God, neighbor, and self is in the Scottish tradition of natural law expounded by Gershom Carmichael; the psychological analysis draws on the scientific method of Francis Bacon and the descriptive psychology of John Locke and Thomas Reid; and the political economy builds on that of the Physiocrats and Adam Smith. In describing the content of his thought, we will focus on his distinctive rationalist contribution to this intellectual inheritance in the theories of perception, freedom, and economic value.

Mylne's thought was not published in his lifetime, other than in a few unrepresentative fragments,[1] though several of his students went on to publish books that drew on the ideas in his lectures.[2] However, his thought

---

1. A prospectus of his course of Political Economy survives from 1804. His other main publications were a brief obituary of John Millar (1835–1801) and editions of Millar's *Works* of which he was joint editor.

2. These include: William Jevons *Systematic Morality* (1827); George Payne *Elements of Mental and Moral Science* (1828); John Young *Lectures on Intellectual Philosophy* (1835).

can be recovered in some detail from manuscript lecture notes or "minutes" left by students, amounting to around 250,000 words. These exemplify the advanced note-taking skills students acquired in George Jardine's Logic class and are in substance mutually corroborating.[3] Whilst this is established in detail in the collation submitted with my thesis (see the appendix for example), at this stage of "Mylne studies," what is most required is an overall interpretation of the general direction and central elements of the philosophy based on the lecture transcripts. The student notes and minutes represent a scorecard of philosophical debate amongst the future opinion forming classes of Glasgow over a period of thirty-eight years.

The lectures demonstrate that philosophical opinion in Glasgow differed substantially from the philosophies of Frances Hutcheson, Thomas Reid, and Dugald Stewart.[4] It is apparent that the Scottish moral sense and common sense traditions represented by Hutcheson, Reid, and Stewart are "in the air"; with the course at times following Stewart's lecture guide *Outlines of Moral Philosophy* (1792). Whilst Mylne appreciated some of David Hume's empiricist analyses of the mind, he rejects Hume's combination of moral sense and skepticism either through argument or as simply "extravagant." Instead, we find a continuation of the English empiricist tradition following John Locke in the series of writers who studied or taught in the Dissenting Academies. These include David Hartley, Joseph Priestley, and William Godwin. The Calvinist influence brought by these writers is reinforced by that of Jonathan Edwards of America, whose *Freedom of the Will* (1754) Mylne particularly admired. This constructive empiricist project is further strengthened by Mylne's reception of recent French philosophers, including the naturalist Buffon, Helvetius, Condillac, and in the later lectures, Destutt de Tracy. The most central of the French writers is Condillac, who provides a non-skeptical account of external perception that, Mylne argues, improves on Reid's reply to Hume.

3. In addition to a capacity for grasping and summarizing argument, there were motives to accuracy as firstly, Mylne's work was not available in print and secondly, student notes were occasionally reviewed by Mylne himself. The resulting documents corroborate the main lines of a coherent argument, whilst for many details there is a lesser degree of corroboration from the facts that they are (a) consistent with the published works cited, (b) consistent with third party summaries of Mylne's thought and (c) logically connected and relevant to the principal line of argument.

4. Of the six surviving sets of notes on moral philosophy, I have transcribed the four legible ones and they amount to around 200,400 words (1799/1800 66,200; Mackenzie 66,300; Pollock 25,800; Wicksteed, 42,100). When collated, they would amount to a fair-sized book. Of the two sets of lectures on political economy, I have transcribed one (the other being in shorthand) and it amounts to 43,900 words. See introduction to bibliography. Obviously the evidence is not ideal, as what was heard and written may diverge from what was said.

We begin with two chapters on Mylne's view of the nature of cognition, his response to Condillac and Reid and his non-skeptical account of our knowledge of externality. Next we turn to the centrality of cognition to "the passions" and to the relations of reason and conscience as a background to the content of duties to God, man, and self. The succeeding essay focuses on Mylne's distinctive intellectual view of belief. I then relate his political commitments to local Whig doctrines. Finally, I turn to the political economy course and identify the primacy of use-value as distinguishing Mylne's political economy from that of Adam Smith and underpinning his concept of the merchant.

CHAPTER 7

The Lectures on Intellectual Philosophy

THE MORAL PHILOSOPHY COURSE that Mylne taught remained stable in form throughout his tenure.[1] Much of it contains material similar to other eighteenth- and nineteenth-century Scottish courses and books on moral philosophy, despite the distinct purposes that animate it. Parallel to Mylne's lectures, his students read Francis Bacon, for whom philosophy as a whole was one species of a tripartite division of learning into poetry, philosophy and history, and Cicero's *On Duties*, which introduced them to ancient moral philosophy. They had been exposed also in George Jardine's Logic class to the rhetoric of Quintilian in which knowledge of philosophy is part of the armory of the orator. In the lectures, Mylne draws on the scientific method of Bacon and the descriptive psychology of John Locke to interpret and justify Stoic and Epicurean concepts of duty and the good life as found in the class study of ancient philosophy and the Christian concept of piety preached on in the College's Sunday sermons. These concepts of public duty, welfare, and piety were part of a common European cultural and educational tradition. The division of duties into those to God, neighbor, and self is likewise in a Scottish and European tradition of natural law expounded by Gershom Carmichael, though not without dissent.

Alongside a critique of Hutcheson's moral sense theory, Hume's skepticism, and the common sense responses of Reid and Stewart, Mylne used the resulting vindicated rationality to engage with the socio-religious and economic problems of his day. This is a neglected aspect of Scotland's philosophical heritage. His philosophical position can be summed up in a

1. This is indicated by the surviving student notes.

popular phrase of the day, as a species of "rational piety."[2] Under the banner of reason, Mylne's analyses of the intellect, mind and society are shot through with a commitment to seeing the unity of the mind through the multifarious phenomena presented by naive experience. This gives his work as a whole a religious ethos. Reason in this sense is not simply one amongst our mental powers, but the harmonious operation of them all together. In his own words: "By reason I mean that compound of all our mental powers by which we perceive the causes of things."[3]

If, as Mylne argues, comparison is always possible between parts of experience and a criterion of preference is available to the mind through the intrinsic qualities of the parts of experience concerned, then a unitary good must emerge from rational inquiry. "Reason is considered to be cold and uninteresting by many," he says, "because it has often been employed about dry and uninteresting objects."[4] Whilst reason is a spontaneous fact of mental life, it is also at work in the philosophical sciences. In this sense, moral and even religious philosophy have the historical task of retracing and, where possible, correcting the work of spontaneous reason.

The Scope and Place of Moral Philosophy

The course of moral philosophy covered all of mental and moral philosophy, whilst touching on social, religious, and political concerns. Indeed in terms of ground covered, he was more ambitious than the Reid of the *Inquiries*. The earliest lecture notes begin with a course description:

> The first object is to explain some of the most important faculties of the human understanding and analyse them. The principles of practical morality and of civil society are only to be sought for in these faculties.[5]

We have seen that Mylne's justification for this in terms of his mode of vindicating reason at the expense of common sense was distinctive, though the practice of prefacing lectures on moral philosophy with treatment of

---

2. The phrase is used in the obituaries of Thomas Reid (*GC* 8/10/1796) and fellow minister John McCaul "a man of a sound judgement, of sincere and rational piety, of strict integrity and uprightness of heart" (*GC* 10/1/1797).

3. Pollock notes of Mylne's lectures, GUL:MSGen/1355/101, lecture of 22 January 1821.

4. Pollock notes, GUL:MSGen/1355/103, lecture of 29 March 1821.

5. 1799/1800 notes of Mylne's lectures, GUL:MS 207, 33.

general and intellectual philosophy was not. He then turns to moral philosophy proper:

> We shall next inquire into those principles by which man is prompted into action, or the active principles. There are some principles that act upon us independently of the good or evil thereof. We can't reduce them all into the desire of good or the fear of evil. [. . .] We shall then discuss some questions such as regard habit, will and [the] liberty of human actions, etc, then those circumstances that influence the moral character both national and individual.[6]

The independent principles seem to be an acknowledgement of propriety and other modifications of utility. Only then does he turn to the content of human duty, both individual and social:

> Human duties come [next] and first those that regard almighty God, or natural theology, and [we shall also] point out those circumstances that nature shews, that reason points out, about the immortality of the soul, etc. Then come the different leading branches of practical duties to others, as justice and benevolence, and then [duties] to ourselves to secure our dignity and happiness. The remainder shall examine man in society; the principles that lead him to civil and political society; government; the form of it; its object; the moral effects produced by it, etc.[7]

The priority of duties to God is an important point in common with contemporary preacher Ralph Wardlaw, author of *Christian Ethics*. Mylne remained true to the full range of this project throughout his long teaching career. In this chapter I recount the principal arguments and positions expounded in the introductory lectures and in the succeeding lectures on intellectual philosophy.

At the outset of the course, Mylne divides Philosophy, or Science, into Natural and Moral. Science he characterizes as a systematic knowledge of causes, or of the laws of nature. He characterizes it also as the result of a systematic inquiry that yields knowledge of principles. This is a non-skeptical position. At the start of his course, Mylne told his students:

> Don't be alarmed at the name of metaphysics. Ridicule may fall on the mode of pursuing the subject, but not on the subject itself. The enquiry is regarding our own mind and its feelings, and we may be as certain of our facts as in physics. We draw our

---

6. 1799/1800 notes, GUL:MS207, 36.
7. 1799/1800 notes, GUL:MS207, 37. Punctuation slightly amended.

information from our own feelings and from what we observe in others.[8]

This project leads Mylne to incorporate into the course an account of human knowledge, at which point the strong intellectualist bias of his thought emerges in another aspect. As moral action depends on knowledge of duty, he argues, and moral philosophy aims to improve this knowledge, human nature and its cognitive powers should first be investigated.

In place of the vindication of freedom found in such diverse writers as Joseph Butler, Thomas Reid and Immanuel Kant, we find instead in Mylne a combination of Calvinist intellectualism and piety. Whenever he introduces a new mental faculty, Mylne pauses to exclude the possibility or intelligibility of a motiveless choice in its exercise. He argues that the exercise of our active and moral powers presupposes intellectual judgement which is implicit in any hope, fear, plan, or motive. Our actions are determined by conceptions, but those conceptions are such as our mental constitution determines, not a consequence of motiveless free will. This theme culminates in his discussion of belief in the existence and attributes of God.

On Art and Science

Mylne proceeds to develop a contrast between art and science based on the kind of knowledge characteristic of each. Mylne distinguishes Moral Philosophy as a particular Science from the Art of Morals, identifying its purpose as the improvement of that Art. The Art of Morals in contrast comprises rules of thumb drawn originally from experience, which vary over time and place and are capable of improvement. Science "facilitates the progress of the artist; it gives him stability."[9] The temporal priority of rules of art such as those of Hesiod and the book of Proverbs, over moral systems was noted by Adam Smith.[10] The relation of art and science was later developed by William Hamilton, in his *Lectures on Metaphysics*.[11] Such continuity of themes between authors locates them in a tradition of Scottish academic teaching.

Thereafter, Mylne addresses four objections to the idea of science as a guide to the art of morals. The art of morals might be guided instead by conscience conceived as quasi-instinctual; by uncontroversial appeals to reason; by the wisdom of the ancients; or by Revelation. This discussion represents

---

8. 1799/1800 notes, GUL:MSMurray 207, 33-4.
9. Pollock notes, GUL:MSGen1355/101/3.
10. Smith, *Wealth of Nations* (1937), 724.
11. William Hamilton, *Lectures on Metaphysics*, 1:115-18.

an apparent change in the course. In 1799, Mylne presented his students simply with a course outline and an exhortation that it deals with matters of "infinite consequence." What develops in the interim however, is a more systematic defense of both the subject and of a "scientific" approach to it. In this, we may identify a response to some contemporary lines of thought.

Firstly, Mylne defends his model of inquiry against the moral sense theory, which he likens to a view of morals as instinctive. Secondly, he criticizes the view that reason itself produces morality without giving rise to controversy. These arguments might be compared with the dispute over the value of moral philosophy between Frances Jeffrey (1773-1850) and Dugald Stewart (1753-1828).[12] In some respects, Mylne agrees with Stewart.[13] However, whilst Stewart stresses the use of the subject for the individual student as a means of general education, Mylne sketches an argument that moral science itself is a principal agent of social reform. This is the first sign in the lectures of their social and political implications which recurs as the course progresses.

Thirdly, the reference to reliance on ancient authority might be taken as a reference to Burkean traditionalism, then politically in the ascendant. Mylne opposes this by adverting to the errors of ancient thought and to changes which are reckoned improvements. A confidence in our rational powers is implicitly a repudiation of Burke's later views.

Fourthly, there is a response to the growing evangelicalism of the West of Scotland, which attained its most coherent expression in the work of Ralph Wardlaw (1779-1853). Against reliance on revelation, Mylne fleet-footedly cites Scripture: "I speak to you as wise men; judge ye what I say,"[11] and elaborates on the uses of reason to identify and interpret revelation.

Positively, Mylne argues that mental philosophy is a necessary groundwork for understanding human action and human society because of the close connections between reason, belief, and action. His successor William Fleming confirms this:

> Next to the opinion that our perceptions of external nature are empirical, rather than intuitive, the doctrine which he maintained with most earnestness was that of the connection which subsists between our powers of knowledge and our principles of

---

12. Davie, *Crisis of the Democratic Intellect*, 3. Jeffrey and Stewart's essays are reproduced in Flynn's anthology *Enlightened Scotland*.

13. Stewart, *Philosophy of the Human Mind* (1862), chapter 2: "Of the utility of the philosophy of the human mind." There is no comparable discussion in Beattie's *Elements of Moral Science*, a work which Mylne's course in some other respects follows closely, which suggests Mylne and Stewart are here contributors to an emerging debate.

14. Pollock notes, MSGen1355/101/7; 1 Cor 10:15.

action. [. . .] The strength and subtlety of argument with which he came to the conclusion that our feelings, affections and passions, even the most sudden, fantastic and apparently lawless, do yet proceed upon a judgment passed in the intellect,—and the glowing eloquence with which, on all occasions, he urged the important truth that Reason is the dominant faculty in man, the supreme guide and ultimate arbiter of his conduct;—these were the characteristics of the Lectures of my distinguished predecessor, which will not soon be forgotten by those who heard them.[15]

In this respect the influence of Condillac is seen in both the empirical nature of perception and the philosophical program of deducing all mental life from unifying principles. This unifying ambition distinguishes Mylne from the common sense school of Reid. The core of Mylne's metaphysics is the study of the mind and the interpretation of the unity of the mind, including the unity of thought and action, through the concept of reason.

Methods of Inquiry into the Mind and Analysis of the Intellectual Powers

Mylne turns next to the study of the human mind; and then to the study of the intellectual powers. He develops his rationalist critique of the "common sense" school, particularly as represented by Reid, whilst also acknowledging some limitations of rational inquiry into human action. The study of mind was to be based on observation. Mylne commences by endorsing the project of an empirical science of the mind, conceived on the analogy of the science of nature advocated by philosophers such as Francis Bacon. The validity of observational and experimental methods had been endorsed by Thomas Reid in his *Inquiry into the Human Mind* (1764).[16] However, Mylne thinks that Reid's reliance on this method has unwarrantedly multiplied the number of primary powers of the mind through lack of analysis.

The idea was that natural science can proceed by collecting observations drawn from the senses (e.g., of the properties of plants) with a view to making generalizations concerning them (e.g., all plants require sunlight). Thus similarly, mental science ought to proceed by collecting observations about mental acts (e.g., of instances of generosity) in order to create similar generalizations (e.g., a favor freely conferred produces gratitude). The

---

15. Fleming, "Moral Philosophy Chair," 11.

16. In addition, there are important reflections on method in Condillac, *Essai sur les Connaissances humaines*, Part 2.2 and in *Traité des systèmes*. This latter criticizes Descartes for overestimating deduction at the expense of observation.

criterion in both cases is consciousness. This theme was later taken up by William Hamilton in his lectures on metaphysics.

There follows a discussion of analogy. This occurs where experience in one field is taken as a guide to another. It may, Mylne suggests, originate in poetry, yet contribute to science. Mylne himself draws analogies between the complexities of chemical compounds and the passions of the mind and between the methods of inquiry into matter and mind.

He proceeds to respond to a series of objections based on the uncertainty of our knowledge of the mind. This spells itself into several specific complaints. Firstly, it is said that the "essence" of mind is unknown. Mylne replies that so too is the essence of matter. This seems to be a version of the debate arising from John Locke's discussion of the concept of essence attributed to Aristotelians. Next, a comparison is drawn with physical theory, where experience, observation, and experiment are all possible. Mylne acknowledges that there are less opportunities for experiment as such in moral science, but argues that equivalent sources of information are sometimes available and that, as in the case of astronomy, where we cannot experiment on the stars, knowledge may still be attainable through observation.

Thirdly, he argues that moral science presupposes universal laws of nature, applicable both to the material and immaterial world. He acknowledges that this is difficult to prove, as it is a universal proposition and experience only gives us particular instances. However, he still regards it as a presupposition of inquiry. Mylne argues that moral science presupposes universal laws of nature applicable both to the material and immaterial world, and this negates Reid's theory of free will.

All in all, the course introduction stands comparison to similar contemporary works by James Beattie and Dugald Stewart and to the later lectures of William Hamilton. In the published records of their views, Beattie for example begins straight off with psychology;[17] Stewart starts with the nature and utility of mental science;[18] whilst Hamilton gave seven lectures on the utility, nature, causes and division of philosophy in general before moving on to psychology.[19] Mylne's course introduction is both theistic and intent on a vindication of "reason" (as later defined) to create and underpin projects of social reform.

Having surveyed method, Mylne moves on to discuss what he takes to be the individual elementary powers of the mind: sensation, memory, and

17. Beattie, *Elements of Moral Science*.
18. Stewart, *Elements of the Philosophy*.
19. Hamilton, *Lectures on Metaphysics*.

judgement. This is less ambitious than Condillac, who had hoped to interpret all experience as "transformed sensation," but instead reflects Hume's distinction between impressions and ideas as original mental contents and reason as their beholder. As it is a condition of the others, he turns first to sensation.

Sensation

Mylne turns then, to discuss sensation in the abstract. The objection that it is impossible to discuss sensation in isolation, when it is always combined with the work of other faculties in real experience, is dismissed. He relates sensation to his model of perception as a complex process:

> The faculty of sensation furnishes materials for perception; memory retains these materials; judgement perceives the sameness and difference of the impressions [. . .] Perception therefore, is the result of sensation, memory and judgement.[20]

This is a much more restricted number of primary faculties than those of Reid, who represents as primary many faculties that Mylne regards as complex, with no guarantee that his treatment is exhaustive.

The primary topics within Mylne's treatment of sensation relate to moral philosophy, namely whether pleasure and pain are distinct sensations or properties of sensation discerned by judgement; the role of prolongation in dulling sensation and directing attention; and the extent to which sensation is subject to the laws of the bodily constitution.

Mylne retains Reid's suspicion of David Hartley's material hypothesis (of "vibrations" in *Observations on Man*), but nonetheless elaborates on the material basis of sensation drawing on Hartley, whom he cites by name, and others. Mylne gives an account of the material basis of sensation, distinguishing observation from the deduction of laws. Mylne's distinction of facts from laws of sensation again reappears in William Hamilton's distinction between phenomenology and nomology and it is apparent that John Young's *Lectures on Intellectual Philosophy* (1835) also owes much to his treatment.

The lectures on sensation conclude that "All tempests, earthquakes &c are subjected to the government of nature and most likely all mental tempests also." This foreshadows his later arguments against free will.

---

20. Pollock notes, MS Gen1355/101/15.

Memory

In the treatment of memory, Mylne's first material assertion is that memory is an "original faculty of mind" distinct in particular from sensation. This argument was developed by Thomas Reid. However, Mylne amends Reid in that what Reid ascribes to memory alone, Mylne attributes to judgement acting through comparison on the material of both memory and sensation. Thus he says:

> When I say an object is black, I must have a present and a past sensation, then compare them in order to find their agreement or disagreement. That such a thing is black can only be determined by recalling other colours and comparing them. Also, I say a burning heat is painful. Here I must remember that other degrees are not painful.[21]

This is brought out again later in the course in Mylne's treatment of the concept of an "idea." Whilst for Hume, this is a simple mental element, "a faint and languid" copy of an impression,[22] for Mylne it is a complex structure whose apparent simplicity and effortless presence to the mind stems from habit and neglect of the history of concept formation.

Mylne distinguishes memory in the sense of retention from memory through recollection, that is, the recovery of concepts or items of knowledge of past events after a period of apparent forgetfulness. There is a paradox here that if I try to remember something, say the name of an actor in a play, I must in some sense already know it, or else I would not know that my attempts to remember are not correct. To explain this, Mylne argues that recollection proceeds by the association of ideas. I know a complex fact (the name and face of the actor) in some particulars and through association can recall the others.

Mylne also uses the cases of fever and palsy to illustrate the dependence of memory on the bodily frame, though he argues that this does not imply materialism. At first sight, there seems to be little movement in discussions of memory between Aristotle and Mylne: we find much the same distinctions, observations and paradoxes. However, looked at closely, Mylne operates with greater precision than Hume and Reid and identifies more clearly the role of reason in complex memories.

---

21. Appendix, collation of memory lectures, proposition 6.
22. Hume, *Treatise of Human Nature* (1978), 9.

Judgement

The two lectures on judgement distinguish it as a primary faculty from unaided sensation and memory. For the most part, they recapitulate the role of the former two faculties, but with a further layer of abstraction removed. In the lectures a shift is underway from a Humean view of the mind's unity as founded on a unity of kind (impressions, sensation) to one based on judgement (or the comparison of different mental entities presupposed as co-present to the mind.[23] In relation to his predecessors, Mylne here adopts Reid's idea of judgement as an independent faculty, in opposition to Hume and Condillac. He says "As a simple element of mind, judgement perceives the differences between our sensations and feelings."[24] As a primary faculty, it cannot be further decomposed or defined, but its fundamental nature can be indicated. The concept of judgement requires to be supplemented by theories of ideation and inference to complete the idea of reason, to which Mylne attributes a central role in mental life. It thereafter forms a central theme of the lectures as a whole.

It is also noteworthy that the theme of opposition to absolutist ideas of human freedom is reiterated here as throughout the lectures: for judgement is not subject to the will. In this sense, Mylne is again defending the "Calvinist" views of Jonathan Edwards and Leibniz against the "Arminian" views of Thomas Reid and others. We discuss this in a separate chapter.

The Compound Mental Faculties

Mylne regards all mental acts other than the above three to be complex and regards them as compounds on analogy with the chemistry of the day. Hence he deals in the remainder of the lectures on the intellectual faculties successively with external perception, including discussion of the distinction between primary and secondary properties of matter, followed by the compound faculties of attention, association, and conception.

---

23. The concept of judgement as comparison was later developed by William Hamilton in his *Lectures on Metaphysics*, 1:333–35, but it is fully expressed beforehand by Hume and Mylne. This can be seen as a move towards Ferrier's and the later Glasgow idealist view of the mind in which the self to which diverse matters are present through judgement is seen to be a presupposition of the unity of experience. Mylne is thus a transitional figure in the arguments of the Scottish philosophers as well as a representative of an enduring tradition of philosophical analysis of memory.

24. Pollock notes, MSGen1355/101/40.

Perception of the External World

We shall devote a further separate chapter to Mylne's analysis of touch and external perception, but in the context of the lectures, this represents the first application of the account of the elementary faculties to explain the mind in action. In addition to this, there is a discussion of skepticism. It is not enough, Mylne argues, merely to have the idea, if we cannot judge of its truth. Judgement presupposes a comparison. In analyzing the comparison of sensation with the idea of externality, he recurs to the Humean idea of causality:

> But after this process, how are we to believe that these judgments are true? May we not be deceived all the while? Berkeley was a sceptic of this kind. Mr Mylne knows of no demonstrative argument to prove the truth of our judgments about the existence of an external world. Neither can the contrary be demonstrated.[25]

Mylne repudiates the solution of "the pious, but whimsical Malebranche" that only Scripture proves the existence of the external world, but finds himself at last driven back on common sense: "This is whimsical and instead of it here I would call [on] the aid of common sense."[26] The line of argument is taken up by John Young, in his *Lectures on Intellectual Philosophy* (1835). Young concludes:

> I cannot believe the sun to be a modification of my own mind, and when I have travelled forty weary miles in a day over a barren country, I can believe the pain and fatigue resulting from this operation to be impressions on my own mind; but I feel it impossible to resist the belief that these had some cause, or that the sun and the road were two different things from my own self.[27]

Mylne's engagement with the philosophy of perception and his drawing on contemporary French theorists is an ancestor of the similar analyses of his pupil William Hamilton in his critique of Brown.[28] This was summarized in 1840 by Felix Ravaisson in a review of the French translation of Hamilton's *Edinburgh Review* essays.[29] Ravaisson argued that, whilst both Locke's "way of ideas" and Kant's position led to skepticism, their premises had been challenged in French work from Condillac to Maine de Biran

---

25. Pollock notes, MSGen1355/102/ 6.
26. Ibid.
27. Young, *Lectures on Intellectual Philosophy*, 495.
28. Hamilton, *Discussions on Philosophy*, article on perception.
29. Review of *Fragments de philosophie de Hamilton* by Ravaisson in *Revue des deux Mondes* (Nov 1840, 210 et seq.) cited in Madinier, *Conscience et mouvement*, 269.

(1766–1824). Ravaisson argues that "touch is the native language of perception, the other senses give only translations."[30] Versions of this analysis were available to later Scottish thinkers,[31] but Mylne had already introduced it into Scottish debates.

Primary and Secondary Qualities

Mylne next discusses the distinction between primary and secondary qualities of matter. Of the authors he cites (Locke, Reid, and Stewart), only Reid devotes a whole chapter to the distinction. Mylne criticizes this distinction, based on ideas similar to Joseph Priestley's natural philosophy. The discussion soon turns to the mathematical properties of matter and the application of mathematics to experience. The Mylnean idea relies on two empirical sources of spatiality (sight and touch). Thus an explanation has to be found for the certainty attributed to geometry and arithmetic, which contrasts with the fallibility of empirical knowledge.

Mylne's theory of mathematics is probably informed by Dugald Stewart.[32] In *Elements of the Philosophy of the Human Mind* (1792) Stewart discusses the nature of mathematics, disagreeing with Reid that mathematics is concerned with the primary qualities of matter. Instead, he thinks it is concerned with our abstract idea of space, the properties of which are shared by matter. His enjoyable discussion is informed, relaxed, and notably undogmatic. Whilst he raises clearly the questions of why mathematical truths should be universal and why, if they relate to abstract ideas, they are applicable to natural objects, he is skeptical of proposed answers. Mylne's position is:

> Abstract notions of quantity etc are entities of our own making. [. . .] Reid is perhaps wrong when he asserts that the

---

30. See Azouvi, *Maine de Biran*, 276.

31. Le Roy considers that Condillac's insistence on identity of principle subverts his acute sense of psychological observation. Biran thinks that psychology aims instead to particularize its descriptions. See Azouvi, *Maine de Biran*, 210. The rejection of Condillac's mechanical identities (e.g., "attention *is* exclusive sensation") is inherited by John Macmurray.

32. Stewart's competence in mathematics was high. In this respect, it is relevant that Mylne too studied mathematics at St. Andrews, where the standard of teaching was considered high. In addition, he knew the mathematician Brown and Mylne's library, auctioned on his death, contains a collection of mathematical works collected through his life. Mylne's earliest discussion dates from 1799, which is prior to both the second edition of *Elements of the Philosophy of the Human Mind* in 1802 and to the Leslie controversy in 1805.

mathematician is employed about primary qualities. They are employed about nothing which actually exists in matter.[33]

He instances mathematical points and surfaces. Mylne's theory, as recorded, leaves unanswered the question of why geometry is applicable to nature, given that its object is abstract ideas. One would not expect analysis of an idea abstracted from particular sense experiences to lead to universally applicable truths.[34]

Attention

There is a considerable subtlety of argument in these lectures which only becomes apparent when the different lecture notes are collated. The argument has several stages. With attention, Mylne begins an attempt to construct synthetically from the three primary faculties the derivative internal and active powers of mind. This takes up most of the rest of the lectures. The initial analysis of the powers of mind has distinguished the three primary powers of sensation, memory and judgement at work in the process of external perception. He now begins the presentation of the derivative internal and active powers of mind with attention.

The theme of freedom recurs as he argues that attention is not an exercise of a new power of free will, but even in its voluntary form, is subject to laws of the mind, in particular to the laws of sensation and association by which we attend to the strongest sensations. However, time lessens the sensation as the novelty is lost. Mylne then asserts that. "If a man in pain were told that his son was raised to some unexpected honour, he would forget his toothache."[35] The other notes clarify that whilst he thinks the pain would still be felt, the thoughts attending it would be banished. Mylne then instances a case where the man tries without such external stimulus to withdraw his attention from his pain. This is voluntary attention. Here he observes that the notion of retiring from pain itself "produces a stronger emotion that the pain from which he wishes to escape."[36] Hence no new faculty is required to explain such instances of voluntary shifts of attention: the same rule of attending to the sensations of greatest energy explains both voluntary and involuntary shifts of attention.

---

33. Pollock notes, MSGen1355/102/8–9.

34. In later Scottish work Edward Caird discusses Kant insightfully in *The Critical Philosophy of Immanuel Kant* and begins to sketch a critique of Kant's intuitionism.

35. Pollock notes, MSGen1355/102/10.

36. Ibid.

This argument is another precursor of the explicit and detailed treatments of free will and providence later in the lectures. This theme frequently gives direction and conviction to Mylne's presentation of particular issues. It shows him in an unexpectedly orthodox light as a Calvinist sympathetic to the English rational dissenters.

Mylne quotes Dugald Stewart's claim of originality on the subject of attention, but considers it overstated. However, detailed treatment of attention appears to have developed after Locke, Berkeley, and Hume.[37] Mylne takes the role of critic, both of Stewart's history of the subject and of his own views. This is similar to the treatment in Hamilton's *Lectures on Metaphysics*. Hamilton too takes issue with Stewart's historical observations, indicating that he cannot find the views Stewart attributes to Reid in Reid's *Works*, of which he was the editor.[38] Mylne identifies the absence of an account of attention in Reid.

Association

We might expect an extended view of association from Mylne in the light of his empiricist account of experience and this is what we in fact find. Association plays the explanatory role that might otherwise have to be attributed to distinct mental faculties. The association of ideas forms the second of three derivative mental faculties he discusses in the 1820 course, the others being attention and conception.

Mylne inherited a developed debate and positions his own rationalist account of the mind in relation to his predecessors. Association plays a subsidiary role in the philosophy of Locke. However, Hume, having dethroned reason, gives to association a larger role in mental life, attributing phenomena to custom and habit that were formerly considered to have a rational basis. In this respect, Reid and Stewart appear as rationalists: they reject Hume's attribution of the work of reason to subsidiary mental principles. However, in place of a return to a unitary reason, they offer an unlimited number of "contingent first principles" and "desires" by which mental life is regulated and which jostle in the mind for the attention of the conscious subject.

Mylne first argues that association is not an elementary power of the mind. He offers two reasons. Firstly, it cannot clearly be conceived. Secondly,

---

37. The history of attempts to explain abstraction by means of attention is examined in Davie, *Scotch Metaphysics*.

38. In longer trajectory, following Hamilton's treatment, attention appears in James' *Principles of Psychology*.

when it is conceived, it appears to be a property of either memory or judgement. If only memory were at work, objects and events would be recalled in the order they happened. Where this is not so, he concludes that judgement has been at work, for example if events in one country call up earlier but similar events in another.

He then analyzes association according to his earlier identification of primary mental faculties. Thus much association is the work of memory. This he calls direct association. However, much association appears to be more creative. This he attributes to judgement and names it indirect association. Finally, he relates this secondary association to the life of the mind in general. Here he finds that associations follow our interests and that there is a historical progress under which errors caused by accidental associations are replaced by knowledge of their true causes.

In terms of classification of associations, Mylne endorses a general rule attributed to Stewart that "any relation has a tendency to call up thoughts." Whereas Aristotle and Hume sought to reduce relations under a few heads, Mylne is more sympathetic to Stewart who adds to their classifications, such as the resemblance, contiguity and causation of Hume. This corresponds to the large role that association has in his intellectual project.

Conception

Conception is the last of the three "compound intellectual powers" that Mylne addresses before moving on to the active powers of the mind. Mylne argues that conceptions originate in a mixture of memories and judgements and thus are not the work of a simple power of mind. Only the simple powers of sensation, memory and judgement have real natures and Mylne observes that as a result the use of the term conception varies in different writers. His own definition is that conception is "a lively idea of mental objects."

In the 1820 lectures Mylne proceeds by way of a close critique of Reid and Stewart. Reid's treatment of conception is found in a dedicated chapter of the *Essays on the Intellectual Powers* (1785). Typically, Reid considers the term capable of illustration but also as (in contrast to Mylne) an elementary concept. He argues that the idea of conception as "an image in the mind" is metaphorical and that conception is a simple power that accompanies the operations of other faculties. Some difficulty arises in disentangling the scope of what Mylne says on conception as he distinguishes his own sense of the term conception from those of Reid, who interprets conception as "simple apprehension," which he identifies as a mental activity abstracted from belief.

In Reid, the comparison of conception with painting is prominent. Stewart makes two uses of the comparison with painting in his *Philosophy of the Human Mind* (1792) by discussing the case of a painter painting the picture of an absent friend to explore the notion of conception and later in his discussion of belief. Mylne develops his own account of conception by re-analyzing the situations of the reader, portrait painter and the theatre audience as described by Stewart. He denies that a reader of fiction believes what he reads. The future poet Robert Pollock records him saying: "Milton's description of Paradise and its inhabitants evokes the strongest conceptions, but we never really think that we see that grand piece of architecture or its inhabitants."[39] In the case of the portraitist, what Stewart attributes to conception can be explained by acts of memory and judgement. He takes issue with Stewart's idea that conception is attended by belief in the theatre audience. Stewart says that the belief is momentary, but the conception continues while the belief disappears. Mylne denies that belief is present, arguing that real belief would be accompanied by action. This extends into a criticism, similar to Reid's, of Hume's conception of belief as a lively idea. In a typical turn of phrase, Mylne dismisses Hume's view as "extravagant."

We are here at the threshold of discussions of belief and imagination. At this point, Mylne breaks off and turns to the active faculties for which, he argues, conception is a central ingredient and reason is the leading element.

Conclusions

The first third of Mylne's course of moral philosophy introduced students to a model of systematic empirical inquiry into the human mind based on general philosophical considerations on the acquisition of knowledge derived in part from the writings of Francis Bacon. His view of inquiry as aimed at the knowledge of universal laws already shows that the concept of freedom can play only a subsidiary role. Mylne structures the inquiry, not according to the senses (of sight, hearing, etc.) as in Condillac, but according to the mental faculties in operations. However, the treatment of touch in the context of perception comes from Condillac. Mylne identifies sensation, memory, and judgement as elementary faculties. He identifies universal properties of sensation that will be invoked later for their explanatory power in more complex mental operations. At each stage of the argument, he excludes the possibility of arbitrary decision in favor of the omnipresence of reason.

The treatment of sensation as having relatively painful and pleasant qualities will be drawn on later in the utilitarian theory of ethics of the later

---

39. Pollock notes, MSGen1355/102/13.

lectures and the large role given to association is consistent with the project of reforming habits of association for purposes justified by utilitarian considerations. The result is a picture of the mind that supports an ideology of rational social reform at the expense of the moral project of individual reform for which metaphysical freedom and moral exhortation are central. This makes a contrast between Mylne one the one hand and Reid and Beattie on the other, although it must be acknowledged that each of these philosophers were complex figures who found room for both aspects of thought in their lectures. In the opposition Hume draws between "cold" and "warm" approaches to morality, Mylne thus comes down on the cold analytical side of Hume and Millar rather than the warm side of exhortation advocated and practiced by Reid and Beattie and in Mylne's later years by his rival and critic Ralph Wardlaw. However, he differs from the skepticism of Hume or the Deism of Millar in retaining a religious compass, which equates roughly with that of the English rational dissenters, wavering somewhat between Unitarian sympathies and endorsement of the more orthodox Christian doctrines of the contemporary Baptists.

CHAPTER 8

Encounters with Condillac and Thomas Reid

WE HAVE SEEN THAT James Mylne drew in his lectures on a variety of philosophers on specific topics. He deprecated the wholesale adoption of any system, recommending that "The authority of great names should not be too closely adhered to."[1] This was noticed by William Fleming, who says: "by a kindly critic, his philosophy may be characterised as eclectic; for, instead of surrendering to the exclusive influence of any leading tenet, he rather liked to cull from the various systems what seemed to be true and good."[2]

Amongst the most decisive of these encounters for his intellectual philosophy were those with Condillac and Thomas Reid. We have seen that Mylne rejects the attempt by Condillac's school to deduce all mental life from sensation. Instead, he sees memory and judgement as co-ordinate mental faculties operating on material at first furnished through sensation. In this respect, he agrees with Thomas Reid. However, having reverted to a broadly Humean project of mental science that rejects the foundational role ascribed by Reid to "common sense," Mylne requires a response to the skepticism about knowledge of the material world that Hume draws from Berkeley. He finds the best such response in Condillac's analysis of the sense of touch. It should also be noted that Mylne speaks of "French writers" when the school of Condillac is meant. In the later lectures, this includes Destutt de Tracy, whose treatment of habit Mylne singles out for praise.

---

1. Wicksteed notes, GUL:MSGen97/103, 36b.
2. Fleming "Moral Philosophy Chair."

Abbé de Condillac: Biography and Reception

Étienne Bonnot, Abbé de Condillac was born in Grenoble in France in 1714. He studied for the Roman Catholic priesthood and moved successively to Lyon and Paris, where he participated in the Salon culture of the *Philosophes*. He was described by the historian of French philosophy, Victor Cousin, as the principal French philosopher of the eighteenth century[3] and was an acknowledged influence on Mylne's French contemporaries,[4] as well as on Mylne himself.

Condillac represents a Christian thread in French enlightenment philosophy.[5] Although it is said that he conducted his studies of theology "sans enthousiasme,"[6] the religious content of his published works contrasts with the mockery of the church by Voltaire and Helvetius. His first book is set in a theological framework by reference to the story of the fall in Genesis, though no further use is made of this remark in the rest of the work.[7] He reintroduces the theme of revelation in a discussion of the metaphorical nature of the statement attributed to Moses "And God said: Let there be light!"[8] This is developed in connection with an evaluation of a translated section of Bishop Warburton's *Divine Legation of Moses* on hieroglyphics. The language of Scripture, Warburton argues, owes some of its metaphorical style to its relation to hieroglyphic script. A government is represented by a star, for example. Thus biblical passages saying that "the stars of heaven shall fall" have a concrete reference to changes of government and are, so to speak a kind of "speaking hieroglyphics," the obscurity of which is owing to our having lost the key of the script. In the *Traité des Sensations*, he sketches an account of the origins of natural religion. As in Mylne and the English rational dissenters, there is an attempt to interpret Scripture in the light of reason.

---

3. Cousin, *Philosophie Morale au XVIIIe Siècle* II, Sensualisme.

4. Destutt De Tracy, Cabanis, French-Swiss writer Charles Bonnet, and Maine de Biran, though perhaps only the first and third of these thinkers were known to Mylne.

5. As usual with French philosophers, there is debate on the sincerity of Condillac's Christianity. I take it that his attitude is expressed in his advice to the prince of Parma: "You cannot be too pious, my lord, but if your piety is not enlightened, you will forget your duties. [. . .] It is not your place that you should live in your court as in a cloister" (Condillac, *Cours d'Études*, tome 10, 4). His views on the existence of God and the origins of Christianity were orthodox for their day, for example his question why, if the Apostles invented their stories of miracles, they themselves believed. He attributes it partly to miracle, partly to the fulfillment of prophecy.

6. Le Roy, *La Psychologie de Condillac*, 5.

7. Condillac, *Essai sur l'Origine des Connaissances humaines* (1973) 1.1.1

8. Ibid., 1.2.11.

There was a sustained market for French literature in Scotland that survived the wars with France. For example, in July 1801, Glasgow's New Circulating Library advertised French and Latin classics "from the Stereotype press in Paris."[9] The following month Dunlop & Wilson advertised French biography, novels, and theater.[10] The following October James and Andrew Duncan "having opened a correspondence with a house in Paris" receive French books,[11] advertising further receipts in June 1803 and urging customers to order quickly "as the intercourse with France is now shut." In 1808, A Murdoch at Brunswick Place advertised a "new English and French circulating library." In January 1811, A and J Duncan advertised that they had "the opportunity for two weeks of ordering foreign publications, both from France and Germany." The Reverend William McCartney (1762–1828), a near contemporary and minister of a neighboring parish to Mylne's, noted in 1798 that until recently "there was no chance of understanding ordinary conversation completely without a knowledge of the French language, French phrases poured in so plentifully."[12] In Edinburgh, Dugald Stewart remarked that translations of philosophical works from French into English were unnecessary, so prevalent was a knowledge of that language amongst their intended readership.[13] All the same, the depth of Mylne's knowledge of French literature is unusual amongst contemporary Scottish philosophers, covering mental philosophy, political economy, mathematics, and modern drama.

Mylne acquired a French edition of Condillac's three-volume *Oeuvres* (1777), perhaps when he was still at St. Andrews.[14] We can see from the date that he may have acquired this edition when he was twenty, though perhaps he bought it secondhand later on. However, subsequent editions appeared in 1782, 1787, and 1792. This suggests that first-time buyers of the 1777 edition may have bought it within five years of publication.[15] There is also a copy of the 1777 edition at St. Andrews University Library. Mylne at that time already had some French and was aware from 1774 of the admiration

9. GC 14/7/1801.
10. GC 22/8/1801.
11. GC 9/10/1802.
12. McCartney, notes to Cicero, *The Treatise of Cicero De Officiis*, 318–19.
13. Schulthess, *Correspondance*.
14. Skirving catalogue III-47 in GUL.
15. The first edition of the three-volume *Works* was 1769 (Jean Sgard, *Corpus Condillac*). In addition, I have found no reference to the local availability or knowledge of Condillac's *Works* in Paisley and Glasgow during Mylne's time there after an extensive search of book shop adverts in the local press and local library catalogues. The only argument against early ownership would be the likely price of the book.

for John Locke in France from reading Voltaire.[16] It is possible that he may have travelled to France and Italy. However that may be, it is apparent from his lectures that he had certainly digested Condillac's arguments thoroughly by the time he began to teach.

The early edition of Condillac owned by Mylne contains three principal books: the *Essai sur l'Origine des Connaissances Humaines* (1746), the *Traité des Systèmes*, and the *Traité des Sensations* (1754), with the *Traitè des Animaux* (1755) included as an appendix to the latter.[17] These works form the backbone and terminology of much of Mylne's intellectual philosophy. As was Hutcheson for John Cook, they are central texts for Mylne, with which he largely agreed, but to which he also responded creatively. Mylne also had ready access to all Condillac's later works, but his principal debt is to the content of this early edition.[18] This influence is evident from the lectures themselves and further confirmed by second hand reports from former students. Alexander Campbell Fraser for example, summarizes the common view of Mylne's philosophical position: "He [Mylne] was, I believe, inclined to the school represented by Hartley in England and Condillac in France, rather than to the spiritual realism of Reid."[19] The use of Condillac distinguishes Mylne from the philosophical radicals with whom he is sometimes grouped, who preferred Hartley.[20]

---

16. He borrowed Voltaire's *Lettres sur les Anglais* from St. Andrews University Library in 1774 ((LY207/1 Vol 2).

17. Condillac, *Oeuvres* (Paris, 1777). There are copies of the 1777 edition in St. Andrews, Edinburgh and Lausanne University Libraries. For editions of Condillac, see *Corpus Condillac*, edited by Jean Sgard. Many early editions contain these three volumes, prior to the 1798 edition. The 1777 edition does not have the "Extrait Raisonnée" (found in the modern Fayard edition) to the *Traité des Sensations*, but it does have the other appendices, including the "Dissertation sur la Liberté."

18. Mylne also owned Condillac's *Course of Study for the Prince of Parma* (1798 edition) and the posthumous *Langue des Calculs* (1798), thus giving him access to all the works of the posthumous 1798 edition of Condillac other than the *Logique* (Skirving catalogue, GUL II-37 & III-59). Mylne would have found the schoolboy history of much of the *Course of Study* thin gruel compared to other history available to him. The *Langue des Calculs* appears also to be drawn on in some of Mylne's remarks on mathematics, though his own personal knowledge of mathematics would also be brought into play. These latter works seem most in his mind in the 1799/1800 lectures, whilst the earlier works are the most enduring influences.

19. Fraser, *Biographia Philosophica*, 42.

20. Mylne's lecture notes indicate the influence of Condillac more than that of Hartley. In this respect, there is a contrast with James Mill, who gave the *Traité des Sensations* to his son "quite as much for a warning as for an example" (Mill *Autobiography*, chapter 3) and with John Stuart Mill himself, who claimed a "metaphysical creed [...] quite different from that of the Condillac school," based rather on Hartley's and his father's. See Letters 111 of 14 October 1834 to John Pringle Nichol in Mill, *The Earlier*

Condillac's first book, the *Essai sur l'Origine des Connaissances Humaines* (1746)—hereafter the *"Essai"*—was intended to supplement Locke's account of experience by a systematic account of the generation of the cognitive faculties out of "sensation." This is accompanied by an account of thought as largely dependent on language of which there is little trace in Mylne.

The second book, *Traité des Systèmes* (1749), deals with questions of method, the role of hypothesis, abstraction, and analysis. This is relevant to the subjects Mylne himself principally worked on, namely mental philosophy and political economy, though the questions of method are discussed by Mylne at the outset of his course as well as in incidental asides throughout it. It is easy to see similarities with Mylne's lectures here, though these may be due to a common reliance on Francis Bacon.

The third book, the *Traité des Sensations* (1754)—hereafter the *"Traité"*—concerns in particular the growth of our knowledge of the external world from sensation and, in particular, from the sense of touch. Mylne draws heavily on this work. It is also likely that he draws on the *Traité des Animaux* (1755) which, like the work on sensations is closely related to the writings of Buffon. This latter book addresses the light which the mental life of animals might shed on that of man. In addition, there is some light reference to Condillac's later works.[21]

Mylne and Condillac shared some significant common reading. Condillac adopts as his own the reform of the sciences projected by Francis Bacon (1561–1626) and the psychology of John Locke (1632–1704), as in turn does Mylne. Although Condillac did not speak English, he had access to Bacon's *Novum Organum* in Latin,[22] a book which was studied (also in Latin) in Mylne's class, and he knew Locke's *Essay Concerning Human Understanding* (1689) in French translation.[23] Locke's thought had been made known in France previously by Voltaire, but its development there owes much to Condillac.[24]

The intellectual philosophies of Mylne and Condillac are both complex conceptual structures that do not map perfectly onto each other. However, they shed light on each other to a considerable degree. They share a

---

Letters, 12:237. See also Mill, *Autobiography* on the "insufficiency of the merely verbal generalisations of Condillac" (ch. 3).

21. There are also references to Condillac's late work *Cours d'Études* and *La Langue des Calculs* (1798).

22. Condillac cites Bacon in the *Essai sur l'origine des connaissances humaines* (1973), 2.2.3.

23. Locke's *Essay on Human Understanding* (1689) was translated into French in 1700 by the Huguenot refugee Pierre Coste.

24. Voltaire, *Lettres Anglaises* (1733), a work known to Mylne.

common vision over a range of subjects within intellectual philosophy, but bordering also on morals and theology. The principal areas in which I shall elaborate on this interpretation are:

- the development of the mind from sensation to reason;
- the role of touch in the perception of the external world; and
- the conceptual aspect of desire.

In addition to this, there are several borrowings of ideas and illustrations that are passed on from Condillac to Mylne. The following areas however, involve central sections of their philosophical agenda.

From Sensation to Reason

Firstly, Condillac's philosophy paints a vision of human reason as a bringing together of diverse experiences comprised ultimately of sensations and memories before the bar of judgement, whereby thought acquires a sense of direction and plans of action emerge. Both philosophers share a common starting point in raw sensation and a common goal in reason. The central message of the primacy of reason is brought out in the *Essai* where, for Condillac, the operations of the mind result in one that, "so to speak, crowns the understanding, that is, reason."[25] They further share a two-stage deduction of the developed mind from elementary, then from derivative faculties, though here their accounts differ in detail.

Condillac rejects the method of doubt practiced by Descartes (1596–1651) as a means of placing human knowledge on sure foundations. To doubt an idea, he argues, does not change its content, but only our attitude towards it.[26] In examining the origin of our ideas then, he concludes, Locke is pursuing a more fruitful path towards the reconstitution of our knowledge advocated by Bacon. Locke in turn though, assumes the faculties of the mind in composing, combining and comparing ideas as ready-made. This Condillac considers unwarranted, whilst Mylne too studies the genesis of different operations to find their common elements.

The starting point for both philosophers then, is sensation (though in Condillac's earliest writings the term "perception" also plays this role). Here we find an explanation for the absence in Mylne's lectures of an account of consciousness, for in Condillac, sensation includes consciousness: the term "sensation" refers to the impression in the mind as such; whereas

25. Condillac *Essai* (1973), 1.2.11
26. Ibid., 2.2.3.

consciousness includes the idea of the mind alerted to its own existence by the impression.[27]

At this point, the paths of the two thinkers diverge. Whereas Condillac considers that all acts of the mind are "transformed sensation,"[28] Mylne concludes that memory and judgement are autonomous aspects of experience. His position is recorded as follows:

> Two French philosophers attempted to reduce memory and judgment to modifications of sensation. Certainly these are feelings, but not such as they would have them. Sensation, memory and judgement are elementary—absolutely simple—and essentially different from each other. Such a reduction of memory and judgment to matter of feeling is carrying simplification to an excess.[29]

The philosophers are not named, but it is clear that the school of Condillac is meant. The explanation for this divergence may be found partly, not in a substantial difference of opinion, but in the French locution *se sentir* (literally "to sense oneself"), which retains the reference back to sensation in speaking of judgement, where English prefers the locution of "to feel" (e.g., "to feel myself ready").[30] In vindicating the autonomy of memory and judgement Mylne concurs with Reid.

For Condillac on the other hand, attention plays a larger role at first than in Mylne. A further difference is that the ability to voluntarily represent situations is made largely dependent on the emergence of a "language of action" in Condillac. In both philosophers however, the end point is the ability to form "conceptions" subject to rational evaluation.

Mylne and Condillac then, shared a loose conception of the unity of the mind involving the omnipresence of sensation and a two-stage

---

27. Condillac, *Essai*: "Ainsi la perception et la conscience ne sont qu'une même chose sous deux noms. [. . .] En tant qu'on ne la considère que comme une impression dans l'âme, on peut lui conserver celui de perception; en tant qu'elle avertit l'âme de sa présence, on peut lui donner celui de conscience" (119). The use of *perception* in the *Essai* corresponds to the later term *sensation*.

28. Condillac, *Traité des Sensations*, 11: "Judgement, reflection, the desires and passions, etc, are only sensation that transforms itself differently."

29. Collated from three sources: 1) GUL/SpecColl: MSGen466/27; 2) Mitchell manuscript: T-MJ/603/1, in Mitchell Library, Glasgow for November 18, 1819; and 3) Pollock manuscript: GUL/MSGen1355/101/17-18.

30. *Larousse Maxipoche 2008* equates it with *s'estimer, se juger* (1278). Thus, in the *Traité des Sensations*, the statue "feels itself equally in both" its hand and the part of its body that the hand touches (104).

deduction of the developed mind from elementary, then from derivative faculties, though the details of their respective deductions are not the same.

The Role of Touch in External Perception

Secondly, we come to the question of contribution of reason to our perception of the external world. Whilst Condillac knew of Berkeley indirectly through Voltaire and Diderot,[31] he did not draw on, or apparently know of, Hume's philosophy and so his thought cannot be seen as a response to Hume's skepticism.[32] In response to Berkeley's idealism though, the *Traité des Sensations* sought to show how the existence of the external world can be deduced from touch.[33] This represents an alternative line of thinking to the response of Thomas Reid to Hume. Mylne adopts Condillac's exposition as his own and here, as on the question of freedom and the number of mental faculties, takes issue with Reid. It should be noted though, that Condillac's account of touch develops between the successive editions of the *Traité*, the later editions stressing movement.[34]

Condillac develops his argument by means of the supposition of a statue which he has the power to endow with the sensations of one or more of the five senses of smell, hearing, taste, sight, and touch. The statue reappears directly in James Mylne's lectures in the guise of an "imagined being."

Unlike in the *Essai*, the *Traité* notes a difference in kind between touch and the other four senses. In the experience of a scent, there is no distinction of self and other, Condillac explains. In fact, he imagines, a sentient statue that had experienced only the scent of a rose would judge that it *was* the scent of the rose. If the scent changed, say to violet or carnation, it would judge that *it* had changed. Nothing in the experience as such allows us to distinguish what is *in us* from what is not. I find this plausible, though it must be remembered that we are to abstract from the motor aspect of

---

31. See Voltaire's *Elements de la philosophie de Newton* (1738) and Diderot's *Lettre sur les aveugles* (1749), cited in Le Roy, *Psychologie de Condillac*, 156, 91–92.

32. He did know Hume's history of the Stuarts though, as it is used in the *Cours d'Études*. The argument is that Condillac did not know English in 1746 (see *Essai* Pt 2.1.15 para 155) and appears never to have learned. Hume's philosophical works were not translated until after Condillac had published (Le Roy, *La Psychologie de Condillac*).

33. Adam Smith possessed copies of both these and several other of Condillac's works. Indeed, his essay on the external senses is little more than a précis of Condillac, though George Davie treats it as an original contribution to a self-contained "Scottish philosophy."

34. Bréhier, *Histoire de la Philosophie*, 1067 gives a more detailed description of developments from the 1754 to 1778 editions.

breathing in and out that belongs rather to touch and that we are to enter imaginatively into the experience of the statue. Condillac comes to the same conclusion in his examination of hearing and taste.

More controversially, he feels that nothing in the phenomena of sight in isolation gives us the sense of distance. In this respect, he draws from the arguments of Berkeley, as made known by Voltaire's *Élémens de la Philosophie de Newton* and also the case of the blind boy described by the surgeon Cheselden, who reported that he had to *learn* to see. Condillac describes, for example, the boy's initial judgement that the objects he saw were no bigger than his eye and his surprise that the people he liked best were not also the most beautiful.

The principal innovation comes next in Condillac's treatment of touch, which is an important and original contribution to phenomenology. Here, he thinks, lies the origin of the judgement of an external world. Like Mylne, he analyzes the concepts required into the aspects of solidity, resistance and impenetrability. These in turn involve contiguity and continuity. Solidity presupposes a continuous surface; whilst resistance and impenetrability require the contiguity of two surfaces in contact.

In the 1829 lectures, Mylne refers to those who ascribe externality "wholly to resistance." This would appear to be a reference to Destutt de Tracy, who deduced externality from muscular motion and resistance, but Mylne says explicitly at this point in 1829 that on externality "Condillac's explanation is better." Mylne states in the same set of notes that he learned of Destutt's work only around 1817.[35] It is also notable that he borrowed Destutt's Works from the College Library in 1824 and 1825 and owned an 1817 copy of his works.[36]

There is a contrast here with Thomas Brown, who lectured on moral philosophy in Edinburgh from 1810 and is thought to have derived his theory of external perception from Destutt.[37] Mylne and Brown agree in rejecting Condillac's attempt to deduce all mental operations from sensation alone.[38] They agree also that muscular effort produces ideas of resistance and extension (Mylne refers to "continuity"). However, Brown ascribes externality to resistance. When an object is placed in a child's hand, says Brown, "he ascribes the feeling of resistance to something that is foreign

---

35. Wicksteed notes, GUL:MSGen97, lecture 19 and for reference to Destutt, lecture 37.

36. GUL Professors' receipt Books and Skirving catalogue.

37. Dixon, introduction to Thomas Brown, *Selected Philosophical Writings*, 19–20. I also owe this point to a talk from Christina Paoletti at the Thomas Reid Tercentenary conference in Aberdeen, March 2010.

38. Brown, *Selected Philosophical Writings*, 123–24,

to him."³⁹ Mylne rejects an explanatory role for resistance in the genesis of the concept of externality in favor of Condillac's analysis of the dual nature of sensations of touch applied to our own and external bodies. However, the difference between the rival analyses of Brown and Mylne is bridged by the nature of the principal organs of active touch (the hands and mouth), the sentient parts of which naturally touch each other where no object is enclosed by them.

Condillac decries the possibility of deducing the concept of continuity from an experience that does not already contain it. This constrains him to look for an experience that does contain continuity. This he finds in the experience of touching my own body with my hand. This reflects Condillac's analysis of the *sentiment fondamentale*⁴⁰ deriving from bodily sensation, and his consequent view that under my hand when I touch my skin, I feel "a continuity of self."⁴¹ When I move my hand over my skin, there is an uninterrupted response of "I am here" and thus a double sensation. The first surface of which I have experience then, is of my own skin. However, when I touch an object other than myself, the answering sensation disappears and what is left is experienced, still as a surface, but as other. It is by a series of such experiences that I infer the existence of my own body as bounded by objects that are *not me*. We shall see that Mylne turns this analysis against Thomas Reid. He identifies Reid as arguing against Hume's skepticism, but prefers Condillac to either.

On Concept and Desire

Thirdly, in contrast to Hutcheson's account of our "moral sense," which Mylne follows Hutcheson's English critics in assimilating to a putative instinct, Condillac undertakes to deduce the active principles of mental life, other than instinct itself, from the data of sensation.

Condillac undertakes to prove this by way of the assumption that all sensation is either pleasant or painful. There is little in the way of argument for this, though he suggests that, when a painful sensation is removed, that is already pleasant. He then argues that pleasure and pain always determine the action of our faculties. Action arises from a felt need, but need arises from recognizing a past state as better than our present one and thus wishing for its return.⁴² Desire operates on a scale from unease through discontent

39. Ibid., 106.
40. Condillac, *Traité des Sensations*, 89.
41. Ibid., 104.
42. Ibid., 26.

through to torment. However in each case it is directed at an object of which we feel a need. In the case of the imaginary statue that identifies itself with its own mental states: "All desire thus supposes that the statue has the idea of something better than what it is at the moment; and that it judges about the difference of two states that succeed each other."[43] The intellectual nature of desire is a central idea of Mylne that in all likelihood originates here. Mylne illustrates the point that thought is present in passion with the example of a man who hits a dog or servant out of what he calls an "uncontrollable passion." Yet, Mylne observes, were the dog a mastiff or a servant a burly fellow with a short temper, the passion would be curbed and the influence of judgement thereby made manifest. Condillac sees philosophy as a systematic reform of such human habits.[44] This vision is also the governing spirit of Mylne's lectures on intellectual philosophy, though Mylne discusses in more detail than Condillac the implications for the active powers of the mind. In this respect the influence of Condillac ran far deeper in Mylne than in Stewart and the other Scottish thinkers.[45]

Thomas Reid

The common ground shared by Mylne and Thomas Reid can be characterized as "rational piety":[46] both philosophers were Ministers of the Church of Scotland who at times projected an image of piety, Reid accompanying the advert for his *Essays on the Intellectual Powers of Man* (1785) with the scriptural citation "Who hath put Wisdom in the inward parts?"[47] whilst Mylne in his lectures taught the division of duties into those to God, neighbor and self.[48] Their works both contain nuanced accounts of the workings of human rationality. However, Mylne's reason is not reined in by the fixed "common sense" premises of Reid.

Mylne and Reid were both members of the Glasgow Literary Society in the 1780s and 1790s, while Mylne was minister of the second charge at

43. Ibid., 67.

44. Condillac, *Traité des Animaux* in *Traité des Sensations* (Fayard, 1984) edition.

45. Stewart's dependence on Reid supports this. George Davie points out that Adam Smith's essay on the external senses may be the source of Stewart's analysis. However, Smith draws on Condillac and Buffon. Stewart owned only Condillac's *Logique*, though he borrowed other works from EUL in 1790 (see Crawford, *Stewart and His Library*).

46. It is used in an obituary of Reid, GC 8/10/1796.

47. *Glasgow Mercury* 4/8/1785, citing Job 38:36.

48. Adam Smith's division in *Theory of Moral Sentiments* had been into duties to others and to ourselves.

Paisley Abbey church and Reid was (emeritus) Professor of Moral Philosophy at Glasgow.[49] A contemporary witness notes that Reid was opposed at these meetings by John Millar, who argued for a version of Hume's philosophy.[50] After his appointment as Professor of Moral Philosophy in 1797, Mylne was in the reformist camp headed by Millar.[51] In his college teaching, he also took a critical stance to the inheritance of common sense philosophy derived from Reid and then associated with Dugald Stewart in Edinburgh.[52]

Turning to mental philosophy, Mylne agrees with Reid in making judgement an independent faculty of the mind in addition to sensation and memory, though his list of elementary mental faculties stops with these three. These are not necessarily the same as the more complex operations that go by the same names. For example, a memory *that* something happened in the past already includes elements of conception (of the something) and judgement (that the something happened). Mylne's simple sensation and memory correspond instead roughly to Hume's impressions and ideas. Simple judgement is a primitive act of comparison which has for its object at least two sensations or memories. For example, the primitive judgement that it is getting colder involves a comparison of a present sensation of cold with the memory of a past sensation of relative warmth. This too corresponds roughly to Hume's reason or judgement.[53] Mylne's conception of mature reason is judgement operating on more complex or abstract mental objects, typically mediated by conceptions and guided by considerations of causality. Mylne's basic philosophical project is thus to explain how human mental life (including Reid's judgements of common sense) is built up from these three primitive or simple mental operations.

A contrast thus emerges between Mylne and Reid's respective views of the relations of reason and common sense. Mylne gives the leading role to reason over all other considerations. He thus attacks Reid and Stewart's limitation of reason by fixed first principles of common sense that, according to Reid, "reason can neither make nor destroy."[54] This is a guiding thread

49. "The Literary Society of Glasgow" in Duncan, *Notices and Documents*, 133–34.

50. Craig, "Account of the Life," lxi.

51. William Taylor asserts this in a letter to Ilay Campbell dated 1800, but all contemporary observers agree.

52. Dugald Stewart's *Elements of the Philosophy of the Human Mind* (1792), *Outline of Moral Philosophy* (1793) and *Philosophical Essays* (1810) are cited in the lecture notes.

53. "All kinds of reasoning consist in nothing but a *comparison*" (Hume, *Treatise of Human Nature*, 73).

54. Reid, *Inquiry into the Human Mind on the Principles of Common Sense*, in *Works*, 1:130. The discussion concerns the argument of the *Inquiry*, chapter 5 section 7.

running through Mylne's course of lectures and manifesting itself on several particular issues. Thus he cites critically Reid's observation that the mind is "inspired with the various principles of common sense"[55] by degrees, arguing that this "inspiration" is in fact the discovery of general conclusions "in proportion to our knowledge and experience."[56] On two subjects that form major set piece arguments in his moral philosophy lectures this disagreement has content: the first is the role of touch in perception and the second is free will.

Mylne's general position is that what Reid classes as "principles of common sense" and "active principles" are in fact complex judgements about sensations and memories that have become habitual and of which we are therefore no longer directly conscious. In a remarkably intellectualist analysis of human nature, Mylne goes on to argue that the will is "not a distinct and separate faculty, but only an exercise of judgement."[57] The identity is to be taken literally. He thus identifies active principles with beliefs and insists on their rationality. In support of this, he argues that Reid's work is deficient in analysis of mental phenomena. Mylne told his students:

> Many of the springs of our actions which Dr Reid has treated as the primary active principles are evidently complex. They have been thought simple, but are compounds that may be analysed into their proper elements. Dr. Reid has not handled this subject right; he has not explained distinctly the will and understanding. For ex[ample], what is opinion, it is a principle of action and belongs to the understanding. It is a rational principle, and these are very nearly allied to the intellect. Opinion and a great number of other principles given by Dr Reid are no other than the powers of reasoning and thought.[58]

This refers to Reid's placing of opinion amongst the "animal principles of action" in the *Essays on the Active Powers*.[59] The same thought reoccurs when Mylne expounds his philosophical agenda in his own terms. He notes that "passions, affections, habits and appetites" move us to action and turns to consider passion. He explains firstly in relation to passion in general:

---

55. Thomas Reid, *Inquiry* in *Works*, 1:130.
56. Wicksteed notes, GUL:MS Gen 97/101–103, Lecture 20.
57. Wicksteed notes, GUL:MS Gen 97/102/Lecture 68.
58. I have collated the following passages from the 1799/1800 (MS Murray 207), Pollock (MS Gen 1355/101–103) and Mackenzie (MS Gen 466) notes at GUL. Material in square brackets is either dubious readings or inserted by me to clarify the meaning.
59. Reid, *Active Powers* in *Works*, 1:3.2.7.

The principle of thought is the primary [part] of any of the passions, because we must first think, compare and judge before we have any passion. [For] ex[ample:] we cannot be angry at any[one] until we perceive, reason and pass a judgment, viz. believe an injury to be received. It is thus with all the other passions and affections. [There is] thought in the most sudden gust of passion.

The remaining parts of passion, according to Mylne, are bodily emotion and movement. Reid also makes the point that passions are intentional (about something), but for Mylne this undermines the view that passion and the like are not themselves rational, but akin to instincts. They are "the offspring of reason and modification of it," though, he concedes, "it may be erroneous, ill directed reason."[60] Moral actions, as a special kind of action, are subject to the same laws. He explains of the above analysis:

> If this be true in common actions it must also be true in moral actions. Indeed it is not denied by those who place morality in instincts that these are connected with the intellect. Man is only a moral agent so far as he is an intellectual creature. [Thus] to discover all the principles of action, we must consider the intellect.

Hence Mylne includes an analysis of the intellectual powers in his moral philosophy lectures. It emerges in the course of these that the disagreement with Reid over reason is in part merely verbal. In the *Inquiry* for example, Reid restricts reasoning to deliberate reflective acts. He writes:

> When I hear a certain sound, I conclude immediately, without reasoning, that a coach passes by. There are no premisses from which this conclusion is inferred by any rules of logic. It is the effect of a principle of our nature common to us with the brutes.[61]

The justifications here given equate reasoning with a conscious process of deduction. Mylne on the contrary regards reason as virtually omnipresent in mental life even when not slowed down by deliberation. He said:

> We are not conscious of reason in the greatest number of everyday actions yet reason [is not] unfelt. These operations have been so often performed, [and] are consequently so quickly done, that they pass [as] natural. Reason is not always slow. In general our reason proceeds with the velocity of [that] which

---

60. Pollock notes, GUL:MSGen1355/102/24/1/1821.
61. Reid, *Inquiry* in *Works*, vol. 1, chapter 4 section 1.

we call feeling. In any discourse the rational faculty makes both slow and hesitating steps. Then we know that we act from reason, but when there is no doubt, the velocity [with] which reason [decides] is very great.

In passing, this shows that an idea of unconscious mental activity later associated with Mylne's student William Hamilton[62] is already present in Mylne's lectures. In one of his common argumentative strategies, Mylne seeks to "illustrate" this analysis by reference to "examples." He says:

> Suppose a man to see his house on fire. He is [thrown] into violent agitations, but his reason is not quenched. If the fire be [of little strength] he will endeavour to extinguish it himself; if at another, he cries to his neighbours; if at another, he may not try to extinguish [it], but to rescue the valuable, or the most valuable [of his possessions], out of its way.—In all these different circumstances, he acts from the conceptions which he forms, which the circumstances oblige him to form. [. . .] In the most hurried case [then, his] action must be regarded as springing from reason.[63]

Turning to a moral example, Mylne instances a case where someone in authority denies that he acts out of rational considerations, but out of passion. Mylne said:

> Considerations drawn from reason and reflection also occur where we attribute our actions to passion and thus excuse ourselves by saying our passions are too strong. [. . .] The person who beats his servant or his dog has probably some mixture of cowardice in his action and is sensible that they can't oppose him. The rage will be less shown if it is an equal or superior that has offended him. If he knew that his servant could toss him over the window or that his dog had the strength and ferocity of a genuine bulldog, he would not act thus.[64]

In this case, the intellectual analysis in itself generates a case for moral reform. The observational humor and implied sympathy with the underdog illustrate the broadly Christian and Whig sensibility that are an attractive aspect of Mylne's lectures.

---

62. Hamilton, *Lectures on Metaphysics*, 2:L18.
63. Pollock notes, GUL:MSGen1355/102/ 23/1/1821.
64. 1799/1800 notes, GUL:MSMurray207/231, and Pollock notes, GUL:MSGen1355/102/24/1/1821.

Mylne disagreed with Reid on the role of touch in perception. In this, Mylne seeks to vindicate the rationality of belief in an external world in an exposition drawn largely from Condillac.[65] There is a contrast here between Reid's *Inquiry into the Human Mind on the Principles of Common Sense* (1764) and Condillac's *Traité* (1754). Condillac's central purpose is to derive externality from sensation. Reid appears not to have been familiar with the argument of Condillac's *Traité* when he composed the *Inquiry*.[66] The bulk of Reid's *Inquiry* is taken up with a detailed treatment of sight that deals at length with scientific theories and subsidiary topics such as squinting and double vision. His treatment of touch is relatively sketchy and makes no mention of scientific literature. In contrast, Condillac in the *Traité* treats sight briefly as one of the senses that do not give knowledge of externality, whilst the bulk of his book consists instead of a detailed account of the sensations of touch and an explanation of how the judgement of externality is derived therefrom. This sets the scene for Mylne's critique of Reid on touch.

Mylne takes issue with Reid's view that sensations of touch only "suggest" the conception of an external object which they in no way resemble. In a series of graded thought experiments, Reid asserts in the *Inquiry* that "we need not surely consult Aristotle or Locke, to know whether pain be like the point of a sword."[67] They are quite unlike, he thinks. Mylne's critique points us to the *Inquiry* (quoted by Mylne), where Reid writes of an imaginary person:

> We shall first consider his body fixed, immovably in one place and that he can only have the feelings of touch by the application of other bodies to it. Suppose him first to be pricked with a pin; this will, no doubt, give a smart sensation: he feels pain: but what can he infer from it? Nothing surely with regard to the existence or figure of a pin.[68]

---

65. We have noted that Mylne owned a three-volume 1777 edition of Condillac's *Oeuvres* (see Skirving catalogue III–47, at GUL) containing the *Essai sur l'Origine des Connaissances humaines; Traité des Systèmes; Traité des Sensations* and *Traité des Animaux*. Mylne also owned copies of Condillac's later works.

66. Reid says in the *Inquiry* that advocates of externality on the basis of the ideal system "seem for half a century past to decline the argument" with Berkeley (chapter 5, section 7), which is precisely what Condillac seeks to do. Paul Wood has recently identified from the professor's receipt books held at Glasgow that Reid borrowed Condillac from the library between 1765 and 1773 (see Wood, forthcoming). The significance of this for Reid's later work is beyond the scope of this essay.

67. Reid, *Inquiry* in *Works*, vol. 1, chapter 5, section 7.

68. Ibid., vol. 1, chapter 5 section 6, "Of extension."

The sensations we feel in other situations, Reid argues, if we attend to them only in isolation, likewise do not directly indicate externality.[69] Mylne discusses this and the following passages at length. He argues that Reid is too rash to conclude that no combination of sensation and reflection indicates external reality. Mylne says:

> After different modifications of the same case, the Doctor comes to the sweeping conclusion that philosophers have imposed upon themselves, and upon us, in pretending to deduce from sensation the first origin of our notion of external existences, of space, motion and extension and all the primary qualities of body. How then is this notion acquired? By common sense, says Dr Reid. This common sense can only signify innate ideas, or instinct. It overthrows all investigation. As for the argument, it leads to scepticism instead of curing it.

Mylne proceeds to offer his own account drawn from Condillac:

> If Reid had not concluded so soon, he would have been able to come to the idea of an external world. He is right in saying that those changes in sensation that make his imaginary being feel cannot give him the notion of solidity, extension &c, but he goes too far when he says that no touch will give any notion of the external world. We allow that the first prick of a pin would give no [room] for inference and that certain sensations of touch, however long acting, can give no idea of external matter, any more than any sensations from our other senses. Thus heat and cold, but to pass over these, we shall find that sensation alone gives us no information of external bodies. Memory and judgment are required before we can have perceptions. We need not expect that without the internal faculties to record the sensations of touch, we could have information of the qualities of matter.
>
> [. . .] Let us not be so unreasonable as, like Reid, to confine our being to one spot. Let our man have all his senses, all his powers of motion and all his [internal] faculties, though in a dormant state. In these circumstances it is very amusing to conjecture his feelings, vide Condillac and Buffon, who has written with more elegance but less accuracy.

This refers to Buffon's *Histoire Naturelle*, a work widely available in Glasgow.[70] Mylne goes on to argue that the conception of an external body is composed of three classes of idea derived from touch, firstly ideas of tan-

---

69. Ibid.
70. Buffon's *Histoire Naturelle*, 8. Des sens en général.

gibility arising from sensations of resistance; secondly of figure, which arises from "touch modified" and by "traversing the outlines of things," which would give the ideas of a continuous surface and of its interruption; and thirdly spatial externality, which is at issue. Mylne concludes: "It is gross scepticism to say that such a being cannot [form these] notions, as Dr Reid thinks. The two class[es] of [of tangible and figurate] qualities make up a great portion of our ideas of an external world. Now we only want to find out that they are external."

Following Condillac, Mylne seeks to derive the concept of externality from reflection on the sense of touch. To appreciate what is going on in the moral philosophy classroom here, we must note Condillac's insistence that his argument be thought through as an experiment, that we enter into the spirit of his statue, which in Mylne has become an "imaginary being." The central point at issue is the conclusions that can be drawn from the phenomenon of active touch. Mylne said:

> When we touch our arm with the hand, we have the same kind of feeling as if we were to touch any other substance unconnected with ourselves, but it is a double feeling, both in the arm which [is] touched and the hand which touched. And thus we soon learn to distinguish what belongs to ourselves and what is external, and then we learn to distinguish in idea parts of our body from ourselves, our exterior from our interior frame, and in process of time, mind from body, and thus we carry abstraction to the highest degree.[71]

In this way, Mylne concludes, we would at length learn that the surface of our body was continuous and thus would have the idea of an external world beyond it. The sense of touch, he concludes, is the source of our ideas of externality. In a final twist, he concedes that having the idea of an external world does not guarantee its truth. At this point, he calls in common sense and probability, but not at the expense of investigation. This analysis was developed further in French phenomenology,[72] but in Glasgow appears to have been forgotten until revived in the work of John Macmurray (1891–1976).[73]

---

71. Wicksteed notes, GUL:MSGen97/101, 4.
72. The history of this is given in Madinier's *Conscience et Mouvement*.
73. Macmurray, *The Self as Agent*, chapter 5.

Conclusions

The contrast between Mylne and Thomas Reid over the scope of reason is accompanied by political divergence over its scope in social reform. Reid supported a number of social reforms, including prison reform[74] and abolition of the African slave trade.[75] He had the typical profile of a churchman in support of charitable endeavors, but drew back from reform of political representation when the French revolution led to civil conflict in the early 1790s.[76] We have noted in contrast that Mylne's was the first generation of Scottish thinkers who embraced the French Revolutionary era and, in contrast to many figures of the Scottish establishment (including Reid) he retained a commitment to political as well as economic and social reform. Politically, this led him in later life to actively promote the liberal constitutional agenda that led to the 1832 Reform Act through the Glasgow "Fox Club," named after the leading Whig statesman Charles James Fox (1749–1806).[77]

Émile Bréhier argues that in the late-eighteenth-century arguments about knowledge had a social significance, derived from the role of knowledge in the legitimation of authority in church and state.[78] We may use this to interpret the possible social significance of Mylne's use of Condillac to respond to Reid. There were already political overtones in English dissenter Joseph Priestley's *Examination of Dr Reid's Inquiry into the Human Mind on the Principles of Common Sense* (1774). Mylne was not alone amongst liberal religious figures in Britain in drawing ideas from Condillac. The Reverend Samuel Parr, who visited Mylne,[79] advised a friend to read Condillac, where,

---

74. *Glasgow Journal* has a letter from Reid on the prison reformer John Howard (7/9/1786).

75. Reid joined with businessman David Dale, John Millar and others in publicly supporting the Abolition Bill (*GM* 1/3/1791).

76. Reid supported the French Revolution until 1791 (*Glasgow Mercury* 28/6–5/7/1791), but drew back from the cause of reform in his talk on the "Dangers of Political Innovation" to Glasgow Literary Society in 1794 (*GC* 18/12/1794), which was republished in 1796 and as an appendix to William Richardson's edition of Arthur's *Discourses on Theological and Literary Subjects* in 1803.

77. For example, see *Glasgow Chronicle*, 25/1/1823 for summary of one of Mylne's speeches to the Glasgow Fox Dinners. This group was also known as the "Friends of Civil and Religious Liberty." For sympathetic contemporary witnesses to Mylne's politics see also John Strang's *Glasgow and Its Clubs* (1856), 549; Fyfe, *Autobiography of John McAdam*, 6.

78. Emile Bréhier observes that: "It is difficult to attack prejudices, above all where it is a matter of social and economic prejudices, without also attacking persons or at least established powers." He refers to Hume and Condillac in this connection and specifies both civil and ecclesiastical power (*Histoire de la Philosophie*, 1055)

79. Field, *Memoirs of the Life*, 2:230. Field was a Unitarian and friend of Joseph

he noted "will be found all the principles of Locke, brought into a small compass, and presented in a clear and intelligible form."[80] Parr was known as "the Whig Johnson." He had taught Richard Sheridan, written on Charles James Fox[81] and his criticisms of William Godwin featured in the first *Edinburgh Review*. In philosophy though, he rated Dugald Stewart, whom he had also met in Scotland, lower than Locke or Hartley, concluding of his work, particularly the *Philosophical Essays*, that "by multiplying, almost without bounds, the number of original innate principles, this system throws back, instead of carrying forward, the science of mind."[82] In these respects, he reflects Mylne's own thinking. A rationally grounded program of social reform would naturally find support in a non-skeptical account of cognition combined with the advocacy of empirical inquiry into human nature. The cases of Mylne and Parr suggest that the reception of Condillac in Britain may have been the vehicle of such a Whig reform agenda at this time. Condillac represented a middle position between the atheism of many of the French revolutionaries and the conservatism of the established churches.

However, Mylne also opposed Reid on the question of free will and this is more readily seen as a version of the old conflict between the Calvinist and Arminian species of piety that had long divided the British Protestant churches. In addition, the common ground that Mylne and Reid shared in opposition to the skepticism of David Hume (particularly the Hume of the *Treatise*) is also a significant aspect of the debate in which they were engaged. In these respects, the Christian duty of care of souls may stand behind the analysis and advocacy of faith. There is an agreement that practical belief, although limited in its objects and uncertain in its nature, is neither inconceivable nor internally contradictory.

In general, the influence of Condillac strengthened the emphasis on reason that Mylne had already found in Godwin. The result was an original synthesis of ideas directed against Thomas Reid's invocation of common sense. Whilst Mylne's philosophy recommends itself as a contribution in mental philosophy, his debt to Condillac also bears the significance of a marshalling of the mental powers to interpret and guide the Whig reformist agenda out under the banner of reason. We shall see that this conclusion is borne out the more practical departments of Mylne's thought to which we turn in our chapters on Mylne's politics and political economy.

Priestley.
   80. Ibid., 2:237.
   81. "Samuel Parr" in *DNB*.
   82. Field, *Memoirs*, 2:235.

CHAPTER 9

The Active Powers and Moral Philosophy

HAVING CONSIDERED MYLNE'S INTELLECTUAL philosophy, we now turn to consider his account of the active powers and moral philosophy proper. In this chapter we will summarize the main lines of argument, particularly those behind Mylne's rejection of the "moral sense" theory, and give a flavor of his lecturing style and of the range and content of the surviving material in student notes.

The remainder of the course comprises discussions of the desires and passions, of which those inspired by sympathy form a separate class; analysis of the nature of conscience, by which virtue is discerned; and of the criteria by which it is distinguished from vice; an extended discussion of freedom and agency, to which we devote a separate chapter; three lectures on the diversity of humanity; and the final discussion of duties to God, neighbor and self. The discussion of duties to God includes treatments of the proofs of God's existence and attributes, the nature of Divine providence and the immortality of the soul.

The Passions

We have already discussed Mylne's view that the desires and passions are intentional states. This and the division of the active powers into mechanical, animal and rational he shares with Thomas Reid. Other writers who bulk large here are Dugald Stewart, whose treatment of the desires Mylne contends with, and Thomas Cogan, author of two recent *Treatises on the Passions*. He begins with instinct, appetite and habit, discussing the views of

David Hartley, Thomas Reid, Dugald Stewart, Erasmus Darwin, and Destutt Tracy and attempting to delineate the sphere of intentional action which he takes to be the proper object of moral philosophy. This discussion falls under the head of mechanical principles of action. Mylne speaks with a genial sagacity. The supposed instincts of credulity and veracity do "not arise from instinct [. . .] but from the order and arrangement of things."[1] He presents the sexual appetite as an appetite alongside hunger and thirst, as a gift of a benevolent Creator. Elsewhere he advocates marriage.

The next class of active principles discussed by Mylne is the passions. He orders the discussion by logical divisions into broad classes. He notes their influence on the body. The first division is into those resulting from the ideas of good and evil. Of those resulting from good, the good may be present, giving satisfaction; or absent, giving hope where attainable or despondency where unattainable. He particularly praises hope, disagreeing with those who represent unfulfilled desire as an evil. The good may be the result of our own agency or that of others. The former gives self-satisfaction (as in St. Paul's "I have fought the good fight!"[2]) and the latter gratitude. Turning to passions arising from ideas of evil, he again makes a number of memorable observations. Unlike joy, we often do not wish to share present evil. Passions of absent evil may lead to good, as when fear of poverty gives rise to industry. Shame can be felt even where we are not responsible for an evil when we follow the opinions of others. Where the agency of others is involved we feel anger or resentment, which have the purpose of protecting us from injury.

Mylne next turns to the theory of sympathy. This was developed in Adam Smith's *Theory of Moral Sentiments* which appeared in 1759 and went through many editions. Mylne owned a copy of Smith's *Philosophical Essays* (1795). He offers his own independent view of the role of sympathy. Mylne argues that: "Sympathy is not a mere contagion, but is to be determined by the conception."[3] For example: "if we see a man rejoicing in a trifling case, we might be happy to see him happy; but at the same time he may appear ridiculous for behaving in such a manner." Whilst Mylne finds a role for sympathy in an account of the mind, Thomas Mackenzie records his view that conscience cannot originate in sympathy:

> Smith says the conscience is founded on sympathy or fellow feeling. This theory cannot stand for a moment. With regard to sympathy, we feel with one, that one feels with another &c, thus

1. Pollock notes, GUL:MSGen1355/102/24.
2. 2 Tim 4:7.
3. Mackenzie notes, GUL:MSGen466/179.

it goes round, but where did this feeling begin? How did the first man feel? There is a want of logic in this reasoning also.[4]

Pollock reiterates this in his summary of Mylne on the standard of virtue: "When we sympathise with our neighbour, where does he get his moral feeling? We must go round in an endless search."[5] This is an elegant argument that founding morality on the sympathy of one person with another would lead to an infinite regress. Smith's argument is rather that we moderate our feelings to those of a dispassionate observer, but Mylne's criticism strikes powerfully at any reduction of conscience to sympathy.

The Sentimental School and Its Critics: Hutcheson, Hume, Smith, and Price

Before we turn to James Mylne's treatment of reason, conscience and virtue, we should pause to consider the moral sense school to which he was opposed. Mylne's first deep engagement with moral philosophy was through the writings of Francis Hutcheson (1694–1746), who was the subject of the course of Moral Philosophy given by John Cook at St. Andrews from 1773 on, which would have been on Mylne's curriculum in his third year.[6] Like Hutcheson's, Cook's lectures were delivered in English and he took Hutcheson's Latin *Synopsis Metaphysicae, Ontologiam et Pneumatologiam Complectens* (1742)[7] as text.[8] Mylne borrowed *Hibernicus's Letters* (1729) shortly after matriculating at St. Mary's College.[9] This contained Hutcheson's *Reflections upon Laughter* and *Remarks upon the Fable of the Bees*. In addition, Mylne owned a copy of Hutcheson's posthumous *System of Moral Philosophy* (1755),[10] with the virtual hagiography of Hutcheson by Glasgow Professor of Theology William Leechman.

4. Mackenzie notes, GUL:MSGen466/187.

5. Pollock notes, MSGen1355/102/52.

6. Moral philosophy was a third year class at St. Andrews (see Drummond and Bulloch, *The Scottish Church 1688–1843*, 190, referring to the 1820s). Mylne's third year of attendance (assuming one year's absence) was 1773, the first year of Cook's lectures.

7. There is a copy of the fifth edition (1762) of Hutcheson's *Synopsis Metaphysicae* in St. Andrews University Library. The page references cited by Cook correspond to this text.

8. There is a copy of the lectures in Cook's own hand in St. Andrews University Library (MS38074).

9. Entry for Mylne in St. Andrews University Library records: LY207/2.

10. See Skirving catalogue IV-33. We do not know when Mylne acquired this book: it should be noted that books published prior to 1800 were relatively more expensive

The weakness of Cook's attempted resolution of the problems of Hutcheson's morality of sentiment makes intelligible Mylne's rationalism. Hutcheson can be seen as standing in for the later Scottish common sense school in this respect: Thomas Reid had published only on the philosophy of perception in his *Inquiry into the Human Mind on the Principles of Common Sense* (1764), his other works not appearing until the 1780s; followed by James Beattie's *Essay on the Nature and Immutability of Truth* (1770); whilst the first volume of Dugald Stewart's earliest work, *Elements of the Philosophy of the Human Mind* (1792), did not appear until even later. Mylne's tendency to assimilate Reid's common sense to "instinct" is explained by a prior engagement with Hutcheson.

Hutcheson's philosophical analyses often shift between first principles and concrete description: for example, between the principle that beauty is the perception of unity in variety and the description of the unity that the light of the setting sun gives to a sunset. Cook gives a favorable impression of Hutcheson in these respects, whilst finding fault with his concept of the "moral sense." The purpose of Cook's course is reflected in Mylne's own lectures over twenty years later: "The intention of Moral Philosophy or Ethics is to establish rules for human conduct, and point out the various duties which it is incumbent on mankind to perform."[11]

Despite the intention to moralize, there is little exhortation and Cook's course consists for the most part of arguments in "Pneumatics." This consists of two parts, "the Deity" and "the human mind," these being the only kinds of spirits the existence of which is discoverable by human reason. As with Mylne, the later parts of the course address the immortality of the soul, the nature of freedom and the existence and attributes of God.

Cook considers, though, that Hutcheson's superiority over the "precepts of the ancients" lies in the rational structure of his morality.[12] However, this rationality proves problematic in the face of the objections of "the famous Dr

---

than thereafter, as new methods of paper production and printing machinery reduced prices. Hutcheson's works were not advertised in the Glasgow press prior to 1821 and John Witherspoon observes "their present tendency to oblivion" ("The Athenian Creed" in *Ecclesiastical Characteristics* (Edinburgh, 1763), 41, cited by Drummond and Bulloch, *The Scottish Church 1688–1843*, 105.

11. John Cook, Course of Moral Philosophy, StUL:MS38074, 1.

12. "The method in which Mr Hutcheson treats Ethics is certainly better than that of any who went before him. He has joined Ethics to Pneumatics and deduced the rules of human conduct from the constitution of the human mind. [. . .] The superior excellence of this method of treating Moral Philosophy is obvious, because before we discover the nature of any being we cannot establish rules for the direction of its conduct" (Cook, Course, StUL:MS38074, 2).

Berkeley" and "the celebrated Mr Hume."[13] Cook briefly rehearses Berkeley and Hume's skepticism on the "primary qualities" of matter and the idea of self. Cook replies that we are nevertheless "led by the constitution of our nature" to believe both in matter and mind. He argues that:

> The error of these philosophers arose from this: They were of opinion that they ought not to believe anything for which they could not give a satisfactory reason. [...] But it is to be observed, that we believe many things of which we cannot give a satisfactory account and which we cannot prove by reasoning. The use of reasoning, you will observe, is to prove things that are not in themselves self-evident, by shewing their connection with others, till we come to some self-evident truths which are in their nature intuitive.[14]

Cook names the axioms of mathematics and the testimony of the senses as examples of intuitive truths. When Cook turns to Hutcheson's theory of the "moral sense" the difficulty of Hutcheson's position in identifying the first principles of morals begin to confront him.[15] This first occurs when Hutcheson classifies sympathy as a reflex sense "by which we feel pleasure at the prosperity and pain at the adversity of another, when no controversy, hatred, enmity or detestation [...] hinders us."[16] Cook argues that the feeling of sympathy is not a "distinct sensation as that of music, color, smell." Rather he identifies it as involving an intellectual judgement:

> Our rejoicing at another's prosperity and grieving at his adversity are the natural consequence of the principle of benevolence. If we did not previously love mankind, we would feel neither pleasure nor pain at their prosperity or adversity.[17]

---

13. John Cook, Course of Moral Philosophy, StUL:MS38074, 12. The original is not numbered after page 8.

14. John Cook, Course of Moral Philosophy StUL:MS38074, 13.

15. It is to Cook's credit as a teacher that he does not hide his difficulty from his students, but goes beyond teaching the terms and arguments of a system to illustrating by means of Hutcheson the creative task of comparing any received system judiciously with experience.

16. John Cook, Course of Moral Philosophy StUL:MS38074, 23, quoting, or rather translating, Hutcheson, who confusingly calls sympathy "*sensus communis*" and "*affectum contagio.*"

17. John Cook, Course of Moral Philosophy StUL:MS38074, 23. Cook deals similarly with our "love of praise or honour," which he argues against Hutcheson is "resolvable into other principles of which it is the consequence" (MS 38074, 25). Similar arguments appear in Mylne's critique of Stewart's "active principles."

However, this contrasts with Cook's account of the "moral sense" which discerns what is fitting and proper in action,[18] for in dealing with this he supports Hutcheson's classification of it under sensation. The moral sense, he says, "is very justly ascribed to a particular sense, as it is analogous to the sensation we feel in contemplating other beautiful objects. This feeling is called a sense, because it is instinctive and operates previous to all reasoning."[19] However, Cook finds that the analogy can only be pushed so far:

> But there is one respect in which it differs from our other sensations. The objects of the moral sense, when examined by reason, appear in their own nature excellent or base, independent of our constitution. [. . .] we cannot help thinking these virtues, justice, goodness, fortitude, truth to be really excellent, independent of our opinions or of the constitution of our nature.[20]

In this respect, he judges, there is a difference with, say, music, where our taste is readily enough conceded to be subjective and we may agree to differ. In morals on the other hand, we tend to stand our ground. Cook does not pursue the subject further, but neither does he leave his hearer with the feeling the topic has been exhausted. Over a range of topics then, from perception to the "moral sense," John Cook's course of moral philosophy raised questions of the scope open to human reason in revising, rethinking, or analyzing the conclusions we find most immediately appealing on the content of our experience.

There are elements of moral sense theory present in Adam Smith's *Theory of Moral Sentiments* (1759), which Mylne cites for its treatment of sympathy. Smith judged it "altogether absurd and unintelligible to suppose that the first perceptions of right and wrong can be derived from reason." He justified this by arguing that only the senses make things agreeable or disagreeable "for their own sakes." Smith wrote, "Pleasure and pain are the great objects of desire and aversion, but these are distinguished, not by reason, but by immediate sense and feeling."[21] Mylne takes issue with this too, but chooses Hume, to whom he devotes a separate lecture for his antagonist.

Mylne was not the first to attribute morality to reason. One early response to Hutcheson's moral sense theory was Richard Price's *Review of the Principal Questions of Morals* (1759) which appeared in the same year as Smith's book. Mylne mentions Price in his 1800 lectures in connection with

---

18. Hutcheson's *"sensus decori et honesti."*
19. John Cook, Course of Moral Philosophy StUL:MS38074, 23–24.
20. John Cook, Course of Moral Philosophy StUL:MS38074, 24.
21. Smith, *Theory of Moral Sentiments*, 320.

conscience.[22] The notes state that Dr. Price, "shews that the understanding often forms simple ideas (incapable of definition and analysis); thus the idea of proportion. Now the notion of right and wrong he considers a simple idea."[23]

Whilst Price gives pride of place to reason over sense in his view of conscience, he is intuitionist in relation to its first principles and this distances his view from that of Mylne. In the early lectures, Mylne opposes Price and Hume. However, Price's intuitionist conception of reason is greatly at odds with that of Mylne and so one must be guarded in alleging Price as a source of Mylne's views. In later lectures Price's name appears only in connection with free will. Mylne's rationalism has affinities with David Hartley and Joseph Priestley, with Joseph Butler's account of virtue as a state where "particular passions" are subject to the control of reason and Thomas Reid's concern for "our good upon the whole." However, Mylne claims credit for his own views rather than endorsing the views of others.

Mylne on Conscience

The particular way in which Mylne identifies reason with conscience as the arbiter of morality, i.e., his rejection of the moral sense theory of Hutcheson, the related sentimentalism of Hume and Smith and the intuitionism of Price, is distinctive.

Almost as soon as Mylne moves from metaphysics to consider morality, he asserts his ethical rationalism. We have seen that his lectures on the active principles are structured to show that instincts, passions, desires, etc are subordinate to and the result of reason. In Mylne's lectures on the moral faculty ("conscience"), he discusses the likening of conscience to an instinct, to a moral sense and to reason. He soon dismisses the comparison with instinct. Hutcheson is then identified by name as the theorist of the moral sense. Robert Pollok summarizes Mylne's views:

> Mr Hutcheson gives the name of sense to many of the judgements of the mind—as perception, a sense of the sublime, etc. Virtue he thought we perceived with similar emotions as the sublime, etc so he gave the name of sense to the moral [discernment].[24]

---

22. 1799/1800 notes, GUL:MSMurray 207/263.
23. 1799/1800 notes, GUL:MS Murray207/264.
24. Pollock notes, GUL:MSGen1355/102/51.

Thomas Mackenzie also identifies Hutcheson as the object of criticism in this section. Mylne dismisses two justifications for supposing a moral sense: the speed of moral evaluation is irrelevant and the "great argument" from universal agreement is flawed, for there are moral disagreements. Mylne then applies his general distinction of sensation from judgement. Mackenzie records the argument:

> What is sense? It does not judge: it only furnishes material for judgement &c. The senses only give sensations. If therefore we had moral senses, they could never judge of anything. But it may be said that we have need of these senses to furnish materials for moral judgement. No, we have experience instead of these. These sensibilities of moral feeling arise from our intellects.

It can be seen that Mylne is here applying his own distinction of sensation and judgement against Hutcheson, but drawing on and developing a tradition of argument that goes back to his own undergraduate experience at St. Andrews.

In the following lecture, Mylne opposes the sentimental view of conscience also in several critical remarks directed at David Hume:

> Mr Hume says that everything is virtuous which excites the approbation of others. This power would be [a rather] wandering standard of virtue. What was a virtuous action at one time would be vicious or indifferent at another.[25]

This view is found in both Hume's *Treatise* and *Enquiries*.[26] Mylne notes that Hume sees reason as assisting the "moral sense." In the *Enquiry concerning the Principles of Morals* (1751), Hume supposes that reason and sentiment concur, but gives the last word to sentiment,[27] though he concedes that reason is more prominent in determining utility. Reason is instrumental in that it relates means to ends, but it does not determine the end aimed at. Mylne wishes to extend its role in moral judgement. According to Mackenzie, he said on judgements of first principle: "Will reason do nothing here? Why do we believe an axiom, if the truth of it is not perceived? Therefore reason is [present] in all cases."[28] The 1800 notes give another argument based on Hume's allowing reason a role in correcting moral judgements: "He allows that the erroneous sentiment arises from false views. The just

---

25. Pollock notes, MSGen1355/102/53; c.f. Hume, *Enquiry*, 289.
26. Hume *Enquiry*, chapter 1 and App. 1; Hume, *Treatise of Human Nature*, book 3, part 1.1–2.
27. Hume, *Enquiry*, 172–73.
28. Mackenzie notes, GUL:MSGen466/190.

sentiment must also surely arise from judgment."²⁹ The Wicksteed notes from 1830 contain considerable reference to Hume, whose works were republished in 1826. Wicksteed records another version of the argument:

> Hume says that the ultimate ends of human actions recommend themselves only by sentiment, independent of reason. For instance, if you ask a man why he uses exercise, he will tell you, to procure his health; but why procure his health? To avoid pain he will answer—but why does he hate pain? He can't give any reason—it is a first principle, it is sentiment, from whose decision at first, judgement afterwards forms its conclusions. But "that pain is unpleasant" is an axiom, and a judgement is employed in the very expression of it.

Mylne returns to the theme in the following lecture, where he deploys his distinction of bodily emotion from the mental states from which it arises:

> Mr Hume confounds sentiment with the emotion, but he should remember before the emotion is raised, the judgement must have roused the conception which gave birth to the emotion. He calls sentiment a first principle—good—but is that not judgement? Is it not by judgement that we see that a part is less than the whole? We do not perceive that by instinct. Neither do we see the sentiment or first principle that pain is hateful by instinct, but by judgement or reason.³⁰

We may relate this to Mylne's adoption of Condillac's view that all sensations can be compared for pleasure and pain and his own view that such comparison is the work of a separate mental faculty of judgement. However, Hume acknowledges the role of reason in utility and Mylne's view is supported by his view that utility is the principal criterion of virtue.

The Standard of Virtue

Following the discussion of "conscience," or the principle of approbation, Mylne turns to discuss the content of morality or, as he puts it, the nature of virtue. This discussion corresponds to a section of Adam Smith's *Theory of Moral Sentiments* on the "different accounts which have been given of the nature of virtue."³¹ Mylne discusses five accounts in turn. What is virtuous may be determined by: benevolence, as Hutcheson maintained; propriety,

29. 1799/1800 notes, GUL:MSMurray207/265.
30. Wicksteed notes, GUL:MSGen97/LVII&LVIII.
31. Smith, *Theory of Moral Sentiments*, 7.2.

a view he attributes to the Stoics and Samuel Clarke; the happiness of the agent, as Epicurus supposed; sympathy; conformity to Divine law, which was the view of Warburton; or by a tendency to the general happiness, or utility. This last view is the one Mylne argues for.

Against the identification of virtue with benevolence, he argues that it is not so much wrong, particularly as regards the "amiable virtues," as incomplete. For example, piety is not reducible to benevolence in this way. Richard Price also argues against Hutcheson that benevolence is not the whole of virtue, for it excludes justice, and this is a common position amongst Calvinists.

Secondly, in addressing propriety, he again does not altogether disagree with it as an interpretation, but he argues that the concept of virtue is accessible to those who have no views as to the intrinsic fitness of things. He is thus reluctant to identify the two concepts.

Mylne next considers the view that the happiness of the agent is the standard of virtue. It is true that virtuous conduct produces happiness, but an agent who acts on this principle we admire for his wisdom and steadiness rather than his virtue. Here he makes a muted criticism of Epicurean philosophy, observing that, as a materialist, Epicurus held that intellectual pleasures were a species of sensual pleasure:

> Epicurus therefore held pleasure to be the highest good, and afterwards this doctrine becoming misrepresented was commonly supposed to maintain sensual pleasure to be the greatest good. But Epicurus did not mean it to be so. The pleasures which he recommended as the highest were those of innocence, wisdom, temperance; and his own life and that of many of his followers were in accordance with these precepts. Afterwards dissolute men adopted his system and corrupted it. And this was the grand objection to it, that by not sufficiently distinguishing our highest pleasures of mind from those of mere sense, it had a bad tendency.[32]

This is probably seepage of content from the class reading of Cicero, indicating that Mylne drew his views from a survey of the whole history of philosophy. The conditional preference for Epicurus over the Stoics contrasts with Joseph Butler's moral theory, which Ralph Wardlaw characterized as Stoicism refracted through the medium of Christianity.[33] The treatment of sympathy reprises the arguments of the section on the sympathetic passions.

---

32 Wicksteed notes, MS Gen97/102/23–24.
33. Wardlaw, *Christian Ethics*.

Next, he engages at some length with the view that virtue is conformity with Divine Law as found in Scripture, "against which it would be highly improper to contend with any degree of eagerness."[34] This was a view defended by Ralph Wardlaw in Glasgow. Mylne observes that there is something in virtue that leads us to think that it is the will of God; and those who do not have Revelation (China) still have the idea of virtue. He observes that: "The vigorous exercise of our moral faculty is necessary in order to ascertain what is the will of God."[35] Hence he is unwilling to locate the standard of virtue in the Bible alone.

Finally, Mylne advocates his own view that a tendency to general happiness ("utility") is a criterion of morality accessible to natural reason and applicable to experience, though accompanied by other considerations such as propriety, piety, and convention. He offers four arguments, noting that he is here arguing against Cicero for whom virtue makes utility rather than the other way around. He summarizes:

> [First] it is a test which is applicable to all moral actions, dispositions, affections, etc, and this, we have found, cannot be said of all the doctrines on this subject. Second, its application is easy and obvious. Third, this test furnishes us at once very readily with the judgements which we pronounce and enables us to pronounce between the competing merit of actions. Fourth, this helps us to explain those lively emotions with which we contemplate virtue or vice, a thing which is not very easy with other tests.[36]

The first argument counts against the identification of virtue with the happiness of the agent, which does not readily apply to cases of virtuous self-sacrifice. He also identifies Adam Smith as an important opponent of this theory, adding that his discussion has "an air of ridicule unworthy of a man searching after truth."[37] To the argument that a chest of drawers has utility, he replies that instruments of torture have a fitness for their purpose.

The Account of Duties: "Moral Philosophy Proper"

We now turn briefly to what Mylne calls "moral philosophy proper," i.e., his tripartite division of human duties into those to God, neighbor and

---

34. Wicksteed notes, GUL:MSGen97/102/lecture59.
35. Wicksteed notes, GUL:MSGen97/102/lecture60.
36. Ibid.
37. Wicksteed notes, GUL:MSGen97/102/lecture63.

ourselves that constitute a Godly, righteous, and sober life. When he turns to concrete moral philosophy, we find another instance of theological context, as Mylne follows Reid, Beattie, and Arthur in adopting his exposition of duty from the Bible. Pollok notes:

> The ancient division of moral duty into [fortitude], prudence, temperance, justice, is not a good one. The one Mr Mylne adopts is from the Bible—To live soberly, righteously, and Godly in the world i.e. our duty to God, to our fellow men, and to ourselves.[38]

This division is found in Gershom Carmichael and in this respect, Mylne is returning to a Glasgow tradition, updated by reference to Samuel Clarke's treatment of the arguments for God's existence. The tripartite division is also found in *The Whole Duty of Man* (1657) by English clergyman Richard Allestree, over which David Hume expressed a preference for Cicero's *Offices*,[39] and mentioned it again to Boswell on his deathbed to justify his rejection of Christianity, noting its lengthy enumeration of "duties." Its origin though, is St. Paul.[40]

Mylne is at one with his Congregationalist opponent Ralph Wardlaw in placing piety first amongst the virtues. However, he relies more than Wardlaw on natural religion and in particular draws his account of the proofs of God's existence directly from Samuel Clarke. Interestingly, Epicurus also placed duty to God high in his ethics.[41] This diverges from the humanist division between duties to self and others found in Adam Smith's *Theory of Moral Sentiments*. Mylne begins with a discussion of Samuel Clarke's proofs of God's existence, for our first duty to God is to have a rational belief in his existence. There follows a discussion of the argument from design and David Hume's criticisms of it. Mylne objects to the idea that crystallization and vegetation are unintelligent causes of order on the ground that they are not causes at all, but abstract terms. He turns to the Divine attributes or benevolence and omniscience. In a typical manifestation of his intellectualism, he relates our ideas of the Divine attributes to our affections towards God:

> If our notions of Deity be proper, so will our affections towards him. [...] Reverence and awe to God unsoftened by love would speedily become slavish terror; and love to God without

---

38. Pollock notes, GUL:MSGen1355/103, 4.

39. Hume, *Enquiries*, 319 n.; Greig, *Letters of David Hume*, vol. 1, letter of Hume to Hutcheson 17/9/1739.

40. Titus 2.

41. Diogenes Laertius, *Lives of the Philosophers*, book 10, citing Epicurus, *Letter to Menoeceus*.

reverence [...] would soon degenerate into a no less fatal rapturous and familiar absurdity.[42]

There follows a discussion of providence, which recalls the arguments on free will which we discuss in the next chapter. The treatment of duties towards God concludes with a discussion of immortality in which Mylne prefers Joseph Butler's endorsement of the doctrine to the materialism of Joseph Priestley.

Following the treatment of piety, Mylne turns to "duty to our neighbour," which he divides under the heads of duties of justice and benevolence. Justice is to refrain from harming our neighbor, benevolence is to do all possible good, but the distinction is not absolute. Under justice, Mylne comprehends uprightness (or integrity), candor and veracity. In the treatment of justice, he pauses to criticize Hume's account of justice as an "artificial virtue." There are indeed positive laws, but they are underpinned by a prior sense of integrity which may be developed by the progress of society. Such integrity is a "master within our heart" that is "much better for guiding our conduct than laws."[43] Justice must be connected to benevolence before it renders us virtuous.

He speaks warmly of candor, particularly in literary judgements and evaluations of character. This involves "a willingness to acknowledge the truth from whatever quarter it comes and however contrary it may be to our preconceived opinions."[44] Veracity is the final virtue of justice. Here Mylne discusses the duty to tell the truth and the obligation to honor promises. This duty is high, but at least in theory may be overturned by considerations of utility, when for example concealing bad news would prevent a sick person losing courage and dying. The obligation to honor promises applies not only to formal promises: "A word, a look, silence, may often bind us."[45] These are cases of voluntary honesty. He extends veracity to our duty to avoid involuntary error, which leads to a duty to pursue inquiries into truth to avoid ignorance. This he notes is particularly incumbent on educators.

Under benevolence, he includes humanity; gentleness or urbanity; patriotism; and philanthropy. Humanity he describes as consideration or sympathy for the distressed that goes beyond legal requirements. Gentleness is indispensable to society: "A man may never need my assistance, but every day he may be hurt or pleased by my rudeness or civility."[46] Love of society

---

42. Pollock notes, GUL:MSGen1355/103, 10–11.
43. Pollock notes, GUL:MSGen1355/103/22.
44. Pollock notes, GUL:MSGen1355/103/23.
45. Pollock notes, GUL:MSGen1355/103/25–26.
46. Pollock notes, GUL:MSGen1355/103/28.

is a virtue, according to Mylne, but must be subordinated to the interests of mankind. This leads on to a discussion of philanthropy, or universal benevolence. Mylne asserts its existence: "although some put it at nought, let them not say that others know it not."[47] He associates philanthropy with Christianity rather than the local patriotism of Greece or the military glory sought by Rome. He hopes that in his own age commerce and scholarship may extend the common interests of nations. What we find here again is a combination of the public virtues of the pagan philosophers of Greece and Rome with a more inward Christian sensibility. Amongst the pagan moralists, Mylne's preference for Epicurus over the Stoics is distinctive.

Finally Mylne briefly addresses "duties to ourselves," which include the classical virtues of prudence, temperance and fortitude. He particularly praises an active life as a means to happiness. We should "enter into social intercourse and attempt to remedy rather than lament the evils of life,"[48] and he again warns against a gloomy spirit that draws from religious skepticism. He also said:

> Nothing is said of certain external circumstances: on birth, rank, affluence, splendour, because these are less in our power and bring less happiness than is generally supposed, and because virtue etc can bring more comfort. [. . .] In this view we are apt to coincide with the [Stoics] that external things are of little consequence, that a virtuous man struggling with adversity is an object of envy even to the gods.[49]

In this last remark we again find that Mylne is not contributing novelties, but operating as a teacher of established wisdom.

Conclusions

James Mylne's moral thought contains elements of natural law tradition as found in his predecessor Gershom Carmichael and in popular sermons and moralizing, together with ethical rationalism and contemporary utilitarian principles as found in both Hutcheson and the "philosophical radicals." In his treatment of the passions he speaks almost as a naturalist, identifying the individual and social functions of our appetites and passions and occasionally dispensing moral advice to his audience. In his account of our duties, he integrates piety with a neighborly approach to social relations and

---

47. Pollock notes, GUL:MSGen1355/103/29.
48. 1799/1800 notes, GUL:MSMurray207, 471–72.
49. 1799/1800 notes, GUL:MSMurray207, 474.

personal ambition. These embody the inherited Christian and natural law components of his thought.

Alongside these traditional expressions of age-old moral wisdom, Mylne's approach to moral philosophy made room for rationalism in his view of conscience and utilitarian conclusions in his treatment of the criterion of virtue. Whilst the Calvinist minister William Thom opposed Hutcheson's version of philosophy on biblical grounds,[50] Mylne did so from the standpoint of the rationalist strand of Calvinism.

Mylne's preferences for reason and utility as moral touchstones facilitated arguments for social reform such as those of the Whigs and the "philosophical radicals." Utilitarian considerations would also tend to favor commercial development, for utility is a component of the economic concept of value that Mylne derived from Pufendorf and Hutcheson.

One of the most distinctive themes of Mylne's philosophy is that of free will in which he supports the traditional Calvinism of the Church of Scotland in opposition to the Arminianism of Thomas Reid. Before investigating the social implications of his thought, we now turn to examine the intellectual background of the free will debate in Scottish theology.

50. Thom, *Works*.

CHAPTER 10

Faith, Belief, and Freedom

MYLNE'S VIEW OF THE determinations of will by intellect contrasts with Reid's view of freedom. In this chapter I will elucidate the significance of Mylne's distinctive view that "judgement follows sensation irresistibly, and we cannot keep from judging and comparing one object with another,"[1] by relating it to his view of religious faith. This view is corroborated by the earliest notes, which warn about the logicians' definition of judgement as:

> a comparison between two objects, which is apt to make us believe it is voluntary and that the mind may turn to either side. From this idea much false reasoning has arisen.[2]

This concept is also found in Hume.[3] In addition to Mackenzie cited above, Pollok also records Mylne's view that "no volition enters" into judgement and his warning that:

> want of attention to this or something different from this has caused much error in the philosophy of the moral and intellectual world.[4]

This indicates that the question has significance ("much error") for Mylne. The same point emerges in his treatments of voluntary attention and free will. I shall relate these views to the theory of the intellectual nature of faith, or belief inherited from Sandemanianism by William Godwin. I argue

1. Mackenzie notes, GUL:MS Gen466, 54.
2. 1799/1800 notes, GUL:MSMurray207, 135.
3. "All kinds of reasoning consist in nothing but a *comparison*" (Hume's *Treatise*, 1.3.2).
4. Pollock notes, GUL:MS Gen1355, Lecture 17, 42.

that Mylne's divergence from Reid probably arose also from an engagement with contemporary theological debates and that Mylne's view is thus Sandemanian in this respect.

The contrast is with the defense of free will by Thomas Reid that supports an Arminian rather than Calvinist theology. In what follows, I will interpret Mylne's thought as part of a larger movement of ideas on the significance of belief, or faith. In this, the Glasite or Sandemanian movement played a central role and we have seen that the Reverend James Adams in Kinnaird had taken up his pen against it. The Scottish Free Church minister R. S. Candlish said of Mylne's era that "the intellectual view of faith was, indeed, prevalent at that time and earlier in Scotland" and refers to "the Sandemanians" as prominent examples of this.[5] By way of comparison, the recent historian of the movement John Howard Smith observes of America that "what Sandemanianism lacked in numbers of adherents it compensated for in intellectual heft and theological impact."[6] Smith also identifies the Sandemanian movement as part of the intellectual context of Jonathan Edwards, who was a central figure in Mylne's treatment of free will. Sandeman's main ideas were known to Mylne himself through his reading of William Godwin around 1796, the year before he first delivered his course of moral philosophy. However, having himself studied theology, it is likely that he was familiar with the views of the Glasite church and those under its influence directly long before that.

Belief and Faith

Mylne distinguishes belief from an act of will. Indeed, this concept is one of a few guiding threads that run through the entire lecture series, supported at each stage by argument and illustrations. Thus at the culmination, we find the principle that "as we believe we will feel" playing a central role in Mylne's lectures on Living to God.[7] In these culminating lectures he clearly develops the principle with regard to religion, arguing that "it is natural to believe a perceived truth, indeed we cannot disbelieve it if we would: then it is thus with regard to our affections of piety."[8] The theological context thus explains

---

5. R. S. Candlish, "Thomas Erskine of Linlathen" in *British and Foreign Evangelical Review* (1873), 114–15, cited by Horrocks, *Laws of the Spiritual Order*. Horrocks does not observe that the two theologians he cites in support of this view, Ralph Wardlaw and Thomas Chalmers, were both close to Mylne.

6. Smith, *The Perfect Rule*, 3.

7. Mackenzie notes, GUL:MS Gen466, 256

8. Mackenzie notes, GUL:MS Gen466, 280.

at least in part the earlier direction of argument in the intellectual philosophy, which is anything but a series of discrete or disconnected discussions in a "common sense" or "ordinary language" style, but rather the first steps in a chain of constructive argument whose significance emerges fully in his lectures on God, freedom, necessity, and providence.

This theory of belief illuminates a tension within British Calvinism. The *Westminster Confession* states that the faith of believers "does not originate with themselves but is the gift of God."[9] However, the *Longer Catechism* states that the believer "not only assents to the truth of the promise of the Gospel, but receives and rests on Christ and his righteousness held forth in the Gospel."[10] Robert Sandeman's central objection is to the "receiving" and "resting" in the latter formulation being taken as meritorious acts that obligate God to work salvation through his justice. This theological context explains the elision of the distinction of conception and belief in Mylne's lectures. No importance attaches to the distinction between conceiving and believing something to be the case for Sandeman, who denies the existence of a meritorious act of belief as an aspect of conversion. For Mylne, action distinguishes belief from imagination.

It is thus not arbitrary in conceptual terms to relate Mylne's thought to these profound debates on the nature of religious belief that continued in the Scottish churches throughout his lifetime. Mylne's system can be seen as a healing of the theological division that had opened up between the Sandemanians on the one hand and orthodox Calvinists and English Baptists on the other between preaching aimed at the "head" and that aimed at the "heart": the division of head and heart is not absolute. Thus the theological context of belief serves to explain in some measure the distinctive intellectualist bias of Mylne's philosophy. For this reason, I proceed to sketch the history of the debate both in Scotland and in works known to Mylne.

The Marrow Controversy and the Sandemanian Account of Belief

Firstly, Sandemanian theology (named after the leading Glasite theologian) developed by the Glasite church, centered in Perth and Dundee, offers a perspective on Mylne's own intellectualism. Given that he grew up in the cradle of the Glasite movement and his background as a theologically

---

9. *Westminster Confession*, 11.1.
10. *Longer Catechism*, para 77; cf *Shorter Catechism*, 86.

literate son of the manse, it is unsurprising to find the core of the Glasite theology present in Mylne's philosophy.[11]

As we have seen, the Glasite church was formed in the aftermath of the Marrow controversy in Scotland that arose from republication of Edward Fisher's *The Marrow of Modern Divinity* (1645) in Scotland. Dating from the year before the *Westminster Confession*, the book is in the form of a dialogue and the sweet temper of the debate lends it great charm. Even its opponent James Adams concedes that there is "something like a strain of seriousness and devotion that runs through the whole book."[12] The *Marrow* draws on Luther's *Commentary on Galatians* and its Lutheran strain of piety led to a conflict between its advocates (who became known as the "Marrow-men") and the Calvinist creed dominant in Scotland.

The connection with Mylnean philosophy originates in the doctrine of "justification by faith" where "faith" is equated to "belief."[13] Fisher argues that the "natural bent" of the human mind in working its own salvation is to rely on the Covenant of Works, which he calls *legalism* and repudiates as unattainable in favor of the Covenant of Grace that we enter into on embracing the Christian faith. He acknowledges that this leads to the charge of *antinomianism* (a neglect of duty under the Law). The argument of the *Marrow* thus requires Fisher to reestablish a connection between Faith (belief) and Works. Thus he argues that "believing includes all other duties in it, and they spring all from it" citing Luther's analogy that "The tree must first be, then the fruit [. . .] So faith first maketh the person, which afterwards brings forth works."[14] Fisher not only satirizes the antinomian Londoner in his dialogue, but seeks to persuade him by means of an analysis of belief. This finds strong expression in the concluding peroration of the book on the Soul's Rest:

> According to the measure of your faith, will be your willing obedience to God. [. . .] if the everlasting love of God in Jesus Christ be truly made known to your hearts, according to the measure thereof, you shall have no need to frame and force yourself to love and good works, for your souls will ever stand bound to

---

11. It is reasonable to suppose influence rather than an independent rediscovery by Mylne of ideas already widely canvassed in his religious and educational milieu, though this remains a hypothesis.

12. Adams, *Snake in the Grass*, iv.

13. In Luther's German both concepts are represented by "Glaube" and Luther's *Commentary on Galatians,* which stresses faith as against works, was a key influence, particularly though the *Marrow*.

14. Fisher, *Marrow of Modern Divinity*, 1.3.8.

love God, and to keep his commandments, and it will be your meat and drink to do his will.[15]

The Established Church rejected the arguments of the "Marrowmen" who wished to revive Fisher's book, though only after considerable debate. One key figure in this was the minister of the parish where Mylne grew up, the Reverend James Adams.

James Adams and John Glas

James Mylne Senior's predecessor at Kinnaird was the Reverend James Adams, a noted controversialist who defended his orthodox Presbyterian views in a series of five pamphlets over a period of twelve years between 1719 and 1731. These pamphlets provide a picture of the way in which the arguments of the Calvinist canon of the *Westminster Confession of Faith, Longer and Shorter Catechisms* and pastoral *Directory* was marshaled against the Lutheranism of the Marrowmen. They led him into an engagement with reverend John Glas (1695-1773), founder of what came to be known as the "Glasite church," though the Glasites preferred to call themselves simply Christians.

Adams' first pamphlet, *The Snake in the Grass* (1719), was directed explicitly against the *Marrow*. The danger that puts "the snake in the grass" is when it is argued that the preacher should say that sins are forgiven before lives are reformed.[16] For this reason, he raises the charge of antinomianism that Fisher was concerned to reject, saying "I suspect mightily that this Gentleman and his followers use an unacceptable liberty in decrying the law, under the notion of a Covenant of Works, that they may get fairly rid of it in all other senses."[17] He also rejects the idea that the Gospel is an unconditional promise of life and salvation to believers. Instead, he affirms with Scripture witness that the Gospel is not without sanctions. Fisher had not denied this, but only that the sanctions include damnation of those who have once believed. His most powerful arguments however, do not tell against Fisher's concept of belief, though he denies that persuasion is the essence of faith and describes this as "the most dangerous Part of the Book."[18] In his next pamphlet, *The Cromwellian Ghost Conjur'd* (1720) Adams expresses

---

15. Ibid., 1.4.3.
16. Adams, *Snake in the Grass*, 39.
17. Ibid., 29.
18. Ibid., 32.

the point that the Gospel is not without sanctions even against believers in terms of Christ's kingly authority:

> I wonder what kind of a King this man and his followers would make Christ to be? Or, what Kind of a Government they would assign to him in the World, if there be no Sanction to his Precepts, and Obedience and Disobedience an Indifferent Thing as to Happiness and Misery?[19]

In this sense, Adams prefers the Biblical language of the Law where the *Marrow* draws its image of authority instead from the family, in which God is father and Christ the bridegroom of his Church. In *Marrow-Chicaning Display'd* (1726), he criticizes Ebenezer Erskine's notion of "assurance" on grounds that echo his criticism of the thin notion of faith found in the *Marrow*.

The implications of the thin Glasite concept of belief for Church government appear most fully in John Glas' *Testament of the King of Martyrs* (1729). A version of the Independent scheme of Church government that rejects any authority above the congregation and rejects State interference, written by one of Glas' associates, was already cited by Adams in *The Independent Ghost Conjur'd* (1728), arguing that "our Saviour declared that his Kingdom was not of this World, and consequently that the Interest thereof cannot be promoted by the Rewards and Punishments of this World."[20] The respondent attempts to make this inference good by reference to the nature of intellectual persuasion as well as by appeal to the refusal of dominion by Christ to the Apostles. "Religion," he argues "is the fear of God, it can't be the effect of Power, which is the fear of Man." Again, force "cannot inform, much less convince the Understanding, which is the way Religion must enter the Soul."[21] This view is reflected in the history of the early church.[22] Glas himself had met Adams but did not adopt the views of the respondent, instead publishing his own counter-queries.[23]

We see then, that the Glasite church was founded by those schooled in the *Marrow* concept of belief. The argument was taken forward some years later by the leading Glasite theologian and proselytizer, Robert Sandeman.

---

19. Adams, *Cromwellian Ghost*, 77.

20. Adams, *Independent Ghost*, 2.

21. Ibid., 3.

22. For example Contantine's refusal to enact penal statutes against his pagan subjects: see Veyne, *Quand notre Monde*, 169, citing Eusebius, *Life of Constantine* 2.60.1.

23. Glass, *A Narrative*, 82–83.

Robert Sandeman

Robert Sandeman (1718-71) studied at Edinburgh University from 1734-36, a few years after David Hume.[24] He was impressed by Glas during the latter's brief stay in Perth and married into his family, but proved himself a more forceful and proselytizing character. Sandeman developed his intellectualist theory of "justifying faith" in *Letters on Theron and Aspasio* (1757). This was a discussion of a book by James Hervey (1714-58) *Theron and Aspasio* (1755) which contained a strong version of ideas that troubled Sandeman and which he felt common to the "popular preachers" of his day. Hervey was an Anglican priest with Calvinist views, best known for his devotional book *Meditations among the Tombs* (1746).

Sandeman's principal complaint against the "popular preachers" was the impression they gave that "faith" was an act of will on the part of the audience by which they could properly "hear" the gospel and that this "hearing" was thus meritorious on their part and a means to salvation. Sandeman objects that what is being proposed under the concept of belief as a voluntary act is a new Covenant of Works, where what is intended in Scripture is rather a handing over of saving belief whose power lies wholly in its transforming power over the mind. To Sandeman, the gospel is a gift of God imparted to the understanding of man while still estranged from his Maker and no promise or incentive to belief is attached to it other than what flows from its truth. Its reception was the work of the intellect alone in which there was nothing meritorious.

The second part of his argument concerned the effect of the Gospel on the acts of man, or "faith as a principle of life and action."[25] The Gospel is intended to transform lives. Sandeman argues that this occurs where we act on the new beliefs it has given us. This happens by degrees through the new understanding of God contained in the Gospel and thus strictly speaking is not meritorious on the Christian's part, but the fruits of Christ's work. He writes "here we must carefully distinguish betwixt all works by which men would pretend to acquire faith, and those which faith produces."[26] Sandeman also objects to the idea of "preliminary faith" implied in "high encomiums on the piety of the author"[27] found in the biographies prefaced to the lives of popular preachers and intended to give their works authority.

---

24. Hume's account of "cold" and "warm" theories of human nature in the first *Enquiry* bears some resemblance to Sandeman's central thought.

25. Sandeman, *Letters on Theron and Aspasio*, letter 6.

26. Ibid., letter 6, 2:189.

27. Ibid., 248.

Sandeman had considerable erudition and his book included criticisms of Locke's *Reasonableness of Christianity*, Hume's *Natural History of Religion*, and Lord Kames' *Essays on Morality and Natural Religion* and discusses Voltaire and Jonathan Edwards, all writers cited by Mylne. It gave rise to a considerable controversy and another opponent of Hervey, who knew the Glasite heartlands of Perthshire and Dundee well, the Methodist preacher John Wesley (1703–91) also contributed to the debate. The *Letters* went through several editions and soon drew forth support as well as a critical response amongst the dissenting community in England,[28] by which means it came to the attention of the future political reformer, William Godwin.

William Godwin

Mylne's near contemporary, the English philosopher William Godwin (1756–1836), was the youngest of a quartet of English dissenting philosophers who prefigure Mylne's own rationalism and also share in various degrees his political reformism: the others being David Hartley, Joseph Priestley, and Richard Price. For example, Mylne discusses aspects of both Hartley's and Priestley's philosophies. Price corresponded with societies in France and Mylne discussed his work on population in his political economy course. The engagement extends to philosophical theory.

However, there are well attested intellectual links between Mylne and Godwin that relate specifically to the crucial time when Mylne was composing his course. Mylne owned a copy of Godwin's principal philosophical work *Enquiry concerning Political Justice* (2nd edition 1796), which his friends recommended to Thomas Chalmers in the 1790s, and Godwin also wrote for the *Analytical Review* which Mylne read at the same time. Reflecting this, Mylne alludes directly to Godwin in the earliest surviving version of his moral philosophy lectures from 1800 where he defends Godwin's utilitarianism against outlandish criticism, remarking that "extravagant conclusions may be drawn from any system."[29] Furthermore, the principal divisions of Godwin's work, namely into metaphysical, moral and political parts, are reflected in some degree in Mylne's lectures.

Godwin himself knew something of the Scottish political scene, having engaged with Henry Dundas over the Warren Hastings trial and later

---

28. Further editions appeared in 1759, 1762, 1768, and 1803 (per NLS catalogue). The later editions contain an account of the controversy to which the book gave rise. An American edition appeared in 1760.

29. 1799/1800 lectures, MSMurray207, 416, reference to Thomas Green's *Observations on a New System of Morals* of 1798.

regularly visited the reformers Thomas Muir and Fyshe Palmer during their time in Woolwich jail awaiting transportation to Australia in 1793.[30] Later on, Mylne's grandniece Frances Wright knew some of Godwin's circle, which included the poet Percy Shelley and novelist Mary Shelley.

Godwin acknowledged the influence of Sandemanian ideas on his *Enquiry* as they formed a central part of his education. His early education in the years 1767–70 was as a dissenter under the Reverend Samuel Newton of Norwich. Godwin recollected of Newton that: "he was rather an intemperate Wilkite; but, first and principally he was a disciple of the [more than] supra-Calvinistic opinions of Robert Sandeman, that men could be saved by their creed alone." He added of Newton's influence: "Ductility is a leading feature of my mind; I was his single pupil; and his sentiments quickly became mine."[31] Godwin went on to study at the Dissenting Academy at Hoxton from 1773 to 1778, having been rejected elsewhere "on suspicion of Sandemanianism." Around this time he later recalled: "I subscribed to a circulating library at Rochester, and among other books, procured the writings of Robert Sandeman, that I might compare them with my previous habits of thinking and know whereof I was accused."[32]

Godwin represents Sandeman as asserting that salvation depends on "judgement" and not on "faith." The priority of judgement is reflected in Godwin's *Enquiry concerning Political Justice*, where he argues that "the voluntary actions of men originate in their opinions."[33] In 1800, he identified three cardinal errors in the first edition of the *Enquiry*. Along with Stoicism ("an inattention to the principle that pleasure and pain are the only bases on which morality can rest") and "the unqualified condemnation of the private affections" he criticizes his own former "Sandemanianism, or an inattention to the principle that feeling and not judgement, is the source of human opinions."[34] He wrote in this regard:

> It will easily be seen how strongly these errors are connected with the Calvinist system, which had been so deeply wrought into my mind in early life, as to enable those errors long to survive the general system of religious opinions of which they formed a part.[35]

---

30. Godwin, *Political and Philosophical Writings*, 2:30 et seq.

31. "The Principal Revolutions of Opinion" in Godwin, *Collected Novels and Memoirs*, 1:52.

32. Godwin, *Collected Novels*, 1:42.

33. Godwin, *Enquiry concerning Political Justice*, 1.5.

34. Godwin, *Collected Novels*, 1:53.

35. Ibid., 1:53–54.

He goes on to say that he rejected Stoicism in 1794 for the second edition of his *Enquiry* with the other errors "detected" after reading Hume's *Treatise of Human Nature* and corrected in the third edition, with some relevant remarks in the later sheets of the second. Mylne owned the 1796 London (second) edition of the *Enquiry*,[36] though the first edition had also been distributed in Glasgow two years earlier.[37] He agreed with Godwin's change of heart in making an Epicurean view basic to his view of ethics rather than Stoicism and did not view "private affections" as in conflict with public duty but as a legitimate concern that at times had to give way to broader considerations.

Whilst Godwin had moved away from Christianity as a creed whilst retaining something of its ethos,[38] the content of Mylne's course suggests that he remained to a greater extent within the ambit of Calvinist ideas. Godwin had read Samuel Clarke, Jonathan Edwards, and Joseph Priestley, as did Mylne, but thereafter fell under the influence of D'Holbach's *Système de la Nature* and moved towards Deism and then Atheism.[39] Following his usual practice of selecting from authors what suited his own purposes, Mylne did not follow him along this train of thought.

Scotch and English Baptists

In the Scottish churches in Mylne's lifetime, the admixture of belief as an element of piety emerges as a question: the change is expressed strikingly by several opponents of Sandeman. Those who preached conversion required to understand their task accurately. Sandemanian theology thus continued to have a notable influence on religious philosophy over at least a century. The argument was developed through a debate between the Scots Baptist Archibald McLean (1733–1812)[40] and his English critic Andrew Fuller (1754–1815). Both men's works were widely distributed in Glasgow. Later contributors included Mylne's pupil, the Baptist preacher George Payne (1781–1848) who was also a notable philosopher.

36. Skirving catalogue of Mylne's library in GUL.

37. *GM* 15/4/1794. A further advert by Brash & Reid in *GC* 12/4/1796 may refer to the second edition (the price of 14s compares with 2 guineas for the first edition).

38. Godwin's *Life and Age of Chaucer* was also advertised in Glasgow (*GC* 11/10/1803).

39. Godwin, *Collected Novels*, 1:53 and introduction to Penguin edition of *Enquiry* for Priestley.

40. McLean is not the same as his namesake Archibald MacLaine/McLean who translated Mosheim's *Ecclesiastical History*, a standard work owned by Mylne and reprinted in Glasgow in a cheap edition.

Archibald McLean was educated near Glasgow after which he worked as a printer in London and Edinburgh.[41] He left the Church of Scotland for the Glasite church in 1762 but soon moved again to become a key figure in the Scottish Baptist movement. This transition is illuminated by a published controversy with John Glas on infant baptism. His earlier views on "believer baptism"[42] were a subject of controversy with Mylne's friend Ralph Wardlaw and also debated by the Paisley Pen' folk.[43] In the controversy with Wardlaw, McLean cites John Glas at length in interpretation of the text "Know ye therefore, that they which are of faith, the same are the children of Abraham,"[44] which foregrounds the concept of faith, though without elaborating on the concept. In illuminating the history of the concept of belief in Scotland, McLean's principal work is *The Commission given by Jesus Christ to his Apostles* (1785, 2nd edition 1797).[45] Here he again endorses Glas' views, writing that: "Everybody knows that faith or belief, in the ordinary sense of the word, is that CREDIT which we give to the truth of anything which is made known to us by report or testimony."[46]

He relies on Paul in support of this, writing that "if faith be a work at all, it is not easy to conceive how sinners are justified by faith *without works*,"[47] discussing the meaning of the Greek equivalent ($\pi\iota\sigma\tau\iota\varsigma$) and the related term "bearing witness." Yet his position is qualified by his discussion of the subordination of faith to hope and charity by Paul in the famous passage from 1 Corinthians[48] and the citation that faith "worketh by love."[49] McLean's work is not greatly systematic, though it borrows some strength in depth when seen against its background in Glasite theology.[50] Its chief significance for us is the debate it led to with Andrew Fuller.

41. *DNB*.

42. McLean, *Defence of Believer Baptism*, published in 1777. McLean derives the association of baptism with belief from Christ's words "He that believeth, and is baptised, shall be saved" (Matt 16:16).

43. McLean, *A Review of Mr Wardlaw's Lectures*.

44. Gal 3:7.

45. His works were collected posthumously in 1823.

46. McLean, *Commission*, 74.

47. Ibid., 77, citing Rom 3:28.

48. 1 Cor 13:13.

49. McLean, *Commission*, 84.

50. Talbott in *The Search for a Common Identity* argues to some effect in his first two chapters that the contributions of the Scottish dissenting churches to theological debate are underestimated by many scholars and his case would only be strengthened by recognizing the relations of the "Scotch Baptists" led by McLean with the Glasites.

Perhaps the most perceptive critic of both McLean and Sandeman was the Baptist theologian Andrew Fuller, though scripturally his task was made easier by the publication of Alexander Cruden's *Complete Concordance of the Old and New Testaments*.[51] Fuller also notes the influence of Sandemanian ideas beyond the Glasite sect, in particular amongst Presbyterians and Baptists.[52] He had first visited Glasgow during a trip to Scotland in 1799, when he met McLean and some local Christians close to Mylne including David Dale[53] and he returned in 1802, visiting Glasgow and Paisley to raise funds for missionary work in India along with several later trips.[54] As we have seen, Dale worked closely with the Sandemanian Robert Ferrier. Fuller's trips were prominently reported in the Glasgow newspapers as they involved public fundraising and preaching and his principal writings were also advertised.

Fuller's *Strictures on Sandemanianism* (1810)[55] takes flight from a dispute with McLean that had lasted twenty years, which it seeks to close by taking on the whole "system" behind his views.[56] The key philosophical part of the *Strictures* is chapter 5 "On the Connexion between Knowledge and Disposition," though the book's considerable philosophical and theological acuity operate in tandem, as the ordinary language of a religious community looks to Scripture for the authoritative use of its key terms.

Fuller undertakes to respond to McLean's charge of "maintaining that the understanding, or perceptive faculty in man, is directed and governed by his will and inclinations."[57] He relates this to Jonathan Edwards's theory that the mind is determined by its perception of the "greatest apparent good,"[58] observing that Edwards concedes that the cause of the agreeable appearance may be "the state, frame of temper of the mind itself." Thus, Fuller infers, Edwards thinks that the understanding may be determined by the mind as a whole. Fuller concedes that there is such a thing as "simple knowledge," but notes that "knowledge is much more frequently used in the scriptures *as including approbation*," as when the Lord is said to "*know* the righteous"

---

51. Available in Glasgow from 1803 (GC 14/5/1803).
52. Fuller, *Strictures on Sandemanianism*, 15.
53. "Memoirs of Mr Fuller," lxi, in *Works* (1831).
54. See GC 25/9/1802. For later trips in 1805, 1808 and thereafter see "Memoir" in *Works*.
55. Nottingham, the 1810 copy in NLS also marked "for J&A Duncan, Glasgow."
56. Fuller, *Strictures on Sandemanianism*, introduction.
57. Ibid., 103.
58. Citing Edwards, *Freedom of the Will*, 1.2.

and "never to have known the works of iniquity."[59] McLean concedes that the term "heart" includes the intellectual faculty and generally denotes all mental faculties in the soul of man "as they all concur in our doing good or evil."[60] Thus the terms "head" and "heart" in the Bible do not equate to the concepts of "understanding" and "will" in moral philosophy if these are conceived as separable.

Fuller's insights embodied a widespread feeling about the limits of Sandemanian theology. For example, some of the Sandemanian literature was translated into Welsh[61] and the doctrine was widely known but eventually rejected in Wales. One famous Welsh preacher, Christmas Evans (1766–1838), gave thanks for his deliverance from Sandeman's "cold and sterile regions" through a vision of Christ that he felt like "mountains of frost and snow dissolving and melting within me" and which enabled him to deliver Anglesey from its grip.[62] Another critic spoke of it as a "horrid blast from the North."[63] It would seem then, that Fuller's views had prevailed.

However, the influence of Sandemanianism can be traced in later American theology and even philosophy. Henry James Senior (1811–82), the father of psychologist and expounder of pragmatism William James, edited an edition of Sandeman's *Letters on Theron and Aspasio* in New York (1838), describing it as "a far more faithful exhibition of Gospel truth than any other work."[64] The appeal of the doctrine for James senior is said to have lain in the implied egalitarianism of all Gospel hearers in the face of God.

Mylne on Free Will and Necessity

Let us turn to Mylne's lectures on free will. Thomas Reid had argued for a version of free will in his *Essays on the Active Powers of Man* (1788), according to which freedom is a power of the human mind over the determinations of the will. We are not determined to act necessarily by motives, Reid argues, but rather we determine ourselves to act freely by means of our own mental self-energy. In contrast, Mylne argues that actions are necessarily determined by motives or reasons. He argues that the dispute is in

---

59. Fuller, *Strictures on Sandemanianism*, 107.

60. Ibid., 110.

61. *Llythyrau rhwng Mr Samuel Pike a Mr Robert Sandeman* (i.e., "Letters between . . .").

62. Sell, *Protestant Nonconformist Texts*, 2:101.

63. Ibid., 2:99.

64. Published in New York: see Frederic Young's *Philosophy of Henry James Sr.*

part verbal, in part technical in nature. His own use of terms appears in the following passage:

> We may act against inclination, but not against will. The lover leaves his mistress much against his inclination, but he has a motive stronger to leave her than to stay, and by this motive his will must be determined.[65]

Mylne gives Reid pride of place as an exponent of free will and summarizes Reid's three arguments in support of it. Briefly, these are: firstly, that such freedom is a common sense belief, for which Reid offers a variety of evidence; secondly, that it is implied by accountability; and thirdly, that it is implied also by our ability to pursue a fixed purpose through time. Other than Reid, he recommends Jonathan Edwards "whose Treatise on this subject is perhaps the most masterly we have." Along with the views of the Church of Scotland, he also mentions on the side of necessity David Hume, Lord Kames, and Joseph Priestley, and on the side of freedom, Bishop Butler, Richard Price, and Bishop Horsley.[66] His own views are interleaved with these expositions and lean to the side of necessity.

Mylne introduces into the argument on free will the intellectualist bias of his general philosophy in opposition to Reid. He says: "The view which we have taken of the will is that it is not a distinct and separate faculty, but only an exercise of judgement."[67] Mylne agrees that we are not pushed around by motives against our will, but that we are determined by our will, which he identifies with reason. He prepares the ground by quoting Reid against himself. Mylne states:

> In the 1st chapter of Reid's second *Essay on the Active Powers*, we find a striking admission: "In all determinations of the will" says he [i.e. Reid], "that are of any importance" (the occasion for inserting this clause is not very apparent) "there must be something in the preceding state of the mind, which disposes us to, and indeed produces, that determination." Now this would seem equivalent to granting that the judgement is concerned in all determinations of the will. And he adds: "If the mind were always in a state of perfect indifference, then our active powers would be given us in vain." That is to say, we require some motives and inducements to act.[68]

65. Pollock notes GUL:MSGen1355, 16/2/1821.
66. Wicksteed notes, GUL:MSGen97/102, 31–32.
67. Wicksteed notes, GUL:MSGen97/102, Lecture 68.
68. Wicksteed notes, GUL:MSGen97/102 citing Thomas Reid's *Active Powers* 2.1, near the end.

As he thinks judgement is not a capricious act, but involuntary recognition of a state of affairs, Mylne is led to accept necessity. He is typically unimpressed with Reid's first appeal to common sense and presents counterarguments that common sense endorses the determination of action by motive. To Reid's second argument, on accountability, Mylne replies that instead: "such freedom is inconsistent with accountability. If we could conceive the moral conduct of man to proceed from self energy without attention to motives, we could give his actions neither praise nor blame." On Reid's third argument deriving free will from persistence in a plan, which Mylne considers unique to Reid, he comments as follows:

> As to Dr Reid's third argument, that a man shews his free-agency by carrying into effect a plan that he has determined upon, in spite of all motives which might lead him to the contrary [...] it ought to be remembered that some motive led him to form the plan, and under the influence of the same motive he continues it. If he finds the plan less favourable than he expected, he may continue it from his pride, or change it for a better: but in either case he would act under the influence of motives.[69]

Mylne ends his exposition with the remark: "Perhaps the objections [to necessity] would not appear so ill if we would substitute the word reason instead of the term motive."[70] In this sense, his position on free will should be seen as an expression of the intellectualist bias of his thought. In this way, as well as in others unconnected with Reid, the significance of Mylne's philosophy appears as a reassertion of the sovereignty of reason.

Other Theological Commitments

Mylne's view of Revelation could be established from his extensive preaching, if only some record of this had survived. However, virtually all record of his preaching as a minister in Paisley and as chaplain of Glasgow College appears to be lost. What we know is thus only what we can infer from the records of the lectures. However, Mylne presents his thought as based in the first instance on natural religion rather than Christian revelation. For example, he cites Christ only twice and then simply as an authority in support of philosophical positions on Providence and knowledge for which he also argues on independent grounds. Whilst he divides duty on a tripartite plan into duties to God, neighbor and self, suggested by a remark of St. Paul, this

---

69. Wicksteed notes, GUL:MSGen97/102, Lecture 71.
70. Mackenzie notes GUL:MSGen466, 246.

was conventional in his day and based on a tradition of natural law theology that goes back in Glasgow at least to Gershom Carmichael.

We have little privileged access to the inner workings of Mylne's mind in the form of private diaries, correspondence, or unguarded comments preserved for posterity. However, his most unguarded comments on religion, in a surviving letter concerning the temporary loss of faith of his niece, Frances Wright, support this reading.[71] He writes of the supposed "atheism or profligacy" (the latter being rejection of marriage) of a document expounding the principles of Wright's Nashoba project that they are "insulting outrages on the fixed principles and the decent feelings of mankind" and continues:

> It is true that she speaks in it of her *denouncing all religious creeds*—but this is ambiguous language which may admit of less offensive interpretation than J[ames] R[ichardson] gives to it. In all the religious creeds that have been proposed to the world some things may be found which a philosopher may be forgiven for denouncing as Fanny calls it.[72]

There is no suggestion that "the language of disappointment of grief of shame, shall I say of anger"[73] that he says he tried to suppress in this letter are anything other than his genuine response to Wright's atheism. This and an earlier private letter, in which he employs terminology similar to his lectures in an undoubted matter of the heart, again concerning Wright, suggest that his publicly declared views and personal opinions were not too far apart.

Conclusions

Mylne's views have a theological context in a developed tradition of reflection on the nature of faith. The view of faith as a non-meritorious intellectual act was developed by John Glas and Robert Sandeman and had followers amongst the Baptist movement. It appealed to the idea of preaching as intellectual persuasion. Its critics came to regard it as failing to appeal to the active and responsible parts of the mind.

One can read Mylne's later evangelical critics such as Ralph Wardlaw, James Begg, and James McCosh as suggesting that there was a similar impetus

---

71. Letter of James Mylne to Julia Garnett Pertz 12 August 1827: The Houghton Library bMS Eng 1304.1(25), held at Harvard College, USA.

72. Letter of James Mylne to Julia Garnett Pertz 12 August 1827.

73. Ibid.

to secularization in his thought as in William Godwin's *Enquiry*. McCosh relates this to the "coldness" of his lecturing style and supposed sympathy with the "Socinian" or Unitarian ideas held by some of his pupils. This reading would make both Mylne and Godwin ancestors of the positivism of Auguste Comte (1798–1857)[74] that arose in the nineteenth century and in Mylne's case would place him alongside the anticlerical traditions of Glasgow.

However, Mylne's views of free will and providence indicate instead that his views on belief retain their original theological context as contributions to the theological debates within the British Calvinism of his day. His reputed "coldness" does not indicate a lack of piety, but rather places him in a Scottish tradition that valued the intellectual nature of faith. This, together with an enduring Christian doctrinal element at the core of his thinking, would make him instead a philosophical precursor of the Glasgow Idealists who were also to inherit his political legacy.

---

74. Buckle's *History of Civilisation in England III*, published in 1857, interprets earlier Scottish intellectual life from a Comtean standpoint and his views are not seriously questioned by modern social historians such as T. C. Smout and Tom Devine.

CHAPTER 11

Political Influences and Doctrines

Introduction

WE NOW TURN TO address Mylne's political opinions in so far as they relate to his general philosophical views. For Mylne politics was, in two distinct senses, a subsidiary sphere of activity: firstly, it is governed by opinion; and secondly, it serves the ends of society. He addresses the first point directly at the outset of his lectures on political economy. Here Mylne said with regard to the principles of political economy:

> Lycurgus complained that the laws he had given the Spartans were not the best, but they were suited to their evil practices and character. How many foolish legislative enactments [are] made because the people wished them, while good and useful ones [are] rejected from an [unacquaintance] with their principles or advantages.[1]

Even in the absence of representative democracy, he argues, government tends to reflect public opinion: "In every country of Europe, indeed, the public opinion is felt by the government, however despotic the government may be in its nature."[2] For example, laws felt to be unjust are circumvented and rulers reluctant to pass or enforce them. His views of belief in general thus have a practical bearing in relation to the transmission of knowledge and opinion.

In this chapter, I firstly review the principal books of political theory Mylne owned and cited to explore the practical implications of the general

---

1. Mylne, *Lectures on Political Economy* (NCL:BOGU3), lecture 1.
2. Ibid.

philosophical ideas on the mind and cognition that he put across in his lectures. Secondly, I discuss how he applied his views to some of the principal grievances of the day and relate these to his mental philosophy, Whig convictions, and personal experience.

Influences

The political influences I will discuss are the theories of the progress and distribution of knowledge of English dissenters Joseph Priestley (1733–1803) and William Godwin, the failed revolutionary program of Thomas Paine, and the Whig analysis of the British constitution of John Millar.

Joseph Priestley

Mylne's lectures and those of his contemporary George Hill in St. Andrews[3] contain numerous references to the English dissenter Joseph Priestley's views across a range of moral and theological subjects. Priestley's work included natural and moral science, history, and theology. Mylne owned Priestley's *Essay on the First Principles of Government* (1771), *Examination of Reid* (1775), three volumes of *Disquisitions relating to Matter and Spirit* (1777),[4] and two volumes of *Lectures on History and General Policy* (1788; Mylne owned a 1793 edition).[5] The early dates suggest some could have belonged to Mylne's father or have been acquired early in life. Priestley was a prominent figure and the events of his life were reported, his works advertised and his views satirized in the Glasgow press up to 1798.[6]

Priestley's *Essay on Government* is based on his distinction between political and civil liberty, where political liberty is power over public offices, e.g., that of voting in elections; and civil liberty is power over our own actions. Priestley's main concern is for civil liberty and in this regard he introduces into the heart of the work two principles on the social distribution of knowledge. The first is that "the more liberty is given to everything which is in a state of growth, the more perfect it will become."[7] The nature

---

3. Hill, *Lectures on Divinity*, passim.

4. Skirving catalogue of Mylne's library in GUL has 1772, which appears inaccurate.

5. Skirving catalogue of Mylne's library in GUL.

6. E.g., *GM* 2/12/1788, *Lectures on History*; burning of his house in Birmingham and characterization as a "Unitarian dissenter" and opponent of government *GM* 19/7/91; satire on Priestley and Paine *GC* 14/12/1793.

7. Priestley, *Of Government*, 258–59.

of knowledge, he argues, is to progress by observation and reflection and hence state regulation of education and religion carries the danger of freezing knowledge in an imperfect state. The second principle is that:

> If the nature of the thing be such, that the attention of individuals, with respect to it, can be applied to more advantage than that of the magistrate; the claim of the former must be admitted, in preference to that of the latter.[8]

The balance of the argument is to advocate a free market in ideas and defend the civil liberty to develop them. The idea of intellectual freedom amongst six "moral causes" of national wealth is found in Mylne's political economy lectures. The first three causes concern what Priestley calls "political liberty," and the latter three concern the content of religion, religious tolerance and "the diffusion of knowledge in general and freedom of inquiry in all subjects." On toleration, Mylne reckons tolerance and "freedom of religious inquiry" of more importance than established religion. Religious intolerance produces "a chilling and benumbing influence over the inhabitants" and he notes that the loss to France of the Huguenots was paralleled by the loss for England of the Puritans who fled to America "where they enjoyed freedom and comfort and there their party have risen to opulence . . . power and . . . dignity."[9] Similarly, Mylne's account of the moral causes of wealth recommends that "no discouragement should be given to free inquiry" and that, as he claims happens in Scotland, "the means of education should be placed in the hands of all."[10]

"A Season of Political Intolerance"[11]

The peaceable development of Mylne's theories was interrupted by the outbreak of the French revolution in 1789. The minister John Young soon wrote: "Never were the minds of men so intent upon political subjects, nor so many pens employed upon political discussions, as since the year 1789."[12] Soon Edmund Burke (1729–97), Rector of Glasgow University in 1783,[13] published *Reflections on the Revolution in France* (1790). Thomas Paine's reply, *Rights of Man* appeared in 1791 with a second and more incendiary

---

8. Ibid., 77.
9. Mylne, *Lectures on Political Economy* (NCL:BOGU3), lecture 25.
10. Mylne, *Lectures on Political Economy* (NCL:BOGU3), lecture 26.
11. The phrase is from Craig's biography of Millar in Millar, *Origins*, xcix.
12. Young, *Essays on the following interesting subjects*, 1.
13. *GM*, 13/11/1783 He gives a speech, reported in *GM*, 1/4/1784.

part the following year.¹⁴ Mylne owned *Rights of Man* (1792) and Paine's American revolutionary pamphlet *Common Sense*.¹⁵ Knowledge of Paine was also common in Paisley where Mylne was then a minister. In the trial of Thomas Muir in 1793 for example, one of the seditious documents alleged was "A Declaration of Rights" published in local papers by a group called "the friends of reform in Paisley,"¹⁶ and Muir was said to have "harangued multitudes" there.¹⁷ A Paisley poet wrote:

> The *Rights of Man* are now well-kenned
> And read by many a hunder,
> For Tammy Paine the buik has penned
> And lent the Court a lounder.¹⁸
> [dealt a blow]

The second part became the occasion of the repression following Burke's speech in the House of Commons in 1792, which was reported in the Glasgow press.¹⁹ This speech showed the Whigs to be unwilling to endorse Paine's views and divided what had hitherto been a united reform movement. This was followed by a royal proclamation and repressive measures against seditious publications and meetings. In January 1793, a five-guinea reward was advertised for any bookseller "after this date" selling or distributing *The Rights of Man*.²⁰ The following month, the book was burned by Ayr Public Library,²¹ but copies were retained and prized by some in radical circles into the 1830s.²² In a family story preserved by Frances Wright, Mylne's brother-in-law in Dundee reportedly dumped copies of the *Rights of Man* that he was distributing in the river Tay.²³ She wrote:

14. Its prohibition indicates that Mylne's 1792 copy was purchased close on publication.

15. Skirving catalogue of Mylne's library in GUL.

16. A copy survives in Paisley town library.

17. Published on 12 March, 1793 according to Metcalfe, *A History of Paisley*, who observes that "The major part of the inhabitants were of saner mind" (369). For Muir, see also Cockburn, *Sedition Trials*, and Mackenzie *Reminiscences*.

18. Alexander Wilson (1766–1813), quoted in Meikle, *Scotland and the French Revolution*, 121.

19. *GC* 17/5/1792.

20. *GC* report 5/1/1793.

21. *GC* 14/2/1793, referring to events on 6 February.

22. *Radical Reformers' Gazette* (Glasgow, 1833), 159–60 [copy in Mitchell Library, Glasgow].

23. See also *The Reasoner: a weekly journal, Unitarian, Republican and Communist*, (London, 1849), vol 6, 325, where the books are said to be burned and medals dumped in the Tay.

He was instrumental in spreading through his own city and neighbourhood, popular translations of French treatises, political and philosophical. He circulated, also, the works of Thomas Paine; and, as having promoted a cheap publication of his *Rights of Man*, became an object of government espionage in 1794.[24]

Mylne used the phrase "rights of man" in a lecture in 1800 and he discussed Paine's account of the national debt in his political economy course in 1815 through a comparison of Paine's views with those of the Scottish philosopher James Beattie in his *Principles of Moral Science* (1792).

Thomas Hardie, Professor of Church History at Edinburgh University, authored a pamphlet against Paine, *The Patriot [. . .] with Observations on Republican Government and Paine's Principles* (1793).[25] This was soon taken up by Glasgow Constitutional Association, along with John Young's *Essays on Government* (1794), which soon reached a fourth edition,[26] and Stevenson MacGill's *The Spirit of the Times* (1792).[27] Hardie was chosen Moderator of the General Assembly in 1793,[28] the first year in which Mylne attended it.[29] The Assembly issued an address to His Majesty George III in which no element of remonstrance was reported to accompany its declaration of loyalty, a distinctively Tory gesture.

Paine's political reputation lived on in the west of Scotland after condemnation of his writings.[30] He was rumored to be intending to accompany a French invasion of Britain in 1804.[31] His late work on religion, *The Age of Reason*, was known by means of published criticisms in the local press.[32] Paine's death in 1809 was noted in the *Glasgow Courier* by means of a eulogy reproduced from the American press which described Paine as a "distinguished philanthropist" and concluded "take him all in all, we shall

---

24. Wright, *Life, Letters and Lectures*, 6.

25. Advertised in *GM* 12/2/1793. For Hardie's authorship, see *GM* 25/6/1793.

26. The third edition is advertised in *GM* 5/8/1794 and the fourth on 28/10/1794.

27. MacGill's *Spirit of the Times* is advertised in *GC* 31/1/1793 and by the Constitutional Association on 19/2/1793.

28. *GM* 14/5/1793.

29. *GM* 26/3/1793. The list of attendees included Rev Thomas Burns (c. 1756–1830), author of *Four Sermons* (Glasgow, 1799–1803).

30. E.g. *GM*, 22/1/1793; *GC* 20/11/1797.

31. Letter of Thomas Paine to the *Philadelphia Gazette*, quoted in *GC* 7/7/1804.

32. Bishop R. Watson. *An Apology for the Bible, in a Series of Letters to Thomas Paine, Author of 'The Age of Reason'* (*GC* 12/4/1796; extracted 28/4/1796.) See also J. Auchinloss. *The Sophistry of Paine's Age of Reason* (*GC* 24/5/1796). Auchinloss was a dissenting minister in Stockport.

never look on his like again."[33] By 1820, a new edition of *The Rights of Man* had been published in Glasgow, whilst another edition was published by Greenock booksellers around 1832. The life of Paine was thus a significant cultural reference point in Glasgow throughout Mylne's life.

Towards the end of his life, we find Mylne at a public dinner held in the Barony of the Gorbals in 1835 celebrating the "downfall of the Self-Elective System" there.[34] The toasts given are bolder than those of the Fox Club with which Mylne was associated, perhaps reflecting the absence of repression after 1832. "The Scotch Reformers of 1793" are openly toasted and "May the soldier never forget that he is a citizen." Scots and Jacobite songs are sung. Although I have identified little contemporary evidence of Mylne's attitudes in the early 1790s, it seems likely that he felt some initial sympathy for Paine's goals, but not his methods, for he warns against rash political actions. This is also suggested by his comparison of Frances Wright with her father on her decision to sail for America, which expresses a kindly exasperation. In this respect, the evolution of his sympathies followed a similar path to those of William Godwin and John Millar.

William Godwin

To revert to chronological order, following the suppression of Paine's writings, the reformist tradition was represented in print by William Godwin's *Principles of Political Justice* (1793). Mylne owned a copy of the second 1796 edition of the *Principles*.[35] The first two editions of *Principles* were advertised in the Glasgow press, the second by Brash & Reid,[36] with the third edition appearing in 1798. Godwin's views were lightly satirized in Elizabeth Hamilton's (1756–1816) novel *Memoirs of Modern Philosophers* (1800), available in Glasgow. In 1803, the first issue of the *Edinburgh Review* endorsed a very Mylnean view of benevolence in its coverage of the dispute between Parr and Godwin. Mylne later acquired Godwin's second and third novels, the *Travels of St. Leon* (1799), which opposed the values of domestic and public life, and *Fleetwood, or the New Man of Feeling* (1805), whose subtitle evokes Henry Mackenzie's novel of that name. Mylne was present

33. From the *New York Public Advertiser*, in GC 11/7/1809.

34. *The Reformers' Gazette*, (1835) vol. 5, 220. The same journal notes later that "Professor Mylne has not resigned." (400).

35. See Skirving catalogue. Godwin's book was also advertised in the Glasgow press.

36. GM 15/4/1794; GC 12/4/1796. Godwin's *Life of Chaucer* (1803) was also advertised in Glasgow and reviewed in the *North British Magazine*, sold by Scrymgeour of Glasgow: see GC 11/10/1803 and review GC 7/1/1804.

in St. Andrews in 1795 at political discussion evenings amongst a handful of political theorists who were, "considered in those days, like Dr Brown, as marked men—ultra Whigs, keen Reformers, and what would now be called Radicals."[37]

Another source indicates that Brown, a mathematician and Foxite Whig, recommended Godwin's *Principles* at this time to the young Thomas Chalmers, who was also present with John Leslie, later professor of mathematics at Edinburgh. Mylne also owned two works praised by Godwin, Jonathan Swift's *Works* (Edinburgh, 1752) including *Gulliver's Travels*, and Fénélon's *Télémache* (London, 1742), a satire on the French court.

Godwin had visited the Scottish radicals Muir and Palmer in Woolwich while they were awaiting transportation. He thought their conduct directed by "an ill-directed zeal for what they thought a good cause" and cites with derision Henry Dundas' comment that "he saw no great hardship in a man's being sent to Botany Bay."[38] Godwin's friend, Joseph Gerrald (1763–96), had been a member at the first Edinburgh reform convention and, like Muir, had been sentenced to fourteen years transportation, dying five months after his arrival in Botany Bay. Godwin's published view in 1794 was that the Scottish sedition trials were "an encroachment upon the Constitution."[39]

There is a direct reference to the critical literature on Godwin in Mylne's 1799/1800 lecture manuscript and the similar lines of argument give us reason to think that Godwin's account of political reform underpinned by the traditions of Calvinist mental philosophy with which he was already familiar was prominent in Mylne's mind around the time he composed his course of moral philosophy delivered from October 1797. In the English dissenting tradition, Godwin seeks a middle way between "an acrimonious spirit of violence and resentment" and "blindness to injustice and calamity."[40] He thus advocates "diffusing in every possible mode, a spirit of inquiry," a term taken up by Mylne. This he justifies in terms of his arguments that opinion is the governing principle of action: "Make men wise, and by that very operation you make them free. Civil liberty follows as a consequence of this; no usurped power can stand against the artillery of opinion."[41] By participating in this project, he argues, we learn patience, but may expect "a mild and

37. NCL: TCP/CHA6.26.70 Letter of James Miller to John Mackenzie 5/7/1847. Brown, *Thomas Chalmers*, 6 cites "CHA 2 Hanna Letters J Miller to W Hanna 21 January 1848" (footnote 17), but dates the letter "1847."

38. Unpublished letter of 3/3/1794 to *Morning Chronicle* in Godwin, *Political and Philosophical Writings*, 2:28–30.

39. Godwin, *Political and Philosophical Writings*, 2:97.

40. Godwin, *Enquiry*, 256.

41. Ibid., 263.

gradual, though incessant advance" towards our evolving goals. We also avoid that indignation which Godwin considers "pregnant with tyranny."[42] These views are strongly reflected in Mylne's lectures. Godwin's book concludes with an account of property, which he described as "the key-stone that completes the fabric of political science."[43] Whilst he decries the pursuit of wealth and advocates equality, Godwin is clear that personal property is a condition of personal independence. He writes:

> Without permitting to every man to a considerable degree, the exercise of his own discretion, there can be no independence, no improvement, no virtue and no happiness. This is a privilege in the highest degree sacred [...] Thus deep is the foundation of the doctrine of property.[44]

This view too is echoed in Mylne's lectures on political economy. Godwin's book may thus have not only justified to Mylne the intellectualist bias of his mental philosophy, but also pointed out the merits of directing his public evening lectures to political economy.

David Hume and John Millar

Mylne owned an early edition of Glasgow Law Professor John Millar's *Historical View of the English Government* (Dublin, 1787; Mylne's copy is marked "London, 1790"), the first edition being 1787. Millar appointed him his joint literary executor along with John Craig and Mylne was thus closely associated with the posthumous edition of *Origins of the Distinction of Ranks* (1771, 4th edition 1806) and is credited as co-editor of the greatly expanded posthumous third edition of Millar's *Historical View of the English Government* (1803).[45] This edition contained two volumes of supplementary essays covering the seventeenth and eighteenth centuries and the governments of Scotland and Ireland. The work was accompanied by an edition of Mylne's predecessor, Archibald Arthur's *Discourses on Theological and Literary Subjects* (1803), edited by William Richardson, who stresses Arthur's caution on constitutional questions, and reprints part of Reid's late essay "Observations on the Utopian System of Government" directed against the idea of political revolution. The two books were thus "militant

---

42. Ibid., 269.
43. Ibid., 701.
44. Ibid., 722.
45. John Craig went on to write *Elements of Political Science* (1814) and *Remarks on some Fundamental Doctrines of Political Economy* (1821).

editions,"[46] representing the Whig and Tory strands of Glasgow opinion. Both were republished in 1812 and Millar again in 1818.

Millar was an open supporter of the Whigs, having dedicated his *Historical View of the English Government* to Fox. He was an opponent of slavery like Adam Smith and the Tory James Beattie, an early member of the Scottish Friends of the People and opponent of the war with France.[47] Millar and Thomas Reid had publicly supported the 1789 French revolution in 1791.[48] In 1793, the Government appealed for support from public figures[49] and other forms of pressure were applied, even within the universities.[50] In 1794, Reid backtracked, arguing that sudden political change was impractical and excessively destabilizing.[51] Millar too recognized revolutionary excesses—he is recorded as shocked at the execution of the famous chemist Lavoisier[52]—though he blamed them partly on external interference.[53] When he joined the professoriate, Mylne joined Millar's party and developed his views in two respects: firstly, the reception of Hume's combination of mental philosophy and politics, and secondly, Millar's analysis of the relations of wealth and political authority.

Firstly, in Mylne's day, David Hume's early *Treatise of Human Nature* (1739–40) was little regarded and long out of print. It was not found in the circulating libraries[54] and even a sale of rare books singled it out as "very scarce."[55] This reflected, not ignorance of Hume, who was very highly

    46. The phrase is from a talk by Laurent Clauzade on Jouffroy (2003) given at Aberdeen.

    47. On slavery, see Millar *Origin of the Distinction of Ranks*, chapter 6, section 4; for the Friends of the People, Craig in Life of Millar in *Origin* (1806), cxv; for opposition to war with France, Millar's *Letters of Crito*.

    48. Strang, *Glasgow and Its Clubs* (1864), 167 n.; see also 204 n. of 1856 edition; GM 28/6&5/7/1791.

    49. Meikle, *Scotland and the French Revolution*, 103. A biographer says of Frances Jeffrey for example: "He joined conscientiously and eagerly the Whig party . . . and in doing so he knowingly cut himself off from all hope of receiving government patronage" (McCosh, *Scottish Philosophy*, 339, probably relying on Cockburn's *Life of Jeffrey*).

    50. According to one historian: "The leading figure in the academic world was Dugald Stewart, the fame of whose teaching attracted students from England and abroad. Yet as an ardent Whig he was a marked man, whom "not a few hoped to catch in dangerous propositions" (Meikle, *Scotland and the French Revolution*, 156, quoting Cockburn's *Memorials*, 153–54).

    51. See Reid's talk on the "Dangers of Political Innovation" to Glasgow Literary Society (GC 18/12/94), republished in 1796.

    52. Craig, "Account of Life," xcv.

    53. See Millar's *Letters of Crito* (1796).

    54. See the Catalogues of Glasgow Circulating Library and Brash & Reid at GUL.

    55. GC 13/2/1798. Dugald Stewart owned a copy; Mylne apparently did not. There

regarded as a historian, but a preference for Hume's later and relatively constructive philosophy, as found in the *Inquiries*. Mylne's own view of Hume was influenced by his reading of Hume's *Dialogues*, which he owned and which he discusses in his lectures on the existence of God. Whilst admiring Hume's "ingenious paradoxes," Mylne is inclined to treat Hume's general skepticism as flimsy and of little practical import, though he adopts Hume's view of causality as a constant conjunction of discrete event-types as vindicated by Thomas Brown's *Inquiry into the Relation of Cause and Effect*, of which Mylne owned a copy. However, Mylne treats our duties to God before our duties to self and others and in this respect speaks as a clergyman and opponent of religious skepticism.

John Millar drew attention to Hume's own preference for his later work. In a comprehensive survey, Millar takes issue in the *Historical View* with Hume's *History of England* by asserting the central constitutional role of Parliament. However, in one remarkable passage he refers to Hume as, "The great historian of England, to whom the reader is indebted for the complete union of history with philosophy."[56] He does not expand on the nature or significance of this "unity," but it acquires content by reference to his later endorsement of Hume's view that "the authority of every government is founded in opinion."[57] As we have seen, this view was associated in the 1790s with William Godwin.

Millar argues, in the *Historical View*, that Britain has moved into a period of "commercial government" since 1603 in which the "corruption" of judgement made possible by public wealth replaces the limitation of the royal prerogative as the principal concern of the Whig party. Turning to public virtue, justice, according to Millar's description, depends on both authority and considerations of advantage, which are the natural provinces of the Tory and Whig parties respectively. "Authority" depends on natural differences of body and mind and on the possession of property, but property is the most important.[58] Millar remarks of "advantage," or utility, that, "Upon the whole, it is evident that the diffusion of knowledge tends more and more, to encourage and bring forward the principle of utility in all political discussion."[59] On moral theory, Millar is a sentimentalist, like Hume and Smith, with regard to the perception of virtue and utilitarian,

---

was an edition of Hume's *Works* in 1826 however and prior to that his name was kept alive by Ritchie's biography.

56. Millar, *Historical View*, 418.
57. Ibid., 589.
58. Ibid., 798.
59. Ibid., 807.

like Hutcheson, on its nature.[60] Mylne of course is rationalist and utilitarian. These considerations point to the significance of an accurate understanding of wealth and utility for the constitution of a political class. Combined with Millar's personal encouragement, this may have pointed Mylne towards lecturing on political economy.

Natural Law and "Physiocracy"

James Mylne's presentation of duties reverts to that published by his predecessor Gershom Carmichael in his edition of Samuel Pufendorf, a work in the "natural law" tradition.[61] His presentation of duties to God, our neighbor, and ourselves deals with the relations of private life and not the public institutions of society. However, he did thereby inherit the tradition of natural law theory.

The concept of natural law is present also in the writings of the "French economists," or Physiocrats. Mylne owned two physiocratic works, both of which he praises in his lectures and both of which set out to locate economic thought in a wider political system. The first is an edition of François Quesnay's writings entitled *La Physiocratie* (1768)[62] in the edition of Dupont de Nemours, who contributed to it a long preface on natural law. Quesnay was the founder of the French physiocratic school.[63] As Mylne notes, Quesnay was at first a self-taught physician who attended the French court in that capacity. Several of his medical treatises are held in Glasgow University Library.[64] Mylne further notes two early articles contributed to the *Encyclopédie*, which he dates to 1757. These can be identified as those on *Fermiers* and *Grains*, written in 1756. Mylne then goes on to mention the famous *Tableau Économique* (1758).[65] The term "physiocrat" (the rule

---

60. Ibid., 790.

61. Mylne mentions Grotius, Pufendorf, and Hutcheson in his lectures on jurisprudence, though the surviving notes are too scrappy to merit much attention.

62. Quesnay, *La Physiocratie*; Skirving catalogue of Mylne's library in GUL, II-65.

63. Daire's two volume *Physiocrates* has both biographies and texts. There is a recent paperback edition, without Dupont's introduction.

64. These are: Quesnay, *L'Art de guérir par la Saignée* (Paris: 1736); *Recherches [...] sur l'Origine, sur les divers États et sur les Progrès de la Chirurgie en France* (Paris: 1744); *Essai Physique sur l'Oeconomie animale* (Paris: 1747); *Traité de la Suppuration* (Paris: 1749); *Traité de la Gangrène* (Paris: 1749, 1771).

65. Glasgow University library also contains Mirabeau (1715–89) and Quesnay's three-volume *Philosophie Rurale* (Amsterdam: 1764) subtitled "general and political economy of agriculture, reduced to the immutable order of physical and moral laws, which assure the prosperity of empires." The date of accession of the former is marked

of nature) originated with Dupont de Nemours and refers to the theory of "natural law" as preceding and therefore limiting positive law or statute. Dupont states: "The more the policy of government occupies itself, on the pretext of the general interest, in raising authority above the laws that constitute the natural order [. . .], the more it breaks the links of society."[66] Thus natural order restricts the actions of the contracting parties in such politicizing works as Hobbes *Leviathan* and Rousseau's *Social Contract*. In economic terms, the principal natural law relates to private property. Here, Dupont takes it that personal property is amongst the rights "naturally recognised by all as absolute rights belonging to each man" from which other social institutions follow.[67]

Mylne also owned Mercier de la Rivière's *L'Ordre Naturel et Essentiel des Sociétés Politiques* (London, 1768)[68] whom he identifies, with Quesnay and Turgot, as the "French economists" in his political economy lectures. Mercier too develops a concept of natural law in which property is central. He also has much to say on politics and sovereignty. For Mercier, the central natural law is that of property and this leads on to a consideration of political economy. Finally, Mylne mentions Anne Robert Jacques Turgot (1727–81), who originally trained in theology at the Sorbonne.[69] His principal work was *Réflexions sur la Formation et la Distribution des Richesses* (1769–70). This, like Mylne, sees commerce as a source of wealth. We thus see that Mylne was very familiar with both the dissenting contribution to the British Whig tradition and British and French theories of the relations of property and political authority.

Relations of Mylne's Views with Public Debate

We now turn to relate the content of Mylne's views to his life, philosophy and the Whig thought of the day. It is noticeable that the contents of Mylne's political economy course mirror both the literature of the subject and the events of the day. For example, in 1807 the potato harvest failed in Scotland, leading to an increase in the price of grain. In the following May, we find the prize essay in Mylne's class awarded to an essay on the political economy of

---

as "Cf NUC pre-1956."

66. Dupont de Nemours, in Quesnay, *Physiocratie*, lx.
67. Dupont de Nemours, in Quesnay, *Physiocratie*, xxix.
68. Skirving catalogue III-43.
69. For this account I draw on the introduction by Ravix and Romani to Turgot, *Formation et Distribution des Richesses*.

the grain trade.⁷⁰ Meetings are called and resolutions drawn up on related issues, such as the temporary prohibition on the use of grain in distilleries and we may perhaps detect the hand of Mylne's pupils in the increased vigor of debate.

The Literary and Commercial Society

John Strang mentions several political-economic topics debated by the Literary and Commercial Society on which Mylne lectured or made his views known, including "the Corn Laws, the East India Charter, the Laws of Bankruptcy, and Reform of Parliament"⁷¹ and mentions Mylne's name as a speaker, though not on these particular themes. Strang adds that these meetings continued:

> till most of the subjects which the members had been in the habit of discussing had been settled by legislative enactment. The Corn Laws were abolished, the East India trade thrown open, the Parliamentary and Burgh Reform Acts were passed, the import duties had been modified, great social improvements were made.⁷²

I will compare Mylne's views on these subjects in turn with those of the Glasgow Whigs and relate them to his philosophy, except bankruptcy on which there is no record of Mylne's having a strong opinion, and add education, Catholic emancipation, and the Militia, on which Mylne held strong or distinctive views.

Popular Education

James Mylne argued for popular education. This was partly on grounds familiar to readers of Adam Smith to prevent the stultifying effect of repetitive labor. He spoke of a worker in a nail factory:

> If he have not the advantage of education to make reading and inquiry agreeable to him, he will most probably be very ill-informed, mean and very ignorant. But if he take delight in

---

70. GC, 3/5/1808.
71. Strang, *Glasgow and Its Clubs* (1864), 314.
72. Ibid., 315.

reading and in inquiry, he may be employed with these things even when he is engaged in making nails or any other single object.[73]

The notes address not only discovery, but the communication of knowledge:

> It is requisite for the dis[semination] of knowledge that the means of education should be placed in the hands of all. This is the case with our own country and particularly in Scotland. The expense too is so trifling as almost to be discreditable and knowledge afforded to youth of both sexes.[74]

Unfortunately, the surviving notes do not dwell on the particular nature of the education, though knowledge of reading and the natural effects of curiosity appear to be at the core. The advantage, he continues, of such popular education, is not merely personal to the worker or even economic, but has a public significance in promoting civil liberty. He goes so far as to say that: "the simple [. . .] influence of reading and writing is the best kind of reform, the only sure guard of our civil rights and the sole defence against the horrors of superstition and fanaticism."[75]

After a reference to education combating religious intolerance, Mylne extends the point to politics. The notes continue, "The chief advantage of general education is its [favours] to civil freedom. Liberty cannot exist in a country without knowledge among its inhabitants. Nor can tyrants live where the education of the people is generally attended to."[76] This promotion of education as a means to other goals is obviously at one with the intellectualist bias of his thought as a whole. This advocacy of popular education is mirrored by the Fox Club. For example, we find in 1812 reference to "Mr Joseph Lancaster and the Education of the People"[77]—a theme on which Mylne spoke in 1821 though without recorded reference to Lancaster. The reference is to the passing popularity of the educational theory of the English Quaker Joseph Lancaster (1778–1838) found in his essay on *Improvements to Education* (London, 1803) which advocated the education of the poor by a recursive passing on of knowledge. In 1820, "the Duke of Sussex and the Education of the People" and from 1821 to 1823 "Mr Brougham and the Education of the People" (or "the Poor") are toasted. The Duke of Sussex

---

73. Mylne, *Lectures on Political Economy* (NCL:BOGU3), Lecture 22.
74. Mylne, *Lectures on Political Economy* (NCL:BOGU3), Lecture 26.
75. Mylne, *Lectures on Political Economy* (NCL:BOGU3), Lecture 26.
76. Ibid.
77. *Glasgow Chronicle* 25/1/1812.

(1773–1843), or Prince Augustus, sixth son if George III, supported a range of liberal causes and was then associated with the Society for Educating and Clothing the Children of the Poor. We have noted Henry Brougham's activities for education.

The Fox Club also toasted in connection with the University in 1812 Lord Archibald Hamilton (1770–1827), a Whig politician with associations with Lanarkshire whom we have cited and from 1813–15 Thomas Graham, Lord Lynedoch. References to other Whig figures associated with the University, including James MacIntosh and "the Memory of Professor Millar and may Constitutional Principles ever distinguish our Scottish Universities" feature regularly in the toasts.

The British Constitution

Mylne held, as John Millar had argued, that the mainstay of the British Constitution was allegiance to Parliament rather than to the monarch. Parliament must thus retain legislative power and the Crown prerogative be curtailed. Bogue's political economy minutes record Mylne saying:

> If this [legislative power] be under the sole government of him who manages the executive, if it be wholly his will, there is little likelihood that the laws will be calculated to promote the wealth and prosperity of the country. If on the contrary, the laws are made by the united talent and wisdom of the nation, the happiest effects must result.[78]

Mylne goes on to identify Parliament and in particular the House of Commons as the cause of Britain's national prosperity, through its links with civil liberty:

> It is from the freedom of our Legislature, from one house of Parliament being composed of the representatives of the people, that all our prosperity has arisen. This has been the grand cause. Whatever opinions men entertain with regard to the present [purity][79] of Commons and Parliament, all admit the importance and advantages of the body.[80]

However, the defects of representation weighed more heavily as time passed and Mylne made common cause with the Glasgow Whigs on

---

78. Mylne, *Lectures on Political Economy* (NCL:BOGU3), lecture 24.
79. Or "party" or "parity."
80. Mylne, *Lectures on Political Economy* (NCL:BOGU3), lecture 25.

Parliamentary reform. These views cohere well with the general philosophical views on knowledge that he shared with Millar.

The Glasgow Foxites were moderately republican. They expressed this in their toast to "The House of Hanover, and may they never forget the principles which seated them on the Throne." Mylne supported this. At the level of political economy, he objected to James Beattie's rejection of republican forms of government as requiring poverty. The notes of Mylne's lectures say: "Republics have been said to be of most feeble tendency to wealth,[81] but this is not true." Venice and Genoa were republics, he argues, but prosperous ones. Despite being ruled by a tyrannical aristocracy, they "enjoyed more liberty than the surrounding nations."[82]

The Franchise and Parliamentary Reform

Mylne after 1820 advocated a political strategy in which popular education is accompanied by extension of the franchise. However, gaps in the evidence leaves it open whether he became more critical of the limited franchise or simply bolder in expressing an unchanged opinion. In the light of Fox's long-standing advocacy of parliamentary reform, it is likely that Mylne's views are simply becoming more visible, rather than more radical. His views stopped well short of universal suffrage and the reasons for this are intimated again in Mylne's philosophy: the best judgement of the good of society by legislators is the result of study and inquiry and requires the diffusion of knowledge amongst those who elect them.

As we have seen, James Mylne's views were at one with the Fox Club on this issue, though some went further in their language than he did. Mylne remained a supporter of parliamentary reform until it was achieved in the 1832 Reform Act.

Colonies and the East India Company

The renewal of the East India Company Exclusive Charter in 1812 was the subject of united opposition on the part of the Glasgow commercial establishment that revived the public life in the town. Significantly, it is called a monopoly and the Glasgow Council went so far as to compare it to the French blockade of British commerce on the continent of Europe.

---

81. This is the view of James Beattie in his *Principles of Moral Science*, who instances Sparta.

82. Mylne, *Lectures on Political Economy* (NCL:BOGU3), lecture 24.

This campaign failed, but the energy mobilized was not dissipated, but transferred to agitation against the raising of Corn Law import tariffs in 1814. The surviving text of Mylne's lectures in 1815/16 does not address the issue, though his opposition to monopolies give a presumption that his views would align with the merchants. However, his rejection of colonies, though consistent with the views of Fox on India, is not prominent amongst the Glasgow Whigs, despite their enthusiasm for the independence of Latin American countries and general support for "the Cause of Liberty all over the World." It is uncertain whether a lack of evidence or a real divergence of view is involved here.

The Corn Laws

Mylne includes a detailed treatment of the subject, drawing on Turgot's experience, Adam Smith's *Wealth of Nations* (Book 4 chapter 2)[83] and another work, perhaps Alexander Dirom's *Inquiry into the Corn Laws* (1796). Mylne notes significant changes in the 1773 legislation in force when Smith wrote and decreases in the price of corn where Smith's theory would have predicted increases. Bogue reports Mylne's conclusion:

> On the whole he thought legislative enactments on corn ought to be [withdrawn] and the price of corn left to the influence of natural causes. [...] There was however, great difficulty in deciding absolutely on this point.[84]

This was an issue on which merchants and town dwellers came together across much of the political spectrum. In 1805, the Magistrates and Town Council of Glasgow took initiatives in opposing changes to the Corn Laws that would raise the price of provisions.[85] In this respect in his lectures, the merchant and laboring classes of the town could make common cause against the landowning aristocracy. In 1814, we again find articulate opposition to the Corn Law Bill amongst the Glasgow trades and manufacturing interests.[86] It was argued that "there can be no difficulty, one should think, in perceiving the object in view—namely the increased value of the estates

---

83. Smith, *Wealth of Nations*; see also appendix to book 4.5.
84. Mylne, *Lectures on Political Economy* (NCL:BOGU3), lecture 33.
85. GC, 1804/05.
86. For example, GC 24/2/1814 for meeting of the Glasgow Chamber of Commerce and Manufactures. The *Courier* records further meetings the same year in Paisley (3 May), Hamilton (7 May) and Greenock (17 May).

and revenues of landed gentlemen."[87] This transmitted itself to Parliament via the local MP and the bill was not proceeded with.[88] Public debate on political economy after 1816 was highly political in respect of the Corn Laws.[89] The banners and speeches at a Radical meeting in 1819 continue to reflect the same issue.[90] We find Mylne engaged in communicating the results of a detailed factual enquiry on the subject throughout this period.

Scottish Burgh Reform

Mylne analyzed Burgh reform in his political economy lectures in a presentation that illustrates his approach to practical politics. He begins by summarizing and building on the history of burgh privileges in William Robertson's *History of Scotland* and Adam Smith's *Wealth of Nations*.[91] These were granted, he argues, by sovereigns and feudal lords to encourage arts and manufactures, but in such general form as enabled the passing of further regulations for the "particular interest of their members," witnessed by the great singularity of many Burgh regulations throughout Europe. These regulations, on apprenticeships for example, "gradually excluded all from certain powers but those belonging to corporations" leading, along with import laws and other restrictions on trade, to raised prices. Thus a system once "very beneficial to mankind" in rewarding innovation had become "useless and impolitic." Mylne draws a general lesson from this much in line with the tenor of his mental philosophy, that:

> Nothing can be more erroneous than to conceive that what is now useless and unjust was always so, without considering that circumstances may be greatly changed. It is also still more injurious to assume that regulations once passed ought never to be revoked, for statesmen obstinately to adhere to old practices and laws once their utility is gone.[92]

This applies his philosophical view of reason to historical enquiry. Mylne applies the argument also to geographically indeterminate grants

87. GC 10/3/1814, letter signed "COMMON SENSE."
88. GC 31/5/1814; 9 /6/1814.
89. The Corn laws and Combination Acts are the first subjects discussed in Maxwell, *A Letter to the Honest Reformers of Scotland*, along with religious establishment, rights of property, equality of rank, and revolution (see GC 16/10/1819).
90. See GC 28/8/1819. The "usual" political themes are "Annual Parliaments, Universal Suffrage, the Corn Laws and the Combination Acts."
91. Smith, *Wealth of Nations*, book 3:3.
92. Mylne, *Lectures on Political Economy* (NCL:BOGU3), lecture 34.

of monopoly and patent rights, advocating a further freeing of trade and "neutralising" of old regulations. In political terms, this call combined a political appeal to merchants for greater access to the corridors of power with a popular economic promise of lower prices.

The cause of Scotch burgh reform dates back to his time in Paisley. As far back as January 1787 the Incorporation of Weavers reasserted support for reform to end "the tyrannical system of self-election,"[93] and the same month the Glasgow burgesses, trades, and inhabitants met to discuss burgh reform.[94] Richard Sheridan advocated Scots reform the following year and in June 1788 the issue came before Parliament without apparent effect.[95] Again in 1792, the Glasgow Society for Burgh Reform publicized the cause of the "Rights of Man—the Right of the People to chuse their own Agents and Magistrates, and to call them to an account" adding in biblical tones that "in due time ye shall reap, if ye faint not."[96] Sheridan was again instrumental in initiating a Parliamentary motion on Burgh Reform that year and received the thanks of the Society despite its failure.[97] By December 1792, the attempt to link Parliamentary and Burgh reform had broken down, though Sheridan read out a further petition on the subject from Glasgow the following year.[98]

The impetus to reform seems to have lapsed after this time. According to Mackenzie, the unreformed Tory Town Council held sway in Glasgow and reporters were not allowed to attend its meetings. In December 1817, perhaps in the wake of publication of Watkins *Life of Sheridan* (2nd edition, 1817) or in the quickening political atmosphere of the times, another meeting on Burgh reform in Glasgow took place, opposing self-election and advocating the enfranchisement of burgesses.[99] The issue was discussed in the *Edinburgh Review* the following year[100] and "Success to Scottish Borough Reform" reappears as a toast at the Fox Dinner in January 1818 and the following year "may the legally adjudged rights of Scottish Burgesses never again be superseded by a Ministerial mandate." In September 1820 a House of Commons committee reported on the issue,[101] whilst from 1820 to

93. *GM* 3/1/1787.
94. *GM* 31/1/1787.
95. *GM* 16/1/1788&11/6/1788.
96. *GM* 20/3/1792; *GC* 22/3/1792.
97. *GC* 24/4/1792&17/7/1792.
98. *GC* 16/3/1793.
99. *GC* 20/12/1817&29/12/1817.
100. *GC* 6/6/1818: citing *Edinburgh Review* 60.
101. *GC* 21/9/1820.

1823 the cause was re-endorsed in Mylne's presence by the Glasgow Whigs and associated with Lord Archibald Hamilton. However, reform had to wait until 1833 when the Whigs returned to government in the wake of Parliamentary reform.

The Military

The Fox Dinners also endorsed the views of the role of the military that Mylne had been advocating in his political economy lectures for some years. In 1818, the Navy was praised in a phrase used by Mylne in a toast to "The Wooden Walls of our Islands" and defense made of:

> the yeomanry of the country, as the most powerful against the enemy and the least dangerous to liberty, contrasted with the growing rage for standing armies; the foul slanders, produced by means of hired informers, against the loyalty of the nation in general, and of this City in particular.[102]

Mylne, who had some firsthand knowledge of the military life, included a detailed account of the merits of standing armies, militias and the navy as means of national defense in his political economy course and his views are echoed in the Fox dinner toasts.

Ireland and Catholic Emancipation

The reform activist John McAdam observed that, prior to 1832, "little had been doing since the 'Radical days' unless some expression of sympathy with Catholic Emancipation."[103] Mylne had a track record on religious toleration as concerning Catholics and Irish politics. In February 1829, he was prominent at a meeting where he seconded a motion on Catholic emancipation held at the Tontine Inn in Glasgow to be forwarded to James MacIntosh and presented to Parliament and proposed thanks to Kirkman Finlay for procedural advice.[104] In 1833, we have noted that Mylne chaired another meeting against an "Irish Coercion Bill" in Glasgow. Mylne also notes the drain of money resulting from absentee landlords on Ireland.[105] His role on these issues seems to have been consistent and principled.

---

102. *Glasgow Chronicle* 27/1/1818.
103. McAdam, *Autobiography*, 4.
104. *Times*, 27/2/1829, citing *Glasgow Chronicle*.
105. Mylne, *Lectures on Political Economy* (NCL:BOGU3), lecture 16.

We may relate his views on toleration to his philosophy, according to which faith or belief is an intellectual act that ought not and, strictly cannot, be compelled. In his lectures, he strongly advocates religious tolerance. Such intolerance, he said, may lead to civil war or feuds, but more generally, it inhibits inquiry and "spreads a chilling and benumbing influence over the inhabitants" of a country.[106] He instances the persecutions of the Huguenots under Louis XIV in France and the Puritans under Charles I and II in England.

This outlook corresponds with the Fox dinner toasts on Ireland, which moved from "The Duke of Bedford, and may his conciliatory government to Ireland be an example to his successors" from 1815–19 to "The Duke of Leinster and the Whigs of Ireland" from 1821 and also included "May the Catholics of Ireland never separate their Religious and Political Rights." John Russell (1766–1839), the sixth Duke of Bedford had been Irish Viceroy in 1806–7 when he had introduced a bill to give Catholic officers equal treatment in the army. We may also note Mylne's reception of Daniel O'Connell in 1835, with whom he shared an acquaintance with Henry Brougham.

The Poor Law

On the relief of poverty, Mylne speaks more as a Church minister than as a Whig, for the Glasgow Fox Club had little to say on poverty. In Dundee, the Very Reverend Robert Small had written on poverty. Another colleague of Mylne's, Stevenson MacGill had also addressed "provision for the poor" in his *Discourses and Essays* (1819).[107] This clerical interest is to be expected given the role of the Church of Scotland in Poor law arrangements prior to the 1843 Disruption. Similar views were developed by another Paisley minister from 1811, Robert Burns (1789–1869), whom Mylne may have known through his lectures or the Clerical and Literary Society, "an Association composed of Professors in the University and Clergymen of the City of Glasgow and the immediate neighbourhood."[108] Burns was also interested in moral philosophy and awarded the degree of D.D. from Glasgow University in 1828.[109] Although unlike Mylne, he was "zealously loyal" to government,

---

106. Mylne, *Lectures on Political Economy* (NCL:BOGU3), lectures 24–25.

107. Advertised in *GC*, 4/121819.

108. Jonathan Ranken in Burns, *Testimonials in favour*, 39.

109. "Robert Burns" in *DNB*. See Burn's *Historical Dissertations*. Burns applied for the moral philosophy chair at St. Andrews in 1823.

this did not preclude concern with the alleviation of poverty.[110] Mylne followed this pattern.

In a political economy lecture,[111] Mylne takes issue with Thomas Malthus' theory about the inevitability of poverty and with Henry Home, Lord Kames (1696–1782), who had criticized the English poor-rates in a chapter of *Sketches of the History of Man* (1774; 2nd edition, 1778) as ruinously expensive and productive of dependency.[112] Mylne concedes that the system is "oppressive" to the taxpayer, but describes generalization from the English case as a "most unwarrantable assumption." He goes on to reject frugality as a universal remedy, observing that "there were some classes in society which frugality and parsimony could never save from poverty," but rather plunge them deeper into it. This he knew firsthand from his time in Paisley. Mylne also opposes a voluntary system on the grounds that "such contributions [. . .] would seldom spring from those best able to offer them and would produce general wretchedness." His conclusion, which Bogue records only in outline, was that in some circumstances an active government role would be "proper and beneficial."

Conclusion

In seeking to explain his politics, we find that James Mylne's mental philosophy sheds light on many of his opinions. His view of the primacy of reason in human nature led him to revise the theory of an unchanging natural law in the direction of a reformist vision in which social institutions accommodate themselves to increasing knowledge, commerce, and prosperity.

In addition to this, he was influenced by his Whig political beliefs as expressed by the Glasgow Fox Club, from whom his views rarely diverged. The political agenda sketched in the speeches and toasts of the Fox dinners thus indicates much of the practical hinterland of Mylne's abstract work in the fields of moral thought and political economy.

His personal experience as a chaplain and minister informed his views on a militia and on the relief of poverty. The dominant images of the Scottish Kirk characterize it as in terms of a rivalry between a lukewarm, patrician Moderation, epitomized by Alexander Carlyle and Hugh Blair, and a "Wild," Popular or Evangelical faction held to be, at least in the person of Thomas

---

110. McKay, *The Kirk and the Kingdom*.

111. Mylne, *Lectures on Political Economy* (NCL:BOGU3), lecture 50.

112. Home, *Sketches of the History of Man*, 2.10 "Public Police with respect to the Poor."

Chalmers (1780–1847), socially conservative.[113] The recovery of Mylne's agenda does better justice to the range, temper and intellectual quality of Christian involvement in the reform agenda in Glasgow.

However, Mylne did not endorse key elements of the radical agenda, such as universal suffrage and he had little to say on the Combination Acts, as far as the surviving records tell us. This leads me to classify him as a committed, lifelong *social reformer*, to use the term popularized by his successor, Glasgow Idealist Henry Jones.[114]

The only surviving extended public expression of James Mylne's beliefs about society took the form of his lectures on jurisprudence and political economy. The priority he gave to consideration of the social significance of wealth is a natural result of having followed the reasoning of figures like Priestley, Godwin, Millar, and the French Economists. In 1815, he began his lectures on political economy by asserting that political "alarms and commotions have resulted from our ignorance of political economy."[115] We now turn directly to the content of these lectures.

---

113. Drummond and Bulloch identify state oversight of Patronage as problematic from the fall of Walpole in 1736: see *The Scottish Church 1688–1843*, 62. According to Michael Fry, "clerics were the merest pawns of patronage" on the part of the Duke of Argyle (*The Dundas Despotism*, 25). This reached a height under the influence of Henry Dundas, whose reign was contemporary with Mylne's ministry in the Church and early years as a professor.

114. Jones, *Working Faith of the Social Reformer*.

115. Mylne, *Lectures on Political Economy* (NCL:BOGU3), Lecture 1.

CHAPTER 12

Political Economy

Introduction

WE NOW TURN TO James Mylne's lectures on political economy. The lectures address socio-political and commercial interests and reflect an era in Britain when the enthusiastic reception of the ideas of Adam Smith's *Wealth of Nations* (1776) led to attempts to modify them in detail by thinkers like Lauderdale and Brougham. Continental thinkers, including the "French economists" (Quesnay, Mercier, and Turgot) and the once exiled James Steuart, whose analyses reflected a more agricultural era and the role of an absolutist state are referenced. The era has been characterized by A. M. C. Waterman as one of opposition between the views of the largely Anglican and conservative "Christian political economy" of Thomas Malthus and the radicalism of William Godwin.[1] However, Mylne endorses instead the "correct principles" and "luminous clarity" of Smith's "illustrious work, a work calculated to do immense good."[2] These he contrasts with the "disordered imaginations" of unnamed opponents. Whilst he mentions Malthus shortly thereafter, the opponents could as well include Godwin's radical followers. Waterman describes how the utopian proposals in book 8 of Godwin's *Principles of Political Justice* (1793) had been criticized by the early Malthus in the first edition of his *Essay on Population* (1798) on grounds of an analysis of the effects of scarcity. The early work of Malthus developed into an advocacy of "moral restraint" and small scale property accumulation in later editions of his *Essay* from 1803. Mylne endorses the concept of private property common to both thinkers, but he rests in the

1. Waterman, *Revolution, Economics and Religion*.
2. Mylne, *Lectures on Political Economy* (NCL:BOGU3), lecture 1.

center ground between Godwin and Malthus in his practical conclusions and the focus of his thought is more commercially oriented.

Mylne's lectures, addressed to the merchant community of Glasgow reflect a practical turn in their criticism of Smith's theory of value and appeal to Whiggish attitudes in their occasional rhetorical passages. The general similarity to the contemporary lectures of Dugald Stewart in Edinburgh should not lead us to undervalue the sense of the moral and intellectual energy of the nascent Glasgow merchant community and the original analysis of the nature of commerce found in Mylne.

I will first describe the circumstances and surviving evidence of the course, and thereafter the nature and influence of the content.

The Origins of the Course

Mylne began to lecture in the evenings on "the philosophy of the human mind, on ethics, jurisprudence and political economy" in October 1801.[3] The following year the course focused on entirely on political economy[4] and pamphlets illustrating its content were published in 1804 and 1811.[5] Some observers gave Mylne's work on political economy equal standing with that on moral philosophy.[6] Mylne himself endorsed the view that "Political Philosophy should be his subject as much as Ethical Philosophy."[7] An observer in 1808 in a "Sketch of the University of Glasgow" describes the origins of the course in the circle of reformers around John Millar: "A series of lectures on political economy was long a favourite object with Mr Millar, and within the last few years, his wishes and suggestions have been realised by the establishment of such a course, under the conduct of Mr. Mylne."[8]

This observer goes on to note the "increasing reputation of these lectures" as affording "an honourable testimony to the abilities and industry of Mr. Mylne in his management of this department."[9] The lectures were

3. GC 22/10/1801

4. GC 9/11/1802

5. Copy in British Library. Another version mentioned in GC 12/11/1811 appears to be lost, if it ever existed.

6. Lant Carpenter for example, describes him as "Professor of Moral Philosophy and Political Economy" (see dedication to *Principles of Education, Intellectual, Moral and Physical*).

7. Parliamentary Reports: Reports from Commissioners: Universities, Scotland Volume 12 (London, 1831), 248.

8. From "Sketch of the University of Glasgow" in *The Monthly Anthology and Boston Review* 5 (May 1808), 240.

9. Ibid.

advertised in the local press as part of the University classes annually until 1809.[10] After that, the course was omitted from the annual University press advertisement and Mylne advertised a class separately starting November 1811. He continued to lecture on political economy until late in his teaching career. The Parliamentary Commissioners reported that, "In 1826–7 the class was attended by between 50 and 60 public students of Moral Philosophy and 32 or 33 others."[11]

One of these latter was John Collingwood Bruce (1805–92) from Newcastle studying for the ministry of the Secession Church.[12] Bruce had graduated MA in 1826 having taken Mylne's moral philosophy class that year. Bruce's attendance was thus voluntary and illustrates that the audience was typically more mature and professional in nature than the moral philosophy class. Some years, prior to 1831, Mylne attempted to combine his lectures into a single course, but deemed the attempt unsuccessful. However, the political economy lectures were moved to the daytime and given two days a week.[13] By the late 1830s, political economy was taught on Tuesday and Thursday at 3:00 pm, though it is likely that by this time one of Mylne's assistants such as Fleming would lecture.[14]

Henry Cockburn contrasted Mylne's course with the "short and very general courses" on the same subject by Dugald Stewart in Edinburgh around the same time, which are described in later editions of Stewart's *Outlines of Moral Philosophy* and were later published by Mylne's student William Hamilton.[15] In Edinburgh, this course appears to have been dropped by Thomas Brown between 1810 and 1820 and revived by Mylne's student John Wilson thereafter. Mylne's lectures were thus a prominent means of diffusing ideas about political economy in Scotland.

---

10. The class is included in the annual lists of College classes published in September each year in the *Glasgow Courier* up to 1809, with reminder notices for the Political Economy class in November, shortly before the classes started and class prize winners in May the following year. Mylne's Political Economy is absent from the September 1810 list and there is no reminder thereafter.

11. Parliamentary Reports: Reports from Commissioners: Universities, Scotland Volume 12 (London, 1831), 247–48.

12. Bruce, *Life and Letters of John Collingwood Bruce*, 28. Bruce later became a historian and folklorist.

13. House of Commons Papers, *Reports from Commissioners* (London, 1831), 4:247–48.

14. Hay, *Inaugural Addresses*, xxxix. Hay appears to copy the 1831 report in some places.

15. Cockburn, *Life of Lord Jeffrey*, 1:277.

Reconstructing the Course

It is possible to reconstruct the outlines of Mylne's political economy from a copy of student minutes of the lectures, written by David Bogue (c. 1795–1824), the son of an English minister who went on to study law,[16] supplemented by advertisements, the surviving printed course introduction, and contemporary descriptions. However, the limited corroboration of points of detail makes us reliant on the coherence of the argument in judging the accuracy of the minutes. There are some internal indications that the course underwent more change than did his lectures on moral philosophy.

The Content of the Course

According the course outline published in 1804, after provisional definition of the subject, the course discussed (a) the general wealth of a nation and (b) that portion which is employed by the State, or the Public Revenue.[17] This agrees with the 1815/16 minutes.

The first part on general wealth addressed four questions. The first of these was the sources of national wealth, under which Mylne discussed the principles of the science, in particular the origins of wealth; the nature of exchange and value; the functions of commerce and banking; and capital, division of labor and machinery. The minutes allow us to identify the sources of many of the ideas. The observer from 1808 summarized the first part of the course:

> In that part of the course, which is devoted to a consideration of the various opinions, with respect to the nature and origin of publick wealth, a detailed account is given of the doctrines of the French economists, accompanied by an impartial and satisfactory discussion of their merits.[18]

These were principal authorities of the day. The observer continues: "Mr. Mylne assumes some particular points of difference with Adam Smith, on which he reasons with much ingenuity and force of argument." Local opinion

---

16. Held in NCL Spec. Coll. MS BOGU3. There is also a set of shorthand notes in NLS from 1804/05 by James Yates, which I have not managed to decypher. For Bogue's biography, see Addison, *Matriculation Records*, entry 9044.

17. I draw this description principally from Mylne's *Plan of a Course of Lectures on Political Economy* of 1804, supported by witness accounts and lecture notes.

18. "Sketch of the University of Glasgow" in *The Monthly Anthology and Boston Review* 5 (May 1808), 240–41.

in Glasgow bore witness to the large influence of French thinkers on Adam Smith[19] and Smith devotes a chapter of *Wealth of Nations* to them.[20]

Turning to considerations of macroeconomic policy, Mylne secondly addressed the causes that affect the amount of national wealth, divided into physical, moral, and legislative. Thirdly, he discussed the causes that affect the distribution of national wealth. Fourthly he discusses the causes that check its growth, which includes a critical discussion of Malthus's views on population.

The second part of the course concerned the public revenue. This comprises practical arguments for and against a series of public measures that relate to his late political activity. It addressed three subjects. Firstly, Mylne discusses the objects to which the national revenue may be applied, distinguished into: national defense; internal security and the administration of justice; encouragements to industry; educational institutions; established religion; and institutions for the support of the poor. Secondly he turns to the means of raising the funds necessary for these objects, in other words the theory of taxation. Thirdly, he discusses the national debt, a subject previously addressed by Thomas Paine and James Beattie. We touch on this in our chapter on Mylne's late political activity.

The Principles of Political Economy

I now turn to Mylne's treatment of the principles of political economy. These discussions, comprising the first twenty-three lectures in 1815/16, consist of original syntheses of the literature of the day, principally the "French economists" (the Physiocrats Quesnay, Mercier, and Turgot),[21] Adam Smith, Lord Lauderdale,[22] and Henry Brougham.[23] The latter two were political

19. The obituary of Adam Smith already pointed out the substantial extent to which he drew on the work of French economists, whilst admiring his systematisation of their opinions. The subject was raised again in an introduction to an early posthumous edition of *Wealth of Nations*, which contained a preface by Germaine Garnier discussing the French economists in relation to Smith.

20. Adam Smith, *Wealth of Nations*, 4.9: "Of the Agricultural Systems."

21. Mylne's lectures allow us to identify in some detail his knowledge of French texts, on which he also lectured to the Glasgow Literary and Commercial Society in 1807. In the lectures, he refers specifically to three French authors: the founder of the Physiocratic school, François Quesnay (1694–1774), his principal interpreter Mercier de la Rivière and author and statesman Turgot. It is noteworthy that his approach of critically comparing Scottish and French sources is similar to his approach to mental philosophy, in which he draws from both Condillac and Reid.

22. Maitland, *Inquiry into the Nature and Origin of Public Wealth*.

23. Mylne refers to Brougham's review of Lauderdale in *Edinburgh Review* (July

allies. In 1795, Lauderdale had objected to restrictions on public meetings, which gave rise to a reproving public letter by Edmund Burke.[24] Fox had appointed Lauderdale Governor General of India[25] and negotiator with the French[26] in the brief coalition "Ministry of All the Talents" of 1806. His *Inquiry into the Practical Merits of the Government of India* appeared in 1809.[27] This exploration of the fundamental concepts of his contemporaries culminates in an argument that commerce, rather than agricultural or manufacturing labor, is the principal source of public wealth. Commerce produces a "double good" by bringing laborers and consumers into relation and thereby increasing wealth by giving potential value to things that formerly lacked it.[28] This occasions a rhetorical passage praising commerce for its public benefits over both extravagance and charity.

Mylne's view of the relations of commerce and agriculture are illuminated in a separate talk on Lord Kames' "stadial" theory of human economic history in the moral philosophy course.[29] Kames identified four stages of human development: hunting, shepherding, agriculture, and commerce ("CASH backwards," in the student mnemonic).[30] Mylne notes that Kames' view has been "very generally adopted,"[31] but objects that the first two of these terms do not fit with the physical facts of human nature. He argued, "Man is not fitted by nature for prowling. An unarmed savage could not prowl and the first savages had no arrows. Besides, food much more tempting in those regions is scattered on every side: fruit, herbs, roots . . ."[32] The regions are those "of almost eternal spring." Instead, he sees hunting and shepherding as degenerations from an original state of primitive agriculture. He first turns then, to consider the emergence of commerce from an "agricultural kingdom," as addressed by the French economists, as

---

1804) 343–77.

24. GC 26/11/1795 for the Lauderdale's opposition to the "Bill for the more effectually preventing Seditious Meetings and Assemblies" that was much opposed in Glasgow and stifled public debate for many years; 3/3/1796 advert for Burke's *Letter to a Noble Lord*. The Earl of Bedford to whom Burke also objects was a forebear of the philosopher Bertrand Russell.

25. GC 3/6/1806.

26. GC 7/8/1806; 16/12/1806.

27. Maitland, *Inquiry into the Practical Merits of the Government of India*, advertised in GC 12/10/1809.

28. Mylne, *Lectures on Political Economy* (NCL:BOGU3), lectures 4–5.

29. Pollock notes, GUL:MSGen1355/103/33.

30. Home, *Sketches of the History of Man*, 1:1.1–4.

31. For example, Adam Smith, *Wealth of Nations*, 5.1.1.

32. Pollock notes, GUL:MSGen1355/103/33.

the principal fact of human economic development. Mylne evaluates the French economists at the outset of his 1815 lectures, the "minutes" of which inform us that the discussion of them is abbreviated compared to his previous discussions.

The first section of the course begins by defining the wealth of a nation as "the sum of all the advantages which a nation possesses for the sustenance and enjoyment of its inhabitants."[33] This appears to be a version of Lauderdale's definition of public wealth, which makes no reference to the market and which contrasts with "private riches," for which exchange value is necessary. Lauderdale argues that an abundance of water would contribute to public wealth, whereas only its scarcity would contribute to private riches. For example, a spring would only bring riches to its owner where water was scarce, but society as a whole would not be better off for water being scarce.[34]

After outlining the French economists' distinction of productive, proprietary, and unproductive classes, Mylne turns to evaluate their theory that only agriculturalists are productive. He begins by noting that this is "absurd and contrary to common sense," but makes two specific criticisms:

> It must be admitted indeed that, according to their view of wealth, certainly, the manufacturer and artisan only contributed to it in an indirect way. Yet, though it be indirectly, they may contribute very much to that wealth. [. . .] Besides, the Economists assume that the production of the manufacturer and artisan is only equivalent to his consumption. Now we are not obliged to grant them this principle.[35]

The use of the term "indirect" is not developed, but rather the assumption of equivalence in exchange. This raises the question of what is meant by "equivalent." Mylne takes the example of a farmer who exchanges a day's food for the labor of an "artist" for a day (the word may be "artisan"). Yet the "value" of the items exchanged may vary greatly. He asks, "What then, is meant by an exact equivalent? It is only exact inasmuch as it is agreed to by both parties, but can never be exact in amount, on account of an infinite variety of circumstances."[36]

---

33. Mylne, *Lectures on Political Economy* (NCL:BOGU3), lecture 2.

34. Brougham takes issue with this, arguing that the natural measure of public wealth is value in use and of private riches value in exchange (*Edinburgh Review* (July 1804), 350–51.

35. Mylne, *Lectures on Political Economy* (NCL:BOGU3), lecture 2.

36. Ibid.

He gives an example of an artist who exchanges his produce with a farmer in exchange for living expenses for six months, where "at the end of this period the treasures of the artist were fully equal to those of the cultivator."[37] He concludes:

> It is evident that the concessions of the Economists [destroy] the extravagance of their doctrine and that, though artisans and manufacturers are productive of wealth only indirectly, yet still their share of production is by no means small and, further, we can see that there is not an exact equivalent between the consumption and production of the artisan and manufacturer.[38]

The implication of this appears to be that non-agricultural labor may also be a source of wealth. However, Mylne moves on to criticize also Adam Smith's theory that "productive labour" is the source of wealth. In this, he appears to be drawing on the writings of Lauderdale. Mylne says:

> The principles of Dr Smith are no less untenable than those of the Economists [. . .] There are many objections against Dr Smith's principles about productive and unproductive labour. [. . .] The objections [raised] by common sense against them were certainly supported by reasoning and inquiry.[39]

In his next lecture, he turns to discuss Smith's distinction of "productive" and "unproductive" labor in the chapter "On the Accumulation of Capital, or of Productive and Unproductive Labour" from *Wealth of Nations*.[40] This seems to owe something to Lauderdale and Brougham's criticisms of Smith. Mylne argues that Smith's concept of "productive" labor is arbitrary and that labor is productive even where it does not result in an enduring or saleable commodity. He illustrates his point:

> The higher orders of life do not indeed for the most part sell labour; but along with labour of body and mind, they sell their responsibility and talent and experience. A lawyer produces, by his professional study, skill which can be sold. Dr Smith seems only to regard the labour by which they transfer their goods. This is a very limited view. [. . .] The mind is the object upon which the labour of the literary man has been employed and the value of which has been increased. [. . .] But that labour is really

---

37. Ibid. The abbreviation in the manuscript could be "artist" or "artisan."
38. Ibid.
39. Ibid.
40. Smith, *Wealth of Nations*, 2.3

productive which is useful to him who buys it, even though it should be immediately consumed.[41]

The disagreement here is not significant overall, as Mylne later in the course reinstates something like Smith's distinction in his own discussion of capital accumulation. The concepts developed however, point to the significance of utility (what is "useful to him who buys it") as the primary measure of value and recur in the immediately succeeding discussion of commerce as a source of national wealth. The priority given to utility marks a difference from Smith and a recurrence to (or development of) ideas found in Pufendorf, Hutcheson, and Hume.[42]

The Role of Commerce

Mylne gives commerce priority over agriculture and manufactures in his discussion of the sources of wealth. He follows the method of starting with simple cases to understand a complex process:

> The simplest form of any object is the best state to examine it and consider it. The mechanic never begins his study with the most complex machines, but with the lever, pulley, etc. In like manner, it would be vain to look for the principle of commerce in its most refined and improved state.[43]

Hence he begins by considering barter.

> In the earliest stages of society indeed, there would be but little exchange. As society advanced in [complexity], commerce would increase. Two parties would then arise, the agriculturalists and the artisans. A third party, the merchants, would not at first because not required. Soon after this however, for the sake of convenience and saving of time, the merchant would become employed by the agriculturalist and the artisan. Yet in its original state, commerce would not include the idea of a separate profession.[44]

There follows a series of three arguments to the effect that commerce diffuses, maintains, and increases wealth, starting from the idea that "all transactions of exchange are commercial agreements." The first argues

---

41. Mylne, *Lectures on Political Economy* (NCL:BOGU3), lecture 3.
42. See Deleule, *Hume et la Naissance du Libéralisme économique*, 54–59, esp 59.
43. Mylne, *Lectures on Political Economy* (NCL:BOGU3), lecture 5.
44. Mylne, *Lectures on Political Economy* (NCL:BOGU3), lecture 4.

simply that commerce brings parties acting from self-interest into contractual relations. The second argues that "wealth diffused by commerce is always preserved," and that in this respect it is superior to benevolence. He illustrates his point thus:

> In exchange, there is an equivalent on both sides. The man who gives a week's provision to a person from pure charity is to be commended for his charity, but does little or no good to [a] comm[unity]; whereas the man who requires a week's labour for the week's provision he gives, perhaps benefits the man as much and certainly does tenfold more good to society.[45]

In other words, the equivalent in the case of a commercial transaction, i.e., the labor of the employee in this case, functions to maintain the economic resources of society as a whole.

The most powerful argument in support of commerce however, is the third. Here Mylne distinguishes two causes of poverty in a country. The first occurs "where it is destitute of means of providing subsistence for its inhabitants," which he illustrates by "Lapland, Greenland, Iceland; some parts of Africa and Asia." There is a second case however, where there are valuable objects, but circumstances prevent their value being realized. This he illustrates by the case of a city, which he might but does not name as Glasgow, separated from abundant coal mines by "impassable hills." Here there is a role for commercial initiative:

> But let commerce be introduced by a bridge being formed, a canal dug or a way cut through these mountains and a commerce opened between this city and those coal mines. Wealth flows into both parties and each species of poverty is destroyed. [. . .] Commerce in [my] view [is] always productive of the double good illustrated in this case. It connects those who want and therefore are poor and those who do not want, but from the objects they possess not being valuable, are also poor.[46]

This illustration serves as the background of a more general discussion of the concept of value assumed in the concept of a potentially "valuable object."

---

45. Ibid.
46. Mylne, *Lectures on Political Economy* (NCL:BOGU3), lectures 4 and 5.

The Theory of Value

Mylne here makes some trenchant and detailed criticisms of Smith's account of value. Smith had stated that the term value "has two different meanings": use-value and exchange-value[47] and goes on to argue that labor is the measure of exchange value. Mylne argues instead that usefulness is the fundamental sense of the term and that exchange value derives from use value. Smith, Mylne argues, conceives use abstractly. He says, "No man or woman will say that *water* abstractly considered is not more valuable than diamonds. It is not however, by the abstract utility of a thing that we are to decide its value and use."[48] What matters is what people actually want. Here, thinks Mylne, Smith is limiting his concept of use arbitrarily so as to exclude it as a source or measure of value. Smith gives the example of diamonds, which he says have "little or no value in use" but a great value in exchange. Mylne rejects Smith's claim that an object in demand may have no use at all. He argues the point thus in a passage that evokes the commodities of the day:

> If utility be taken in the rigorous sense of Dr Smith, everything beyond the common necessities of life will become totally useless. Utility then must be made more comprehensive. It must include everything that will be beneficial to a man, or that a man thinks valuable to gratify his lawful wishes: whether from the rough wool cloth to the scarlet coat or Brussels lace; from a beef steak to venison and turtle soup; or whether from small beer to champagne and burgundy.[49]

Use value depends on the judgements of men, even where these are erroneous or whimsical. This makes it dependent on the "desires and passions" of individuals, or on "the tastes and circumstances of individuals who estimate the objects in question." This returns the theory of value from Smith to the natural law tradition of Gershom Carmichael, for whom "suitability, real or imaginary" enters into his account of scarcity as part of the estimate of value.[50] Value is thus something subjective and "altogether relative." Mylne says:

> A thing may be useful to me that is not useful to my neighbour. An old Greek manuscript may not be thought very valuable by

---

47. Smith, *Wealth of Nations*, 28.
48. Mylne, *Lectures on Political Economy* (NCL:BOGU3), lecture 5.
49. Ibid.
50. Carmichael, *Natural Rights*, 106–7.

me, but esteemed very invaluable by a Greek scholar. Our ideas of value in use are then much affected by relative circumstances.

Mylne argues successfully that use value must thus precede and always conditions exchange value. The minutes conclude:

> value in exchange always depends on [the] value in use of the object. This view was in opposition to Dr Smith. It is impossible for a thing to be an object of exchange, if nobody puts a high value on it in use. It depends therefore on some person who is eager to possess it and desirous to consume it.[51]

Having argued plausibly that use value is a factor in exchange value, Mylne turns consider other components that affect price. Here too he qualifies Smith's positive account of exchange value, particularly the famous "labor theory of value" and the distinction of natural and market price. Mylne notes that Smith's view of labor as a fixed standard of value has a moral element:

> Smith was led into this view by various maxims he maintains, as that labour is the price for the blessings nature has bestowed on us, etc. Yet though true, it was questionable whether these maxims were applicable to the [science] of political economy.[52]

It is likely that there was a moral undercurrent in acceptance of the labor theory of value also in the Marxist tradition, and that this compromised the positive analysis of exchange. Mylne argues that the value of labor is itself subject to modification and that it is thus not uniquely privileged as a "standard" of value. He brings in the literary marketplace and quips:

> If so, many old theological works which cost their authors immense labour and researches would not now be allowed to sleep quietly on the shelf, while the flimsy compositions of the present day are widely read and put money into their authors' purse.[53]

He refers to Lauderdale and Brougham for support. Mylne proceeds to argue that the distinction of natural and market price is obscure. The minutes state:

> the natural or philosophical price of any commodity will never affect its market price. The man who is endeavouring to sell his goods will get no more for them, from his saying he has

---

51. Mylne, *Lectures on Political Economy* (NCL:BOGU3), lecture 6.
52. Ibid.
53. Ibid.

bestowed so much labour and trouble and care about them. [...] It is only the philosopher who considers what ought to be the natural price of an object, and even the philosopher, when he goes to market forgets every other consideration and endeavours to make as good and cheap a purchase as he can.[54]

One might argue however, that this underrates the ultimate centrality of labor to cost calculations, though Mylne does proceed to make some remarks that might be seen as relevant to this.

Mylne then explains how markets shape the character of the merchant through self-interest. For example, avarice that raises prices may encourage competitors to outbid him on price; whilst a merchant's trade "depends vitally on his probity and honour."[55]

Money

Following the discussion of commerce in the abstract, Mylne turns to discuss money in various forms as a medium of commercial transactions. This contrasts with Adam Smith, who begins with the division of labor. This again reflects the priority Mylne gives to commerce as an agent of economic development. He begins with the development of money from barter, the role of gold and silver. He concludes that "The value of money ought to be left to be decided by the ordinary operations of commerce and not restricted by any legal enactments." Despite fluctuations of values, he judges that "if a man conduct his affairs with prudence, he will not suffer much from variations in value of gold and silver." He endorses the idea of an international currency, writing that "if this simple proposal were carried into effect, we should know the price of an article in every part of Europe, as we know it now in London."[56]

He then turns to paper money, which was a prominent though not exclusive feature of Scottish commerce and banking. One form of this was Bills of Exchange between merchants, an "expedient of commercial men to facilitate the barter of their commodities." Soon however, this was supplemented by banks, for which he identifies several social functions. Firstly, banks have the same effect as the commerce they facilitate, "The banking system has a tendency to extend and facilitate commercial transactions

---

54. Mylne, *Lectures on Political Economy* (NCL:BOGU3), lecture 6.
55. Mylne, *Lectures on Political Economy* (NCL:BOGU3), lecture 7.
56. Mylne, *Lectures on Political Economy* (NCL:BOGU3), lecture 11.

between count[ries] and people totally unconnected before."[57] This encourages both merchants and manufacturers. In addition though, it puts to use idle funds deposited with it. Thirdly, Mylne notes that it increases frugality and encourages saving "particularly amongst the lower classes." This coincides with the founding of the Trustee Savings Bank in 1810 by the Reverend Henry Duncan (1774–1846). Duncan incidentally, was in charge of the early education of the Scottish philosopher James Frederick Ferrier.

Barring cases of malfeasance, which are not in the bankers' interest, Mylne asserts the general soundness of the private banking system even in the occasional absence of liquidity:

> The person who takes the banker's notes knows perfectly well that the banker is not merely accountable with the cash he has in hand or in all solid or paper money; but in every species of property he possesses. [...] Nothing can be more absurd than to say that because persons cannot pay all debts at once, therefore they cannot ever discharge them.

Despite the skepticism of "poets and satirists" and problems of fictitious bills, he concludes that banking serves important social functions. As banking and prosperity have gone together in Britain over a long period, he remarks, we are entitled to be skeptical of its critics. Mylne refers his hearers to Adam Smith and Sir James Steuart for further information on banks.

There follows a long treatment of the suspension of cash payments by the Bank of England from 1792. In this, he defends the "common honesty" of William Pitt who required the Bank of England to loan money to government to finance war. This illustrates Mylne's political moderation that lent his voice authority on those occasions when he did speak out on the political questions of the day.

On the whole then, in this series of connected discussions, we can see a theoretical justification for a class of active merchants who identify the "lawful wishes"[58] of the community and match them with the economic resources necessary to meet them, supported by the inventors of machines who maximize the value of labor and create new economic possibilities. For many years, this provided for economic development in the West of Scotland. For example, Mylne's two younger sons were respectively a merchant and an engineer. It is possible to sketch some likely lines of influence for Mylne's economic ideas.

---

57. Mylne, *Lectures on Political Economy* (NCL:BOGU3), lecture 12.
58. Mylne, *Lectures on Political Economy* (NCL:BOGU3), lecture 5.

Capital, Division of Labor, and Machinery

Having discussed commerce and money, Mylne turns to a relatively brief discussion of the roles of capital and labor in generating wealth. He defines capital as wealth applied to the increase of property. He defends Smith against Lauderdale on the virtue of parsimony in describing the origin of capital. Once created, capital, he thinks, has three principal functions: supporting laborers; constructing tools; and bringing together establishments for particular purposes, such as the levelling of roads or building of bridges.

Mylne gives less priority than Smith to the division of labor and unlike Smith he thinks it may arise from human sagacity independent of barter. However, his account of its benefits in shortening labor time required for a given task; improving skill and dexterity; and encouraging the improvement of tools, is similar to that of Smith. He endorses Smith's view that education is desirable to counteract the narrowing effects of specialized work.

Mylne relates advances in machinery to the demand for mechanization consequent on the division of labor. He defines machinery generally, saying: "What is a ship but a machine, a wagon than a machine?"[59] Whilst he does not endorse Smith's view that the workmen themselves will invent machines, nor does he clearly take up Lauderdale's criticism that the invention of machines is also an instance of the division of labor, being the work of a specialized engineering profession. It is typical of his general rationalism and optimism that, in contrast to Lauderdale, he sees no upper limit to capital accumulation: "Human ingenuity will always furnish new demands for the laying out of capital."[60]

The Causes of National Wealth

Mylne turns to a discussion of the macroeconomic causes of national wealth, which he divides into physical, moral and legislative. We cover many of the moral and legislative causes in our chapter on his politics. This results in particular from his method of investigation, which is to study Britain and only bring in comparisons thereafter to confirm or refute lessons he is inclined to draw on the basis of the British experience.

Mylne downplays the influence of physical geography on national wealth, pointing out that it does not act uniformly, as similar environments produce quite different levels of wealth; whilst the supposed natural advantages of Britain such as its wheat fields are the product of labor. He makes

---

59. Mylne, *Lectures on Political Economy* (NCL:BOGU3), lecture 23.
60. Ibid.

two exceptions to this, for extreme physical conditions that ingenuity cannot overcome, such as in the Arctic and Britain's island status. In this latter case, he summarizes John Millar's account of the lack of a standing army and the consequent alliance of Crown and Commons against the Nobility that led to the rights of the House of Commons.

The moral causes of national prosperity we have largely covered in the politics chapter and, where they differ from common opinion, they generally reflect his Whig convictions. These moral causes are: an equitable distribution of power; good legislators, which he stresses as a key point; the administration of justice; a religion that favors economic activity; religious toleration; and the diffusion of knowledge, on which he also lays particular stress. He makes a final observation that the moral causes are "mutually connected and influential." Civil freedom might lead to religious freedom and the advance of knowledge for example. In Britain's case this may have been so, but we could not conclude that it would always or generally be so. The primacy of these joint causes he judges "a conjecture of high probability," with the qualification "unless some superior causes can be discovered."

Turning to those he describes as "legislative causes" of national wealth, he divides these into internal or domestic laws; those affecting foreign trade; and those related to colonies. The first receive the most detailed treatment and are divided in turn into those affecting population, agriculture and commerce.

Population, Agriculture and Commerce

On population, Mylne argues that it is wrong to increase population by state intervention, as did Louis XIV, arguing that this may be left to personal choice. Instead he states, "The number of a population of any country will ever be regulated by nature. She well can fix the bounds of [national] population."[61] His attention is directed instead to the problem of Highland depopulation resulting from emigration. Here he defends the right to emigrate. He opposes state support for agriculture where this is not profitable and questions why private commerce could not encourage manufactures. However, he sees a role for government in the construction of canals, roads, and bridges in the Highlands, a process underway as he spoke. He also advocates exemption from tax except for large estates, which would encourage small proprietors.

There is no explicit acknowledgement in this of Malthus' argument that the tendency of population is to rise until there is pressure on resources.

61. Mylne, *Lectures on Political Economy* (NCL:BOGU3), lecture 27.

Mylne comments instead that: "We are in fact not well qualified to judge in the economy of nature and often mistaken,"[62] which leads him on to an account of the national census, which commenced in 1801 and provides factual data on population. The census shows that British population was increasing, as was national wealth. However, Mylne does note that "Perhaps in some cases sufficient encouragement is not given to marriage."[63] This may represent an engagement with Malthus. His later remarks dedicated to Malthus however, see the impetus of his work as opposition to Godwin's theories of human perfectibility and are decidedly negative in tone. Whilst Mylne does not make this argument, we may comment that Malthus' theological interpretation of life as a period of probation is intertwined with a theory of free will scarcely consistent with Mylne's residual Calvinism.

In the course of Mylne's treatment of agricultural legislation, he encourages his audience to "Respect the sacred right of property."[64] This reflects the view of Godwin, but is accompanied by dismissal of Thomas Paine's levelling views which would locate Mylne's own views in the Whig tradition. The bulk of his treatment opposes price control on the price of foodstuffs and draws on the free market opinions on the French Physiocrats (naming Turgot and citing Quesnay) and Adam Smith. As with Malthus on population, he attempts to find empirical confirmation of their abstract reasoning, which leads him to cast doubt on some of their practical conclusions, particularly on the operation of the Corn Laws, but the principles themselves he endorses. He notes the opposition of agricultural and commercial interests in the House of Commons on the subject.

Turning thirdly to legislation on domestic commerce, here we find Mylne endorsing the free market views of Adam Smith over a range of legislative topics. We have discussed Burgh reform in the politics chapter. There are discussions of: grants of monopoly; bounties for inventions; import and export restrictions; and the export of machinery. The exceptions to a free trade model in such goods are typically temporary in nature, intended to prevent the "ruin" of participants by facilitating the withdrawal of capital from declining trades, such as linen manufacture in Scotland. He recommends Smith and Hume over Judge Blackstone, who supported restrictions on the emigration of artisans and the export of machinery. Mercantile laws, e.g., on factoring, solvency, insurance, he thinks a practical matter best decided by judges and jurists. He states that: "there is more advantage to be derived from the internal commerce of a country than from its foreign

---

62. Mylne, *Lectures on Political Economy* (NCL:BOGU3), lecture 29.
63. Mylne, *Lectures on Political Economy* (NCL:BOGU3), lecture 27.
64. Mylne, *Lectures on Political Economy* (NCL:BOGU3), lecture 29.

trade."⁶⁵ The reason for this is that less capital is required and returns on it are quicker. He sees a role for government in organizing improvements in transport (canals, roads, bridges), though even here those expected to benefit should bear the cost. Many such projects were afoot in contemporary Glasgow and Scotland. The uniformity of weights and measures is a government responsibility. On the rate of interest, he argues against Sir Joshua Child that this may be left to the markets, which are best placed to reflect security and risk. The role of government is to increase the security of loans, which reduces risk.

Foreign Trade

We move from domestic legislation to that covering foreign trade and commerce, that is, relations with other sovereign states and nations. The attention given to this perhaps reflects not only Britain's status as a trading nation, but Glasgow's position as a British expanding port. Mylne rejects analogies with a household, which requires to trade. Domestic national wealth can be increased without foreign trade. He also rejects the distinction of "active" and "passive" merchants as a misleading analogy, making a division instead between the foreign trade of consumption and the carrying trade. The former, meaning the import and export of goods for consumption is both necessary (to some) and useful. He states:

> The improvement of one country tends to multiply the intercourse of nations. It gives them the means to purchase and the desire to purchase. It gives rise to improvement of various powers. It promotes [. . .] friendship and goodwill between the nations who carry it on.⁶⁶

He rejects the notion that if one nation gains, another must lose. Where trade between nations is contracted voluntarily, "Both profit much, or no such traffic would be conducted."⁶⁷ With regard to the balance of trade and the export of money, he rejects the analogy of the exporting nation with a spendthrift: money is simply a commodity like any other and commercial rivalry need not lead to hostility.

Mylne is less of an advocate of the foreign carrying trade (that is, the operation of merchant shipping between foreign countries by ships owned by Britain or operated by British crew). He comments that "Dr Smith has

---

65. Mylne, *Lectures on Political Economy* (NCL:BOGU3), lecture 36.
66. Mylne, *Lectures on Political Economy* (NCL:BOGU3), lecture 39.
67. Mylne, *Lectures on Political Economy* (NCL:BOGU3), lecture 40.

ably shewn that little profit is derived from it."⁶⁸ This leads on to a detailed treatment of the Navigation Laws, under which preference was given to British ships and sailors at British and colonial ports. Here again he calls Adam Smith's treatment "masterly." Mylne describes the principal arguments for and against the Navigation Laws, citing Anderson's *History of Commerce* for historical background. They are said to have strengthened the British fleet at the expense of the Dutch. Mylne suggests that British trade prospered whilst they were in effect, but not necessarily because of them. The independence of the former North American colonies does not speak in their favor. He asks whether Glasgow would flourish more if it refused to deal with non-Glaswegian merchants. If it were true that the Laws strengthened the Royal Navy, then he would say "Dash our commerce!" but he doubts this is so and if it were, would other countries not simply reciprocate? In fact, most marines are not taken from merchant ships.

Turning to colonies, Mylne again comes to a negative view similar to that of Adam Smith. The causes of their establishment were accidental and included a search for gold, for a passage to India, religious persecution that sent the American colonists overseas and naval power and glory. British attention was first drawn to the West Indies by the profits to be made from sugar and tobacco; whilst the American War of Independence had arisen over taxation. Mylne finds confirmation of his view of the relation of freedom and prosperity in the contrast between the British, Spanish and Portuguese colonies: "The [reason] why Britain and British colonies [are] flourishing and prosperous is on account of their liberty of government, civil and religious."⁶⁹ The "despotism and superstition" of the Spanish colonies and their independence were regular subjects of comment in the newspapers and his favorable remarks on the "freedom and independence" of North America may have led to his grand-niece Frances Wright's first trip to America, which produced her *Men and Manners in America* (1822).

After this long discussion of the amount of national wealth, there was advertised a discussion of the distribution of national wealth.⁷⁰ We do not have notes of this, though they may still exist in shorthand. The course outline indicates that Mylne considered inequality excessive and advocated "indirect" rather than "direct" methods for its alleviation.

Mylne then turns to discuss laws of the increase and diminution of national wealth. Here he contrasts the stable state of India and North America with the rise and fall of Greece, Venice, and Genoa. His main point

---

68. Ibid.
69. Mylne, *Lectures on Political Economy* (NCL:BOGU3), lecture 43.
70. Mylne, *Plan of a Course of Lectures on Political Economy*, 21–22.

is rejection of comparisons with biological entities (e.g., the ages of man) in discussing societies, where knowledge makes progress possible. Thus Britain, having risen, need not fall again. He introduces "Mr Malthus's book"[71] in a discussion of perfectibility. Unfortunately, the legibility lets us down at this point, but it is clear that Mylne identifies the principle of population as a weak point in Malthus.

It is also apparent that Mylne here begins to summarize material. He refers on March 29, 1816 to "the late period" as justifying brevity and selective treatment. The course ended on April 15. This may explain his omission of a discussion of the distribution of national wealth, the inequality of which he apparently thought should be mitigated, but not abolished. He thus makes way for the second part of the course on public revenue and expenditure.

National Revenue and Expenditure

In the second part of the course, the abbreviated treatment may explain the absence of any treatment of taxation and national debt, though these topics have been mentioned earlier in the course. The three topics examined relate to public expenditure on national defense, the administration of justice and the catch all title of expenditure on objects of "public utility."

National Defense, Courts, Utilities

The fullest treatment deals with the military. Here Mylne discusses at some length the relative merits of a standing army, militia and, the Royal Navy as means of national defense. He contrasted his own views with Adam Smith's preference for standing armies, giving as counter instances the militias of Switzerland and the Netherlands who had taken the field against Austria and Philip the Second of Spain. A standing army can be disciplined and efficient. However, it is also costly; it can be a danger to liberty, as Machiavelli and Lord Liverpool have argued; soldiers can be led into lives of dissipation, which affects the lower classes; an army is a temptation to rulers to start wars, as under Charles V and in Prussia and Russia; the purchase of military service hurts national spirit; and military honor, though this last point Mylne considers mere declamation.

A standing army is necessary though, to an absolute monarchy that rules by fear. This is not so in the case of a militia, which Mylne favors. He

---

71. Mylne, *Lectures on Political Economy* (NCL:BOGU3), lecture 45.

qualifies this statement: "Before however, a nation can adopt this plan, the government must accord with the feelings of the people."[72] He conceives a militia as arising from a universal obligation to military training and service for which no substitution is permitted. He deals with several objections. It is held that this would be oppressive to citizens, but this would be forestalled by the universality of the requirement. It may be objected that it would obstruct industry, to which he replies that taxation for a standing army also has this effect. Neither would it induce dissipation more than a standing army. It may be objected that it would raise sedition and tumult. Mylne cites Lord Liverpool against this. In ancient Rome and Carthage, the soldiers overthrew the government, not the people. Military power would be in the hands of those most interested in prosperity and peace. It is objected that a militia would be inefficient. Mylne replies that civic virtue and military skill could be combined to deter an invader. In conclusion, he cites the Scottish patriot and republican theorist Andrew Fletcher in favor of a militia: "The only difference, says Mr Fletcher between a free man and a slave is the former being allowed to bear arms.[73] Where the government only is armed, there despotism must exist."[74]

Mylne turns to consider the use of a navy for the defense of Britain, a subject which, he comments Adam Smith neglected to cover. This is relatively favorable to civil liberty, as sailors cannot easily be used to coerce the citizenry. In addition, Mylne is impelled at this point to praise the "value and benefits" of Britain's "wooden walls," before turning to its disadvantages. These he enumerates as the great expense of ships and equipment; the danger to other countries of the power it bestows; the operation of the Impress service (the notorious "press gangs"); and the rendering of commerce subservient to the Navy. Despite these, he concludes, the Royal Navy is both popular and necessary.

Mylne turns to the administration of justice, which he characterizes as a means of "defence from internal foes."[75] His main line of argument is that, whilst justice is necessary, it would be better to reduce the expense associated with duties, stamps, bills, and the fees and salaries of advocates

---

72. Mylne, *Lectures on Political Economy* (NCL:BOGU3), lecture 46.

73. "The possession of arms is the distinction of a free man from a slave" (Fletcher, *Selected Political Writings*, 83). Fletcher's pamphlet *A Discourse of Government with relation to Militias* also contains several arguments similar to those of Mylne and is included in his *Political Works* (1732 and Glasgow, 1749). On the context, Pocock's *The Machiavellian Moment* and Paul Scott's *Andrew Fletcher and the Treaty of Union*, chapter 8.

74. Mylne, *Lectures on Political Economy* (NCL:BOGU3), lecture 47.

75. Mylne, *Lectures on Political Economy* (NCL:BOGU3), lecture 48.

and judges. Legal procedures could be rationalized: "if a simplification was made in legal enactments and regulations, the administration of the law would be soon attended with less expense." To this end he would prefer the use of "simple words and perspicuous language."[76] He takes issue with Adam Smith's proposal that judges be paid from fees, which would promote delays. He accepts the case that they should be paid by salaries.

Finally, Mylne turns to the catch all title of "objects of public utility." Here he recapitulates the argument already developed that those who benefit from roads, bridges, and harbors should bear the cost; whilst bounties for inventions are unnecessary as, if they are useful, they are profitable to the inventor. He concludes the course with a lecture on the relief of poverty.

Relations with Debate in Glasgow

There is little doubt, in the light of the popular content and sustained local delivery of his views, that Mylne was a significant disseminator of economic ideas in the West of Scotland Through the lectures, the Glasgow Literary and Commercial Society and personal acquaintance, Mylne came into contact with the commercial middle class of Glasgow.

Tom Lee notes that the merchant classes in Glasgow were less inclined to attend college classes than their counterparts in Edinburgh.[77] However, this needs to be qualified in the case of Mylne's lectures.[78] The 1808 witness describes the audience as "numerous, comprehending not only many of the students who are regularly engaged in the business of the college, but some of the most respectable inhabitants of Glasgow, and its neighbourhood." John Strang too notes that, in the absence of the principal Scottish Law Courts, Glasgow's merchant community played a role in public life similar to that of the law in Edinburgh. He adds that consequently, it is "quite a mistake to suppose that Glasgow has ever wanted among its merchants, as well as professional men, individuals of high classical attainments and classical taste."[79] Even before this time, John Millar too felt warranted in referring to the "universal approbation which this new doctrine"—political economy—"has met with in the higher classes of mercantile people."[80]

76. Ibid.

77. Lee, *Seekers of Truth*.

78. Literary and Commercial Society debates and Mylne's political economy class were open to the public, so non-attendance at College does not imply lack of interest in commercial or general education.

79. Strang, *Glasgow and Its Clubs* (1864), 315.

80. Millar, *Historical View*, 717.

Mylne also spoke on political economy to the Glasgow Literary and Commercial Society. As with the lectures, these talks drew ideas from both Adam Smith and the French economists. They included consideration of the fundamental concepts and first principles of the science we have discussed above as well as more technical matters.[81] As we shall see, he met there several other noted contributors to the debate and it appears that merchants were a conduit of Mylne's influence in Glasgow.

Mylne also knew several businessmen through political activity. These included the Christian philanthropist and factory owner David Dale (1739-1806), who had formed the New Lanark Mills along with Richard Arkwright, whom he had later bought out. Dale later acted as Glasgow agent for the Royal Bank of Scotland, which operated a substantial business discounting bills of exchange in the city.[82] Mylne also knew Robert Grahame from at least 1809 through the committee of management of Glasgow Public Library.[83] Grahame was a lawyer and had been Secretary of the Glasgow Society for abolition of the slave trade, one of whose meetings Dale chaired.[84] Grahame had defended Thomas Muir in 1793. Thereafter he had co-founded the St. Rollox chemical works, which produced bleach for local industry. In January 1820, he served as Steward of the Friends of Mr. Fox meeting at which Mylne spoke.[85] He went on to become Lord Provost of the city in 1833 in a victory for the liberal "Clique" to which Mylne was also party.[86]

Another liberal businessman was the banker James Dennistoun, who seconded a motion with Grahame at a public meeting in December 1820 along with others associated with Mylne calling for dismissal of the government.[87] Dennistoun had earned a fortune from trade (a district of Glasgow was named after lands purchased by him) before forming the Glasgow Bank in 1809. As with Dale, this discounted bills of exchange on a large scale.

---

81. Mylne's talks on political economy are: "On the Law of Fixing the Rate of Interest," March 1807; "On the Doctrine of the French Economists," December 1807; "Some Observations on Adam Smith's doctrines about productive and unproductive labour," April 1812; and "On the Importance usually attached to Foreign Commerce," January 1816. Interestingly, Thomas Reid also spoke on interest rates (See Holcomb, "Thomas Reid in the Glasgow Literary Society," in Hook and Sher, *The Glasgow Enlightenment*, 99, quoting GUL MS 3061.
82. Checkland, *Scottish Banking*, 146.
83. GC 17/1/1809.
84. GC 4/2/1792.
85. GC 18/1/1820.
86. Mavor, *Glasgow*.
87. *Glasgow Herald* 22/12/1820.

Mylne and Dennistoun also shared an interest in the economic development of the Highlands.[88]

Mylne's neighbors in Fairley, who constructed the three villas there and occupied the other two, were Hugh Tennent (1780–1864), owner of the Drygate and Well Park brewery in Glasgow, and Charles Parker, partner in McInroy Parker, West India merchants,[89] who imported sugar and coffee from Sandbach Tinne of Liverpool, which owned plantations in Demerary, British Guiana (now Guyana).[90] However, there appears to be no evidence on how well they knew one another.

It is likely that Mylne drew his knowledge of commerce and banking partly from these sources.[91] For example, banking and specifically bills of exchange figure largely in the activities of both Dale and Dennistoun and this is reflected in the detail with which they are treated in Mylne's lectures. Certainly he had ample opportunity to compare his limited personal and reading knowledge of commerce with that of several articulate and politically sympathetic individuals who dealt closely with commercial activity.

Not only did some of Mylne's pupils become eminent in commerce, as might be expected,[92] but some relations can be glimpsed between college and business life. In 1824, the young accountant James McClelland (1799–1879) opened for business in the Trongate near the College. McClelland went on to be a major influence on the development of accountancy in Scotland as the first president of the *Institute of Accountants and Actuaries in Glasgow* (IAAG),[93] founded in 1854, in which role he guided the accounting profession.[94] Over the years he took on several of Mylne's students as trainees and drew several other students who went on to important commercial or literary careers, as well as providing a considerable part of the initial

88. For Dennistoun Glasgow Herald 15/1/1827; for Mylne see Polecon lectures.

89. Maclehose, *Memoirs and Portraits*, 315.

90. Private letters: http://www.victorianweb.org/history/letters/sandfin.html.

91. James Steuart's *Principles of Political Economy* (1767) also discusses banking though.

92. Donald Cuthbertson (1784–1864), from a merchant family, attended Mylne's class around 1799 and became a director of the Caledonian Insurance Company, a founder of IAAG and, along with McClelland and Watson, a founder of *Glasgow Athenaeum*. The lack of interest in Mylne's lectures in insurance perhaps reflects the fact that this was an Edinburgh speciality.

93. This was a predecessor body to the current *Institute of Chartered Accountants of Scotland* (ICAS). Like ICAS and similar organizations, it was a chartered body which restricted membership to those it deemed qualified.

94. He wrote "The Origin and Present Organisation of the Profession of Chartered Accountants in Scotland" (1869). There are biographies in *The Accountants' Magazine* (1897) 294–300 and Maclehose, *Memoirs and Portraits*.

membership of IAAG.[95] McClelland appears to have been a member of the Literary and Commercial Society, which he seems to have attended with fellow accountant Robert Aitken (1806–90), a student of Mylne from a merchant family.[96] McClelland was also a friend of the Edinburgh philosopher George Combe, who wrote *The Constitution of Man in Relation to External Objects* (1828) and works on phrenology.[97] The tradition of public discussion of commerce continued after Mylne. McClelland was a co-founder of a successor discussion group, the *Glasgow Athenaeum*, started in 1847, as were many of his former trainees. Also involved in the *Athenaeum* venture was James Watson (1800–89), the "father of stockbroking in Glasgow," who had attended Glasgow University briefly.[98] Watson had founded the Glasgow Stock Exchange Association in 1844, which played a major role in directing capital into new enterprises and thus in the expansion of Glasgow and was also a founder of IAAG. He wrote on *The Present Railway Crisis* (1846), on sanitation (1877), and on artisan's housing (1879). The railway crisis was in part behind the creation of IAAG, as accountancy in Glasgow was often an adjunct to stockbroking. It would seem then, the culture of combining liberal and commercial pursuits in which Mylne participated persisted in the business community through much of the nineteenth century.

Later Versions of the Course

I have identified no surviving information on versions of Mylne's course after 1816. One may speculate on the direction of debate in Glasgow by taking account of the similar work of John Craig, the co-editor with Mylne of Millar's works and author of a three volume *Elements of Political Science* (1814). This work has three parts, dealing respectively with the Constitution, Duties, and Revenues of Government. Craig advertised it as giving "a connected and systematic view of politics, and of that branch of the Science

95. McClelland's trainees included several founding members of IAAG. These included Walter Mackenzie (1817–98), who studied at Glasgow University from 1831–34, including "philosophy." Another was Charles Gairdner (1824–99), who attended Glasgow University after Mylne had effectively retired. He became a banker and economist, who later founded the Adam Smith club and published papers read there. In all, McClelland and his trainees represent seven of forty-one founding members of IAAG.

96. See list of members: "Robert Aitken jun." is 135 (Aitken's father was also Robert) and "James McLelland" follows as 136 (variant spellings of surnames are common at this time).

97. Lee, *Seekers of Truth*, 45.

98. The "Dr James Watson" in the Commercial Society records is probably a different person as Watson seems to have had no such qualification.

usually denominated Political Economy."⁹⁹ Craig went on to write *Remarks on Fundamental Questions in Political Economy* (1821).

Relations with Other Political Economists

In addition to Craig, Mylne had opportunities to meet several other economists. Thomas Chalmers (1780–1847) spoke on Malthus and Pauperism. Chalmers had first published in political economy in 1808 as a minister. At that time, his political economy was still represented by his *Enquiry into the Extent and Stability of National Resources* (1808), a book incorporated into the four-volume edition of his works that appeared in 1817. Any influence on economic questions would appear to be from Mylne to Chalmers, for Mylne in his lectures rejected Thomas Malthus' views on population that Chalmers relied on.¹⁰⁰ Malthus' *Essay on the Principle of Population* first appeared under his name in 1803.¹⁰¹ The work argued against Godwin's theory of the perfectibility of man on the basis of arguments about the relation of population to national resources. Malthus' views were known outside academia: one student, Theodore Rathbone, who knew Mylne well, discussed Malthus' views with his family.¹⁰² JP Nichol discussed Thomas Chalmers' work in correspondence with John Stuart Mill.¹⁰³ Mill claimed to have derived from Chalmers' later work "an entirely new view of the order in which the truths of the science ought to be arranged."¹⁰⁴

Whilst Mylne rejected the Anglican political economy of Malthus, his views also differ from those of contemporary radicals. Principal amongst these was Robert Owen (1771–1858),¹⁰⁵ who spoke to the Literary and Commercial Society on "The manufacturing system, with hints for the improvement of those parts of it which are injurious to health and morals" in 1818.¹⁰⁶ His views were opposed by some political reformers as prioritizing

99. *GC*, advert, 15/3/1814.

100. Mylne, *Lectures on Political Economy* (NCL:BOGU3), lecture 44.

101. An anonymous version had appeared in 1798.

102. Theo Rathbone, Letter from Glasgow December 1818.University of Liverpool Rathbone collection RP VIII 1.1A. Rathbone was from a business family in Liverpool and stayed with Mylne at college (notes in Rathbone papers by TW Rathbone).

103. The discussion concerned Chalmers' *On Political Economy in Connexion with the Moral State and Moral Prospects of Society*. See Letters 112 of 26 November 1834 to John Pringle Nichol in Mill, *The Earlier Letters of John Stuart Mill 1812–1848*, 12:237.

104. See Letter 109 of 30 August 1834 to John Pringle Nichol in Mill, *The Earlier Letters of John Stuart Mill 1812–1848*, 12:231.

105. For Owen and Mylne's relations, see Eckhardt, *Frances Wright*, 19 and passim.

106. See "List of Essays read by members of the Literary and Commercial Society

social over political rights.[107] By 1817, he had also attracted conservative criticism in Glasgow for mixing his personal religious speculations with practical reform agenda.[108] Mylne considered his views to be "extravagant."[109] John Pringle Nichol, Mylne's colleague and later professor of Astronomy, had written highly regarded articles on the subject in *Tait's Magazine* and popular articles on the Corn Laws for the radical press.[110] He had been recommended for Say's chair of political economy at the Collège de France by both James Mill and Nassau W Senior (1790–1864) on the basis of his early writings.[111] However, when Mylne retired, political economy at Glasgow was taught by the Conservative William Fleming.

In Britain, David Ricardo's *Principles of Political Economy and Taxation* appeared in 1819. Technical issues such as the return to the gold standard were debated between followers of Ricardo and Lauderdale thereafter.[112] The intended effect of the policy was a kind of control on inflation in relation to one commodity (i.e., gold) considered of relatively stable absolute value.

Mylne and Craig's work shared a focus on the analysis of market transactions in terms of utility that contrasts with Ricardo and Marx who accept and refine Smith's labor theory of value. Socialist sentiment achieved philosophical expression in Scotland with James Hutchison Stirling's *The Secret of Hegel* (1865). This contains an extended attack on Smith's "night watchman state," modeled on the rhetoric of Thomas Carlyle. Despite this changing mood, Mylnean ideas however, persisted in popular opinion in the West of Scotland. Socialist speakers in the 1880s and later addressing audiences of working men reported a hostile audience for socialist ideas, though they

---

of Glasgow from Session 1806 to Session 1830," copy in *A Collection of Glasgow Tracts and Pamphlets* Vol VIII, series B, David Murray, GUL:Spec.Coll Mu22-a, 8.

107. *Radical Reformers Gazette*.

108. GC 28/8/1817 & 1/10/18.

109. Letter to Julia Pertz 12./8/1827. Houghton Library (USA) bMS Eng 1304.1(25).

110. He wrote on the Corn Laws in the *Fife Herald*, a widely circulated radical newspaper published in Cupar. The articles are mentioned in Letters 102 of 15 April 1834 and 109 of 30 August 1834 to John Pringle Nichol in Mill, *The Earlier Letters of John Stuart Mill 1812–1848*, 12:222, 232. In Fife at this time, *Tait's Magazine* (NS III, March 1836. 195) claimed that "reading and Radicalism are nearly universal." See also Letter 111.

111. See Letters 65 of 16 January 1833 to John Pringle Nichol in Mill, *The Earlier Letters of John Stuart Mill 1812–1848*, 12:136 n. See also Letter 71 to William Tait 30 March 1833 and 79 to Nichol of 10 July 1833, where Nichol's lack of a "high European reputation" is thought to have excluded him (165).

112. GC 20/3/1819.

were given a fair hearing.[113] Some Scottish Church history assumes various forms of broadly Socialist analysis that identify early radicalism with socialism.[114] Mylne's thought embodies the prior liberal tradition that might usefully be recovered as a mode of economic analysis.

In relation to his European contemporaries, Mylne may have met the French economists Jean-Baptiste Say (1767–1832) and perhaps his successor Adolphe Blanqui (1798–1854) during their respective visits to Glasgow in 1815 and 1823.[115] Mylne owned an 1821 edition of Say's *Catechisme d'Économie Politique* and some other French works,[116] though not Say's *Traité d'Économie Politique* (1803), the second edition of which Craig cites in 1821. Blanqui later wrote a letter in support of the young accountant[117] Pierre-Joseph Proudhon when the latter's income was threatened by the Besançon trust that had financed his *Qu'est-ce que la Propriété* (1840).

Conclusion

Mylne's political economy matches neither the concept of a "Christian political economy" of Waterman's *Revolution, Economics and Religion*, embodied in figures such as Thomas Malthus and Thomas Chalmers, nor the concept of a secular "philosophical radicalism." Waterman identifies an opposition between William Godwin's radical optimism and the views of Malthus, who justified Anglican practices on the basis of considerations of economic scarcity which arises because population pressures eliminate per capita gains in production. The institutions of marriage and private property, he argues, are necessary to maintain per capita wealth above subsistence levels. In my view, Waterman's contrast misrepresents Godwin, who strongly supports private property as distributing power widely amongst members of society and as a condition of intellectual independence. In contrast to Malthus, the emphasis on scarcity as underpinning the institutions of society is largely absent in Mylne's lectures. The role of scarcity in Mylne is rather the more

---

113. Maxton, *Lenin*, 29; McCormick, *The Flag in the Wind*, 14.

114. Smith *Passive Obedience and Prophetic Protest*. See also Mathieson, *The Church and Reform in Scotland 1797–1843* and Mechie, *The Church and Scottish Social Development 1780–1870*.

115. See Bain *Les Voyageurs Français*, 132 and 158, citing Say, *L'Angleterre et les Anglais* and Blanqui, *Voyage d'un Jeune Français en Angleterre et en Ecosse*, 130 et seq.

116. Skirving catalogue. By way of comparison, Dugald Stewart in Edinburgh owned copies of Quesnay and Turgot, as well as Say's *Catechisme*.

117. He kept the books of a canal enterprise based in Lyon: see Introduction to *Qu'est-ce que la propriété*, 8. Blanqui's younger brother was the republican socialist Louis Auguste Blanqui (1805–81).

general one of setting prices that underlies commerce. Mylne also rejects the notion of population pressure as the motor of scarcity. His emphasis is on political structures that support commerce and on the role of commerce itself in creating economic activity and thus wealth.

Whilst Mylne refers at times to the "laws of Providence," the phrase is synonymous with the "laws of nature" and the focus of his economic thought is secular. However, in developing the idea of a Christian merchant community, conceptually equipped to seek out and meet the "lawful desires" of the citizens of neighboring communities in which it was located, he perhaps reflects the idealized self-image of the actual merchant community of Glasgow with whose leading Whig members he was closely acquainted. The sharpened analysis of "value" developed by criticism of Adam Smith, which emphasizes desire, approximates more closely to the market prices observable by actual merchants.

Neither does Mylne embody the concept of a largely secular "philosophical radicalism" developed by Andrew Seth and others. Whilst he was prepared to give radical ideas a hearing, he clearly distinguished his own views from those of Thomas Paine and Robert Owen. He stops short of radical levelling views and prefers to see potential harmony of interests rather than conflict in the relations of rank and wealth. Instead, he is closer to the contemporaneous Whig political economy lectures of Dugald Stewart in Edinburgh.

Mylne's engagement with the ideas of John Millar, Adam Smith, Lord Lauderdale, and Andrew Fletcher justify our placing him instead as a continuer in his political economy lectures of Scottish and Whig intellectual traditions of inquiry. His numerous disagreements with Smith on both on the nature of value and on matters of detail show that he was an independent figure, despite the frequent congruence of their views. The memorable phrase from Mylne's lectures: "The great mine from which all wealth is drawn is the intellect of man"[118] reflects his rationalism and the spirit of inquiry embodied by the Glasgow merchant community in its Reading Rooms, scientific and technical innovations, and trading ventures. Mylne's economic thought inculcates such a spirit of inquiry that encompasses both the needs of the consumer and the production process, without being restricted to them, and which relates economics to broader sociological and psychological analyses. In these respects, his agenda both reflects his own situation and remains relevant to the contribution of economics to society. It has an equal title with Malthus to the title of Christian.

---

118. Mylne, *Lectures on Political Economy* (NCL:BOGU3), lecture 26.

Conclusion

WE TURN NOW TO review the results of our study. Our initial biographical approach has shown that the intellectualist bias of James Mylne's mental philosophy occurred in the context of the extraordinary commercial and scientific achievements of Britain and the consequent prominence of reason as an arbiter in adjusting customs and institutions to changing social realities, but that his philosophy also had religious origins in the rationalism of the Scottish and English dissenting traditions.

We have seen that Mylne's father had experienced the democratic ethos of Scottish Presbyterianism when his future congregation's right to choose its minister was vindicated by the highest courts of the Church of Scotland. We have followed Mylne's own origins as a son of the manse in a farming community in Carse of Gowrie in the heartland of the dissenting Glasite movement and his education at St. Andrews University, where he was introduced to mental philosophy and where his lifelong interest in mathematics and French literature were nourished. We noted his prize essay on the limits of religious tolerance.

We then noted his choice of the ministry of the Church of Scotland and first post as deputy chaplain of the 83rd Regiment of Foot, stationed in the French-speaking Channel Islands during the American War of Independence. We have seen the scientific, literary, and political interests he shared with his clerical colleagues. The military events that he witnessed may lie behind his later endorsement of patriotism, general opposition to war, and preference for a militia as a means of national defense. In covering his subsequent fourteen-year ministry in Paisley, we drew attention to the literary accomplishments of his fellow ministers and their wide range of political opinions, whilst in society at large radical views were expressed by Thomas Muir and others in the wake of the French revolution. We also noted that Mylne was drawn to the literary society where he would have met his predecessors in the moral philosophy chair Thomas Reid and Archibald Arthur and the Whig constitutional historian and sociologist John Millar. We know from his library that Mylne kept himself abreast of both political and intellectual developments during this period.

After his appointment in 1797, Mylne became known as a diligent and effective teacher in the moral philosophy chair at Glasgow. His views were noted as reformist and in his lectures he argued against the "moral sense" and "common sense" views of his predecessors Frances Hutcheson and Thomas Reid. The class also read Francis Bacon and Cicero. He added topical material in his lectures on political economy, which were addressed to an older audience and held in the evening.

James Mylne lived a full and rewarding domestic life, though not without tragic losses. His friends and acquaintances included many prominent businessmen, reformers, and public intellectuals. We have seen that he was drawn into local politics after 1815, though he was known to some as a Whig from the 1790s. Politics at this time was generally divided into Tory, Whig, and Radical factions, with the latter two weakened by mutual disagreements on the means of achieving reform. Mylne associated with the Glasgow Whigs who included many prominent local businessmen. He was most closely associated with Whig reformer Henry Brougham. Mylne operated within and defended the British reform agenda based on the press, public meetings and petitions to Parliament.

He prepared his moral philosophy course at a time when he was influenced by the radicalism of William Godwin, but his political conclusions were more modest and always guided by reason. For example, he warned in a remark that survives from after the 1820 Radical Wars: "We ought to inquire how far we are likely to succeed in any attempt to promote universal interest. This would prevent many a foolish expedient."[1] Whilst he was at ease in the company of prominent radical sympathizers like Robert Grahame, William Cobbett and Daniel O'Connell, he also distinguished himself from the "extravagant" utopianism of Robert Owen and later from his own grandniece Frances Wright. Instead, he lent sustained support to an achievable Whig reform agenda based on inquiry and rational persuasion. By the close of his life, many of the constitutional and social reforms he advocated had been legislated for by the reform parliament and the Whig Ministries of Earl Grey and Lord Melbourne.

---

1. Pollock notes, GUL:MSGen1355/103/31 (April 1821).

CONCLUSION

In the second thematic part of our study, we have located Mylne's mental and moral philosophy as a constructive corrective to the sentimentalism or "moral sense" theory of Francis Hutcheson and the "common sense" philosophy of Thomas Reid. This involved Mylne in a comprehensive treatment of mental philosophy starting with the intellectual powers. In his account of the intellectual powers, he uses Condillac to reject Humean skepticism and the "common sense" reply of Thomas Reid. As a result, he returned to the empirical standpoint of John Locke. We have seen him arguing in favor of a radically Calvinist view of free will and against the low estimate of the powers of reason implicit in skepticism. At the same time, we noted that duties to God were central to Mylne's ethics.

We have thereby challenged the identification of Scottish philosophy with either the secularizing and skeptical empiricism of David Hume (the current ideology of the "Scottish enlightenment") or the Common Sense school of Thomas Reid. Mylne thus appears as an original figure on the Scottish intellectual scene. Our account is corroborated by an amusing character sketch of Mylne that survives by the hand of Robert Pollock, one of the student note takers. It has the form of a short story containing a dream of an exam.[2] He writes:

> Again the tread of a foot was heard, and, in a moment, Jacobus Mylne, the illustrious metaphysician, sat down before us. The ghost of Locke sat on his right hand, the graceful shade of Cicero took his left, with the book of 'Offices' under its arm; and the passionate spectre of Cogan whispered behind him, "Passions are the result of conceptions of the mind, or conceptions themselves." [. . .] On the blast, the goblin of Reid, actuated mostly by mechanical and animal principles, was heard wailing its confusion while in the flesh. It admitted, that it had never been able to prove the existence of an external world; but "neither," grumbled it, "does Mylne's yearly-created man prove it?" On our duty to God, to man, and to ourselves, we were now judged. [. . .] and we rejoiced because we were acquitted. The great metaphysician went out and left us, and with him departed the ghosts of Cicero, Locke and Cogan; and multitudes of those spirits, which had cut themselves into numberless pieces when dwelling in their earthly tabernacles, shrieked away after him, beseeching him to bind up their wounds; thus offering an awful

---

2. Russel confirms Mylne's role in the Blackstone examination in Glasgow in *View of the System of Education*, 159.

lesson to those who would wickedly divide that ever whole-acting thing—the soul of man.³

Mylne did indeed incorporate the writings of Thomas Cogan on the passions into his course, though his lectures on the subject predate their publication. Pollok draws our attention to two distinctive Mylnean doctrines, the primacy of reason and the unity of the mind. The argument on the role of touch in external perception which Pollock draws attention to has the significance of a vindication of the rational powers; as does the primacy of judgement in action in moral theory, including the account Mylne gives of piety.

We noted that Mylne's confidence in the powers of reason was associated with support for a series of well-thought out political, social, and economic reforms that he gave expression to in his evening lectures on political economy and, in a more partisan spirit, in his support for the Whigs of the Glasgow Fox Club and later the Friends of Civil and Religious Liberty and Glasgow Reform Association. The achievements of this set of activists included Parliamentary reform, the end of slavery in the British Empire and restrictions of child labor in the Factory Acts that are still widely lauded as markers of progress.

In relation to political economy, it is worth drawing attention to the relation between the notion of utility in Mylne's moral philosophy and the notion of use-value in his political economy lectures. His conception of exchange value and hence economic activity in general as determined and measured by value in use, i.e., the utility to the buyer of a good or service differs from the labor theory of Adam Smith. This underpins Mylne's notion of the role of the merchant class in creating value by matching consumer wants with production.

When we turn to the historical significance of these ideas, we find that Mylne's philosophy can be traced in the writings and other actions of his pupils in the main English-speaking countries. In assessing this influence, we may recall J. D. Morrell's observation that:

> From what I have learned of those who attended his lectures, and what I have seen of the impulse they gave in prosecuting the work of intellectual analysis, I think there can be little doubt but that his mind told forcibly upon the philosophy of Scotland during the many years of his professorship.⁴

---

3. Pollok, *The Life of Robert Pollok*, 169.
4. Morrell, *An Historical and Critical*, 390.

Mylne's influence on his former students flows naturally from his philosophy and was often acknowledged. The result allows us to collect together hitherto neglected intellectual and religious developments that were based on a modernizing empiricist outlook and, in social terms, looked favorably on democratic reforms subject to the requirement of an educated electorate. This influence includes university appointments in Britain and overseas, on the English dissenting community and locally in the West of Scotland amongst figures held in high esteem by the Glasgow Idealists.

We have seen that Mylne's former students Robert Buchanan and William Fleming came to occupy the chairs of Logic and Moral Philosophy at Glasgow University in the generation following him. Other former students, including Norman MacLeod and the theologian John McLeod Campbell, author of *The Nature of the Atonement* (1856) were Scottish Churchmen publicly honored by the early Glasgow Idealists John and Edward Caird and John Nichol. Nichol's father, the Professor of Astronomy John Pringle Nichol, who had offered to take over Mylne's course in the 1830s, was a transitional figure in the growing interest in Glasgow in German philosophy. This interest dates back to Mylne himself, as a teacher of German in Glasgow, A. F. M. Willich, co-dedicated an early book on Immanuel Kant, *Elements of the Critical Philosophy* (1798), to Mylne.[5] Other contemporaries or Whig acquaintances of Mylne interested in German thought include the merchant William Buchanan (1797–1883)[6] and John Strang, author of *Germany in MDCCCXXXI* (1836), whilst many other of his students studied in Germany. However, Mylne himself is on record only as having "scouted transcendentalism," in a remark recorded long after by George Gilfillan (1813–78) who knew him in the late 1820s.[7] For Mylne himself, German thought may have been associated with the conservatism of Coleridge and Mme. De Stael.

In Edinburgh, Mylne's former student John Wilson occupied the chair of Moral Philosophy after 1820 and William Hamilton that of Logic and Metaphysics after 1836. As a charismatic Tory, Wilson derided Mylne's philosophy and politics: "I believe he followed the French, for he hated Reid. But though an acute man, I cannot think he had any wisdom; he was continually nibbling at the shoe-latchets of the mighty."[8] Yet Wilson had won a class prize in Mylne's Ethics class.[9] Moreover, on his appointment in

5. The other dedicatee is William Miller (1755–1846) of Glenlee, Bart, a senator of the College of Justice of Scotland; Willich, GC 8/4/1794.

6. MacLehose, *Memoirs and Portraits*.

7. Gilfillan, "Reverand David Young," 194; Gilfillan, *History of a Man*, 89. Gilfillan matriculated in 1825 (Addison, *Matriculation Albums*, entry 11783).

8. Gordon, *Memoir of John Wilson*, 218.

9. GC 6/5/1802.

Edinburgh Wilson wrote to John Smith, the Glasgow publisher, for a copy of Mylne's lectures.[10] He wrote:

> I am anxious to know if you can get me Mylne's notes. [...] I am anxious to have before me a vista of my labours, and this might be aided by a sight of his or any other lectures. But all this is confidential, for my enemies are numerous and ready, and will do all they can to injure me in all things.[11]

There are thus reasons beyond their intrinsic similarity for thinking that the views of the relations of sight and touch in Wilson's lectures and the writings of his son-in-law James Frederick Ferrier[12] may date back to Mylne. An article in the *North British Review* in 1857 described Wilson's colleague William Hamilton's philosophy as, "a determined recoil against the method and systems of Mylne and Brown, the two professors who, in Hamilton's younger years, were exercising the greatest influence on the opinions of Scottish students."[13] The two men were in contact in the 1830s; whilst the two *Edinburgh Review* essays on *The Philosophy of the Unconditioned* (1829)[14] and *Perception* (1830) that made his reputation address central topics in Mylne's lectures. However, Hamilton's own erudition and the influence of Reid and Kant clearly overlay any influence from Mylne.

At Belfast Academical Institution, Mylne's former pupils William Cairns, John Young, and John Ferrie occupied the equivalent chairs to Hamilton and Wilson at Edinburgh. William Cairns acknowledged that Mylne's "ingenious mode of analysis has given a salutary impulse and direction to many ardent and inquisitive minds."[15] William Hamilton likens Young's views to "Professor Mylne of Glasgow, whose views of mental philosophy are well known to have closely resembled those of M. De Tracy."[16] Young and Cairns however, diverge from Mylne in their treatments of free will. After Young's death in 1829, John Ferrie of Glasgow was appointed

10. Gordon, *Memoir of John Wilson*, 215.

11. Letter to John Smith, Glasgow publisher, 22 July, 1820, quoted in Gordon, *Memoir of John Wilson*, 231.

12. "The Metaphysician III" in *Blackwood's Edinburgh Magazine* (1836) 258–59; Ferrier refers to Mylne's attendance at a Whig dinner in 1834 in Wilson, *Works*, 4:208 n.

13. Book review headed "Scottish Metaphysicians," in *North British Review* (1857), 226.

14. In the *Notes to Reid*, Hamilton applies his general analysis of the Unconditioned explicitly to human rather than divine freedom and takes issue with the concept of freedom for involving an infinite regress of free acts. Hamilton, *Reid* (1872), 2:599 n. (note to *Active powers* 4.1 and references on).

15. Cairns, preface to Young's *Lectures on Intellectual Philosophy*, xii.

16. Hamilton, *Works of Thomas Reid* (1872), 2:968 n.

in a contested appointment with support from Mylne. One contemporary related Ferrie and Mylne:

> Professor Mylne elucidated and explored the whole vast field of metaphysics [. . .] He was a powerful metaphysician, and possessed of uncommon powers of analysis. Many of his views were new and original. [. . .] Professor Ferrie, of Belfast College, has also carried out many of them in his lectures to his classes, with great ability.[17]

James Thomson, who returned to Glasgow, and James McCosh, later associated with Princeton in the U.S., also taught at Belfast Academical Institution.

Amongst the English dissenters, we find both Unitarians and Evangelicals acknowledging Mylne's influence. Amongst the Evangelicals, the Congregationalist George Payne (1781-1848), who studied at Glasgow from 1804,[18] wrote a significant philosophical work, *Elements of Mental and Moral Science* (1828), which went through four editions and had some popularity in the U.S.[19] Alan Sell describes it as "one of the most substantial of Nonconformist works on moral philosophy."[20] Another Evangelical student, John Hoppus (b. 1791-1875), became the first Professor of Logic and Mental Philosophy at University College, London from 1829 to 1866.[21] Hoppus had taken Mylne's class in 1820-21 and in 1823 published some of his student essays on a variety of subjects in a book dedicated to Mylne and his colleague Meikleham.[22] The essays on ethics and general philosophy closely reflect the views of Mylne and are critical of Stewart, for example on the subject of attention. Hoppus' best known student was perhaps the banker and author, Walter Bagehot (1826-77), who was from a Unitarian family and author of *The English Constitution* (1867) and *Lombard Street* (1873).[23] Henry Forster Burder (1783-1864) and Joseph Fletcher (1784-1843) had studied alongside Payne at Glasgow and also went on to develop philosophical ideas.[24] Both had studied previously at Hoxton Academy and

---

17. Scott, *Life, Letters and Remains*, 96.

18. Addison, *Matriculation Albums*.

19. For Payne's biography, see Sell: *Philosophy, Dissent and Non-conformity*, 151 et seq.

20. Ibid., 151.

21. Addison, *Matriculation Albums*, entry 10435.

22. Hoppus, *Recollections, Juvenile, Miscellaneous and Academical* (1823); Addison, *Matriculation Albums*, entry 10435.

23. *DNB*.

24. John Kendrick ("Memoir of Turner") mentions H[enry] F Burder and [Joseph]

graduated MA at Glasgow University in 1807 going on to teach philosophy at Hoxton and Blackburn dissenting academies. Burder's early book *The Scripture Character of God* (London, 1822) gives a luminous account of the metaphysical and moral attributes of God and his *The Pleasures of Religion* (London, 1823) also draws on Mylne's lectures on Duties to God. He also played an active part opposing slavery in America.[25] Joseph Fletcher's course of Intellectual Philosophy at Blackburn Independent Academy comprised thirty-eight lectures, based on Reid, Stewart, and Mylne,[26] indicating a similar level of detail to Mylne's lectures on the same subject. Fletcher's *Lectures on the Principles and Institutions of the Roman Catholic Religion* (London, 1817) takes as its target Claude Buffier's *First Truths*, a work in the common sense tradition that was known to Mylne.[27] A Congregationalist student, Richard Alliot (1804-63) studied at Homerton and Glasgow University before teaching Theology and Mental Philosophy at Western College, Plymouth. He wrote a valuable and far from outmoded book, *Psychology and Theology* (London, 1855), which defends the Mylnean view that natural reason can generate the idea of God.

In Australia, former pupils associated with philosophy in Sydney include John Dunmore Lang (1799-1878) and Charles Badham (1813-84),[28] whilst the first Australian philosopher, Barzillai Quaife (1798-1873), was educated by Mylne's pupils at Hoxton.[29] In an early sketch of his system, Quaife applies Mylne's chemical analogy in his analysis of the intellectual faculties. He writes: "We reach back to Conception as a compound of Suggestion and Reason, and to Perception as a similar compound of Sensation and Reason."[30] Two of Quaife's sons later studied at Glasgow University.[31]

Fletcher as later prominent Independent Churchmen.

25. *DNB*.

26. Sell, *Philosophy, Dissent*, 123.

27. Fletcher became a minister in Lancashire and London who wrote for the *Eclectic Review* and was awarded DD by Glasgow in 1830 (*DNB*). Mylne had a copy of Buffier's book.

28. Addison, *Matriculation Albums*, entries 12026, 12204, 12758, for matriculation under Mylne. After leaving Eton, Badham was elected to Wadham College in June 1830. However, according to the Wadham College records, he did not matriculate there until May 1831, so presumably attended Glasgow from October 1830 to May 1831. See also *Australian Dictionary of Biography* (vol. 3).

29. "Barzillai Quaife," *Australian Dictionary of Biography*.

30. Quaife, *Intellectual Sciences*, 1:103.

31. Frederick Harrison Quaife, who graduated in 1867 (Addison, *Roll of Graduates*) and practiced medicine, went on to build the Italianate villa Hughenden in Woollahra, reminiscent of Mylne's residence in Fairley.

The "other Scottish tradition" identified by Selwyn Grave in *A History of Philosophy in Australia* (1984) may thus date back to Mylne.

Several of Mylne's Unitarian students acknowledged his influence. These include Lant Carpenter (1780-1840), who took Mylne's class at Glasgow in 1799/1800 and further private classes the following year and kept in touch later.[32] Mylne, he said, "gave his mind the first decided bias to philosophical investigation"[33] and he dedicated his *Principles of Education* (1820) to Professors Young, Jardine, and Mylne. William Jevons (1794-1873) matriculated at Glasgow in 1810.[34] He published *Systematic Morality, or a Treatise on the Theory and Practice of Human Duty, on the Grounds of Natural Religion* (1827), dedicated to Mylne. Amongst other pupils who developed Unitarian ideas, John Kendrick (1788-1877) and John James Tayler (1797-1869) went on to teach at Manchester College. John James Tayler studied with Mylne and Jardine at Glasgow from 1816 under whose influence James Martineau says he acquired "that tincture of philosophic thought which ever after penetrated and organised his historical and literary judgements."[35] More distantly James Martineau (1805-1900) was taught almost entirely by former students of Mylne, including Lant Carpenter, John Kendrick, and John Tayler, who appears to have spoken favorably of Mylne to him.[36] He also knew Charles Wicksteed in Liverpool, whose notes of Mylne's lectures are now held at Glasgow. Martineau was Professor of Mental and Moral Philosophy at Manchester New College from 1841. The opposition of another pupil of Mylne, William Gaskell (1805-84), to Martineau's later introspective view of religion is reckoned pivotal in nineteenth-century Unitarian history.

In relation to the Church, James Mylne comes across to me as an undogmatic Christian, whose rationalist religious views brought him into conflict with supporters of the Evangelical revival associated with William Wilberforce and Thomas Chalmers. In this, there was perhaps a misunderstanding of the Glasite doctrines familiar to Mylne. Hence his intellectual account of belief was questioned by James McCosh and Ralph Wardlaw, his sympathy with one of his Unitarian students associated him with the Unitarian controversy and his attitude to the Bible was rejected by James Begg. The priority he gave to reason over revelation and his deflated theological

---

32. Carpenter, *Memoirs*, 92, 130, 172. Testimonial and letter from Mylne to Carpenter in Manchester College, Oxford: MS Lant Carpenter 1, fol31-37.

33. Carpenter: *Memoirs*, 73.

34. Addison, *Matriculation Albums*, entry 8007; Logic prize, see Addison, *Prize Lists*, 140.

35. Martineau, *Essays, Reviews and Addresses*, 1:382.

36. Ibid.

commitments on questions like miracles ally him in some respects to the Moderate agenda in the Church of Scotland. It is common for some such combination of classical and Christian ideals to exist side-by-side in higher education in Europe in this era.

Our study as a whole has shown that James Mylne contributed significant ideas on perception, the unity of the mind and the nature of economic value to British thought. In addition, he is significant both in the history of philosophy and the broader history of Scottish society:

The history of philosophy in the eighteenth century is sometimes presented as a progressive shipwreck of empiricism in the work of Locke, Berkeley, and Hume, making way for the new projects of Reid and Kant. For example, Thomas Hill Green thought this in relation to Hume and Kant and Victor Cousin suggests an equivalent history in France. This evaluation was not accepted by Mylne or by many of his students and much work in the nineteenth century continued to combine empiricism with a religious ethos. This renders explicable several subsequent intellectual developments, for example Alan Sell's observation that "Reid never had the impact upon nineteenth-century English and Welsh Non-conformists that he had upon American Presbyterians of the same century."[37] The idea of the unity of the mind implicit in the idea of judgement also makes Mylne a forebear of the Glasgow or Scottish Idealists. Recovery of Mylne's work thus fills in the first half of a near eighty-year gap in the history of philosophy in Glasgow between Reid's *Essays on the Active Powers of Man* (1788) and the first idealist work, James Hutchison Stirling's *The Secret of Hegel* (1865). There is still a generation gap between the idealists and Mylne.[38] However, through such continuities of ideas, the Mylnean ethos can be identified as passing from Mylne to the early idealists.

Secondly, Mylne's work sheds light on the progress of society in Glasgow. The priority he gave to investigation over common sense in the study of the mind leads out naturally into investigations of the social acts of the mind that shed light on the work of the liberal professions. For example, Mylne was closely involved with the merchant community of Glasgow, which played a leading role similar to the legal profession in Edinburgh. The priority he gives to utility in his reworking of the theory of value in his political economy lectures arguably forms a bridge between mental philosophy and political economy that supports the tasks of investigation that contribute to commercial progress. In terms of church history, we have shown that

---

37. Sell, *Philosophy, Dissent*, 206.

38. To my mind, the writings of William Fleming are pale copies of Reid and Mylne.

Scottish Christianity can claim through Mylne and his friends a contribution to the movement of ideas that led to the 1832 Parliamentary Reform Act. Mylne was an influence on social reformers through example and through commitment to historical investigation. For many, the philosophical ideas of reason and utility found practical application in social reform. James Mylne's contributions to philosophy and social reform thus merit a place in the history of philosophy and in Scottish history, both as neglected achievements and potential precedents. The published volumes of Scottish philosophy from the nineteenth century are the fruits of great traditions of reflection and teaching. The living plant which produced them however was the commitment to reason and investigation espoused by James Mylne.

Appendix

The following is a collation of Mylne's introductory lecture on moral philosophy, derived from student manuscripts.

Object of the Course; of Natural and Moral Philosophy

1. Philosophy, which is a knowledge of the causes of things, is divided into two great branches – physical and moral. Moral science or philosophy may be known from its name "moral" and distinguished from natural philosophy. The nature of the science may be learned either from the subjects of which it treats or the object it has in view.

[Our subject matter]

2. Moral is distinguished from physical philosophy because the latter concerns objects that strike the external senses. A physical cause produces a physical effect. It is a cause which operates upon the external world and objects around us. Natural philosophy comprehends no other objects. A moral cause is that which operates on the mind. It produces a moral effect. If it is right to examine causes and effects in the physical world, it is no less so in the objects of the human mind, as its laws, movements, &c. The mind is the subject of this science. Moral science embraces a wide field: the affections, passions etc of man as well as the mind to which these belong. The subject of moral philosophy does not affect the senses at all, but the mind only.

[Our aim or object]

3 The great and proper object of moral philosophy is to make us more acquainted with our duty. This is our great design. This then, is surely an interesting study. Whence arise almost all human ills? From the want of a just view of the relations we bear to other beings, and the duties which must flow from them. Were this understood, human ills would dwindle into physical causes only. Even physical evils may be made more tolerable by moral philosophy. The light of moral philosophy is next best to revelation for conducting us to honour and happiness.

4. The object of moral philosophy may be known by attending to the object of the natural philosopher. Physical philosophy tends to turn the rude things of nature to man's use and convenience &c. Ex[ample] coals, minerals, the useless ore into useful metal &c. Thus it gives man power over nature. In like manner moral philosophy has for its object to change the mind of man from its original uncultivated state by showing [men] the proper motives which ought to regulate their actions and showing them their duties &c. The natural philosopher has in his view to add to the comfort and happiness of man by attending to external objects. This happiness respects this world. The moralist has the happiness of man in his view, both with regard to time and eternity. Morals and Ethicks are synonymous terms with duties.

Morals an art or a science?

5. The subject of Morals or Ethics may be regarded in a twofold point of view, viz, as an art or as [a] science. An art consists of a system of rules for compassing any particular end. An art signifies only rules suggested by experience. These may be impressed without principles, as in common arts. Some rules are abandoned for those that are better. As an art then, Morals consists of a set of rules - of rules for regulating our duties. These rules may be followed without any knowledge of science. Arts may be improved both by experience and science. They may be improved by experience without any inquiry into the general laws from which these rules rise. As a science, Moral Philosophy considers the principles on which these rules are founded.

6. The art of morals consists of rules for regulating our conduct suggested by experience.[1] As such it must have been a very early art. At first however, although of great use, these rules must have been imperfect and odious &c. Since these times they have been improved. In the rudest state

---

1. This view derives from Adam Smith, who refers to Proverbs as examples of early rules.

there are some rules of duty, but [few], and different, perhaps erroneous. This art advances with the advancement of civilisation. Improvements in civilisations however, do not necessarily produce improvements in this art. In periods of refinement there are deviations from morality, as notions of false honour &c. (This is granted by the way of indulgence.) It receives more improvements from the science which enquires into the faculties by which we are fitted to form moral judgments &c.

7. Science in general means the knowledge of the constitution or foundation of the laws of nature. Science has been defined also to be that knowledge that can be demonstrated, but this is too limited a definition. More properly, it may be defined to be a knowledge of the laws of nature – this is science in general. When we speak of the science of astronomy, [it] is the knowledge of the laws of nature as far as they respect astronomy. Science investigates the rules of arts.

8. The great design of science is to discover, from a kn[owledge] of the laws of nature, the rules of art. Its object is the discovery of principles on which it may securely rest the rules which constitute an art. Science enables men to prepare rules. It is calculated to throw light on kindred arts, on which it sheds its [benevolent] influence. Science facilitates the progress of the artist; it gives him stability and by its study we improve in arts &c. By the investigating into the laws and constitutions of nature many arts are invented. Ex[*amples*]: the art of navigation is indebted to astronomy for much and by it the mariner can plow the largest ocean; how much is done in chemistry by science.

9. The science of morals inquires into the various principles of action and of thought. It inquires into the principles of vice and virtue, of merit and demerit, right and wrong in conduct. It looks into the nature of all these active principles of [man's] affections. It investigates into the active principles of men, by which they are prompted, stimulated and directed. It inquires in[*to*] the order &c of these principles, and into virtue and vice by the eternal laws of the moral world. There is a reciprocal influence of this [on knowledge] of the intellectual principles. We inquire which of these should be supreme or subordinate. It inquires into vice and virtue, a sense of duty, what is right and wrong. It [looks] into the relations which man [has][2] to his Maker and the other creatures around him and into the consequences of these relations, into the consequences and result which may be expected from human conduct. From these relations it examines what duties result from these relations.

2. Mitchell has 'have.'

Science of morals more likely to improve them

10. It is to moral science that we are to look for the improvement of this art. From these enquiries he expects to discover some more sure rules than are furnished by the art or by the experience on which that art is founded. It is from a scientific inquiry into these, and not from rules of art to which the philosopher looks for the improvement of this moral art. By this science the moralist expects to find better rules and [*also*] he [i]s[3] led to abandon those which are faulty and to erect a standard of conduct in his life &c. Such is the use, effects and importance of moral philosophy.

11. A great deal of the reformation of man is wrought by this science.[4] It would be wrong to ascribe all refinement to this science, but a great deal of it may [*be*]. A most important improvement has taken place in general conduct, a great part of which may be attributed to the cultivation of the science of Ethics since the Reformation. The thoughts of men are greatly changed since the revival of literature. The art of morals respects the rules of good conduct; by their improvement morality has been much improved [from] three, or four centuries ago. From want of it revelation was darkly understood in the scholastic ages. It brought man out of the dark ages, which the Bible failed to do, being misunderstood. In the ignorance of scholastic ages the worship of God was turned to a mere ceremony.[5] No hypocritical confessor dare now insult and wound the moral feelings of men. To prevent such things the minister should be both a philosopher and a priest. It has done much since the reformation, and morality is visible throughout all Europe both in nations and private families. Much vice still [remains] in Europe, but if the philanthropist will consider what has already been done in the world with regard to morals he will find much pleasure and much pain will vanish. A century or two will convince man that [vice] simply does harm to ourselves.

---

3. Mackenzie's text is corrupted here.

4. In this opinion, unfortunately not developed further, Mylne diverges from Stewart's treatment of the same subject.

5. This view was considered seriously by the Church of Scotland: see Davie, *The Democratic Intellect*, chapter 2. Also: 'Be it enacted [. . .] That, previously to the enrolment of any student as a Student of Divinity, he shall be examined by the Presbytery within which he resides, upon Literature, Science and Philosophy' (Anon, *The Principal Acts of the General Assembly*, 29; see also, 27).

A question

12. But is there any need for science on this subject, for the deep research of philosophy, which few understand? – Can the [art of morals] not persuade man to [shun] vice and follow virtue? How comes science to be necessary for morals, since, though every person cannot study the science, everyone needs morals to direct him? All have duties to perform; therefore the art is necessary, but the rules may be safely followed without a knowledge of the science. All men ought to follow the rules of morality but the science cannot extend to a great many. Why in a word are morals not treated as an art?

13. [We] answer: The art of morals may be used when the [science] cannot be studied, but [we] wish to see the ground of these rules. It is natural for us to inquire into the foundation of [rules]. Are they founded in nature? Show me whence these rules of yours proceed? These cannot be answered without science. Some science is best suited for the improvement of other arts. It will be so in morals too. Science helps us to remember the rules of art and to understand them and on what foundation they are built. Lectures of this kind are useful. There is a greater inducement for our application to the science of morals, viz that we cannot be perfectly certain of the truth of [our rules] unless we study the science.

[Four objections & replies]

14. Some indeed who undervalue science appeal for the truth of their rules other authorities. Such despisers of philosophy, who seek answers from another quarter, must and have admitted certain principles.

15. Firstly, some send you to conscience, to the moral feelings of man, for a proof of the rectitude of their precepts and rules of duty. [They hold] that there is in man a certain moral principle, like instinct in brutes, which guides us to do whatever we should do.[6] Now these must allow that there is an instinct in man to show him all his duty, as that it is so easy, that no philosophical inquiry is necessary, no doubt or [scarcely] is about morals. If this was the case there would be no need for science [any][7] more than there is need for a scientific power in brutes to point out what kind of food they ought to eat.

---

6. This is Mylne's gloss on Hutcheson's 'moral sense'.
7. Mackenzie has 'no more'.

16. This must not be admitted rashly, for the conscience or moral feelings of man [arise in] different people very different[ly]. No blind principle in man prompts him to his duty. It is not right to appeal to the moral feelings, for these may be perverted, as they are not perfect and invariable. It is wrong for a teacher of morality in particular to appeal to the moral feelings, and to ask if the rules laid down are not consistent with their feelings, because this supposes man's moral feelings to be something like instinct. This makes man a brute without reflection. There is no such thing in man, else they must suppose that every rational creature may perceive at once what he ought to do, and what he ought not. We cannot depend on the unaided moral feeling for it is apt to err, in morals as in every other thing. Conscience is just judgements of the understanding. If therefore, the understanding be closed, so will the conscience.

17. Second, it is argued that there is no difficulty in any method of action— that reason is able to guide us easily. This is easily seen to be an unfounded supposition because we can easily imagine circumstances in which it may be extremely difficult to discover the right method of acting. Our duty is not so easy and obvious as to appear without research. We see men disagreeing what rules they should follow. Some will not eat flesh on certain days; others not at all. A man may be asked why he [enforces] such rules – then he must have recourse to science which will give him a knowledge of principles.

18. Third, the moralist who appeals not to science appeals to the science of the ancients. If we examine those maxims however, we will soon see that they are not more free of faults than any other set of rules. Some lay great stress on the antiquity of morals and rely on authority; but the ancients were only men, and as apt to err as we are. For example, it was a maxim with them to require a "tooth for a tooth and an eye for an eye".[8]

19. Fourth, God is some[times] appealed [to]. The teacher of morals gives his precepts as commandments of God: the rules he prescribes are the laws of heaven. Indeed when the teacher shows clearly that he had a divine commission all doubt about them rests and all submission is to be shown. But

---

8. And the suicide of Cato is also used to illustrate this point in the lectures in ancient philosophy. The following satirical passage from Strang's *Clubs of Glasgow* on the Tory Camperdown Club, founded in 1797 after the British naval victory of that year, is also relevant: "They detested the French, without knowing much about them, and swore against democracy and democrats as most pestilential to the well-being of the social system. They were aristocrats in their own way, and in imitation of their idols, the great *fruges consumere nati* ["Born to consume the fruits of the earth" Horace. Ep liber 1:2.], they held that there was no wisdom to be relied on, save the wisdom of their ancestors" (1864 edition, 198; 1856 edition, 242).

how is this to be determined? How do we distinguish between the true laws of God or of weak or wicked men? There are many who say they have divine laws; how are we to decide in favour of any one, for they all make great pretensions! We see those whose rules differ widely agree in referring them to the Deity. Shall we refrain from examining their rules?[9]

20. Those men that were really sent by God submitted their precepts to the inquiry of the wise: "I speak to you as wise men; judge ye what I say &c."[10] We must examine the rules themselves—and what standard are we to use?—The standard of human nature. But this standard cannot be discovered without science.

---

9. Edward Caird applies this idea in his reading of Maurice: "I think that to say that conscience in itself gave us the Representation of a Tyrannical God only is equally far from the truth [as the idea of a Propitiate God, whose mercy contradicts his justice] – There is a sense in which Law is above God – His Character above his Will." (MS Gen 516/4: Letter to A MacQuisten, Letter 27 undated circa 1857.) Surprisingly, there are similar remarks in Wardlaw's *Christian Ethics*. However, Caird goes on to argue: "I do not think we can refuse a doctrine, because it is not altogether satisfactory to our moral sense, unless we are sure that we *comp*rehend the doctrine, and in all questions where sin is brought in this is impossible" (ibid) giving the startling example of the Israelites who "might have refused to massacre the Canaanites" (ibid).

10. Wardlaw criticises Mylne's use of this text in his *Christian Ethics*.

Bibliography

Principal Manuscripts, Newspapers, and Journals

THERE ARE FOUR SETS of student notes from James Mylne's philosophy class in Glasgow University Library (GUL). Two from 1820/21 are by the poet Robert Pollok (1798–1827) and the Church of Scotland minister Thomas Mackenzie. A third from 1829/30 is by the English dissenting minister Charles Wicksteed, along with an anonymous set from 1799/1800. There is another set from a member of the founding Mitchell family in the Mitchell Library in Glasgow. I have not located another by Principal Lee of Edinburgh, in EUL (MS 117); and a sixth from 1804/5, unfortunately in shorthand, is in the National Library of Scotland. There is a set of class essays that reflect the work of his class more indirectly in Mitchell Library, Glasgow.

There are two sets of manuscript lectures of Mylne's evening course of lectures on Political Economy. The first dates from 1804/5 and is in the National Library of Scotland. Unfortunately it is in shorthand. This includes the lectures on mental philosophy. A printed course outline for this year exists in the British Library. The second set (Bogue's "Minutes" from 1815/16) is in New College, Edinburgh. Political Economy in Mylne's day was a nascent discipline and thus works on it often combine material of a more general political nature.

Mylne's library records ("Professors' Receipt Books") and the Skirving catalogue of books sold at the time of his death are at GUL. Copies of letters between the Mylne, Wright, Dale, Owen and Millar family circles in Glasgow exist in Cornell University in the USA. There is a letter of Mylne to Julia Garnett-Pertz, dated 12 August 1827, in Houghton Library at Harvard

University (Ref: hou00634 Letter 25). GUL Special Collections also has letters and other material relating to Mylne, his colleagues and contemporaries, including George Jardine, Robert Buchanan and William Fleming. The senate minutes (held in GU Archives) contain some basic information. Scottish church records are held at the Mitchell Library and National Archives of Scotland (NAS). Scottish records of births, marriages and deaths are at NAS.

To reconstruct the social, literary and political life of the times, I consulted newspapers, principally the *Glasgow Mercury*, copies of which are held in the Mitchell Library, Glasgow, the *Glasgow Courier* and the *Glasgow Chronicle*, with copies at both the Mitchell Library and the National Library of Scotland, Edinburgh. These contain the adverts of local booksellers and circulating libraries, with news and discussion concerning social, political and Church controversies. Whilst the *Mercury* and *Courier* in particular were aligned politically to the establishment of the day, much information about the range of contemporary opinion can be gleaned by a critical reading. I supplemented this with online searches of Gale Group British newspaper records and other websites, including googlebooks for out of copyright printed books and journals and JSTOR for academic articles.

Books, Pamphlets, and Articles Consulted

Adams, James. *The Cromwellian Ghost conjured, &c, and put from creeping into Houses, &c, or Epaphroditus and Epaphras, called to a new conference, in vindication of the author of The Snake, etc.* Edinburgh, 1720.

———. *The independent Ghost Conjur'd, being a review of three letters clandestinely sent to a minister in the presbytery of Dundee, in answer to his queries concerning the lawfulness of national covenanting.* Edinburgh, 1728.

———. *Marrow-Chicaning Display'd, in a Letter to Mr Ebenezer Erskine.* [Edinburgh], 1726.

———. *The Snake in the Grass, or remarks upon a Book entitled "The Marrow of Divinity."* Edinburgh, 1719.

Addison, W. Innes, ed. *Matriculation Albums of the University of Glasgow.* Glasgow: Maclehose, 1913.

———. *Prize Lists of the University of Glasgow from Session 1777–78 to Session 1832–33.* Glasgow: Carter, 1902.

———. *Roll of Graduates of the University of Glasgow.* Glasgow: MacLehose, 1898.

Aitken, David. "Extract from the Diary of the Late Rev. David Aitken." *Scottish Review* 24 (1894) 106–25.

Akenside, Mark. *Poetical Works, with Memoir and Critical Dissertation by George Gilfillan.* Edinburgh: James Nichol, 1857.

Alexander, William Lindsay. *Memoirs of the Life and Writings of Ralph Wardlaw.* Edinburgh: Black, 1856.

Alison, Archibald. *Essays on the Nature and Principles of Taste.* 1790.

Allestree, Richard. *The Whole Duty of Man*. 1657; London: Rivington, 1826.
Alliot, Richard. *Psychology and Theology*. London, 1855.
Anderson, Adam. *A Historical and Chronological Deduction of the Origin of Commerce, containing an History of the Great Commercial Interests of the British Empire*. London: Walter, 1787–89.
Anderson, James M. *The Matriculation Roll of the University of St Andrews, 1747–1897*. Edinburgh: Blackwood, 1905.
Anon [or multiple authors]. *Actes des États de l'Ile de Jersey*. Société Jersiaise, 1911.
———. *Catalogue of Books of the Late Professor Mylne [. . .] sold by Barclay and Skirving*. Glasgow, 1840.
———. *Chambers' Cyclopaedia of English Literature*. Vol 7. New York: American Book Exchange, 1880.
———. "Critique of Our Late 'Notice of the University of Glasgow.'" *Edinburgh Magazine* (June 1825) 647–51.
———. *Dictionnaire Maxipoche 2008*. Paris: Larousse, 2007.
———. *Fortuna Domus: A Series of Lectures Delivered in the University of Glasgow in Commemoration of the Fifth Centenary of Its Foundation*. Glasgow: Glasgow University Press, 1952.
———. *Kilmarnock Mirror, or Literary Gleaner*. Numbers 1–13. Kilmarnock: Mathie and Lochore, 1818–19.
———. *Largs and Fairlie: Ayrshire Directories*. Pigot, 1837.
———. *Literary and Commercial Society Records*. Glasgow, 1831.
———. *A Memorial and Remonstrance Concerning the Proceedings of the Synod of Glasgow and Ayr, and of the General Assembly . . . in the Case of Dr. William McGill. By Some Members of the Church of Scotland who Took an Active Part in that Prosecution*. Edinburgh, 1792.
———. *A Narrative of the Whole Process respecting some late publications of the Rev. Dr. William McGill: with remarks on the late conduct and decision of the very Reverend the Synod of Glasgow and Ayr, in that cause: to which is subjoined an appendix containing the substance of the report of the committee of inquiry, appointed by the Presbytery of Ayr relative to said publications*. N.p. [Scotland], 1790. [Copy in GUL.]
———. "Notes on the Current State of St Andrews." *Edinburgh Magazine* (January 1826).
———. "Notes on the Present State of the University of St Andrews." January 1826, 90–93.
———. "Notice of the University of Glasgow: Its Professors and Students." *Edinburgh Magazine* (May 1825) 513–23.
———. *The Principal Acts of the General Assembly of the Church of Scotland*. Edinburgh: Waugh, 1826.
——— ["Friends of Truth"]. *The Procedure of our Church Courts in the Case of Dr William M'Gill of Ayr: with a complaint lately exhibited against him; and a narrative of the rise, progress and termination of a prosecution carried on against him before our church judicatories, by the laity of Scotland: to which is added a conclusion, containing reflections on the defection of our church courts*. N.p., 1792. [Copy in GUL.]
———. *Proceedings*. Royal Philosophical Society of Glasgow. Richard Griffin for the Royal Philosophical Society of Glasgow, 1848–1955.

———. *Register of the Society of Writers to Her Majesty's Signet.* Edinburgh, 1983. [Copy in NLS.]

———. *Report made to his Majesty by a Royal Commission of Inquiry into the State of the Universities of Scotland.* [London]: House of Commons, 1831.

———. *Report of the Royal Commissioners Appointed to Inquire into the Universities of Scotland.* Edinburgh: HMSO, 1878.

———. "Scottish Metaphysicians." *North British Review* 26–27 (1857) 216–34.

———. *Sessional Papers of the House of Lords.* 1839, vol. 37, 1837 Report of the Glasgow University Commissioners.

———. "Sir Daniel Keyte Sandford." *Hogg's Weekly Instructor* 26 (August 23, 1845) 403–5.

———. *Société Jersiaise Bulletin Annuels.* [Copies in Public Records Office, London.]

———. *Westminster Confession of Faith and Catechisms in Modern English.* 1644–49. Edited by Rowland Ward. Wantirna: New Melbourne, 1994.

Anselm, Saint. *Anselm of Canterbury: Major Works.* Edited by Brian Davies and G. R. Evans. Translated by D. P. Henry et al. Oxford: Oxford University Press, 1998.

Armour, Richard, W. *Barry Cornwall: A Biography of Bryan Waller Procter.* Boston: Meador, 1935.

Arthur, Archibald. *Discourses on Theological and Literary Subjects.* Edited by William Richardson. Glasgow, 1803.

Azouvi, François. *Maine de Biran: La Science de l'Homme.* Paris: Vrin, 1995.

Bacon, Francis. *Essays Civil and Moral.* London: Ward, 1910.

———. *Novum Organum.* Glasgow: Scrymgeour, 1803.

Badham Charles [senior]. *Essay on Bronchitis.* 2nd ed. London, 1814.

Badham, Charles [junior]. Introduction to Plato's *Philebus*. Pages iii–xx. London, 1855.

———. *Life of James Deacon Hume.* London, 1859.

———. *Speeches and Lectures delivered in Australia.* Sydney: Dymock, 1890.

———. *Thoughts on Classical and Commercial Education.* Birmingham, 1864.

Baker, Richard. *German Pulpit.* London: Rivington, 1829.

Balleine, George. *History of Jersey.* Edited by Marguerite Syvret and Joan Stevens. London: Phillimore, 1992.

Bailey, Samuel. *Critical Dissertation on the Nature, Measure and Causes of Value.* London: Hunter 1825.

———. *Essays on the Formation and Publication of Opinions.* 2nd ed. London: Hunter, 1826.

———. *The Rationale of Political Representation.* London, 1835.

Baillie, Joanna. *The Collected Letters of Joanna Baillie.* Edited by Judith Slagle. 2 vols. London: Associated University Press, 1999.

———. *A Collection of Poems, Chiefly Manuscript, and from Living Authors.* London: Longman, Hurst, 1823.

Bain, Alexander. *James Mill: A Biography.* London: Longmans, 1882.

Bain, Margaret. *Les Voyageurs Français en Ecosse 1770–1830 et leurs curiosités intellectuelles.* Paris, 1931.

Baker, D. W. A. *Days of Wrath.* Melbourne: Melbourne University Press, 1985.

Bartlett, Elizabeth. *Liberty, Equality, Sorority.* New York: Carlson, 1994.

Beattie, James. *Elements of Moral Science.* 2 vols. Edinburgh: Cadell, 1790–93.

———. *Essay on the Nature and Immutability of Truth, in opposition to Sophistry and Scepticism.* 1770.

Bell, James. *Sermons, preached before the University of Glasgow*. London: Strahan, 1790.
Bell, James, and James Paton. *Glasgow: Its Municipal Organization and Administration*. Glasgow: Maclehose, 1896.
Bell, Robert. *Treatise on Leases*. 3rd edn: Edinburgh: Constable, 1820.
———. *Treatise on the Election Laws as they relate to the Representation of Scotland*. Edinburgh: Constable, 1812.
Bellantone, Andrea. *Hegel en France*. 2 vols. Paris: Hermann, 2011.
Belsham, Thomas. *Elements of the Philosophy of the Mind, and of Moral Philosophy, to which is Prefixed a Compendium of Logic*. London: Johnson, 1801.
Blanqui, A. *Voyage d'un Jeune Français en Angleterre et en Ecosse*. Paris, 1824.
Boileau, Daniel. *Nature and Genius of the German Language*. London: Boosey, 1820.
Boims, J. D. "The Scottish Democratic Movement in the Age of the French Revolution." PhD diss., Edinburgh University, 1983.
Bonnot, Étienne [see Condillac, Abbé de].
Bono, Paola. *Radicals and Reformers in Late Eighteenth Century Scotland: An Annotated Checklist of Books, Pamphlets and Documents printed in Scotland, 1775–1800*. Frankfurt-am-Main: Lang, 1989.
Boog, Robert. *Discourses, Selected from the Manuscripts of the Late Robert Boog D.D.* Edited by James Mylne. Glasgow: Glasgow University Press, 1824.
———. *History of the Abbacy of Paisley*. [compiled from newspaper clippings, copy in PCL.]
Braudel, Fernand. *The Mediterranean and the Mediterranean World in the Age of Philip II*. London: Collins, 1972.
Bréhier, Émile. *Histoire de la Philosophie*. Paris: PUF, 1964.
Brewster, Patrick. *The Claims of the Church of Scotland*. Paisley, 1835.
———. *The Heroism of the Christian Spirit*. Edinburgh, 1833.
———. *Reply to the Attacks made on Mr Brewster in the Synod of Glasgow and Ayr for attending the O'Connell Dinner*. Paisley, 1835.
———. *Seven Chartist and military Discourses*. Paisley, 1843.
Brougham, Henry. *Inaugural discourse of Henry Brougham, Esq., M.P., on being installed Lord Rector of the University of Glasgow, Wednesday, April 6, 1825*. Glasgow: John Smith, 1825.
———. Review of Lauderdale's *Inquiry* in *Edinburgh Review*. Edinburgh, 1804.
Brown, Stewart Jay. *Thomas Chalmers and the Godly Commonwealth*. Oxford: Oxford University Press, 1982.
Brown, Thomas. *Inquiry into the Relation of Cause and Effect*. 3rd ed. Edinburgh: Constable, 1818.
———. *Lectures on the Philosophy of the Human Mind*. 4 vols. Edinburgh: Tait, 1820.
———. *Observations on the Zoonomia of Erasmus Darwin M.D.* Edinburgh: Mundell, 1798.
———. "Review of Viller's *Philosophie de Kant*." *Edinburgh Review* (1803).
Bruce, Gainsford. *Life and Letters of John Collingwood Bruce*. Edinburgh: Blackwood, 1905.
Bruce, John. *History of the Parish of West or Old Kilpatrick*. Glasgow: John Smith, 1893.
Brühlmeier, Daniel. "Price, Burke, Smith, Millar: Réactions Britanniques face à la Révolution Française." In *La Révolution Française dans la Pensée Européenne*, edited by Daniel Schulthess and Philippe Muller, 169–88. Lausanne: PAN, 1989.

Buckle, Henry. *History of Civilisation in England III: Scotland and the Scotch Intellect.* Oxford: Oxford University Press, 1904.
Buffier, Claude. *Œuvres Philosophiques du Père Buffier.* Edited by Francisque Bouillier. Paris: Charpentier, 1853.
Buffon. *Histoire Naturelle.* Paris: Gallimard, 1984.
Burder, Henry. *Mental Discipline or Hints on the Cultivation of Intellectual and Moral Habits, addressed particularly to Students in Theology.* Andover, 1827.
———. *The Pleasures of Religion.* London, 1823.
———. *The Scripture Character of God.* London, 1822.
Burke, Edmund. *Reflections on the Revolution in France.* Oxford: Oxford University Press, 1993.
Burns, Robert. *Memoir of Stevenson MacGill.* Edinburgh, 1842.
Burns, Robert [minister]. *Historical Dissertations on the Law and Practice of Great Britain, and particularly of Scotland, with regard to the Poor.* Glasgow, 1819.
———. *Testimonials in Favour of the Rev. Robert Burns [. . .] for the vacant Chair of Moral Philosophy in the University of St Andrews.* 1823. [copy in NCL.]
Burns, Robert Ferrier. *The Life and Times of the Rev. Robert Burns.* Campbell, 1872.
Butler, Joseph. *The Analogy of Religion.* Glasgow: Collins, n.d.
Butler, Samuel. *Hudibras.* Edited by Zachary Grey. London: Warne, n.d.
Cadet, Félix. *Histoire de l'Economie Politique: les Précurseurs.* New York: Franklin, 1970.
Cage, R. A. *The Scottish Poor Law, 1745–1845.* Edinburgh: Scottish Academic Press, 1981.
Caird, Edward. *The Evolution of Religion.* 2 vols. Glasgow: Maclehose, 1892.
Caird, John. *Faiths of the World.* Edinburgh, 1881.
———. *Spinoza.* Edinburgh: Blackwood's, 1888.
Cairns, William. "Memoir of the Author." In *Lectures on Intellectual Philosophy* by John Young, xv–xxxii. Glasgow: Reid, 1835.
———. *A Treatise on Moral Freedom, containing Inquiries into the Operations of the Intellectual Faculties.* London: Longman, 1844.
Campbell, John McLeod. *The Nature of the Atonement.* Edinburgh: Handsel, 1996.
Campbell, Thomas. *Inaugural Discourse of Thomas Campbell, Esq., on being installed as Lord Rector of the University of Glasgow, Thursday April 12th, 1827.* Glasgow: John Smith, 1827.
Cant, R G. *The University of St Andrews.* Edinburgh: Scottish Academic Press, 1970.
Carlyle, Thomas. *Sartor Resartus.* Oxford: Oxford University Press, 1987.
———. "Signs of the Times." [Untitled review] *Edinburgh Review* 49 (June, 1829) 439–59.
Carmichael, Gershom. *Natural Rights on the Threshold of the Scottish Enlightenment.* Edited by Knud Haakonssen, James Moore, and Michael Silverthorne. Indianapolis: Liberty Fund, 2002.
Carpenter, Lant. *Principles of Education: Intellectual, Moral and Physical.* London: Longman, 1820. [Originally part of the Abraham Rees's *Cyclopaedia, or Universal Dictionary*; dedicated to John Young, George Jardine and James Mylne.]
———. *A Review of the Labours, Opinions and Character of Rajah Rammohun Roy.* London: Rowland Hunter, 1833.
———. "Social improvement and Unitarian Prospects in Scotland." Letter to editor of *Christian Reformer* (1837).

———. *A View of the Scriptural Grounds of Unitarianism*. London: Longman Hurst, 1811.
Carpenter, Lant, W. Shepherd, and J. Joyce. *Systematic Education, or Elementary Instruction in the Various Departments of Literature and Science with Practical Rules for Studying Each Branch of Useful Knowledge*. 2 vols. London: Longman, 1815.
Carpenter, Russell. *Memoirs of the Life of Lant Carpenter*. Bristol: Philp, 1842.
Carter, Matthew. *T H Green and the Development of Ethical Socialism*. Exeter: Imprint Academic, 2003.
Chalmers, Thomas. *An Inquiry into the Extent and Stability of National Resources*. Edinburgh: Oliphant & Brown, 1808.
———. *On Political Economy in Connexion with the Moral State and Moral Prospects of Society*. Glasgow, 1832.
Chambers, Robert. *Biographical Dictionary of Eminent Scotsmen*. Edited by Thomas Thomson. Glasgow: Blackie, 1855.
Chambers, Robert. *The Threiplands of Fingask: A Family Memoir "Written in 1853."* London: Chambers, 1880.
Checkland, Sydney G. *Scottish Banking: A History, 1695-1973*. Glasgow: Collins, 1975.
———. *The Upas Tree: Glasgow 1875-1975, A Study in Growth and Contraction*. Glasgow: Glasgow University Press, 1976.
Chichester, Henry. *The Records and Badges of every Regiment and Corps in the British Army*. London: Gale, 1900.
Chitnis, Anand. *The Scottish Enlightenment and Early Victorian English Society*. London: Croom Helm, 1986.
Cicero, Marcus Tullius. *De Officiis*. Edited by Harry G. Edinger. Indianapolis: Bobbs-Merrill, 1974.
———. *The Treatise of Cicero De Officiis, or his essay on moral duty, translated and accompanied with notes and observations*. Translated by William McCartney. Edinburgh: Bell, 1798.
Clark, Sylvia. *Paisley: a History*. Edinburgh: Mainstream, 1988.
Clarke, Samuel. *A Collection of the Promises of Scripture*. Edited by Ralph Wardlaw. Glasgow: Collins, 1831.
———. *A Demonstration of the Being and Attributes of God*. Edited by Ezio Vailati. Cambridge: Cambridge University Press, 1998.
———. *Discourse concerning the Being and Attributes of God, the Obligations of Natural Religion and the Truth and Certainty of Christian Revelation*. London: Knapton, 1732.
Clauzade, Laurent. *L'Idéologie: ou la révolution d'analyse*. Paris: Gallimard, 1998.
Cobbett, William. *A Tour in Scotland and in the Four Northern Counties of England*. London, 1833.
Cockburn, Henry. *An Examination of the Trials for Sedition Which Have Hitherto Occurred in Scotland*. 2 vols. Edinburgh: Douglas, 1888.
———. *Letter by the Late Rector of the University of Glasgow*. n.p., 1833.
———. *Life of Lord Jeffrey, with a Selection from his Correspondence*. 2nd ed. Edinburgh: Black, 1852.
———. *Memorials of his Time*. Edinburgh: Thin, 1988.
Cogan, Thomas. *An Ethical Treatise on the Passions, founded on the Principles investigated in the Philosophical Treatise*. Bath: Hazard, 1807.

———. *A Philosophical Treatise on the Passions*. 2nd ed. London: Hazard, 1802.
Colley, Linda. *Britons: Forging the Nation, 1707–1837*. London: Pimlico, 1992.
Combe, George. *The Constitution of Man in Relation to External Objects*. London: Longman, 1828.
———, [presumed ed.]. *Testimonials on behalf of George Combe as a Candidate for the Chair of Logic at the University of Edinburgh*. Edinburgh: Anderson, 1836.
Comte, Auguste. *Cours de Philosophie Positive*. Paris, 1835–.
Condillac, Abbé de [Étienne Bonnot],.*Cours d'Etudes pour l'instruction du Prince de Parme*. Parme: 1775; 1798.
———. *Essai sur l'Origine des Connaissances humaines*. 1746; Auvers-sur-l'Oise : Galilée, 1973.
———. *La Langue des Calculs*. 1798. Repr. Lille: Presses Universitaires de Lille, n.d.
———. *Oeuvres*. 3 vols. Paris, 1777.
———. *Traité des Sensations*. 1754; Paris: Fayard, 1984.
———. *Traité des Systèmes*. La Haye, 1749; Paris: Fayard, 1991.
Constant, Benjamin. *Écrits Politiques*. Paris: Gallimard, 1997.
Cook, George. *Life of the Late George Hill*. Edinburgh: Constable, 1820.
Cooper, Anthony Ashley [Earl of Shaftesbury]. *Characteristicks of Men, Manners, Opinions, Times, etc*. 1694; Edited by John Robertson. 2 vols. Gloucester: Smith, 1963.
Cousin, Victor. *Philosophie Sensualiste du XVIIIe Siècle*. 3rd ed. Paris: Librairie Nouvelle, 1856.
Coutts, James. *History of the University of Glasgow, 1451–1909*. Glasgow: Maclehose, 1909.
Craig, John. "Account of the Life and Writings of John Millar, Esq." In *Origins of the Distinction of Ranks*, by John Millar, i-cxxxiv. Edinburgh: Blackwood, 1806.
———. *Elements of Political Science*. 3 vols. Edinburgh: Blackwood, 1814.
———. *Remarks on Some Doctrines of Political Economy*. Edinburgh: Constable, 1821.
Crawford, George. *History of the Shire of Renfrew*. Paisley, 1818.
Crawford, Kenneth, *Dugald Stewart and His Library*. London: Serendipity, 2004.
Crawford, Thomas. *Boswell, Burns and the French Revolution*. Edinburgh: Saltire Society, 1989.
Crouan, Katharine. *John Linnell: A Centennial Exhibition*. Cambridge: Cambridge University Press, 1982.
Curtis, Edward. *The Organization of the British Army in the American Revolution*. Wakefield: E.P., 1972.
Daire, Eugène. *Les Physiocrates*. Paris: Guillaumine, 1846.
Darwin, Erasmus. *The Botanic Garden*. New York, 1798.
———. *Zoonomia, or the Laws of Organic Life*. Dublin: Byrne, 1796.
Davidson, John. "Dunbartonshire." In *Statistical Account of Scotland, 1791–1799*, edited by John Sinclair. Wakefield: E.P., 1976.
Davidson, Randall, and William Benham. *Life of Archibald Campbell Tait*. London: Macmillan, 1891.
Davie, George. *Crisis of the Democratic Intellect: The Problem of Generalism and Specialisation in Twentieth-Century Scotland*. Edinburgh: Polygon, 1986.
———. *The Democratic Intellect: Scotland and Her Universities in the Nineteenth Century*. Edinburgh: Edinburgh University Press, 1961.

———. *Ferrier and the Blackout of the Scottish Enlightenment*. Edinburgh: Centre for the History of Ideas in Scotland, 2003.
———. *A Passion for Ideas: Essays on the Scottish Enlightenment 2*. Edinburgh: Polygon, 1994.
———. *The Scotch Metaphysics: A Century of Enlightenment in Scotland*. London: Routledge, 2001.
———. *The Scottish Enlightenment and Other Essays*. Edinburgh: Polygon, 1991.
Deleule, Didier. *Hume et la Naissance du Libéralisme économique*. Paris: Aubier, 1979.
Descartes, René. *Philosophical Works*. 2 vols. Translated by Elizabeth Hamilton and G. Ross. Cambridge: Cambridge University Press, 1911.
Destutt de Tracy, A. L. C. *Élemens d'Idéologie*. 4 vols. Paris: Librairie pour les Mathématiques, 1804.
Deuchar, Robert. *Brief Review of Ancient and Modern Philosophy*. Edinburgh: Thin, 1864.
Dewar, Daniel. *Elements of Moral Philosophy*. 2 vols. Glasgow: Ogle, 1826.
Dewaule, Léon. *Condillac et la psychologie anglaise contemporaine*. Paris: Alcan, 1892.
Dick, Thomas. *The Christian Philosopher: or the Connection of Science and Philosophy with Religion*. Glasgow: Chalmers, 1825.
Dirom, Alexander. *Inquiry into the Corn Laws*. Edinburgh: Creech, 1796.
Douallier, Stéphane. *Philosophie: France XIXe Siècle: Écrits et opuscules*. Paris: Livre de Poche, 1994.
Drummond, Andrew L., and James Bulloch. *The Scottish Church, 1688–1843*. Edinburgh: St. Andrew, 1973.
Duncan, Henry. *The Sacred Philosophy of the Seasons*. Boston: Marsh, 1839.
Duncan, John. *An Essay on Genius: or, the Philosophy of Literature*. Edinburgh: Blackwood, 1814.
———. *Philosophy of Human Nature, containing a Complete Theory of Human Interests, to which is added an Essay on the Origin of Evil*. Edinburgh: Oliver & Boyd, 1815.
Duncan, William J., ed. *Notices and Documents illustrative of the Literary History of Glasgow, during the Greater Part of Last Century*. Glasgow: Maitland Club, 1831.
Dunckley, Henry. *Lord Melbourne*. 2 vols, London: Low, 1890.
Dunlop, Robert. *Daniel O'Connell and the Revival of National Life in Ireland*. London: Putnam's, 1908.
Dunn, William. "Kirkintilloch." In *Statistical Account of Scotland, 1791–1799*, edited by John Sinclair. Wakefield: E.P., 1976.
Durant, Thomas, ed. *Memoirs and Select Remains of an Only Son, who died November 27, 1821 in his 19th Year while a Student in the University of Glasgow*. Andover: Newman, 1823.
Eckhardt, Celia Morris. *Fanny Wright: Rebel in America*. Cambridge, MA: Harvard University Press, 1984.
Edmonds, Angus A. "Political Philosophy." Emmanuel College, University of Queensland. 1997. Online: http://www.emmanuel.uq.edu.au/Lang/political.html.
Edwards, Jonathan. *The Freedom of the Will*. 1754. Indianapolis: Bobbs-Merrill, 1969.
———. *Treatise concerning the Religious Affections*. 1746. Grand Rapids: Sovereign Grace, 1971.
Ellis, Peter Berresford, and Seumas Mac a'Ghobhainn. *The Scottish Insurrection of 1820*. London: Pluto, 1989.

Emerson, Roger L. *Academic Patronage in the Scottish Enlightenment: Glasgow, Edinburgh and St Andrews Universities.* Edinburgh: Edinburgh University Press, 2008.

———. "Politics and the Glasgow Professors 1690–1800." In *The Glasgow Enlightenment*, edited by Andrew Hook and Richard B. Sher, 21–39. East Linton: Tuckwell, 1995.

Enfield, William. *History of Philosophy, from the earliest Times to the Beginning of the present Century, drawn up from Brucker's Historia Critica Philosophiae.* Dublin: Ershaw, 1792.

Epicurus. "Letter to Menoeceus." In *Lives of the Philosophers*, by Diogenes Laertius. Translated by D. H. Hicks. Loeb Classical Library 10. London: Heinemann, 1925.

Ewan, Elizabeth L., et al., eds. *The Biographical Dictionary of Scottish Women.* Edinburgh: Edinburgh University Press, 2007.

Eyre-Todd, George. *History of Glasgow.* 3 vols. Glasgow: Jackson Wylie, 1934.

Farmer, John S. *The Regimental Records of the British Army.* London: Grant Richards, 1901.

Fénélon, Francois. *Télémache.* London, 1742.

Ferguson, DeLancey. "An Inedited Burns Letter." *Modern Language Notes* 58/8 (1943) 617–20.

Fergusson, David, ed. *Scottish Philosophical Theology, 1700–2000.* Exeter: Imprint Academic, 2007.

Ferrier, James Frederick. *Lectures on Greek Philosophy and Other Philosophical Remains.* Edited by Alexander Grant and E. L. Lushington. 2 vols. Edinburgh: Blackwood, 1866.

Field, William. *Memoirs of the Life, Writings and Opinions of the Rev. Samuel Parr.* London: Colburn, 1828.

Findlay, Robert. *The Divine Inspiration of the Jewish Scriptures or Old Testament.* Cadell, 1803.

Fisher, Edward. *The Marrow of Modern Divinity.* Montrose, 1803.

Fisher, Joe. *The Glasgow Encyclopaedia.* Edinburgh: Mainstream, 1994.

Fitzpatrick, Martin. "Varieties of Dissent: Scottish and English Style." *Enlightenment and Dissent* 7 (1988) 35–36.

Fleming, William. *A Gazetteer of the Old and New Testaments, to which is added the Natural History of the Bible.* Edinburgh: Edinburgh Printing, 1838.

———. *A Manual of Moral Philosophy.* Glasgow: Richardson, 1854.

———. "Moral Philosophy Chair: Hutcheson, Smith, Reid and Mylne." In *The Peel Club Papers for Session, 1839–40*, 8–12. Glasgow: Richardson, 1840.

———. *The Vocabulary of Philosophy, Mental, Moral and Metaphysical; with Quotations and References for the Use of Students.* Glasgow: Griffin, 1858.

Fletcher, Andrew. *Selected Political Writings and Speeches.* Edited by David Daiches. Edinburgh: Scottish Academic Press, 1979.

Fletcher, Joseph. *Lectures on the Principles and Institutions of the Roman Catholic Religion.* London, 1817.

Flynn, Philip. *Enlightened Scotland: A Study and Selection of Scottish Philosophical Prose from the Eighteenth and Early Nineteenth Centuries.* Edinburgh: Scottish Academic Press, 1992.

Fortescue, John. *A History of the British Army, 1763–1793.* London: Macmillan, 1911.

Foucault, Michel. *Histoire de la Folie à l'Age classique.* Paris: Gallimard, 1972.

Fraser, Alexander Campbell. *Biographia Philosophica: A Retrospect*. Edinburgh: Blackwood, 1904.
———. *Thomas Reid*. Famous Scots. Edinburgh: Oliphant, 1898.
Fry, Michael. *The Dundas Despotism*. Edinburgh: Edinburgh University Press, 1992.
Fuller, Andrew. *The Calvinistic and Socinian Systems compared as to their Moral Tendency* in *Works*. 1841. Edinburgh: Banner of Truth, 2007.
———. *Strictures on Sandemanianism*. 1810. Edinburgh: Banner of Truth, 2007.
Galloway, William Brown. *Philosophy and Religion with their Mutual Bearings comprehensively considered and satisfactorily determined on Scientific Principles*. London: Smith, 1837.
Garnier, Germaine. "A View of the Doctrine of Smith, compared with that of the French Economists; with a method of facilitating the Study of his Works." In *An Inquiry into the Nature and Causes of the Wealth of Nations*, by Adam Smith. Edinburgh: Mundell, 1809.
Gilfillan, George. *The History of a Man*. London: Hall, 1856.
———. *Life of the Rev. William Anderson LLD, Glasgow*. Glasgow: Hodder, 1873.
———. "Memoir and Critical Dissertation." In *Poetical Works, with Memoir and Critical Dissertation by George Gilfillan*, by Mark Akenside, v–xxiii. Edinburgh: James Nichol, 1857.
———, ed. *Poetical Works of Beattie, Blair and Falconer*. Edinburgh: Nichol, 1854.
———. *Remoter Stars in the Church Sky*. London: Jackson, 1867.
———. "Reverend David Young." In *Our Scottish Clergy*, edited by John Smith. Edinburgh: Oliver, 1849.
Gilmour, David. *Reminiscences of the Pen' Folk*. Gardner: Edinburgh and Paisley, 1879.
Glas, John [or Glass]. *Letters of Correspondence: Robert Sandeman and John Glas*. Dundee: MacIntosh, 1851.
———. *The Marrow of Ancient Divinity, showing the Import of John 1.17, by John Glas, to which is attached an Essay on the Song of Solomon by the Late Mr R Sandeman*. Whitehaven, 1800.
———. *A Narrative of the Rise and Progress of the Controversy about National Covenants*. Edinburgh, 1728.
———. *Testament of the King of Martyrs*. 1729.
———. *Works*. 5 vols. Perth, 1782.
Godwin, William. "Autobiography." In *Collected Novels and Memoirs of William Godwin*, edited by Mark Philps, 1:1–38. London: Pickering, 1992.
———. *Collected Novels and Memoirs of William Godwin*. Edited by Mark Philps. London: Pickering, 1992.
———. *An Enquiry concerning Political Justice, and its influence on general Virtue and Happiness*. Harmondsworth: Penguin, 1985.
———. *Fleetwood, or the New Man of Feeling*. London: Philips, 1805.
———. *Political and Philosophical Writings*. Edited by Mark Philp. 7 vols. London, Pickering, 1993.
———. "The Principal Revolutions of Opinion." In *Collected Novels and Memoirs of William Godwin*, edited by Mark Philps, 1:52–54. London: Pickering, 1992.
———. *St Leon, a Tale of the Sixteenth Century*. London, 1799.
———. *Things as they are, or the Adventures of Caleb Williams*. London: Crosby, 1794.
Gordon, Mary Wilson. *"Christopher North": A Memoir of John Wilson*. Edinburgh: Edmonston, 1862.

Grave, Selwyn. *A History of Philosophy in Australia*. Queensland: Queensland University Press, 1984.

———. *The Scottish School of Common Sense*. Oxford: Clarendon, 1960.

Green, Thomas. *An Examination of the leading Principle of a new System of Morals, as that Principle is stated and applied in Mr. Godwin's Enquiry concerning Political Justice*. London: Green, 1798.

Griscom, John. *A Year in Europe*. New York: Collins, 1824.

Hamilton, Elizabeth. *Memoirs of Modern Philosophers*. Dublin, 1800.

———. *Translation of the Letters of a Hindoo Rajah*. London: Robinson, 1796.

Hamilton, John Andrew. *Life of Daniel O'Connell*. London: Allen, 1888.

Hamilton, William. *Discussions on Philosophy and Literature, Education and University Reform*. New York: Harper, 1855.

———. *Fragments de Philosophie*. Translated by L. Peisse. Paris: Ladrange, 1840.

———. *Lectures on Logic and Metaphysics*. Edited by John Veitch and H. L. Mansel. 4 vols. Edinburgh: Blackwood, 1869.

Hanna, William *Memoirs of the Life and Writings of Thomas Chalmers*. Edinburgh: Sutherland, 1849–52.

Hardie, Thomas. *The Patriot [...] with Observations on Republican Government and Paine's Principles*. 1793.

Harris, James. "Mylne, James." In *The Dictionary of Nineteenth Century British Philosophers*, edited by W. J. Mander and Alan P. F. Sell, 2:843–45. Bristol: Thoemmes, 2002.

———. *Of Liberty and Necessity: The Free Will Debate in Eighteenth Century British Philosophy*. Oxford: Clarendon, 2005.

Hartley, David. *Address to the Committee of Association of the County of York, on the State of Public Affairs*. York: Almond, 1781.

———. *Observations on Man: his Frame, his Duties and his Expectations*. London, 1749.

Hay, John Barras. *Inaugural Addresses by Lord Rectors of the University of Glasgow, to which are prefixed an historical sketch and account of the present state of the University*. Glasgow: Robertson, 1839.

Hegel, Georg Wilhelm Friedrich. *The Difference Between Fichte's and Schelling's System of Philosophy*. Translated by H. S. Harris. Albany: SUNY, 1977.

———. "The English Reform Bill." In *Hegel's Political Writings*, 295–330. Translated by T. M. Knox. Oxford: Oxford University Press, 1964.

———. "How the Ordinary Human Understanding Takes Philosophy (as Displayed in the Works of Mr. Krug)." In *Between Kant and Hegel: Texts in the Development of Post-Kantian Idealism*, edited by George di Giovanni, 292–310. Translated by H. S. Harris. New York: New York University Press, 1985.

———. *Philosophy of Right*. Translated by T. M Knox. Oxford: Oxford University Press, 1952.

Heinemann, Helen. *Restless Angels: The Friendship of Six Victorian Women*. Athens: Ohio University Press, 1983.

Helvetius, Claude-Adrien. *De l'Esprit*. Edited by François Châtelet. Verviers: Gérard, 1973.

Herder, Johann Gottfried. *Oriental Poetry: containing the dialogues of Eugenius and Alciphron on the Spirit and Beauties of the Sacred Poetry of the Hebrews*. Strahan, 1801.

———. *Outlines of a Philosophy of the History of Man.* Translated by T. O. Churchill. London, 1800.
Hicks, G. Dawes. "A Century of Philosophy: University College, London." *Journal of Philosophical Studies* 3/12 (October 1928) 468–82.
Hill, George. *Lectures in Divinity.* Edited by Alexander Hill. Edinburgh: Waugh, 1821.
———. *A View of the Constitution of the Church of Scotland.* Edinburgh: Hill, 1817.
Hoeveler, J. David. *James McCosh and the Scottish Intellectual Tradition: From Glasgow to Princeton.* Princeton: Princeton University Press, 1981.
Hogg, James. *Memoirs and Confessions of a Justified Sinner.* 1824.
Holcomb, Kathleen. "Thomas Reid in the Glasgow Literary Society." In *The Glasgow Enlightenment*, edited by Andrew Hook and Richard B. Sher, 95–110. East Linton: Tuckwell, 1995.
Home, Henry [Lord Kames], ed. *Sketches of the History of Man.* 2nd ed. Edinburgh, 1778.
Hook, Andrew, and Richard B. Sher, eds. *The Glasgow Enlightenment.* East Linton: Tuckwell, 1995.
Hoppus, John ["Edinensi-Glasguensis" per attribution in NLS catalogue]. *Account of Lord Bacon's Novum Organum.* London, 1827.
———. *The Continent in 1835: Sketches in Belgium, Germany, Switzerland, Savoy and France.* 2 vols. London: Saunders, 1836.
———. *The Crisis of Popular Education.* 1847.
———. *Ireland's Misery and Remedy: A Discourse.* London, 1835.
———. *Recollections, Juvenile, Miscellaneous and Academical.* London, 1823.
———. *Schism, as opposed to the Unity of the Church.* 1839.
Horrocks, Don. *Laws of the Spiritual Order: Innovation and Reconstruction in the Soteriology of Thomas Erskine of Linlathen.* Carlisle: Paternoster, 2004.
Hughes, Gillian. "James Hogg, and Edinburgh's Triumph over Napoleon." *Scottish Literary Journal* 4/1 (Spring 2003) 98–111.
Hume, David. *Enquiries Concerning Human Understanding and the Principles of Morals.* 1748; Oxford: Clarendon, 1975.
———. *The History of England: From the Invasion of Julius Caesar to The Revolution in 1688.* 6 vols. Indianapolis: Liberty, 1983.
———. *Letters of David Hume.* Edited by J. Y. T. Greig. 2 vols. Oxford: Oxford University Press, 1932.
———. *Natural History of Religion.* In *Essays, Literary, Moral and Political*, 514–52. London: Ward. n.d.
———. *Philosophical Works.* 4 vols. Edinburgh: Black, 1826.
———. *Philosophical Works.* Vol. 1. Edited by Thomas Hill Green and Thomas Hodge Grose. London: Longmans, 1874.
———. *Treatise of Human Nature.* 3 vols. London: Noon, 1739–40.
Hutcheson, Francis. *Philosophical Writings.* Edited by Robin Downie. London: Everyman, 1994.
———. *Synopsis Metaphysicae, Ontologiam et Pneumatologiam Complectens.* 1742; Glasgow: Foulis, 1762.
———. *System of Moral Philosophy.* Edited by Francis Hutcheson [Jr.] and William Leechman. London, 1755.
Hutton, Joseph. *Unitarian Christianity Vindicated.* London, 1832.

Innes, Arthur D. *History of England and the British Empire.* Vol. 3. New York: Macmillan, 1914.
James, William. *Pragmatism.* Edited by A. J. Ayer. Cambridge, MA: Harvard University Press, 1975.
———. *Principles of Psychology.* 2 vols. New York: Dover, 1950.
Jardine, George. *An Outline of Philosophical Education.* Glasgow: Duncan, 1818.
Jessop, Ralph. *Carlyle and Scottish Thought.* New York: St. Martin's, 1997.
Jevons, William. *Systematic Morality, or a Treatise on the Theory and Practice of Human Duty, on the Grounds of Natural Religion.* London: Hunter, 1827.
Jones, Henry. *The Working Faith of the Social Reformer.* London: Macmillan, 1910.
Jones, Peter. *Hume's Sentiments.* Edinburgh: Edinburgh University Press, 1982.
Kaner, Jennifer. "York and the Battle of Jersey." *York Historian* 6 (1985) 72–82. [Société Jersiaise archives BJ1/34.]
Kant, Immanuel. *Critique of Pure Reason.* Translated by Norman K Smith. London: Macmillan, 1929.
———. *Groundwork of the Metaphysic of Morals.* 1785.
———. *On Perpetual Peace.* London, 1796.
Kendrick, John. "Memoir of the Late Rev. William Turner Jun., MA" *The Christian Reformer* (March 1854) 129–43.
Kitzmiller, John M., II. *In Search of the "Forlorn Hope": A Comprehensive Guide to Locating British Regiments and Their Records (1640–WW1).* 2 vols. Salt Lake City: Manuscript Publishing, 1988.
Knight, William. "Unpublished Letters from John Stuart Mill to Professor Nichol." *Fortnightly Review* (May 1898) 660–78.
Knowles, Dudley. "Review of Edward Caird: *Hegel*." *Journal Scottish Philosophy* 1/2 (Autumn 2003) 187–89.
Koyré, Alexandre. *Études d'histoire de la pensée philosophique.* Paris: Gallimard, 1971.
Lambton, John. *Speeches of the Earl of Durham delivered at Public Meetings in Scotland and Newcastle in 1834.* London: Ridgeway, 1834.
Lancaster, Joseph. *Improvements to Education.* London, 1803.
La Rochefoucauld François. *Maxims.* 1665; Harmondsworth: Penguin, 1959.
Laurie, Henry. *Scottish Philosophy in its National Development.* Glasgow: MacLehose, 1902.
Lee, Tom. *Seekers of Truth.* Amsterdam: JOA Elsevier, 2006. [Copy in ICAS Library, Edinburgh].
Lehmann, William. *John Millar of Glasgow, 1735–1801: His Life and Thought and His Contributions to Sociological Analysis.* Cambridge: Cambridge University Press, 1960.
Lenman, Bruce. *Scotland 1746–1832.* London: Arnold, 1981.
Le Roy, Georges. *La Psychologie de Condillac.* Paris: Boivin, 1937.
Linnaeus, Carl [Carl von Linné]. *Systema Naturae.* 1735.
Locke, John. *An Essay Concerning Human Understanding.* Edited by A. S. Pringle-Pattison. Ware: Wordsworth, 1998.
Lockhart, John Gibson. *Memoirs of the Life of Sir Walter Scott.* Edinburgh, 1837.
———. *Peter's Letters to his Kinsfolk.* London: Nelson, 1952.
Lubac, Henri de. *The Unmarxian Socialist.* London: Sheed, 1948.
Lucretius. *On the Nature of the Universe.* Edited by Ronald E. Latham. Harmondsworth: Penguin, 1951.

Ludwig, Christian. *Teutschenenglisches Lexicon*. Leipzig, n.d.
Lyall, William. *The Intellect, the Emotions and the Moral Nature*. Edinburgh: Constable, 1855.
MacGill, Stevenson. *The Connexion of Situation with Character, considered with a View to the Ministers of Religion*. Glasgow, 1796.
———. *Discourses and Essays on Subjects of Public Interest*. Edinburgh: Waugh, 1819.
———. *Lectures on Rhetoric and Criticism and on Subjects Introductory to the Critical Study of the Scriptures*. Edinburgh: Oliphant, 1838.
———. *Remarks on Prisons*. Glasgow, 1810.
———. *The Spirit of the Times, considered in an Address to the People of Eastwood*. Glasgow: Reid, 1792.
Mackenzie, E. *A Descriptive Account of the Town and County of Newcastle*. Newcastle, 1827.
Mackenzie, Peter, ed. *Glasgow Electors: List of the Names and Designations of the Persons who voted in the First Election of Two Members to serve in Parliament for the City of Glasgow under the Scotch Reform Bill, 18th & 19th Dec. 1832*. Glasgow: Muir, 1832.
———. *The Life of Thomas Muir, Esq. Advocate, Younger of Huntershill, Near Glasgow, One of the Celebrated Reformers of 1793, who was Tried for Sedition Before the High Court of Justiciary in Scotland, and Sentenced to Transportation for Fourteen Years*. Glasgow: Muir, 1836.
———. *Reminiscences of Glasgow and the West of Scotland*. 3 vols. 2nd ed. Glasgow: Tweed, 1866.
MacLehose, James [senior]. *Memoirs and Portraits of 100 Glasgow Men who have Died during the Last Thirty Years, and in their Lives did Much to Make this City what it now is*. Glasgow: MacLehose, 1886.
MacLehose, James. *Books Published by James MacLehose from 1838 to 1881 and by James MacLehose and Sons to 1905 Presented to the Library of University of Glasgow*. Glasgow: Glasgow University Press, 1905.
———. *The Glasgow University Press 1638-1931*. Glasgow: MacLehose, 1931.
MacLelland, James. "The Origin and Present Organisation of the Profession of Chartered Accountants in Scotland." 1869.
MacLeod, Donald. *Memoir of Norman MacLeod*. London: Daldy, 1876.
Macmillan, Dorothy, and Douglas Gifford, eds. *A History of Scottish Women's Writing*. Edinburgh: Edinburgh University Press, 1997.
Madinier, Gabriel. *Conscience et Mouvement*. 2nd ed. Paris: Alcan, 1967.
Maitland, James [Lord Lauderdale]. *Inquiry into the Nature and Origin of Public Wealth*. Edinburgh: Constable, 1804.
———. *Inquiry into the Practical Merits of the Government of India*. Edinburgh: Constable, 1809.
Malthus, Thomas Robert. *An Essay on the Principle of Population*. Oxford: Oxford University Press, 1993.
Mandeville, Bernard. *The Fable of the Bees*. 1714; Harmondsworth: Penguin, 1970.
Martineau, James. *Essays, Reviews and Addresses*. London: Longman, 1901.
———. *The Rationale of Religious Inquiry*. 2nd ed. London, 1836.
Marx, Karl. *Capital*. Vol. 3. Translated by David Fernbach. London: Penguin, 1991.
Mathieson, W. L. *The Church and Reform in Scotland, 1797-1843*. Glasgow: MacLehose, 1916.
Mavor, Irene. *Glasgow*. Edinburgh: Edinburgh University Press, 2000.

Maxton, James. *Lenin*. Daily Express, 1932.
Maxwell, John. *Letter addressed to the Honest Reformers of Scotland, with remarks on the Poor Rates, Corn Law, Religious Establishments, Right of Property, Equality of Ranks, and Revolution*. Glasgow: Duncan, 1819.
Mayne, Richard, *The Battle of Jersey*. London: Phillimore, 1981.
McAdam, John. *Autobiography of John McAdam*. Edited by Janet Fyfe. Edinburgh: Scottish History Society, 1980.
McCarthy, Mary. *A Social Geography of Paisley*. Paisley: Paisley Public Library, 1969.
McCormick, John. *The Flag in the Wind*. London: Gollancz, 1955.
McCosh, James. *The Life of James McCosh: A Record Chiefly Autobiographical*. Edited by William M. Sloane. New York: Scribner, 1896.
———. *The Scottish Philosophy: Biographical, Expository, Critical, from Hutcheson to Hamilton*. London: Macmillan, 1875.
McKay, Johnston. *The Kirk and the Kingdom*. Edinburgh: Edinburgh University Press, 2011.
McLean, Archibald. *The Commission given by Jesus Christ to his Apostles*. 2nd ed. Glasgow, 1797.
———. *Defence of Believer Baptism*. Edinburgh, 1777.
———. *A Review of Mr Wardlaw's Lectures on the Abrahamic Covenant and its (supposed) Connection with Infant Baptism*. Edinburgh, 1807.
McNair, Alexander. *Scots Theology in the Eighteenth Century*. London: Clarke, n.d.
Mechie, Stewart. *The Church and Scottish Social Development, 1780–1870*. Oxford: Oxford University Press, 1960.
Meikle, Henry. *Scotland and the French Revolution*. Glasgow: Maclehose, 1912.
Mercier de la Rivière, Pierre-Paul. *L'Ordre Naturel et Essentiel des Sociétés Politiques*. Paris: Fayard, 2001.
Metcalfe, W. N. *A History of Paisley*. Paisley: Gardner, 1909.
Metz, Rudolph. *A Hundred Years of British Philosophy*. London: Allen Unwin, 1938.
M'Gill, William. *A Practical Essay on the Death of Jesus Christ*. Edinburgh: Mundell, 1786.
Mill, John Stuart. *Autobiography*. Oxford: Oxford University Press, 1924.
———. *The Earlier Letters of John Stuart Mill, 1812–1848*. Vol. 12 of *Collected Works*. Edited by F. E. Mineka. Toronto: Routledge, 1963.
Millar, John. *Historical View of the English Government, from the Settlement of the Saxons in Britain to the Revolution in 1688. To which are subjoined, some Dissertations connected with the history of the Government*. Indianapolis: Liberty, 2006.
———. *Letters of Crito on the Causes, Objects, and Consequences of the Present War*. 2nd ed. Edinburgh: Scots Chronicle, 1796.
———. *The Origin of the Distinction of Ranks: or, An Inquiry into the Circumstances which give rise to Influence and Authority in the Different Members of Society*. 4th ed. Edinburgh: Blackwood, 1806.
Millar, Richard. *De morbi venerei natura*. Glasgow: Foulis, 1789.
Miller, Perry, ed. *The American Transcendentalists: Their Prose and Poetry*. New York: Anchor, 1957.
Milton, John. *Paradise Lost*. Edited by Northrop Frye. New York: Reinhart, 1951.
Moir, James. *The Scripture Doctrine of Redemption stated and defended, being an answer to a Practical Essay on the death of Jesus Christ by William McGill*. Glasgow: Chapman, 1787.

Monteath, John. *The Divine Precepts and Promises with the Dispensations of Providence, the Continual Source of Instruction and Comfort to the Church.* Glasgow, 1785.

Montesquieu, Charles-Louis de Secondat. *L'Esprit des Lois.* 2 vols. Paris: Flammarion, 1979.

Morrell, John B. "The Leslie Affair: Careers, Kirk, and Politics in Edinburgh in 1805." *Scottish Historical Review* 54 (1975) 63–82.

Morrell, John Daniel. *An Historical and Critical View of the Speculative Philosophy of Europe in the Nineteenth Century.* New York: Carter, 1846.

Morrison, James. *Elements of Bookkeeping.* London: Longman, 1813.

Mossner, Ernest. *Life of David Hume.* Oxford: Oxford University Press, 1980.

Murray, David. *Memories of the Old College of Glasgow: Some Chapters in the History of the University.* Glasgow: Jackson Wylie, 1927.

Muston, Christopher. *Recognition in the World to Come, or Christian Friendship on Earth.* London: Holdsworth, 1830.

Mylne, James. "Account of the Late Professor Millar." *Glasgow Courier,* June 13, 1801.

———. [involvement uncertain]. *Catalogue of Books belonging to the Ethics Class Library.* Glasgow, 1815.

———. "Introduction to Robert Boog's *Discourses.*" Glasgow: Glasgow University Press, 1824.

———. *Plan of a Course of Lectures on Political Economy, delivered in the University of Glasgow.* Glasgow: Scrymgeour, 1804. [Copy in British Library, London.]

———. *A Statement of the Facts Connected with a Precognition Taken in the College on March 30 and 31st, 1815.* Glasgow, 1815.

Mylne, James William, et al., eds. *Reports of Cases determined in Chancery.* 4 vols. London: Saunders, 1832, 1834, 1837, 1848.

Mylne, Margaret. *Woman, and Her Place in Society.* London: Green, 1872.

Nichol, John. *Byron.* London: Macmillan, 1909.

———. *Carlyle.* 1892; London: Macmillan, 1905.

Nichol, John Pringle. Contributions to *Cyclopaedia of Biography.* London: Griffin, 1854.

———. "Introduction to Joseph Willm: *The Education of the People.*" 1847.

———. "On the Existing Obstructions to a National System of Education." *National Education: Report of the Proceedings of a Meeting of the Glasgow Public School Association.* Glasgow: Robertson, 1851.

———. *The Phenomena and Order of the Solar System.* Edinburgh: Tait, 1838.

———. *Views of the Architecture of the Heavens.* Edinburgh, Tait, 1837.

Nicole, Pierre: *Les Pretendus reformés convaincus de schisme.* Paris, 1684.

O'Brien, Conor Cruise. *Edmund Burke.* Edited by Jim McCue. Dublin: New Island, 1997.

O'Connell, Daniel. *The Correspondence of Daniel O'Connell.* Edited by Maurice O'Connell. Shannon: Irish University Press, 1972.

Olson, Richard. *Scottish Philosophy and British Physics, 1750–1880.* Princeton: Princeton University Press, 1975.

Paine, Thomas. *The Age of Reason, Being an Investigation of True and Fabulous Theology.* New York: Dover, 2004.

———. *Common Sense, Addressed to the Inhabitants of America.* New York: Dover, 1997.

———. *The Rights of Man.* London: Everyman, 1915.

Paley, William. *Natural Theology, or Evidence of the Existence and Attributes of the Deity Collected from the Appearances of Nature*. Oxford: Oxford University Press, 2006.

Payne, George. *Elements of Mental and Moral Science*. London: Holdsworth, 1828.

———. *Remarks on the Moral Influence of the Gospel upon Believers [...] occasioned by Mr Walker's Letters on Primitive Christianity*. Edinburgh, 1820.

Paoletti, Christina. "'An Open Revolt Against the Authority of Reid': Thomas Brown and the Developments of Common-Sense Philosophy." Paper at the Thomas Reid Tercentenary conference in Aberdeen, March 2010.

Passmore, John. *100 Years of Philosophy*. Harmondsworth: Pelican, 1968.

Pertz, Carl. "Georg Heinrich Pertz's Leben und literarische Wirksamkeit." In *Wissenschaftliche Beilage der Leipziger Zeitung*. Leipzig, 1882.

Petry, Michael J. "Hegel and the 'Morning Chronicle.'" In *Hegel-Studien* 11. Bonn: Bouvier, 1976.

———. "Propaganda and Analysis: The Background to Hegel's Article on the English Reform Bill." In *The State and Civil Society: Studies in Hegel's Political Philosophy*, edited by Z. A. Pelczynski, 138–58. Cambridge: Cambridge University Press, 1984.

Philip, Adam. *The Evangel in Gowrie*. Edinburgh: Oliphant, 1911.

Pictet, Benedict. *Christian Theology*. Translated by Frederick Reyroux. Philadelphia: Presbyterian Board, n.d.

Pictet, M.-A. *Voyage de Trois Mois en Angleterre, en Ecosse et en Irelande pendant l'Été de l'An IX*. Geneva, 1802.

Pike, Samuel. *Llythyrau rhwng Mr Samuel Pike a Mr Robert Sandeman* ["Letters between . . ."]. Carmarthen: Ross, 1765.

Plato. *The Collected Dialogues of Plato*. Edited by Edith Hamilton and Huntington Cairns. Translated by Lane Cooper et al. Princeton: Princeton University Press, 1961.

Playfair, James. *Of the Care and Knowledge of Bees*. Unpublished manuscript. [Copy in NLS: MRB.214.]

———. *Sermon on the Centennial Day of the Revolution in Great Britain*. Dundee, 1788.

Pocock, J. G. A. *The Machiavellian Moment*. Princeton: Princeton University Press, 2003.

Pollok, David. *The Life of Robert Pollok*. Edinburgh: Blackwood, 1843.

Pollok, Robert. *The Course of Time*. 4th ed. Edinburgh: Blackwell, 1828.

Porteous, William. *The New Light Examined*. Glasgow: Niven, 1800.

Price, Richard. *Review of the Principal Questions of Morals*. Oxford: Clarendon, 1974.

Priestley, Joseph. *Essay on the First Principles of Government, and on the Nature of Political, Civil and Religious Liberty*. 2nd ed: London: Johnson, 1771.

———. *Examination of Dr Reid's Inquiry into the Human Mind on the Principles of Common Sense* [etc]. London: Johnson, 1775.

———. *Lectures on History and General Policy, to which is prefixed an Essay on a Course of Liberal Education for civil and active Life*. Birmingham: Johnson, 1788.

———. *Priestley's Writings*. Edited by J. A. Passmore. New York: Collier, 1965.

Proudhon, Pierre-Joseph. *Qu'est-ce que la propriété?* Paris : LGF, 2009.

Pucelle, Jean. *L'Idéalisme en Angleterre de Coleridge à Bradley*. Neuchatel: Baconnière, 1955.

Quaife, Barzillai. *The Intellectual Sciences*. 2 vols. [Sydney], 1873.

———. *Lectures on Prophecy and the Kingdom of Christ, delivered in the Scots Church, MacQuarrie Street*. Sydney, 1848.

———. *The Rules of the Final Judgement*. Sydney, 1846.
Quesnay, François. *L'Art de guérir par la Saignée*. Paris, 1736.
———. *Essai Physique sur l'Oeconomie animale*. Paris, 1747.
———. *La Physiocratie*. Edited by Jean Cartelier. Paris: Flammarion, 1991.
———. *Recherches [...] sur l'Origine, sur les divers États et sur les Progrès de la Chirurgie en France*. Paris, 1744.
———. *Traité de la Gangrène*. Paris, 1771.
———. *Traité de la Suppuration*. Paris, 1749.
Quillien, Jean, ed. *La Réception de la Philosophie Allemande en France aux XIXe et XXe Siècles*. Lille: Presses universitaires de Lille, 1994.
Quintilian [Marcus Fabius Quintilianus]. *On the Early Education of the Citizen-Orator*. Indianapolis: Bobbs-Merrill, 1965.
Rabbe, F. "Sir William Hamilton." *Revue Contemporaine* 87 (1870) 524-48.
Rammohun Roy, Raja. *Translation of Several Principal Books, Passages and Texts of the Vedas and some controversial Works of Brahmunical Theology*. London: Parbury Allen, 1832.
Ranken, Alexander. *History of France*. 8 vols. London: Cadell, 1801-20.
Redford, George. *Body and Soul: or, Life, Mind and Matter*. London: Churchill, 1847.
———. *The True Age of Reason*. London: Holdsworth, 1821.
Rees, Abraham, ed. *The Cyclopaedia, or Universal Dictionary of Arts, Sciences and Literature*. London: Longman, 1820.
Reid, Stuart. *British Redcoat 1740-1793*. Oxford: Osprey, 1996.
Reid, Thomas. *The Works of Thomas Reid, D.D.* Edited by William Hamilton. 2 vols. Edinburgh: MacLachlan, 1872.
Rendall, Jane. "Prospects of the American Republic, 1795-1821: The Radical and Utopian Politics of Robina Millar and Frances Wright." In *Enlightenment and Emancipation*, edited by Peter France and Susan Manning, 145-59. Lewisburg, PA: Bucknell University Press, 2007.
———. "'Women that would plague me with rational conversation': Aspiring Women and Scottish Whigs, c.1790-1830." In *Women, Gender and Enlightenment*, edited by Sarah Knott and Barbara Taylor, 326-48. Basingstoke: Macmillan, 2005.
Richardson, Mary, ed. *Autobiography of Mrs Fletcher*. Cambridge: Cambridge University Press, 2010.
Richardson, William. *Philosophical Analysis and Illustration of Some of Shakespeare's Remarkable Characters*. London: Murray, 1774.
Roach, W. M. "Radical Reform Movements in Scotland, 1815-22." PhD diss., Glasgow University, 1970.
Robertson, George. *Topographical Description of Ayrshire*. Irvine: Cunninghame, 1820.
Robertson, Paul. "The Finances of the University of Glasgow before 1914." *History of Education Quarterly* 16/4 (Winter 1976) 449-78.
Robertson, William. *History of Scotland*. 1759.
———. *History of the Reign of the Emperor Charles V*. London: Routledge, 1894.
Rogers, Charles. *Four Perthshire Families*. Edinburgh, 1887.
———. *The Scottish Branch of the Norman House of Roger*. London, 1872.
Rosenkranz, Karl. *Hegels Leben*. Berlin: Duncker, 1844.
Ross, James. *A History of Congregational Independency in Scotland*. Glasgow: MacLehose, 1900.
Rousseau, Jean-Jacques. *Émile, ou de l'éducation*. Paris: Flammarion, 1966.

Russel, Michael. *View of the System of Education at present pursued in the Schools and Universities of Scotland*. Glasgow: Duncan, 1813.

Rutherford, Donald. *In the Shadow of Adam Smith: Founders of Scottish Economics, 1700-1900*. Basingstoke: Macmillan, 2012.

Sandeman, Robert. *Letters on Theron and Aspasio*. Edinburgh, 1759.

Sandford, Daniel Keyte. *Inaugural Lecture delivered in the Common Hall of the University of Glasgow, November 6th, 1821*. Glasgow: Glasgow University Press, 1822.

Say, Jean-Baptiste. *L'Angleterre et les Anglais*. Paris, 1815.

———. *Catechisme d'Economie Politique* in *Cours d'économie politique*. Edited by Philippe Steiner. Paris: Flammarion, 1996.

Schelling, Friedrich Wilhelm Joseph. *Jugement de M. de Schelling sur la Philosophie de M. Cousin, traduit de l'allemand et précédé d'un Essai sur la Nationalité des Philosophies*. Translated by J. Willm. Strasbourg: Levrault, 1835.

Schlegel, Friedrich. *Lectures on the History of Literature: Ancient and Modern*. Edinburgh: Blackwood, 1818.

Schneewind, J B. "Review of A Broadie's *Cambridge Companion to the Scottish Enlightenment*." *Journal of Scottish Philosophy* 2/1 (March 2004) 78-83.

Schulthess, Daniel. *Correspondance Dugald Stewart-Pierre Prevost*. Forthcoming.

Schulthess, Daniel, and Philippe Muller, eds. *La Révolution Française dans la Pensée Européenne*. Lausanne: PAN, 1989.

Scott, David, ed. *The Engineer and Machinist's Assistant*. Glasgow: Blackie, 1856.

Scott, Hew. *Fasti Ecclesiae Scoticanae: The Succession of Ministers in the Church of Scotland from the Reformation*. [1st edition: 3 volumes, Edinburgh, 1866-71] 2nd edition: Vol III: Synod of Glasgow & Ayr. Edinburgh: Oliver & Boyd, 1920. Vol. V: Synods of Fife, Angus & Mearns, 1925.

Scott, James. *Life, Letters and Remains of Rev. Robert Pollok*. New York: Carter, 1848.

Scott, Paul H. *Andrew Fletcher and the Treaty of Union*. Edinburgh: Saltire Society, 1994.

Scott, Walter. *Minstrelsy of the Scottish Border*. London: Harrap, 1931.

Sell, Alan P. F. *Philosophy, Dissent and Non-Conformity, 1689-1920*. Cambridge: Clarke, 2003.

———, ed. *Protestant Nonconformist Texts*. Aldershot: Ashgate, 2006.

Sgard, Jean. *Corpus Condillac*. Paris: Slatkine, 1981.

Silliman, Benjamin. *A Journal of Travels in England, Holland and Scotland and of two Passages over the Atlantic in the Years 1805 and 1806*. New Haven: Converse, 1820.

Sinclair, John, ed. *The Statistical Account of Scotland, 1791-1799*. Reissued by general editors D. J. Withrington and I. R. Grant. 20 vols. Wakefield: E.P., 1973-83.

Small, Robert. *An Account of the Astronomical Discoveries of Kepler*. London: Mawman, 1804.

———. *Defence delivered by Dr Small at the Bar of the General Assembly 1800*. Dundee: Lesslie, 1800.

———. *The importance of the poor illustrated: in a sermon preached, December 15th, 1793, on the occasion of making a charitable contribution, for the support of the Sunday-schools*. Dundee, 1794.

Smart, Robert N. *Biographical Register of St Andrews 1747-1897*. St. Andrew's University Library, 2004.

Smeal, William G. "Glasgow's Share in the Anti-Slavery Struggle." *Old Glasgow Club Transactions* 1, Sessions 1900-08. 9-11 and 30-32.

Smith, Adam. *An Inquiry into the Nature and Causes of the Wealth of Nations*. Edited by Germaine Garnier. Edinburgh: Mundell, 1809.

———. *The Theory of Moral Sentiments*. Edited by D. D. Raphael and A. L. Macfie. Oxford: Clarendon, 1976.

Smith, Donald C. *Passive Obedience and Prophetic Protest: Social Criticism in the Scottish Church, 1830-1945*. New York: Lang, 1987.

Smith, James [from Glasgow]. *The Case of James Smith later Minister in Newburn and Robert Ferrier, late Minister at Largo, truly represented and defended*. Edinburgh, 1768.

Smith, James [from Paisley]. *Evidences of a Special Divine Providence attending the late signal Successes obtained over the Enemy*. Paisley, 1814.

Smith, John Howard. *The Perfect Rule of the Christian Religion: A History of Sandemanianism in the 18th Century*. Albany: SUNY, 2009.

Smith, Sarah. "Retaking the Register: Women's Higher Education in Glasgow and Beyond, c1796-1845." *Gender and History* 12/2 (July 2000) 310-35.

Smith, Thomas, ed. *Memoirs of James Begg D.D.* Edinburgh: Gemmell, 1885.

Smith, William Robertson. *Lectures on the Religion of the Semites*. New York: KTAV, 1969.

Snodgrass, John, *An Effectual Method for Recovering our Religious Liberties*. Glasgow, 1770.

———. *The Leading Doctrines of the Gospel*. Paterson, 1794.

———. *The Means of Preserving the Life and Power of Religion in a Time of General Corruption*. Dundee: Colvill, 1781.

Somerville, James. "The Trojan Horse of the Scottish Philosophy." *Philosophy* 82 (2007) 235-57.

Spence, David. "South and East Perthshire, Kinross-shire." In *Statistical Account of Scotland*, edited by John Sinclair, 11:280-88. Wakefield: E.P., 1976.

Spence, John. "Perth." In *The New Statistical Account of Scotland*, 10:228-32. Edinburgh: Blackwood, 1896.

Spinoza, Benedict de [Baruch]. *Ethics, and on the Correction of the Understanding*. London: Everyman, 1963.

———. *Opera Posthuma*. Amsterdam, 1677.

———. *A Theologico-Political Treatise*. New York: Dover, 1951.

Staël-Holstein, Anne Louise Germaine [Mme de Staël]. *De L'Allemagne*. London: Murray, 1813.

Steuart, James. *Principles of Political Economy*. Edited by A. S. Skinner. Chicago: Chicago University Press, 1966.

Stewart, Dugald. "Account of the Life and Writings of Adam Smith." In *Biographical Memoirs*, 1-152. Edinburgh: Creech, 1811.

———. *Biographical Memoirs*. Edinburgh: Creech, 1811.

———. *Dissertation: Exhibiting the Progress of Metaphysical, Ethical, and Political Philosophy, since the Revival of Letters in Europe*. In *Collected Works*, edited by William Hamilton, 1:. Edinburgh: Constable, 1854.

———. *Elements of the Philosophy of the Human Mind*. Edited by Francis Bowen. Boston: Munroe, 1862.

———. *Outlines of Moral Philosophy*. Edinburgh: Creech, 1792.

———. *Works*. Edited by William Hamilton. 10 vols. Edinburgh: Constable: 1854-.

Stewart, George. *Curiosities of Glasgow Citizenship, as Exhibited Chiefly in the Business Careers of its Old Commercial Aristocracy*. Glasgow: Maclehose, 1881.

Stewart-Robertson, Charles. "The Pneumatics and Georgics of the Scottish Mind." *Eighteenth Century Studies* 20 (Spring 1987) 296–312.

———. "The Rhythms of Gratitude: Historical Developments and Philosophical Concerns." *Australasian Journal of Philosophy* 68 (1990) 189–205.

———. "A Scottish Horse-Tale: Ideology, Conspiracy and the Fall from Enlightenment." *Rivista di Storia della Filosofia* 43/3 (1988) 443–78.

Stirling, Amelia Hutchison. *James Hutchison Stirling: His Life and Work*. London: Unwin, 1912.

Stirling, James Hutchison. *Darwinianism: Workmen and Work*. Edinburgh: Clarke, 1894.

———. *Lectures on the Philosophy of Law*. London: Longman, 1873.

———. "Review of Alexander Campbell Fraser's *Biographia Philosophia*." *Mind* (1905) 85–92.

———. *The Secret of Hegel*. Edinburgh: Oliver, 1898.

———. *Sir William Hamilton: The Philosophy of Perception*. London: Longmans, 1865.

Story, Alfred T. *The Life of John Linnell*. London: Bentley, 1892.

Strang, John. *Germany in MDCCCXXXI*. 2 vols. London: MacCrone, 1836.

———. *Glasgow and Its Clubs: or Glimpses of the Conditions, Manners, Characters and Oddities of the City, during the Past and Present Centuries*. 3rd ed. Glasgow: Tweed, 1864.

Sullivan, Alvin, ed. *British Literary Magazines*. 4 vols. London: Greenwood, 1983.

Swift, Jonathan. *Gulliver's Travels*. 1726.

Talbot, Brian. *The Search for a Common Identity: The Origins of the Baptist Union of Scotland, 1800–1870*. Milton Keynes: Paternoster, 2003.

Tayler, John James. *Christian Aspects of Faith and Duty*. New York, 1851.

———. *Christianity: What Is It and What Has It Done?* London, 1868.

Taylor, Isaac. *Elements of Thought*. London: Holdsworth, 1824.

———. *The Natural History of Enthusiasm*. London: Holdsworth 1830.

Taylor, John. *Examination of Dr Hutcheson's Scheme of Morality*. Waugh, 1759.

Taylor, William. *An Answer to Mr Carlile's Sketches of Paisley*. Paisley, 1809.

Thom, William. *The Works of the Rev. William Thom, late Minister of Govan, consisting of Sermons, Tracts, Letters, etc.* Glasgow: Dymock, 1799.

Thomas, Arthur. *Gallery of Portraits with Memoirs*. London, 1833.

Toland, John. *Christianity not Mysterious*. 1696.

Tulloch, John. *Movements of Religious Thought in Britain during the 19th Century*. New York: Scribner, 1901.

Turgot, Anne Robert Jacques. *Réflexions sur la Formation et la Distribution des Richesses*. In *Formation et Distribution des Richesses*, edited by J.-T. Ravix and P.-M. Romani. Paris: Flammarion, 1997.

Turner, William. *Lives of Eminent Unitarians, with a Notice of Dissenting Academies*. London: Unitarian Association, 1840–43.

Upton, Charles. *Dr Martineau's Philosophy: A Survey*. London: Nisbet, 1905.

Ure, Andrew. *Outlines of Physical Science: A Compound of Mechanical and Chemical Philosophy*. Lang, 1806.

———. *The Philosophy of Manufactures*. London: Knight, 1835.

Veitch, John. "A Memoir of Dugald Stewart." In *Works*, edited by William Hamilton, 10:i–clxxvii. Edinburgh: Constable, 1858.

———. *Memoir of Sir William Hamilton*. Edinburgh: Blackwood, 1869.

Veyne, Paul. *Quand notre Monde est devenu Chrétien*. Paris: Michel, 2007.

Villers, Charles de. *Philosophie de Kant, ou principes fondamenteaux de la philosophie transcendentale*. Metz: Collignon, 1801.

Voltaire [François-Marie Arouet]. *Candide, L'Ingénu, L'Homme aux quarante écus*. Paris: Armand Colin, 1957.

———. *Lettres sur les Anglais*. Harmondsworth: Penguin, 1980.

———. *Micromégas*. In *Zadig and Other Stories*, edited by H. T. Mason, 51–71. Oxford: Oxford University Press, 1971.

Wardlaw, Ralph. *Christian Ethics: or Moral Philosophy on the Principles of Divine Revelation*. 3rd ed. London: Jackson, 1837.

———. *Discourses on the Principal Points of the Socinian Controversy*. Glasgow: Duncan, 1814.

———. *Man Responsible for His Belief: Two Sermons*. Glasgow: Glasgow University Press, 1825.

———. *Memoir of the Late Rev. John Reid*. Glasgow: Maclehose, 1845.

———. *Systematic Theology*. Edited by James Campbell. 2 vols. Edinburgh: Black, 1856.

———. *Unitarianism Incapable of Vindication*. London: Longman, 1816.

Warnock, Geoffrey. *English Philosophy since 1900*. Oxford: Oxford University Press, 1969.

Warnock, Mary. *Ethics Since 1900*. Oxford: Oxford University Press, 1960.

Waszek, Norbert. "Hegels Excerpte aus der "Edinburgh Review" 1817–1819." *Hegel-Studien* 20 (1985) 79–112.

———. "Hegels schottische Bettler." *Hegel-Studien* 19 (1984) 311–16.

———. *The Scottish Enlightenment and Hegel's Account of "Civil Society."* Dordrecht: Kluwer, 1988.

———. "A Stage in the Development of Hegel's Theory of the Modern State. The 1802 Excerpts on Bonaparte and Fox." *Hegel-Studien* 20 (1985) 163–72.

Waterman, A. M. C. *Revolution, Economics and Religion: Christian Political Economy 1798–1833*. Cambridge: Cambridge University Press, 1991.

Watkins, John. *Memoirs of the Public and Private Life of the Right Honourable Richard Brinsley Sheridan*. 2nd ed. 2 vols. London: Colburn, 1817.

Watson, James. *A Paper on the Present Railway Crisis, read at a Meeting of the Literary and Commercial Society of Glasgow*. Lang, 1846.

Watson, Robert. *History of Phillip 2nd of Spain*. London, 1777.

Wellek, René. *Immanuel Kant in England, 1793–1838*. Princeton: Princeton University Press, 1931.

Welsh, David. *Account of the Life and Writings of Thomas Brown*. Edinburgh: Tait, 1825.

White, A S. *Bibliography of Regimental Histories of the British Army*. Dallington: Naval & Military, 1992.

Whytock, Jack. *"An Educated Clergy": Scottish Theological Education and Training in the Kirk and Secession, 1560–1850*. Milton Keynes: Paternoster, 2007.

Wilberforce, William. *A Practical View of the prevailing religious System of professed Christians in the higher and middle Classes in this Country, contrasted with real Christianity*. 6th ed. London: Cadell, 1798.

Williamson, W. *The Proceedings at Large on the Trial of Moses Corbet Esq., Lieutenant Governor of Jersey, tried by a Court-Martial held at the Horse Guards, 1 May 1781, taken in short-hand*. London: Stockdale, 1781.
Willich, A. F. M. *The Elements of Critical Philosophy*. London: Longman, 1798.
Willm, Joseph. *The Education of the People*. 2nd ed. Edinburgh: Nichol, 1850.
———. *Essai sur la Philosophie de Hegel*. Levrault, 1836.
———. *Histoire de la Philosophie allemande depuis Kant jusqu'à Hegel*. 4 vols. Paris: Ladrange, 1847–49.
Wilson, Alexander. *The Chartist Movement in Scotland*. Manchester: Manchester University Press, 1970.
Wilson, John. *The City of the Plague*. Edinburgh: Constable, 1816.
———. *Isle of Palms*. Edinburgh: Longman, 1812.
———. "The Metaphysician." *Blackwood's Edinburgh Magazine* 39 (1836) 798–805.
———. *Noctes Ambrosianae*. Edited by Shelton Mackenzie. 5 vols. New York: Widdleton, 1866.
———. *Works of Professor Wilson*. Edited by James Frederick Ferrier. 4 vols. Edinburgh: Blackwood, 1855–56.
Wilson, William, and Robert Rainy, eds. *Memorials of Robert Smith Candlish*. Edinburgh: Black, 1880.
Wilson. *History of Renfrewshire*. Paisley, 1812.
Winch, D. *Riches and Poverty: An Intellectual History of Political Economy in Britain, 1750–1834*. Cambridge: Cambridge University Press, 1996.
Wolterstorff, Nicholas. *Thomas Reid and the Story of Epistemology*. Cambridge: Cambridge University Press, 2001.
Wright, Frances. *Course of popular lectures as delivered by Frances Wright in New York, Philadelphia, Baltimore, Boston, Cincinnati, St. Louis, Louisville, and other Cities, Towns and Districts of the United States with three addresses on various public occasions and a reply to the charges against the French reformers of 1789*. 4th ed. New York: Free Enquirer, 1831.
———. *England the Civiliser: Her History developed in Its Principles*. London: Simpkin Marshall, 1848.
———. *A Few Days in Athens: Being the Translation of a Greek Manuscript Discovered in Herculaneum*. London: Longman Hurst, 1822.
———. *Life, Letters and Lectures*. New York: Arno, 1972.
———. *Views of Society and Manners in America*. Cambridge, MA: Harvard University Press, 1963.
Yates, James. *A Vindication of Unitarianism, in Reply to Mr Wardlaw's Discourses on the Socinian Controversy*. 2nd ed. Glasgow: Eaton, 1818.
Young, Frederic. *Philosophy of Henry James Sr*. New York: Bookman, 1951.
Young, John. *A Criticism on the Elegy Written in a Country Churchyard*. 2nd ed. Edinburgh: Ballantyne, 1810.
Young, John. *Essays on the following interesting Subjects . . .* [advertised as *Essays on Government*]. 3rd ed. Glasgow: Niven, 1794.
Young, John. *Lectures on Intellectual Philosophy*. Glasgow: Reid, 1835.
———. *Testimonials in Favour of John Young AM, Professor of Moral Philosophy in [. . .] Belfast Institution, produced on the occasion of his applying for the Moral Philosophy Chair in the University of Edinburgh*. 1820. [Copy in NCL.]

Index

A

Adams, James, 15–16, 19–21, 20n26, 21nn28–31, 22, 22n33, 22nn38–39, 178, 180, 180n12, 181–182, 181nn16–18, 182nn19–21
Adamson, Professor, 56
Addison, W. Innes, 5n14, 99n16, 101nn28–29, 102nn39–40, 103nn47–48, 104n56, 107n70, 114n111, 114n113, 116n125, 220n16, 251n7, 253n18, 253nn21–22, 254n28, 254n31, 255n34
Aitken, George, 16
Aitken, Robert, 241
Alexander, Boyd, 87
Alexander, William Lindsay, 26n64
Allan (from Edinburgh), 64
Allestree, Richard, 173
Alliot, Richard, 254
Anderson, Adam, 235
Anderson, John, 52, 52n73
Anderson, William, 9n27, 24n51, 25n57
Argyle, Duke of, 216n113
Aristotle, 74, 133, 139, 157
Arkwright, Richard, 239
Armour, Richard W., 102n34

Arthur, Archibald, 2n1, 49, 56, 58, 60n130, 70, 118, 119n139, 160n76, 173, 201, 248
Aspland, Robert, 107
Atkinson, T., 112–113n107
Auchinloss, J., 198n32
Augustus (son of George III), 208
Austin, John, 117, 117n126
Austin, Sarah, 117n126
Azouvi, François, 136nn30–31

B

Bacon, Francis, 25, 33, 73, 74, 74n70, 121, 125, 130, 140, 146, 146n22, 147, 248
Badham, Charles, 108, 254, 254n28
Bagehot, Walter, 253
Bailey, Samuel, 117
Baillie (father of Joanna Baillie), 100
Baillie, Helen, 100
Baillie, Joanna, 100, 100n19, 100n24, 102, 102nn36–37, 119
Bain, Alexander, 23n41
Bain, Margaret, 244n115
Balfour, Robert, 52, 52n78, 55n100
Bannatyne, D., 112–113n107
Bannatyne, John, 6
Bartlett, Elizabeth, 104n52, 104n54

INDEX

Beattie, James, 1–2, 2n1, 26n61, 119n139, 129n13, 131, 131n17, 141, 165, 173, 198, 202, 209, 209n81, 221
Bedford, Duke of, 82, 214
Bedford, Earl of, 222n24
Begg, James, 107, 107n71, 192, 255
Bell, James, 60, 61n133
Bell, Robert, 86
Belsham, Thomas, 107
Belsham, William, 47n44
Benham, William, 101n32
Bentham, Jeremy, 104
Berkeley, George, 135, 138, 149, 150, 157n66, 165–166, 256
Biran, Maine de, 135–136, 136n31, 143n4
Black, Adam, 114
Blackie, George. *See* Blaikie, George
Blackstone, Judge, 233
Blaikie, George, 16, 17, 18n18, 103
Blair, Hugh, 60, 215
Blake, William, 114
Blanqui, Adolphe, 244, 244n115, 244n117
Blanqui, Louis Auguste, 244n117
Bogue, David, 79, 208, 210, 215, 220, 220n16
Bolingbroke, Lord, 23
Bonnet, Charles, 143n4
Boog, Robert, 7n20, 45–46, 45n27, 45nn29–30, 46n32, 47, 48, 50, 51, 52, 54, 55, 55nn100, 57n112, 58n121, 97, 112
Boog, William, 45, 112, 112n104
Boswell, James, 47, 173
Brahé, Tycho, 33
Braudel, Fernand, 25n53
Bréhier, Émile, 149n34, 160, 160n78
Brewster, David, 95n82
Brewster, Patrick, 94–95, 95nn82–83
Brougham, Henry, 82, 89, 89n59, 90, 91, 94, 95, 95n86, 101, 108, 110, 110n94, 113, 207, 208, 214, 217, 221, 221n23, 223n34, 224, 228, 248
Brown, James, 24, 24n47, 56, 109n83, 136n32

Brown, Stewart Jay, 24n47, 109nn83–84, 116n125, 200n37
Brown, Thomas, 3n8, 4–5, 6, 113, 135, 150, 150nn37–38, 151, 151n39, 200, 203, 219, 252
Brown, William Galloway, 101
Bruce, Gainsford, 73n58, 219n12
Bruce, John, 43nn12–13
Bruce, John Collingwood, 73, 219, 219n12
Brühlmeier, Daniel, 2n2
Buchanan, Robert, 59, 59n129, 70, 251
Buchanan, William, 251
Buckle, Henry, 193
Buffier, Claude, 61, 254, 254n27
Buffon, Georges-Louis Leclerc, Comte de, 122, 146, 152n45, 158, 158n70
Bulloch, James, 44, 44n20, 84n17, 164–165n10, 164n6, 216n113
Burder, Henry Forster, 253, 253n24, 254
Burke, Edmund, 2n2, 3, 44n25, 68, 82, 129, 196, 196n13, 197, 222, 222n24
Burns, Robert (author), 99n11
Burns, Robert (minister), 214, 214nn108–109
Burns, Robert (poet), 55
Burns, Thomas, 198n29
Burton, Edward, 108
Butler, Bishop, 190
Butler, Joseph, 54, 60, 128, 168, 171, 174
Butler, Samuel, 26, 26n63, 27, 27n65

C

Cabanis (French-Swiss writer), 143n4
Caird, Edward, 3n8, 10, 78, 78n102, 103, 137n34, 251, 265n9
Caird, John, 103, 251
Cairns, William, 252, 252n15
Calvin, John, 27
Campbell, C. A., 10
Campbell, Ilay, 43, 67, 69, 70, 101, 153n51

INDEX

Campbell, John MacLeod, 10nn31–32, 251
Campbell, Thomas, 64n7, 91
Candlish, R. S., 178, 178n5
Canning, George, 37n49
Cant, R. G., 27n68, 28nn73–74
Carlile, Alexander, 215
Carlile, James, 111
Carlyle, Thomas, 102n34, 243
Carmichael, Gershom, 121, 125, 173, 175, 192, 204, 227, 227n50
Carnie, David, 38n59
Carpenter, Lant, 75–76, 78, 106, 106n63, 218n6, 255, 255n32
Carpenter, Russell, 75nn81–82, 78n99, 255nn32–33
Cato, 264n8
Chalmers, Thomas, 1, 2n3, 24n47, 47, 49, 56, 58, 64, 64n5, 65–66, 65nn19–20, 69, 71, 71n49, 83, 84n17, 106, 106n68, 107, 109, 109n86, 109nn83–84, 110, 110n92, 111, 178n5, 184, 200, 200n37, 215–216, 242, 242n103, 255
Chambers, Robert, 19n22
Chapman, George, 44n22
Charles I (King of England), 214
Charles II (King of England), 214
Charles V, 236
Checkland, Sydney G., 239n82
Cheselden (surgeon), 150
Chichester, Henry, 36n44, 38n61
Child, Joshua, 234
Chitnis, Anand, 56n109
Chrystal, William, 112n106
Cicero, Marcus Tullius, 26, 73, 74, 125, 144n12, 171, 172, 173, 248, 249
Clarke, Samuel, 27, 60, 108, 171, 173, 186
Clovis, 51
Cobbett, William, 92, 93, 93nn71–73, 248
Cockburn, Henry, 41, 41n3, 67, 67n29, 115, 115n118, 116, 117, 117n130, 197n17, 202nn49–50, 219, 219n15
Cogan, Thomas, 162, 249, 250

Coleridge, Samuel Taylor, 251
Collins, Anthony, 60
Combe, George, 114, 114n112, 114n115, 241
Comte, Auguste, 104, 193
Condillac, Abbé de, 2, 7, 61, 75, 104, 106, 122, 123, 130, 130n16, 132, 134, 135, 136n31, 140, 142, 142n1, 143, 143n5, 143nn7–8, 144, 144n15, 145, 145n17–18, 145–146n20, 146, 146nn21–22, 147, 147nn25–26, 148, 148nn27–28, 149, 149nn32–33, 150, 151, 151nn40–42, 152, 152nn43–45, 157, 157nn65–66, 158, 159, 160, 160n78, 161, 170, 221n21, 249
Condorcet, Marie-Jean-Antoine-Nicolas Caritat, Marquis de, 61
Constant, Benjamin, 105n58
Constantine, 182n22
Cook, George, 15n2
Cook, John, 25–26, 25nn58–59, 28, 28n72, 145, 164, 164nn6–8, 165, 165nn11–12, 166, 166nn13–17, 167, 167nn19–20
Cooke, Henry, 72n55
Copernicus, 33
Copley, John, 36, 36n41
Corbet, Moses, 34, 35, 35n38, 36
Cornwall, Barry, 102n33, 102n34
Cornwallis, Charles, 36, 37
Cousin, Victor, 6–7, 119, 143, 143n3, 256
Coutts, James, 68n32, 112nn102–103, 116, 116n125
Cowper, James, 112n102, 112–113n107
Craig, James, 53
Craig, John, 38nn56–57, 67n26, 71n45, 77, 77n92, 97, 97n3, 98, 98n5, 98n7, 100n18, 153n50, 196n11, 201, 201n45, 202n47, 202n52, 241, 242, 243, 244
Craig, Margaret, 97
Crawford, Thomas, 3n5
Crawfurd, George, 92
Cronstedt, Axel Fredrik, 60
Cruden, Alexander, 188

INDEX

Cullen, Margaret, 98
Curtis, Edward, 31nn5–6, 31n12, 34n28
Cuthbertson, Donald, 240n92

D

Daire, Eugène, 204n63
Dale, David, 3, 46, 46n31, 57, 83, 103, 160n75, 188, 239, 240
Dalling, John, 37
Darwin, Erasmus, 163
Davidson, Archibald, 43, 56, 68, 69
Davidson, Christopher, 42
Davidson, Grizel, 42n6, 43n17, 68
Davidson, James, 42
Davidson, John, 42, 42n5, 42nn9–10, 43, 43n11, 67
Davidson, Randall, 101n32
Davidson, Robert, 42, 42n8, 43, 56, 68
Davie, George, 3n7, 24n45, 65nn17–18, 93, 108n79, 129n12, 138n37, 149n33, 152n45, 262n5
Deleule, Didier, 225n42
Dennistoun, Alexander, 103nn43–44
Dennistoun, James, 88, 239, 240, 240n88
Dennistoun, John, 103nn43–44
Descartes, René, 147
De Stael, Madame Anne-Louise-Germaine Necker, Baronne, 251
Destutt de Tracy, A. L. C., 105n58, 122, 142, 143n4, 150n35, 163, 252
Devine, Tom, 193
Dewar, Daniel, 110
D'Holbach, Paul-Henri Thiry, 186
Dick, Robert, 103n43
Dickens, Charles, 102n34
Diderot, Denis, 149, 149n31
Diogenes Laertius, 173n41
Dirom, Alexander, 210
Douglas, George, 102
Douglas, Neil, 86, 86n36
Drummond, Andrew L., 44, 44n20, 84n17, 164n6, 164–165n10, 216n113
Drummond, Thomas, 95, 95n87

Duncan, Andrew, 144
Duncan, Henry, 230
Duncan, James, 144
Duncan, William J., 58n122, 99n12, 153n49
Dunckley, Henry, 98n4
Dundas, Henry, 28, 38n63, 44, 67, 68–69, 69nn36–37, 83, 90, 119, 184, 200, 216n113
Dundas, Ralph, 32
Dundas, Robert, 28n74
Dunlop, Alexander, 83
Dunlop, Robert, 95n84
Dunn, William, 50, 52, 55n100, 57n111
Dupoint, de Nemours, 204, 204n63, 205, 205nn66–67
Durant, Thomas, 75, 75n78, 76
Durham, Earl of. *See* Lambton, John

E

Eckhardt, Celia Morris, 98n8, 100n18, 105nn58–60, 242n105
Edwards, Jonathan, 122, 134, 178, 184, 186, 188, 188n58, 190
Elliot, A., 100n24
Emerson, Roger L., 69n37, 70n39, 98n6
Enfield, William, 59, 61
Epicurus, 104, 171, 173, 173n41, 175
Erskine, Ebenezer, 182
Erskine, Henry, 90
Erskine, Thomas, 178n5
Eusebius, 182n22
Evans, Christmas, 189
Ewan, Elizabeth L., 102n38

F

Faichney, Janet, 17
Falconer, William, 76n88
Fanshawe, Henry, 34
Farmer, John S., 38n60
Fénélon, Francois, 61, 200
Fenton, Isobel, 23n41
Ferguson, Adam, 60

Fergusson, Robert, 24, 24n46
Ferrie, John, 111, 113, 252, 253
Ferrier, James Frederick, 94, 134n23, 230, 252, 252n12
Ferrier, Robert, 57, 188
Ferrier, William, 58n117
Field, William, 100n21, 160–161n79, 161n80, 161n82
Findlay, Robert, 49, 50, 68, 106, 106n69
Finlay, Kirkman, 47, 112, 112–113n107, 213
Fisher, Edward, 180, 180n14, 181, 181n15
Fisher, Joe, 39n64
Fitzgerald, Augustus, 89
Fleming, William, 5, 6, 24n49, 78n102, 106, 106n67, 115–116, 117, 118–119, 129, 130n15, 142, 142n1, 219, 243, 251, 256n38
Fletcher, Andrew, 40, 237, 237n73, 245
Fletcher, Archibald, 99
Fletcher, Elizabeth, 98, 99, 99n15, 119
Fletcher, Grace, 99
Fletcher, Joseph, 253, 254, 254n24, 254n27
Flynn, Philip, 129n12
Fortescue, John A., 36n44
Fox, Charles James, 44–45n25, 67, 82, 84, 85, 160, 161, 209, 210, 222
Fraser, Alexander Campbell, 3n7, 10, 10n30, 10n31, 17n14, 94, 94n79, 145, 145n19
Frazer, William, 88n50
French, William, 43
Frend, William, 60
Fry, Michael, 44n23, 68n33, 216n113
Fuller, Andrew, 186, 187, 188, 188nn52–53, 188nn56–57, 189, 189nn59–60
Fulton, Mary, 45
Fyfe, Janet, 91n62, 160n77

G

Gairdner, Charles, 241n95
Galloway, William Brown, 116, 116n124

Garnett, Thomas, 53, 53n82
Garnier, Germaine, 221n19
Gaskell, William, 255
George III (king of England), 198, 208
Gerrald, Joseph, 58, 200
Gilfillan, George, 7–9, 7n22, 8n23, 9nn25–27, 70, 70n40, 72, 76, 76n88, 114, 251, 251n7
Gilfillan, John, 38n59
Gilmour, David, 58nn118–119
Glas, John, 20, 21, 57, 181, 182, 182n23, 183, 187, 192
Godwin, William, 22, 22n35, 32, 59, 61, 62, 114, 122, 161, 177, 178, 184, 185, 185nn30–35, 186, 186n38–39, 193, 195, 199, 199nn35–36, 200, 200nn38–41, 201, 201nn42–44, 203, 216, 217, 218, 233, 242, 248
Gordon, Major, 38n59
Gordon, Mary Wilson, 251n8, 252n10, 252n11
Graham, James, 69, 69n37, 117
Graham, Thomas, 86, 208
Grahame, Robert, 64, 80, 85, 88, 89, 89n54, 90, 92n68, 112, 112–113n107, 239, 248
Grant, Mrs. [Tory], 100
Gray, George, 65, 76
Green, Thomas, 184n29, 256
Gregory, David, 24
Greville, 95n86
Grey, Charles, 89, 94, 248
Griscom, John, 100, 100n22
Grotius, 204n61

H

Hamilton, Archibald, 82, 208, 213
Hamilton, Elizabeth, 199
Hamilton, George, 64
Hamilton, Grizel, 42
Hamilton, James, 42n6, 43, 43n15
Hamilton, John Andrew, 94n79, 95n86
Hamilton, Margaret, 42, 43

Hamilton, William, 3n8, 5, 9, 26n61, 83, 113, 114, 116, 117, 119, 128, 128n11, 131, 131n19, 132, 134n23, 135, 135n28, 138, 138n38, 156, 156n62, 219, 251, 252, 252nn14–15
Handaside, John, 17n13
Hanna, William, 24n47, 109nn83–84, 200n37
Hardie, Thomas, 198, 198n25
Harris, James, 10
Hart, Rachel, 24n50
Hartley, David, 122, 132, 145, 145–146n20, 161, 163, 168, 184
Hay, John Barras, 64n6, 65n21, 66n25, 71nn4–47, 73nn63–64, 108n76, 219n14
Helvetius, Claude-Adrien, 61, 65, 122, 143
Hemery, Captain, 35, 35n35
Hervey, James, 183, 184
Hill, Alexander, 28n73
Hill, George, 15, 15n2, 28, 28nn73–74, 44n24, 195, 195n3
Hobbes, Thomas, 205
Hogg, James, 23, 23n42, 55, 65n16, 84n22, 114n116
Holcomb, Kathleen, 239n81
Home, Henry. *See* Kames, Lord
Hook, Andrew, 69n37, 239n81
Hoppus, John, 110, 111, 114, 253, 253n22
Horace, 60, 264n8
Horrocks, Don, 178n5
Horsley, Bishop, 190
Howard, John, 160n74
Hughes, Gillian, 84n22
Hume, David (nephew), 66n23–24
Hume, David (the philosopher), 2, 7n20, 24, 25, 26, 26n62, 37n49, 65, 65n14, 66, 66n23–24, 77, 122, 125, 132, 133, 133n22, 134, 134n23, 138, 139, 140, 141, 142, 149, 149n32, 151, 153, 160n78, 161, 164, 166, 167, 168, 169, 169nn25–27, 170, 173, 173n39, 174, 177, 177n3, 183, 183n24, 186, 190, 201, 202, 203, 203n55, 225, 233, 249, 256
Hume, Joseph, 108
Hunt, Leigh, 102
Hunter, Robin, 2n3
Hutcheson, Francis, 2, 25, 50, 68, 69n36, 71, 74, 111, 118, 122, 125, 145, 151, 164, 164n7, 164–165n10, 165, 165n12, 166, 166nn15–17, 167, 167n18, 168, 169, 170, 171, 173n39, 175, 176, 204, 204n61, 225, 248, 249, 263n6
Hutton, Joseph, 76, 76n83

J

James, Henry (senior), 189
James, William, 138n38, 189
James the Pretender, 22
Jardine, George, 72, 72n54, 73, 73n60, 74, 76, 78, 85n26, 101n27, 113, 122, 125, 255
Jeffrey, Francis, 65, 66, 129, 129n12, 202n49, 219n15
Jesus Christ, 54
Jevons, William, 121n2, 255
Johnson, Joseph, 59, 59n126
Johnson, Samuel, 24n46, 60, 65
Johnstone, 94n80
Jones, Henry, 216, 216n114
Jones, Peter, 7n20
Jones, Thomas, 36n44
Jurieu, Pierre, 60

K

Kames, Lord, 46, 64, 67, 184, 190, 215, 215n112, 222, 222n30
Kant, Immanuel, 128, 135, 137n34, 251, 252, 256
Kendrick, John, 75, 75n80, 76, 76n89, 77n91, 106, 106n65, 107, 253n24, 255
Kepler, Johannes, 33
Kitzmiller, John M., 38n60

L

La Coutour, Francis, 35n38
Laertius, Diogenes, 74
La Fayette, General, 104–105, 105n58
Lamb, Charles, 102
Lamb, Frederick, 97, 98
Lamb, William, 97, 98, 248
Lambton, John, 94, 94n76
Lancaster, Joseph, 207
Lang, Gilbert, 55n100
Lang, John Dunmore, 254
Lapslie, James, 55
Lauderdale, Earl of. *See* Maitland, James
Lavoisier, Antoine, 202
Lawless, John, 91
Lee, Tom, 238, 238n77, 241n97
Leechman, William, 50, 52, 52n76, 164
Leibniz, Gottfried Wilhelm, 134
Leinster, Duke of, 89, 214
Lemprière, William-Charles, 35n37
Lenman, Bruce, 38n63
Le Roy, Georges, 136n31, 143n6, 149nn31–32
Leslie, Alexander, 31
Leslie, John, 24, 56, 200
Linnell, John, 114, 114n117
Liverpool, Lord, 236, 237
Locke, John, 2, 5, 5n13, 27, 54, 121, 122, 125, 131, 136, 138, 145, 146, 146n23, 147, 157, 161, 184, 249, 256
Lockhart, John Gibson, 66n24, 71, 71n49, 74, 74n68
Louis XIV (King of France), 51, 60, 214, 232
Lucretius, 74
Lushington (professor), 117, 117n132
Luther, Martin, 180, 180n13
Lycurgus, 194
Lyon, John, 114

M

MacFarlan (principal Rev.), 112n102

MacGill, Stevenson, 44n22, 46, 46n34, 49, 49nn57–58, 106, 198, 198n27, 214
Machiavelli, Niccolò, 40, 236
MacIntosh, James, 71, 87, 91, 208, 213
Mackenzie, Henry, 199
Mackenzie, John, 200n37
Mackenzie, John Morell, 9, 107
Mackenzie, Peter, 79, 80, 81n3, 84–85, 85n24, 85n27, 88, 88n46, 92n65, 106, 106n64, 178nn7–8, 197n17, 212
Mackenzie, Thomas, 122n4, 154n58, 163, 163n3, 164n4, 169, 169n28, 177, 177n1, 191n70, 262n3, 263n7
Mackenzie, Walter, 241n95
Macklin, Charles, 68–69, 69n34
Maclaurin, Colin, 60
MacLehose, James (senior), 240n89, 240n94, 251n6
Macleod, Donald, 21
MacLeod, Norman, 251
Macmurray, John, 136n31, 159, 159n73
MacQuisten, A., 265n9
Madinier, Gabriel, 135n29, 159n72
Maitland, James, 18n20, 33, 37, 38, 82, 217, 221, 221nn22–23, 222, 222n24, 222n27, 223, 224, 228, 231, 243, 245
Malebranche, Nicolas, 135
Malthus, Thomas, 215, 217, 218, 221, 232, 233, 236, 242, 244, 245
Martinaeu, James, 255, 255nn35–36
Marx, Karl, 243
Mathieson, W. L., 244n114
Mavor, Irene, 87n41, 88n50, 239n86
Maxton, James, 244n113
Maxwell, John, 87, 87n41, 88, 88n50, 89, 211n89
Mayne, Richard, 36n44
McAdam, John, 79, 83n12, 84, 84n18, 85, 87, 87n44, 91n62, 92, 92nn63–64, 160n77, 213, 213n103
McCarthy, Mary, 57n110
McCartney, William, 144, 144n12
McCaul, John, 51n68, 126n2

McClelland, James, 240, 240n92, 241, 241nn95–96
McCormick, John, 244n113
McCosh, James, 3, 4n9, 7, 7nn20–21, 75n77, 106, 106n66, 107, 109, 118n134, 119, 192, 193, 202n49, 253, 255
McCulloch, Reverend, 44n21
McFarlan, Duncan, 24n48
McGrigor, Alexander, 112–113n107
McIndoe, David, 52, 52n77
McKay, Johnston, 215n110
McLean, Archibald, 186, 186n40, 187, 187nn42–43, 187nn45–47, 187nn49–50, 188, 189
McLelland, James. See McClelland, James
McNair, Alexander, 54
McTear (divinity student), 86
McTurk, William, 64, 106
Mechie, Stewart, 244n114
Meek, James, 50
Meikle, Henry, 3n5, 197n18, 202nn49–50
Meikleham (Natural Philosphy Teacher), 73n59, 84, 253
Melbourne, Viscount. See Lamb, William
Mercier, de la Rivière, 205, 217, 221, 221n21
Metcalfe, W. N., 197n17
M'Gill, William, 51, 53–54, 54n94, 54n96, 55, 55n100, 55nn102–104, 62, 111
Mill, James, 23n41, 145–146n20, 243
Mill, John Stuart, 117n126, 117n132, 145–146n20, 242, 242nn103–104, 243n110
Millar, Agnes, 97, 98, 100
Millar, Ann, 99
Millar, Archibald, 99
Millar, James, 85n26, 98, 99
Millar, Janet, 99
Millar, John, 2, 2nn2–3, 10, 10n33, 38, 39, 39n67, 40n69, 44n18, 56, 59, 59n125, 61, 64, 66–67, 66n22, 66n24, 67nn26–28, 69, 73n59, 77, 81–82, 89, 89n55, 97, 97n3, 98, 98n5, 100n19, 121n1, 141, 153, 160n75, 195, 196n11, 199, 201, 202, 202n47, 202n53, 203, 203nn56–59, 204, 204n60, 208, 209, 216, 218, 232, 238, 238n79, 241, 245, 248
Millar, Margaret, 99
Millar, Richard, 44n18
Millar, Robina Craig, 98
Millar, William, 98, 99
Miller, James, 109n84, 200n37
Miller, Richard, 85n26
Miller, William, 251n5
Miln, James. See Mylne, James
Milton, John, 140
Mirabeau, 204n65
M'Lerie, William, 58, 58n117
Moir, James, 54
Monteath, John, 49
Montesquieu, Charles-Louis de Secondat, 47, 67
Montrose. See Graham, James
Morrell, John B., 109n83
Morrell, John Daniel, 4, 4n10, 5, 5nn16–19, 6, 24n47, 250, 250n4
Morrison, James, 67, 67n30
Morton, Alexander, 24
Moses, 143
Mosheim, Johann Lorenz, 60
Mossner, Ernest, 66n23
Motherwell, William, 93
Muir, Thomas, 32, 44, 50, 51, 52, 53–54, 53n86, 55, 56, 58, 62, 80, 185, 197, 197n17, 200, 239, 248
Muirhead, Lockhart, 64
Murdoch, A., 144
Murdoch, John, 59
Murison, Professor, 24
Murray, David, 9, 74, 74n67, 74n71, 77n96, 78n97, 78n101, 99n9, 100n23, 117n130, 243n106
Muston, Christopher, 114, 114n114
Mylne, Agnes, 97, 98, 100, 101
Mylne, Anne, 17–18
Mylne, Archibald, 101, 103
Mylne, Elizabeth, 17
Mylne, George, 17–18
Mylne, Isobel, 17

INDEX

Mylne, James, 1–10, 4n9, 7n20, 10n33, 13, 15, 15n1, 17–29, 23n43, 24n46, 24n51, 24nn48–49, 25n54, 28nn70–71, 30, 32–40, 32n17, 38n57, 38n63, 39n68, 40–54, 42n8, 44n18, 44nn21–22, 44nn24–25, 45n26, 45n29, 47n40, 50n64, 51n72, 56–62, 59n125, 59nn127–128, 60n130, 63–78, 65n13, 67n26, 68n31, 69n36, 70n41, 71n52, 71nn48–49, 73n59, 74n72, 75nn77–79, 78n97, 79–96, 81n4–6, 83n13, 83n15, 85n27, 87n38, 88n47, 89n55, 92nn68–69, 93n71, 95n82, 97–101, 103–119, 103n44, 104n54, 104nn56–57, 110n94, 111n100, 111–112n101, 112n103, 113n110, 115n118, 121–123, 122n3, 125–141, 126n3, 126n5, 129n13, 134n23, 136n32, 142–161, 143n4, 144n15, 145–146n20, 145n18, 146n24, 157n65, 160n77, 162–164, 164nn9–10, 166n17, 167–176, 177–181, 178n5, 180n11, 184–193, 186n36, 186n40, 192nn71–73, 194–211, 194n1–2, 195nn4–5, 196nn9–10, 197nn14–15, 199n34, 202n55, 204n61, 207nn73–76, 208n78, 208n80, 209n82, 210n84, 213–216, 213nn105–106, 215n111, 216n113, 216n115, 217–245, 217n2, 219n10, 220n17, 221n21, 221n23, 222n28, 223n33, 223nn35–36, 224nn37–39, 225n41, 225nn43–44, 226nn45–46, 227nn48–49, 228nn51–53, 229nn54–56, 230nn57–58, 231nn59–60, 232n61, 233nn62–64, 234nn65–67, 235nn68–70, 236n71, 237nn72–75, 238n76, 238n78, 239n81, 240n88, 240n92, 241n95, 242n100, 242n102, 242n105, 245n118, 247–258, 249n2, 252n12, 254n31, 254nn27–28, 255n32, 256n38, 259, 262n4, 263n6, 265n10
Mylne, James (Father), 15–17, 18, 18nn16–17, 19, 22, 56, 60n130, 181, 195, 247
Mylne, James William, 101, 101n30, 102
Mylne, Janet, 17, 23
Mylne, John, 17
Mylne, John Millar, 101, 102
Mylne, Margaret (daughter), 101
Mylne, Margaret (sister), 17
Mylne, Margaret (wife of John Mylne). *See* Thomson, Margaret
Mylne, Mary, 17
Mylne, William Craig, 101, 102, 103

N

Napoléon I. empereur des français, 80, 112n104
Nassau, W Senior, 243
Newton, Samuel, 185
Nichol, John, 112n103, 251
Nichol, John Pringle, 117, 117n126, 117n132, 145–146n20, 242, 242nn103–104, 243, 243nn110–111, 251
Nicole, Pierre, 60, 60n131
North, Lord, 67

O

O'Connell, Daniel, 94, 94n79, 94n81, 95, 95n84, 95n86, 214, 248
Ogilvie, Alexander Fotheringham, 34
Ogilvie, Colonel, 16
Ogilvie, Walter, 18n16
Orme, Trent, 84n23
Oswald, James, 88, 92, 92n68, 96
Owen, Robert, 104, 104n56, 242, 242n105, 245, 248
Owen, Robert Dale, 104

P

Paine, Thomas, 3, 59, 61, 195n7, 196, 197, 198, 198nn31–32, 199, 221, 233, 245
Palmer, Fyshe, 185, 200
Paoletti, Christina, 150n37
Parker, Charles, 240
Parr, Samuel, 100, 160, 161, 161n81, 199
Paterson, William, 47n42
Paul, Saint, 163, 173, 187, 191
Payne, George, 121n2, 186, 253, 253nn19–20
Pertz, Julia, 104nn56–57, 192nn71–73, 243n107
Philip, Adam, 20n23, 22n36
Philip II (king of Spain), 236
Phillips, Richard, 59
Pictet, Benedict, 27
Pictet, M-A, 70n42
Pierson, Major, 35, 36, 36n41
Pike, Samuel, 189n61
Pillans (Professor), 91
Pitt, William, 68, 82, 230
Plato, 74
Playfair, James, 33–34, 34nn26–27, 36, 37
Playfair, John, 34, 34n27
Pocock, J. G. A., 237nn73
Pollok, Robert, 9n24, 76, 76nn84–87, 126nn3–4, 129n14, 132n20, 134n24, 135nn25–26, 137n33, 137nn35–36, 140, 140n39, 148n29, 154n58, 155n60, 156nn63–64, 163n1, 164, 164n5, 168, 168n24, 169n25, 173, 173n38, 174nn42–46, 175nn47–49, 177, 177n4, 190n65, 222n29, 222n32, 248n1, 249, 250, 250n3
Pope, Alexander, 60
Porteous, William, 26n64, 50, 52
Price, Richard, 2n2, 59, 68, 164, 167, 168, 171, 184, 190
Priestley, Joseph, 59, 61, 68, 75, 103, 122, 136, 160, 160–161n79, 168, 174, 184, 186, 186n39, 190, 195, 195nn6–7, 196, 196n8, 216

Procter, Bryan Waller, 102, 102n33
Proudhon, Pierre-Joseph, 244
Ptolemy, 33
Pufendorf, Samuel, 176, 204, 204n61, 225

Q

Quaife, Barzillai, 254, 254nn29–30
Quaife, Frederick Harrison, 254n31
Quesnay, François, 204, 204n62, 204nn64–65, 205, 217, 221, 221n21, 233, 244n116
Quintilian (Marcus Fabius Quintilianus), 74, 125

R

Ranken, Alexander, 51, 51n68, 52n78, 214n108
Rathbone, Theodore W., 72–73, 72n56, 73n57, 100, 100n20, 242n102
Ravaisson, Felix, 135–136, 135n29
Ravix, J. T., 205n69
Redford, George, 68n31
Reid, John, 34, 108, 108n80
Reid, Robert, 24n50
Reid, Stuart, 31n10
Reid, Thomas, 1–2, 2n1, 3n8, 5–6, 9, 10, 17, 25, 26n61, 58, 61, 64, 66, 66n22, 68, 69n36, 70, 71, 75, 77, 95n82, 98n5, 118, 119n139, 121, 122, 123, 125, 126, 126n2, 128, 130, 131, 132, 133, 134, 136, 138, 139, 140, 141, 142, 145, 148, 149, 151, 152, 152nn45–46, 153, 153n53, 154, 154n55, 154n59, 155, 155n61, 157, 157nn66–68, 158, 158n69, 159, 160, 160nn74–76, 162, 163, 165, 168, 173, 176, 177, 178, 189, 190, 190n68, 191, 201, 202, 202n51, 221n21, 239n81, 248, 249, 251, 252, 252n14, 254, 256, 256n38

Rendall, Jane, 98n8
Ricardo, David, 243
Richardson, James, 192
Richardson, Mary, 99n15
Richardson, William, 49, 64, 160n76, 201
Ritchie, Thomas Edward, 203n55
Robertson, George, 99n13
Robertson, William, 25, 44n24, 99n12, 211
Rogers, Charles, 34n27
Romani, P. M., 205n69
Ross, James, 22n34, 57n113, 57n115
Rousseau, Jean-Jacques, 61, 65, 205
Rullancourt, Baron, 35
Russel, Michael, 5, 5n15, 44n22, 73, 73n61, 73n65, 74n66, 74n74, 249n2
Russell, Bertrand, 222n24
Russell, John, 214

S

Sandeman, Robert, 20, 22, 178–179, 182, 183, 183n24–27, 184, 185, 186, 188, 189, 189n61, 192
Sandeman, William, 17n13
Sandford, Daniel, 92
Saunderson, Nicholas, 60
Say, Jean-Baptiste, 243, 244, 244nn115–116
Schulthess, Daniel, 144n13
Scott, Alexander J., 10n31
Scott, David, 103
Scott, George, 34, 35, 36, 37
Scott, Hew, 15n1, 16n11, 17n15, 20n25, 30n1, 32n18, 33n23, 41nn1–2, 42n6, 42n8, 43n14, 43n17, 44n19, 45n28, 50n62, 56nn107–108, 95n82, 100n25
Scott, James, 76n87, 253n17
Scott, John, 37n49
Scott, Paul, 237nn73
Scott, Walter, 23, 23n42, 66n24, 91

Sell, Alan P. F., 189nn62–63, 253, 253nn19–20, 254n26, 256, 256n37
Seth, Andrew, 245
Sgard, Jean, 144n15, 145n17
Shaftesbury, 65
Shelley, Mary, 185
Shelley, Percy, 114, 185
Sher, Richard B., 69n37, 239n81
Sheridan, Richard, 161, 212
Sibbald, Robert, 60
Silliman, Benjamin, 70, 70n43, 71, 71n50, 77n95, 104n55
Simson, Robert, 60
Sinclair, John, 19n21, 20n24, 42, 46nn32–33
Small, Robert, 32n19, 33, 33n21, 34, 37, 46, 46n36, 48, 48nn48–49, 49, 49n52, 55, 214
Smart, Robert, 24n50, 32
Smeal, William, 95n87
Smith, Adam, 1–2, 2n2, 5–6, 18, 26n61, 33, 39, 39n66, 40, 61, 64, 66, 67, 69n36, 71, 77, 77n93, 78n102, 104, 118, 119n139, 121, 123, 128, 128n10, 149n33, 152n45, 152n48, 163–164, 167, 167n21, 168, 170, 170n31, 172, 173, 202, 203, 206, 210, 210n83, 211, 211n91, 217, 218, 220, 221, 221nn19–20, 222n31, 224, 224n40, 225, 227, 227n47, 228, 229, 230, 231, 233, 234–235, 236, 237, 238, 239, 239n81, 243, 245, 250, 260n1
Smith, Donald C., 110n90, 244n114
Smith, James (from Glasgow), 57n114, 57n116
Smith, James (from Paisley), 95n82, 104n56
Smith, John, 59, 252, 252n11
Smith, John Howard, 178, 178n5
Smith, Sarah, 53n82
Smith, Thomas Southwood, 107, 107n71
Smout, T. C., 193
Snodgrass, John, 17n13, 48, 49, 49nn50–51, 55n100
Somerville, James, 10

Speirs, Archibald, 49
Spence, David, 18n17, 19, 20
Spence, John, 18n17
Spiers, Archibald, 88, 89, 92n68
Spinoza, Benedict de, 61
Stanhope, Lord, 59
Stanley, James, 38n59
Sterling, John, 117n132
Steuart, James, 217, 230, 240n91
Stewart, Dugald, 2, 3n8, 4–5, 5n13, 9, 26n61, 61, 66n22, 77nn93–94, 100, 122, 125, 129, 129nn12–13, 131, 131n18, 136, 136n32, 138, 139, 140, 144, 152, 152n45, 153, 153n52, 161, 162, 163, 165, 166n17, 202n50, 202n55, 218, 219, 244n116, 245, 253, 254, 262n4
Stewart-Robertson, Charles, 10
Stillingfleet, Edward, 27
Stirling, James Hutchison, 10, 10n31, 243, 256
Strang, John, 46n31, 57n112, 58, 58n123, 79, 85, 85n28, 92n68, 98n5, 105, 105n61, 107n72, 160n77, 202n48, 206, 206nn71–72, 238, 238n79, 251, 264n8
Stuting, Walter, 112
Sullivan, Alvin, 59n124
Swift, Jonathan, 200

T

Tait, Arichibald Campbell, 101
Tait, William, 243n111
Talbot, Brian, 58n117, 187n50
Tayler, John James, 255
Taylor, Isaac, 114, 117
Taylor, John, 68
Taylor, William, 47, 48n45, 50, 64, 64n4, 64n7, 68, 69, 88, 153n51
Tennant, Charles, 88, 112–113n107
Tennent, Hugh, 240
Thom, William, 50, 50n64, 52, 176, 176n50
Thomas, Arthur, 112–113n107

Thompson, Murray, 103n43
Thomson, James, 253
Thomson, John, 99
Thomson, Margaret, 102, 102n38
Threipland, 19, 22
Ticknor, George, 99, 100n17
Titus, 173n40
Toland, John, 60
Tracy, Destutt de. *See* Destutt de Tracy, A. L. C.
Traill, Thomas Stewart, 113, 113n110
Trimmer, Sarah, 98
Tulloch, John, 54n95
Turgot, Anne Robert Jacques, 205, 205n69, 210, 217, 221, 221n21, 233, 244n116
Turner, William, 75n80, 76n89, 77, 77n91

U

Ure, Andrew, 53, 53n85

V

Veitch, John, 10, 116n123
Veyne, Paul, 182n22
Virgil, 26, 26n60
Voltaire, François-Marie Arouet, 7n20, 27, 50, 61, 106n69, 143, 145, 145n16, 146, 146n24, 149n31, 150, 184

W

Wallace, Robert, 87, 89, 89n54
Wallace, William, 47n40
Warburton, Bishop, 143, 171
Wardlaw, Ralph, 4n9, 7n20, 26n64, 52n78, 56, 75n78, 105, 107, 108, 108n77–78, 108n80, 109, 109nn81–82, 111, 127, 129, 141, 171, 171n33, 172, 173, 178n5, 187, 192, 255, 265nn9–10

Washington, George, 37
Waterman, A. M. C., 217, 217n1, 244
Watkins, John, 212
Watson, James, 240n92, 241, 241n98
Watson, Robert, 24–25, 24n51, 25n52, 25nn55–56, 198n32
Watt, James, 103, 103n50
Wesley, John, 184
White, A. S., 38n60
Whitfield, Herbert, 38n59
Whitman, Walt, 105
Whyte, Colonel, 34
Whyte, John, 37
Whytock, Jack, 27n66
Wicksteed, Charles, 122n4, 142n1, 150n35, 154nn56–57, 159n71, 170, 170n30, 171n32, 172nn34–37, 190nn66–68, 191n69, 255
Wilberforce, William, 109, 109n85, 255
William, Edgar, 86n36
Williams, Daniel, 68
Willich, A. F. M., 251
Wilson, Alexander, 93n70, 197n18
Wilson, John, 77, 80n2, 91, 94, 94n77, 113, 118–119, 219, 251, 251n8, 252, 252nn10–12
Witherspoon, John, 164–165n10
Wodrow, James, 55n100
Wood, Paul, 157n66
Wood, William, 102, 103
Wooler (*Gazette*), 84n20
Wooller, Thomas Jonathan, 92, 93
Wright, Alexander, 17
Wright, Camilla, 104
Wright, Camilla Campbell, 104
Wright, Frances, 3, 15n1, 17, 23, 23n40, 46, 98, 100, 104, 104nn53–54, 105, 105nn58–60, 119, 185, 192, 197, 198n24, 199, 235, 242n105, 248
Wright, James, 104

Y

Yates, James, 56, 78n101, 107, 108, 220n16
Young, David, 7, 7n22, 8, 251n7
Young, Frederick, 189nn64
Young, John (minister), 196, 196n12, 198, 251n7
Young, John (philosopher), 6, 23n44, 111, 113, 113n109, 121n2, 132, 135, 135nn27, 198, 252, 252n15
Young, John (Professor of Greek), 64–65, 65n13, 65n15, 65nn9–11, 71nn48–49, 73n59, 74, 74n69, 99n11, 101n27, 255

www.ingramcontent.com/pod-product-compliance
Lightning Source LLC
Chambersburg PA
CBHW061429300426
44114CB00014B/1610